The Fall of Jerusalem

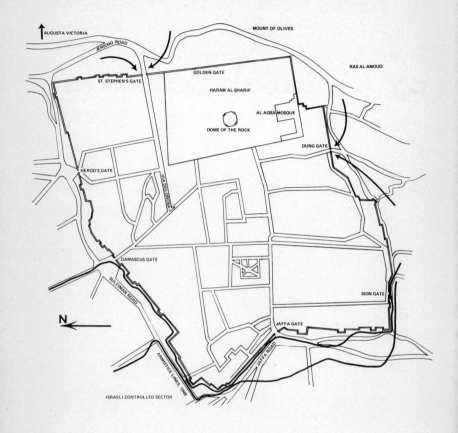

AUGUSTA VICTORIA

MOUNT OF OLIVES

JERICHO ROAD

RAS AL-AMOUD

GOLDEN GATE

ST. STEPHEN'S GATE

HARAM AL-SHARIF

AL-AQSA MOSQUE

DOME OF THE ROCK

DUNG GATE

HEROD'S GATE

VIA DOLOROSA

DAMASCUS GATE

SION GATE

SULEIMAN ROAD

N

JAFFA GATE

JAFFA ROAD

ARMISTICE LINES - 1948

ISRAELI CONTROLLED SECTOR

The Fall of Jerusalem

by Abdullah Schleifer

Monthly Review Press
New York and London

To the people of Arab Jerusalem

Jerusalem–Amman–Beirut
1968–1971

Contents

1. The City

The soul of this city rests in Haram al-Sharif—the "Noble Sanctuary" where history and traditions posit the presence of Abraham, Isaac and Jacob, Jesus, Mary, and Muhammad.

Here is that rock, that Jebusite threshing floor upon which David built his altar and which Solomon enclosed within his temple, where ancient desert genealogy records the act of worship and sacrifice by Malki Sadek, king of the Jebusites, the "gate of Paradise" where the souls of Believers shall gather on the Day of Judgment.

Thirty-four acres, leveled and tiered, carved to the north out of rocky crest and raised up, to the south, by the fill of time and Herod's ambition, the Haram is guarded by high walls and massive gates through which passage has always been a sacramental or at least a solemn occasion.

The Romans tumbled Herod's walls and turned the sanctuary into a mound of rubble. The Byzantines left it as a refuse dump to be cleared away, in 638 A.D., by the hands of the second caliph, Omar ibn-al-Khattab, and his desert warriors, and restored as the center of worship and pilgrimage in their belief that Islam had come, not as a new religion but as restoration of a timeless prophetic Faith.

The strength of Jerusalem lies in its consistent architectural caution, the beauty of massed, faded gray austere stone catching the white Palestinian light, rather than in that recurring brilliance of detail, artifact, and color which flavors the other "museum cities" of Islamic civilization. So it is possible for a single building, Qubbat al-Sakhrah—Dome of the Rock—with its sparkling blue, green, and turquoise Kashan tiles and golden dome, to dominate an entire city.

1

When the Umayyad caliph, Abdul Malik ibn-Marwan, built the Dome of the Rock in 691 A.D., he sought for his own political ends a shrine worthy of a site to rival Mecca. But the Haram is more than a setting for Abdul Malik's maneuver: it is both a shrine and a treasure house harboring mosques, ritual pools, koranic schools and courts, arcades, formal gardens and cypress groves, tombs, and open-air prayer platforms, all of which recall in actual carved inscription or undying legend the names of prophets, holy men, kings, emirs, and caliphs.

"It is said that there is not upon the face of the earth a mosque larger than it," wrote Ibn Battutah. The Haram al-Sharif glows by moonlight like a celestial city.

When Omar received the city from the Byzantine Patriarch, he granted security to the lives, property, and churches of the Christians. And in this time the Muslims allowed the Jews—barred by the Byzantines from Jerusalem for all but one day a year—to worship and dwell here.

So the city took its shape over the centuries under this seal—a rolling skyline of countless domes, pierced by minarets and steeples, fixed finally by the city walls that rose in the early sixteenth century during the reign of the Ottoman Sultan, Suleiman the Magnificent.

Only the grid effect along and across the market streets betrays the city's origin—Aelia Capitolina, the Roman colony built upon the ruins of Herod's city and inherited by Byzantium. According to K. A. Creswell, Jerusalem is one of the most perfectly preserved examples of a medieval Islamic city.

"Jerusalem of Gold," the Israelis sing—and they really mean gold as the Dome of the Rock. And the cobbled lanes and massive houses twisted into that organic maze-effect of insect beauty; the shafts of light filtering down through the vented arched roofs of otherwise opaqued bazaars; the free-flowing headdress of the men and flashes of intricate peasant embroidery as the country women in their long-sleeved, ankle-length gowns glide by, baskets of figs balanced on their kerchiefed heads—these, too, are all images drenched in Arab style.

Even the small but long-established and Arabic-speaking communities of religious Jews who lived here within the walls before the 1948 War—generally indifferent or even opposed to Zionist ambitions—were so much a part of the city's Eastern spirit.

When the Crusaders conquered Jerusalem they quartered their horses in the Haram al-Sharif. The Israelis turned it into a motorpool.

It would be unfair not to note the differences. The Crusaders put an estimated 70,000 Muslim and Jewish noncombatants to the sword—"It was impossible to see without horror that mass of dead," wrote William of Tyre—while the Israelis made a special point of not bombarding most of the holy places and of distributing free bread and milk in part of the city the day after their victory. But to the Arab and Muslim world these are but expressions of a different time and its tensions.

Two great powers—Christendom and Islam—confronted each other in that closing year of the eleventh century; the fate of vast territories, not to mention the Holy City, was to be determined solely by the outcome of the unfolding armed struggle. This was a bloody but direct universe without such modifying forces as the Afro-Asian and Communist blocs condemning the conqueror in a world assembly or without the obvious concern for the fate of this city by powerful religious communions not involved in the combat.

And if history today generally describes the Crusaders as "aggressors" and "foreign intruders," or even as usurpers and settler-colonialists, one can either be cynical about the inevitable morality of history that is usually so unkind to the ultimate loser or, like the Arab and the Muslim, smile with knowing charm.

For no man relishes the title of aggressor, and if the Israelis are absolute in denying accusations that they have usurped Palestine—which would by definition make them the aggressors, whatever the particulars of any specific battle or campaign—it would be unfair to the Crusaders to admit a lesser claim to idealism.

The Holy Land was considered the common fief of all Christendom at the time of the Crusades, and the European knights came using violence only to reconquer what had been taken from them by violence. Little more than four hundred years separated the Crusaders from the mythic source—the fall of Byzantine Jerusalem—and not nearly two thousand years.

The Crusaders had endured years of suffering in their treks through the Balkans to Constantinople, across to Asia Minor, and finally into Palestine, sustained by a vision of Jerusalem and the Holy

Land no less intense than that which has served as central fact to the entire Zionist concept of the "Return from Exile."

When they were but in sight of the Holy City, knights and foot soldiers to a man fell to their knees uttering cries of joy and wept without shame. Like Moshe Dayan, Levi Eshkol, and Ben-Gurion before the Wailing Wall, so walked the Crusader Barons: Robert of Normandy, Godfrey of Bouillon, Tancrède, Raymond of Saint-Gilles—"barefoot, with sighs and tears, through the holy places of the city where Jesus Christ Our Savior lived in the flesh. Devoutly they kissed the places where His feet had trod," wrote William of Tyre.

Here rose the Latin or Frankish Kingdom of Jerusalem, linked by alliance and marriages of state to the other Crusader kingdoms of the north and stretched along the Mediterranean in a shape so strikingly similar to that of the Zionist state. As one commentator aptly put it, the amazing thing about the creation of this artificial state was the rapid development of a new national consciousness based on the Christian Biblical past. Those who remained were aware that they had become citizens of the real home of all Christians.[1]

Certain of the permanence of their colonization, as convinced of their bastion-like place in the Middle East as any contemporary Zionist, Fulcher of Chartres—historian and chaplain to the first Crusader King of Jerusalem, Baldwin I of Boulogne—wrote in *Gesta Francorum Iherusalem*:

> The Italian and the Frenchman of yesterday have been transplanted and become men of Galilee or Palestine. . . . We have already forgotten the land of our birth; who now remembers it? Men no longer speak of it. Here one now has his house and servants with as much assurance as though it were by immemorial right of inheritance in the land. . . . Every day relatives and friends from the West come to join us. They do not hesitate to leave everything they have behind them. . . .

It is impossible to argue over ideological source—be it Crusader, Zionist, Muslim, or Arab. What is discernible is the way men respond to acts. In the eyes of most Arab Christians as well as of all Muslims, the Crusaders were simply the Franks—Europeans, intruders . . . *al-Ifranj;* and the name sticks to this day in the backwaters of the Middle East for any European or European mannerism affected by an Arab.

The people of Palestine—an Arabian (i.e., Semitic) blend of Amorites, Canaanites, Hittites, Jebusites, Phoenicians, Hebrews, and late-Arabians with Philistine, Roman, Greek, and Frankish flavoring—have lived out their centuries and moved from one Semitic tongue to another in a series of religious-political experiences as animists, as Jews, as Christians, and finally as Muslims. And with the adoption of the language of the Quran (Koran) as their ultimate idiom they have taken as a name for their modern cultural identity, "Arab."

The process has been culturally consistent—an Eastern or Asian development—even during the greatest periods of Hellenization. And it is this consistency, marked by the many hundreds of Palestinian peasant villages where an unbroken chain of families has cultivated the land for several thousand years, that was so visibly marred by the armed intrusion of Western ideologues, regardless of their Crusader or Zionist idealism.

The Israelis rejoice that they have "returned" to liberate Jerusalem. The emotion is obviously a genuine and powerful source of morale and a directive for intelligence. And it is almost irrelevant, in the face of such emotion, to recall that the Diaspora as a voluntary phenomenon predates the destruction of even the first Temple and the modest deportations of Nebuchadnezzar, or to consider the recorded existence of thriving communities of Jews in Mesopotamia, Chaldea, and Egypt during the Persian epoch.

Long before the destruction of Jerusalem the great majority of Jews had left Palestine to populate the urban centers of the Roman Empire; of those Jews still in Palestine at the time of Titus and Hadrian, the majority remained and embraced Christianity and/or Islam in the coming centuries.[2] Today, then, many people can visit this part of the world, be struck by the biblical familiarity of Arab ways, and find the Western, the Zionist, sense of "Return" unbearably abstract.

At work in his fields or market stalls, at prayer in the mosque, or secure with his family beneath fig tree and vine—it is the Arab, his movements, manners, and remnant graces that fix every biblical image to this tortured landscape of prophecy and asceticism.

In prewar days, visitors crossing over from Israel into Jordan would comment that the Middle East began at Mandelbaum Gate, that one-time singular and restricted link between New Jerusalem and the Old City. Within a few weeks after the June War the gate was gone, along with all other signs of the old cease-fire line dividing the two Jerusalems. New connecting roads sprang up almost overnight, and old routes—atrophied since the end of the British Mandate—were quickly revived by the Israelis. Street markers in Hebrew lettering, carefully produced to complement the Arabic and English-lettered Armenian decorative tiles, were cemented into place above the Jordanian originals throughout the twisting streets of the Old City.

These were the first days of annexation and it was as if the Israelis were exerting all of this amazing civic energy to convince themselves, the Arabs, and the rest of the world that Jerusalem's "unification" was more than a permanent fact; as if all that could conceivably remain of the past two decades, which in turn flows into millennia of Eastern history regardless of ruling regime or dynasty or tribe, was a vague memory of a highly artificial state of affairs.

But the prewar character sticks. The two "sectors" are actually an Asian city plus its vast twentieth-century semicolonial suburb (or European "city"), and both had gone their separate ways for almost twenty years.

The stigmata of modern and provisional occupations are all visible in Jerusalem: the ending of genuine political life and the search for reasonable collaborators; the banishment of outspoken Arab leaders such as the mayor, the chief justice of the Muslim law court, former Jordanian ministers, educators and trade union organizers, Arab nationalist and Communist leaders; and the arrest, imprisonment, and almost inevitable torture of those suspected of resistance.

The prisons fill up, empty, and fill up again. The occupier—by the iron logic of these affairs—becomes increasingly repressive. In the passage of little more than a year several thousand Arabs in Jerusalem alone have already experienced at least temporary detainment.

Think of Paris under a German garrison during World War II—held but not annexed, administered (in time, terrorized) but not Germanized—or of Santo Domingo in the hands of the Marines, and then understand the particular agony of Arab Jerusalem.

Mass evictions number in the thousands. Hundreds of Arab homes demolished, one-third of the land already expropriated and more inevitably to come—while new housing springs up for thousands of Israelis prepared to settle in what is now known as "East Jerusalem." Impersonal "laws of the market" and intentional boycott are destroying the local economy. All these are reasonable requirements or historical necessities if Israel, in the words of President Zalman Shazar, "is to make the Old City Jewish."

Not long after the war an Israeli cigarette company with a taste for patriotic appeals placed a series of ads on the front page of the Israeli English-language daily, the *Jerusalem Post*. The ads featured photographs of typically beautiful Old City Arab scenes: the old bazaars, an aerial view of the Haram al-Sharif and the Damascus Gate. Above each photo appears the caption "This is your land," and it is clear to the Arab that the message is not meant for him.

The fall of Jerusalem on June 7, 1967—859 years to the day since the Crusader armies first appeared before the walls of the Holy City —and the occupation that has followed are a microcosm of the fate of all Palestine and of the entire Arab-Israeli conflict. And it is still more.

The idea that Europeans, by nature of any number of superior spiritual, historic, or cultural rights, were justified to directly colonize the rest of the world (and in that peculiarly intense racist manner that seems to run like a profound flaw through Western man) has not been fashionable since the end of World War II.

The last great, shameless conquests or colonizations—India, Egypt, North Africa, the Chinese capitulations, Indo-China, Indonesia, the Malay states, the Tartar emirates, southern Africa, the Congo—were all mainly nineteenth-century affairs.

By the end of World War I the gathering mood already required ambiguity and subterfuge—"mandate," "trusteeship"—rather than admit any unembarrassed right of conquest. In the 1930's, when Italy brought 20,000 colonists to Libya and dug up from under the desert some old Roman columns to prove "historic rights," the world snickered.

Who in Europe, besides the hopeless Portuguese, today dares talk about the white man's burden, about missionaries for the heathen, and about gunboats for missionaries bringing light into the jungle? The most stable and powerful of the remaining settler-colonial states is the Republic of South Africa, as dedicated to white rule and apartheid as Israel is to Jewish exclusivity, as ideologically certain of her biblical rights (that business about Ham and Noah and who will forever hew wood and draw water for whom) as David Ben-Gurion thundering on about the Promise to Abraham.

The founder of Zionism—Theodor Herzl—could write without embarrassment in 1895 of his admiration for the "scientific" quality of the colonization of South Africa.[3] But there are nevertheless profound differences in situation and style which have allowed Israel and the Zionist movement to transcend such frankness. The bare bones of Herzl's vision have been fleshed over with a provisional humanism so similar to that other successful venture in twentieth-century liberal empire-building—the American New Deal.

It is not simply a matter of rhetoric and certainly not of cynicism. The cultural formation of the Afrikaner cannot be compared to that of the oppressed European Jew, consciously allied for decades with democratic and even revolutionary movements. There was nothing in the Afrikaner's experience as a European to obscure the hard racial tone inherent in settler-colonialism. And Herzl, who was spared any significant brush with virulent anti-Semitism until the Dreyfus affair, could emotionally afford—unlike his Eastern European followers—to ignore this moral tension.

The South Africans have been stuck with their highly visible natives—unavoidable in a society built on the exploitation of native labor and not, as in the case of Israel, upon the vacated land of the native turned into refugee and upon the abandoned fruits of his labor. (The Israelis have their own economic ambitions for the region that are far more comprehensive, if ever realizable, than the typical Afrikaner's narrow nineteenth-century concept of profit.)

Aside from a remnant of the Palestinians left behind Jewish lines at the end of the 1948 War, the native simply vanished as a calculable element. It is no accident that the "hard" and "hawkish" aspect of Zionism which has plagued the Palestinian for decades has only now become apparent to limited sections of Western public opinion after the June 1967 War, when the Israeli occupation of the remaining portions of Palestine (Jordan's West Bank and Gaza) brought the native back into everyone's focus.[4]

There are vast Anglo-American investments in South Africa; the investors have the power to ensure that anti-apartheid sentiment in the West is never translated into actively effective measures against South Africa. But there are no large, articulate, and influential communities of Afrikaners in the West, manipulated by Pretoria, and then in turn manipulating public opinion in behalf of Pretoria. Ideologically South Africa has been on the defensive for decades.

South Africa's frontiers are as fixed and as old as its self-image; all the Republic basically seeks is buffer space between itself and the African revolution. But Arab Jerusalem, the Golan Heights, Gaza, and parts of the West Bank are fresh fields. Here is a clinic for case studies in a still dynamic settler-colonialism of the most subtle sort, successful to the degree that it has evaded the colonialist label (at least in the West) throughout an anticolonialist epoch. Only in Palestine is it still possible for liberals to cheer cowboys gunning down the Indians or pushing them back into the badlands.

The people of Arab Jerusalem have committed themselves to a holding action against annexation.

If most merchants now must look to Israeli sources for stock, almost none have entered partnerships or turned over their locations for key money despite the frantic barrage of deals offered by Israeli businessmen in the first months after the war. Local lawyers continue to boycott the Israelized courts while discreetly arranging for "Israeli-Arab" attorneys from Haifa to represent their clients.

Government schools function under Israeli direction, Hebrew is taught as a second language, and both students and parents "welcome" it in the sense of a survival course. But on the first anniversary of the fall of the city a new Arab generation revealed itself as thousands of school-age boys and girls, organized in secret, turned out to march for three tense days. Despite periodic police charges and the use of water cannon, these solemn and disciplined children held their ranks and, bearing wreaths, made their way to the Muslim cemeteries just outside the city walls. The koranic inscriptions wrapped about the wreaths were not evasive: "Those who are killed in the service of Allah are not dead; they are still living."

Most of the people, however, rarely dare consider more than listening to the fedayeen radio broadcasts or closing up their shops on a few politically significant days, and do that with great fear of reprisal.

The cost of living soared when the city was incorporated into the relatively high-wage and distinctly tax-prone Israeli economy. The Arab banks remain closed (their assets locked away in the Israeli Central Bank), and aside from the souqs selling vegetables and other staples, stagnancy reigns in the business districts.

The hundreds of thousands of pilgrimage visitors from the Arab and Muslim world who came each year to the great churches and mosques of Jerusalem, filling the many modest hotels or renting rooms in private homes throughout the city and staying on to shop in the old markets and in the modern business district outside of the walls, no longer can come. And so much of what remains of the former flow of Western tourists has been taken in hand by Israeli entrepreneurs. Tourist guides, taxi drivers, travel agencies, the touring bus company, and the modern hotels of Arab Jerusalem languish with few customers. The depression spreads in widening circles to the souvenir shops and to the artisans who fashion and carve olive-wood prayer beads and crucifixes.

The men of Jerusalem who work as teachers or technicians in Saudi Arabia, Libya, and the oil-rich Gulf states—but retain their Jordanian citizenship and return home each summer with money for their families—must now apply through relatives in the hope of receiving severely restricted "visitors'" permits to their own homes.

Hundreds of thousands of Israelis poured into the Old City in the first few weeks after the June War to buy up local stocks of American and European canned goods, fountain pens from China, and plastic trifles from Hong Kong and Japan. The sudden availability of low-cost farm produce from the West Bank also brought swarms of Israeli housewives. Within a month the boom was over: those Arab merchants who had not exhausted their imported stock were taxed Israeli-fashion; West Bank farm produce, livestock, and light manufactured products were barred from direct access to the Arab Jerusalem market, which must now deal almost exclusively with Israeli distributors and at Israeli prices. With the passing of great bargains the Israeli shoppers lost interest in the Arabs, and unemployment depressed the merchants' own local market.

Now and then one hears of a neighbor who has gone away to find work in Kuwait, Qatar, or Abu Dhabi. But most stay on; the shopkeepers master Hebrew to better serve what there is in the way of trade, and the unemployed Arab laborers fan out through the Jewish city to search for work. I know an amazing number of men who once worked as clerks, accountants, or taxi drivers and who now sell soda pop, ice cream, or groceries from little stalls dotting the Old City.[5]

Funds from Amman—loans from friends and family, salaries or grants paid out by the Jordanian government, and bank withdrawals —are carried back by hundreds of Jerusalem residents whom the Israelis allow brief trips across the river, and this invisible income helps keep the Arab city alive.

In the modern business districts within and outside the city walls, retail shops that once sold household appliances or furniture soon began to transform themselves into cafés, bars, restaurants, and nightclubs.

It seems at present that the only viable role for the Arab city within the Israeli economy will be as a night-life quarter to service the Israeli youth who flock to Arab Jerusalem during the Friday night and Saturday Sabbath when the Jewish cities close up. The far-sighted pimps of Tel Aviv and Jaffa have moved their girls here to get in on the boom. The pimps and their women, like all the other under-classes of Israeli life, are invariably Oriental Jews. The Old City could well become a racial tenderloin, like Havana or even Harlem in older times.

But Jerusalem whistles Savonarola's tune. The revolutionary pres-ence so often in the air—grenades exploding in the night, a truckload of dynamite shattering an Israeli-Jerusalem marketplace, a rash of guerrilla attacks not far from the city—makes poor public relations for any solid sort of Arab "sin city."[6]

There are also Arabs to be found who share neither the general discontent nor the will to at least passively resist. Many of the city's very poor—unskilled laborers frequently unemployed in Jordanian times—have found factory or service jobs with Israeli employees at wages far above what was ever possible in the past. A few of these workers rest content unless directly threatened by the waves of land expropriations and sudden evictions.

More typical is the owner of a floundering Arab hotel who eventu-ally hired an Israeli consultant, turned his kitchen kosher, and was immediately rewarded with a stunning summer guest list of eighty-seven visiting teachers and principals from the Hebrew day schools of America.

There is Masswadi, a hardworking if overly ingratiating cook from Hebron whose hommus (boiled chick-peas and sesame oil whip) was considered about the best in the Old City. After the June War someone brought Moshe Dayan to Masswadi's small Oriental restaurant to sample the hommus. Dayan's praises appeared in print and a new age dawned for Masswadi. A rush of Israeli trade, a mysterious source of capital, and he emerged as the owner of a large, modern restaurant and as a new-style effendi, strutting through the streets with his head held high and settling all arguments with his neighbors by invoking the name of his friend Dayan. According to dark Arab rumor, Masswadi has been licensed to carry a gun.

An Arab-Jewish nightclub partnership introduced the striptease to the Old City: "The first floor show in Jerusalem in two thousand years," the Arab partner told me with peculiar pride.

A founder of the Royal Jordanian Air Club turned his struggling suburban hotel into a country club which staged, according to the local press, "chic and daring Arab-Jewish fashion shows" (i.e., Israeli models in streamlined Arab peasant dress). "There's a not-so-ancient saying that Jerusalem is always under curfew. What we mean is that it's dead—completely dead—at night. Too much praying and all that sort of thing," the Arab hotelman told the press. His embarrassed Israeli partner explained: "Reunification also means revitalization!"

Jerusalem has known and thrived upon masses of foreign visitors—at Easter, Christmas, Ramadan, the Feast of Nebi Musa, Eid al-Adha—processionals as great as any of the Israeli crowds that have poured through the city since the war. But then even the most hedonistic made peace with this ascetic, tradition-bound city and saved the partying for Beirut. You would see them, camera-laden and self-conscious, moving through the streets or even within the Haram during brief and regulated visiting hours, transmuted into pilgrims by the dignity of the Arabs and the sight of richly bearded Greek Orthodox clergy, nuns from French, Spanish, and Russian orders, cloaked Franciscans, Armenian priests in their scary black hoods, and turbaned sheikhs of Islamic law, all treading about within the psychic aura of a holy city.

Now, from late morning till past sunset, so many of these narrow streets belong to jostling crowds of Israelis who will not be intimidated by any native's sense of solemnity. Bored or infectiously gay, in

COMBINATORIAL GROUP TESTING AND ITS APPLICATIONS

2nd Edition

Ding-Zhu Du

Department of Computer Science, City University of Hong Kong
Department of Computer Science and Engineering, University of Minnesota, USA
Institute of Applied Mathematics, Chinese Academy of Sciences, Beijing, China

Frank K. Hwang

Department of Applied Mathematics, National Chiao Tung University, Taiwan

World Scientific
Singapore • New Jersey • London • Hong Kong

Published by

World Scientific Publishing Co. Pte. Ltd.

P O Box 128, Farrer Road, Singapore 912805

USA office: Suite 1B, 1060 Main Street, River Edge, NJ 07661

UK office: 57 Shelton Street, Covent Garden, London WC2H 9HE

Library of Congress Cataloging-in-Publication Data
Du, Dingzhu.
    Combinatorial group testing and its applications / by Ding-Zhu Du, Frank K. Hwang. --
[2nd ed.].
        p.   cm. -- (Series on applied mathematics ; vol. 12)
    Includes bibliographical references and index.
    ISBN 9810241070 (alk. paper)
    1. Combinatorial group theory.   I. Hwang, Frank.   II. Title.   III. Series on applied
mathematics ; v. 12.
    QA182.5.D8 2000
    512'.2--dc21
                                                                    99-048251
                                                                        CIP

British Library Cataloguing-in-Publication Data
A catalogue record for this book is available from the British Library.

QA
182
.5
D83
2000

Printed in Singapore.

Preface

Group testing has been around for fifty years. It started as an idea to do large scale blood testing economically. When such needs subsided, group testing stayed dormant for many years until it was revived with needs for new industrial testing. Later, group testing also emerged from many nontesting situations, such as experimental designs, multiaccess communication, coding theory, clone library screening, nonlinear optimization, computational complexity, etc.. With a potential worldwide outbreak of AIDS, group testing just might go the full cycle and becomes an effective tool in blood testing again. Another fertile area for application is testing zonal environmental pollution.

Group testing literature can generally be divided into two types, probabilistic and combinatorial. In the former, a probability model is used to describe the distribution of defectives, and the goal is to minimize the expected number of tests. In the latter, a deterministic model is used and the goal is usually to minimize the number of tests under a worst-case scenario. While both types are important, we will focus on the second type in this book because of the different flavors for these two types of results.

To find optimal algorithms for combinatorial group testing is difficult, and there are not many optimal results in the existing literature. In fact, the computational complexity of combinatorial group testing has not been determined. We suspect that the general problem is hard in some complexity class, but do not know which class. (It has been known that the problem belongs to the class PSPACE, but seems not PSPACE-complete.) The difficulty is that the input consists of two or more integers, which is too simple for complexity analysis. However, even if a proof of hardness will eventually be given, this does not spell the end of the subject, since the subject has many, many branches each posing a different set of challenging problems.

This book is not only the first attempt to collect all theory and applications about combinatorial group testing in one place, but it also carries the personal perspective of the authors who have worked on this subject for a quarter of a century. We hope that this book will provide a forum and focus for further research on this subject, and also be a source for references and publications. Finally, we thank E. Barillot, A.T. Borchers, R.V. Book, G.J. Chang, F.R.K. Chung, A.G. Dyachkov, D. Kelley, K.-I Ko, M. Parnes, D. Raghavarao, M. Ruszinko, V.V. Rykov, J. Spencer, M. Sobel, U. Vaccaro, and A.C. Yao for giving us encouragements and helpful discussions at various stage of the formation of this book. Of course, the oversights and errors are solely our responsibility.

Preface to the Second Edition

Besides the usual tingling of updating results and correcting errors felt by most authors in revising their books, the recent extensive application of nonadaptive group testing to the clone library screening problem provides another irresistible impetus. Thus we expand the meager section on the subject in the previous edition to a full chapter(Chapter 9) here. We know we can never catch up with the fervent development of the subject; but a full chapter provides a much better start to follow it.

Urged by the clone library application, recent study on the group testing theory has focused on the nonadaptive side. To accommodate this reality, we split the original chapter into two, depending on whether the testing design is deterministic (Chapter 7) or random (Chapter 8). We also add the all-important fault tolerant material to the latter chapter.

Detecting counterfeit coins is perhaps the most well-known mathematical problem for general public. There are two motivations to do a new chapter (Chapter 16) on it. One is to put all scattered results into one source; and the other is to report on the recent finding of Alon, Kozlov, and Vu for an interesting connection of this problem with lattice geometry and numerical linear algebra.

We also provide a structure to the book which is lacking in the previous edition. Chapters 2 to 6 deal with sequential group testing, while chapters 7 to 9 with the nonadaptive kind. Chapters 10 to 12 introduce various extended group testing models, while the last 4 chapters introduce other search problems which have the group testing flavor. It is worth mentioning that the chapter in group testing on graphs (Chapter 12) is updated with a solution of our conjecture in the first edition of this book. This new result enable us to remove two old sections.

We would like to thank Mr. J.S. Lee, Dr. C.C. Ho, Mr. H.Q. Ngo, and Ms. D.Y. Li for detecting many errors for us, and the 1999 group testing class at Chiao-Tung University for putting up with one of us in experimenting the material for a one-year research seminar course.

Ding-Zhu Du
Frank K. Hwang
at CityU Hong Kong

Contents

1
Introduction

Group testing has been around for fifty years. While traditionally group testing literature employs probabilistic models, combinatorial models have cut their own shares and become an important part of the literature. Furthermore, combinatorial group testing has tied its knots with many computer science subjects: complexity theory, computational geometry and learning models among others. It has also been used in multiaccess communication and coding, and recently, in clone library screening.

1.1   The History of Group Testing

Unlike many other mathematical problems which can trace back to earlier centuries and divergent sources, the origin of group testing is pretty much pinned down to a fairly recent event-World War II, and is usually credited to a single person-Robert Dorfman. The following is his recollection after 50 years (quoted from a November 17, 1992 letter in response to our inquiry about the role of Rosenblatt):

> "The date was 1942 or early '43. The place was Washington, DC in the offices of the Price Statistics Branch of the Research Division of the office of Price Administration, where David Rosenblatt and I were both working. The offices were located in a temporary building that consisted of long wings, chock-full of desks without partitions.
>
> The drabness of life in those wings was relieved by occasional bull sessions. Group testing was first conceived in one of them, in which David Rosenblatt and I participated. Being economists, we were all struck by the wastefulness of subjecting blood samples from millions of draftees to identical analyses in order to detect a few thousand cases of syphilis. Someone (who?) suggested that it might be economical to pool the blood samples, and the idea was batted back and forth. There was lively give-and-take and some persiflage. I don't recall how explicitly the problem was formulated there. What is clear is that I took the idea seriously enough so that in the next few days I formulated the underlying probability problem

1

and worked through the algebra (which is pretty elementary). Shortly af-
ter, I wrote it up, presented it at a meeting of the Washington Statistical
Association, and submitted the four-page note that was published in the
Annals of Mathematical Statistics. By the time the note was published,
Rosenblatt and I were both overseas and out of contact."

We also quote from an October 18, 1992 letter from David Rosenblatt to Milton
Sobel which provides a different perspective.

"It is now (Fall of 1992) over fifty year ago when I first invented and
propounded the concepts and procedure for what is now called "group
testing" in Statistics. I expounded it in the Spring of 1942 the day after I reported for induction during World War II and underwent blood
sampling for the Wasserman test. I expounded it before a group of fellow
statisticians in the division of Research of the Office of Price Administra-
tion in Washington, D.C. Among my auditors that morning was my then
colleague Rorbet Dorfman."

Considering that fifty years have lapsed between the event and the recollections,
we find the two accounts reasonably close to each other. Whatever discrepancies
there are, they are certainly within the normal boundary of differences associated
with human memory. Thus that "someone" (in Dorfman's letter) who first suggested
to pool blood samples could very well be David Rosenblatt. It is also undisputed that
Dorfman alone wrote that seminal report [1] published in the Notes Sections of the
journal *Annals of Mathematical Statistics* which gave a method intended to be used
by the United States Public Health Service and the Selective Service System to weed
out all syphilitic men called up for induction. We quote from [1]:

"Under this program each prospective inductee is subjected to a
'Wasserman-type' blood test. The test may be divided conveniently into
two parts:

1. A sample of blood is drawn from the man,

2. The blood sample is subjected to a laboratory analysis which reveals the presence or absence of "syphilitic antigen." The presence
   of syphilitic antigen is a good indication of infection.

When this procedure is used, n chemical analyses are required in order to
detect all infected members of a population of size n.

The germ of the proposed technique is revealed by the following possibility.
Suppose that after the individual blood sera are drawn they are pooled
in groups of, say, five and that the groups rather than the individual sera
are subjected to chemical analysis. If none of the five sera contributing

to the pool contains syphilitic antigen, the pool will not contain it either and will be tested negative. If, however, one or more of the sera contain syphilitic antigen, the pool will also contain it and the group test will reveal its presence (the author inserted a note here saying that diagnostic tests for syphilis are extremely sensitive and will show positive results for even great dilutions of antigen). The individuals making up the pool must then be retested to determine which of the members are infected. It is not necessary to draw a new blood sample for this purpose since sufficient blood for both the test and the retest can be taken at once. The chemical analysis requires only small quantities of blood."

Figure 1.1: The idea of group testing.

Unfortunately, this very promising idea of grouping blood samples for syphilis screening was not actually put to use. The main reason, communicated to us by C. Eisenhart, was that the test was no longer accurate when as few as eight or nine samples were pooled. Nevertheless, test accuracy could have been improved over years, or possibly not a serious problem in screening for another disease. Therefore we quoted the above from Dorfman in length not only because of its historical significance, but also because at this age of a potential AIDS epidemic, Dorfman's clear account of applying group testing to screen syphilitic individuals may have new impact to the medical world and the health service sector.

Dorfman's blood testing problem found its entrance into a very popular textbook on probability as an exercise; Feller's 1950 book "*An Introduction to Probability Theory and Its Application*, Vol. I" [2] and thus might have survived as a coffee break talk-piece among the academic circle in those days. But by and large, with the conclusion of the Second World War and the release of millions of inductees, the need of group testing disappeared from the Selective Service and the academic world was ready to bury it as a war episode. The only exception was a short note published by Sterrett [7] in 1951 based on his Ph.D. dissertation at University of Pittsburgh. Then Sobel and Groll [6], the two Bell Laboratories Scientists, gave new meaning to the phrase "group testing" by giving the subject a very thorough treatment and established many new grounds for future studies in their 74-page paper. Again, they were motivated by practical need, this time from the industrial sector, to remove all leakers from a set of n devices. We quote from Sobel and Groll:

> "One chemical apparatus is available and the devices are tested by putting x of them (where $1 \leq x \leq n$) in a bell jar and testing whether any of the gas used in constructing the devices has leaked out into the bell jar. It is assumed that the presence of gas in the bell jar indicates only that there is at least one leaker and that the amount of gas gives no indication of the number of leakers."

Sobel and Groll also mentioned other industrial applications such as testing condensers and resistors, the main idea is very well demonstrated by the Christmas tree lighting problem. A batch of light bulbs is electrically arranged in series and tested by applying a voltage across the whole batch or any subset thereof. If the lights are on, then whole tested subset of bulbs must all be good; if the lights are off, then at least one bulb in the subset is defective.

Call the set of defectives among the n items the *defective set*. Dorfman, as well as Sobel and Groll, studied group testing under probabilistic models, namely, a probability distribution is attached to the defective set and the goal is to minimize the expected number of tests required to identify the defective set. Katona [4] first emphasized the combinatorial aspects of group testing. However, his coverage was predominantly for the case of a single defective and he considered probability distributions of defectives. In this volume a more restrictive viewpoint on *combinatorial group testing* (CGT) is taken by completely eliminating probability distributions on defectives. The presumed knowledge on the defective set is that it must be a member, called a *sample point*, of a given family called a *sample space*. For example, the sample space can consist of all d-subsets of the n items, when the presumed knowledge is that there are exactly d defectives among the n items. The reason that probabilistic models are excluded is not because they are less important or less interesting, but simply because there is so much to tell about group testing and this is a natural way to divide the material.

Li [5] was the first to study CGT. He was concerned with the situation where industrial and scientific experiments are conducted only to determine which of the variables are important. Usually, only a relatively small number of critical variables exists among a large group of candidates. These critical variables are assumed to have effects too large to be masked by the experimental error, or the combined effect of the unimportant variables. Interpreting each variable as an item, each critical variable as a defective, and each experiment as a group test, a large effect from an experiment indicates the existence of a critical variable among the variables covered by the experiment. Li assumed that there are exactly d critical variables to start with, and set to minimize the worst-case number of tests.

Since Li, CGT has been studied along side with PGT for those classical applications in medical, industrial and statistical fields. Recently, CGT is also studied in complexity theory, graph theory, learning models, communication channels and fault tolerant computing. While it is very encouraging to see a wide interest in group testing, one unfortunate consequence is that the results obtained are fragmented and submerged in the jargons of the particular fields. This book is an attempt to give a unified and coherent account of up-to-date results in combinatorial group testing.

1.2   A Prototype Problem and Some General Remarks

We first describe a prototype CGT problem which will be the focus of the whole book. Then we discuss generalizations and special cases.

Consider a set I of n items known to contain exactly d defectives. The defectives look exactly like the good items and the only way to identify them is through testing, which is error-free. A test can be applied to an arbitrary subset of the n items with two possible outcomes: a *negative* outcome indicates that all items in the subset are good, a *positive* outcome indicates the opposite, i.e., at least one item in the subset is defective (but not knowing which ones or how many are defective). We also use the term *negative group* or *positive group* to describe a subset of items not containing a defective. A positive (negative) group is also said to be *contaminated (pure)*. The goal is to find an algorithm to identify all defectives with a small number of tests. This is the prototype problem. It is also called the (d, n)-problem to highlight the two parameters n and d. In the literature the (d, n) problem has sometimes been called the *hypergeometric group testing problem*. We now reserve the latter term for the case that a uniform distribution is imposed on S, since then the probability that a subset of k items containing x defectives follows the hypergeometric distribution

$$\frac{\binom{d}{x}\binom{n-d}{k-x}}{\binom{n}{k}} \ .$$

Note that the hypergeometric group testing problem under this new definition belongs to PGT, not CGT.

There are two general types of group testing algorithms. In a *sequential* algorithm, the tests are conducted one by one, and the outcomes of previous tests are assumed known at the time of determining the current test. In a *nonadaptive* algorithm, no such information is available in determining a test. Thus, it can be interpreted as if all tests are specified simultaneously, although in practice the real reason can be the collection of such information is too time-consuming or too costly. A compromise between the two types of algorithms is realized by the so-called *multistage algorithm* in which tests are divided into several stages where the stages are considered sequential but all tests in the same stage are treated as nonadaptive. Namely, a test can use outcomes of tests conducted in previous stages, but not those in the same stage. If the number of stages is fixed at s in an algorithm, then it can be called an *s-stage algorithm*.

Since a sequential algorithm possesses more information at testing, clearly, it requires fewer number of tests than a nonadaptive algorithm in general. Another way of looking at that is every nonadaptive algorithm can be used as a sequential algorithm by doing the tests one by one in an arbitrary order. An s-stage algorithm is similar to a nonadaptive algorithm for very small s, and is otherwise similar to a sequential algorithm (which must be bounded by a certain number of stages for any finite n). Although the first group testing algorithm proposed by Dorfman was 2-stage, urged by an eagerness to reduce the number of tests, the early history of group testing was all sequential algorithms. Recently, the focus has been shifting due to the general influence of the popularity of parallel computing, and also due to the need of nonadaptive algorithms in the application of clone library screening (see Chapter 9).

Consider a sequential or multistage algorithm A. Then the number of tests used by A to solve the problem depends on which sample point is the problem. For example, let a, b, c be the three items in the $(1, 3)$ problem and let A be the algorithm of testing a and then b. If the sample point is $\{a\}$, then A needs only one test since after the first test, the second test is no longer needed. But if the sample point is $\{b\}$ and $\{c\}$, then both tests are needed. We will use $M_A(d, n)$ to denote the worst-case number of tests required by A, namely, the maximum number of tests over all sample points. If A is nonadaptive then $M_A(d, n)$ is simply the number of tests contained in A.

An algorithm is *reasonable* if it contains no test whose outcome can be predicted from outcomes of other tests either conducted previously or simultaneously. For example, in a reasonable sequential algorithm, if $\{a, b\}$ is tested with negative outcome, then neither $\{a\}$ nor $\{b\}$ should be tested again; while in a reasonable nonadaptive algorithm, the three tests $\{a, b\}$, $\{a\}$, $\{b\}$ cannot co-exist since the outcomes of any two tests determine the third outcome. In particular, no test can repeat itself in a reasonable algorithm. Thus, the number of tests is finite, and consequently, the number of reasonable algorithms is also finite. To minimize the number of tests, clearly, it suffices to consider only reasonable algorithms. Thus we may define

$$M(d, n) = \min_A M_A(d, n) \text{ over all reasonable } A.$$

In general, let S be the sample space of a group testing problem. Then $M_A(S)$ and $M(S)$ can be defined similarly. A is called a *minimax algorithm* for S if $M_A(S) = M(S)$. We give some basic results on $M(S)$.

Let $\lceil x \rceil (\lfloor x \rfloor)$ denote the smallest (largest) integer not less (greater) than x. Also let $\log x$ mean $\log_2 x$ throughout unless otherwise specified.

Theorem 1.2.1 $M(S) \geq \lceil \log |S| \rceil$.

Proof. Since each test divides the sample points into two disjoint sets, and there are $|S|$ sample points to start with, Theorem 1.2.1 gives the well-known *information theory bound*. □

Theorem 1.2.2 $S \subseteq S'$ implies $M(S) \leq M(S')$.

Proof. Every reasonable algorithm for S' is an algorithm for S although it may not be a reasonable algorithm for S. This algorithm for S can be modified to a reasonable algorithm for S by removing some unnecessary tests. Therefore, $M(S) \leq M(S')$. □

Corollary 1.2.3 $M(d, n)$ *is nondecreasing in* n.

One goal of the prototype problem is to solve $M(d, n)$. But this turns out to be a very different problem. In fact, only $M(1, n) = \lceil \log_2 n \rceil$ is known. Even the $(2, n)$ problem is unexpectedly hard and remains open. So most of the available results reported in this book are efforts in pursuing the other goal - obtaining good heuristic algorithms.

1.3   Some Practical Considerations

In practice, one hardly knows d exactly. Thus d is often either an estimate or an upper bound. Note that the algorithms discussed in this chapter all have the property that they will either identify all defectives, if the actual number of defectives is up to d, or they will identify d defectives, if the actual number exceeds d. When d is an overestimate, a (d, n) algorithm still identifies all defectives and solves the problem, although not as efficiently as if the correct value of d is assessed. On the other hand, one could guard against the case that d is an underestimate by applying a test on all remaining items upon the identification of the dth defective. If the outcome is positive, then d must be an underestimate. One would assign a value d' to represent the number of defectives in the remaining n' items and apply a (d', n') algorithm and proceed similarly. When d is known to be an upper bound of the number of defectives, the (d, n) problem will be denoted by $(\bar{d}, n)$.

In practice, one hardly knows d exactly. Thus d is often either an estimate or an upper bound. Note that the algorithms discussed in this chapter all have the property that they will either identify all defectives, if the actual number of defectives is up to d, or they will identify d defectives, if the actual number exceeds d. When d is an overestimate, a (d, n) algorithm still identifies all defectives and solves the problem, although not as efficiently as if the correct value of d is assessed. On the other hand, one could guard against the case that d is an underestimate by applying a test on all remaining items upon the identification of the dth defective. If the outcome is positive, then d must be an underestimate. One would assign a value d' to represent the number of defectives in the remaining n' items and apply a (d', n') algorithm and proceed similarly. When d is known to be an upper bound of the number of defectives, the (d, n) problem will be denoted by $(\bar{d}, n)$. Hwang, Song and Du [3] proved that $M(\bar{d}, n)$ is at most one more than $M(d, n)$.

When the tests are destructive or consummate, as in the blood test application, then the number of tests an item can go through (or the number of duplicates) becomes an important issue. If an item can only go through one test, then individual testing is the only feasible algorithm. If an item can go through at most s tests, then Li's s-stage algorithm is a good one to use.

In some other applications, the size of a testable group is restricted. Usually, the restriction is of the type that no more than k items can be tested as a group. An algorithm can be modified to fit the restriction by cutting the group size to k whenever the algorithm calls for a larger group.

There are some subtle restrictions for sequential algorithms. Call a storage unit a *bin* and assume that all items in a bin are indistinguishable to the tester even though they have different test history. A *b-bin algorithm* can use at most b bins to store items. A small number of bins not only saves storage units, but also implies easier implementation. Since at most stages of the testing process, one bin is needed to store good items, one to store defectives and one to store unidentified items, any sensible algorithm will need at least three bins. An obvious 3-bin algorithm is individual testing.

Yet another possible restriction is on the number of recursive equations defining a minimax algorithm in a given class. A small number implies a faster solution for the recursive equations. For example, individual testing needs one equation (in a trivial way).

Suppose that there are p processors or p persons to administer the tests parallelly. Then p disjoint groups can be tested in one "round." In some circumstance when the cost of time dominates the cost of tests, then the number of rounds is a more relevant criterion to evaluate an algorithm than the number of tests.

There are restrictions other than the above-mentioned. In the line group testing problem the n items are arranged on a line and only subsets of consecutive items from top of the line can be tested. This situation may be appropriate when one inspects items on an assembly line. Similarly, one can study circular group testing and in general, graphical group testing in which only certain subgroups can be tested. In the last problem, the goal can also change from identifying n defective nodes to identifying a prespecified subgraph. The searched items and the searching space can also be geometrical objects.

Let i denote the outcome that the tested subset contains i defectives, and let i^+ denote at least i defectives. The binary outcome $(0, 1^+)$ of group testing can be extended to k-nary outcomes. For example, multiaccess channels in computer communication have ternary outcome $(0, 1, 2^+)$. This has been further generalized to $(k + 1)$-nary outcome $(0, 1, \cdots, k - 1, k^+)$. In particular, when $k = n$ (the number of items), then each test reveals the exact number of defectives contained therein. Other types of k-nary outcome are also possible. For example, a check bit in coding often provides the binary outcome (even, odd).

One big assumption in the prototype problem which may not hold in reality is that tests are error-free. Various error-tolerance methods, in particular, ideas borrowed from coding theory, have been introduced. However, the theory so far can only handle a very small number of errors. Recent application of group testing in clone library screening shows that the easiness of collecting test-sets can be a crucial factor. Two consequences are that the number of tests is no longer the single intention to choose an algorithm, and that we may have to consider algorithms which provide easy test-sets, but do not guarantee finding all defectives. Thus a different kind of error, due to algorithm capability and not to test uncertainty, is introduced into the problem.

The prototype problems as well as all of its variations will be the subject matter in subsequent chapters.

References

[1] R. Dorfman, The detection of defective members of large populations, *Ann. Math. Statist.* 14 (1943) 436-440.

[2] W. Feller, *An Introduction to Probability Theory and Its Applications*, Vol. 1, (John Wiley, New York, 1950).

[3] F. K. Hwang, T. T. Song and D. Z. Du, Hypergeometric and generalized hypergeometric group testing, *SIAM J. Alg. Disc. Methods* 2 (1981), 426-428.

[4] G. O. H. Katona, Combinatorial search problem, in *A Survey of Combinatorial Theory*, Ed. J. N. Srivastava et al, (North-Holland, Amsterdam, 1973).

[5] C. H. Li, A sequential method for screening experimental variables, *J. Amer. Statist. Assoc.* 57 (1962) 455-477.

[6] M. Sobel and P. A. Groll, Group testing to eliminate efficiently all defectives in a binomial sample, *Bell System Tech. J.* 28 (1959) 1179-1252.

[7] A. Sterrett, On the detection of defective members of large populations, *Ann. Math. Statist.* 28 (1957) 1033-1036.

Part I
Sequential Group Testing Algorithms

2

General Sequential Algorithms

In most practical cases, d is a much smaller number than n. Group testing takes advantage of that by identifying groups containing no defective, thus identifying all items in such a group in one stroke. However, the determination of how large a group should be is a delicate question. On one hand, one would like to identify a large pure group such that many items are identified in one test; this argues for testing a large group. But on the other hand, if the outcome is positive, then a smaller group contains more information; this argues for testing a small group. Keeping a balance between these two conflicting goals is what most algorithms strive for.

2.1 The Binary Tree Representation of a Sequential Algorithm

A *binary tree* can be inductively defined as a node, called the *root*, with its two disjoint binary trees, called the *left* and *right* subtree of the root, either both empty or both nonempty. Nodes occurring in the two subtrees are called *descendants* of the root (the two immediate descendants are called *children*), and all nodes having a given node as a descendant are ancestors (the immediate ancestor is called a *parent*). Two children of the same parent are *siblings*. Nodes which have no descendants are called *leaves*, and all other nodes are called *internal nodes*. The path length of a node is the number of that node's ancestors. A node is also said at *level l* if its path length is $l - 1$. The *depth* of a binary tree is the maximal level over all leaves.

Let S denote the sample space. Then a group testing algorithm T for S can be represented by a binary tree, also denoted by T, by the following rules:

(i) Each internal node u is associated with a test $t(u)$; its two links associated with the two outcomes of $t(u)$ (we will always designate the negative outcome by the left link). The *test history* $H(u)$ of a node u is the set of tests and outcomes associated with the nodes and links on the path of u.

(ii) Each node u is also associated with an event $S(u)$ which consists of all the members of S consistent with $H(u)$. $|S(v)| \leq 1$ for each leaf v.

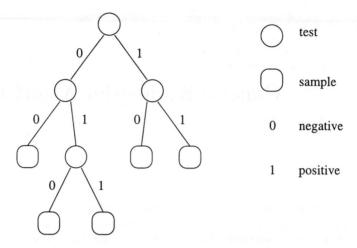

Figure 2.1: The binary tree representation.

Since the test $t(u)$ simply splits $S(u)$ into two disjoint subsets, every member of S must appear in one and only one $S(v)$ for some leaf v.

For a reasonable algorithm each $S(u)$ is split into two nonempty subsets. Thus $|S(v)| = 1$ for every leaf v, i.e., there exists a one-to-one mapping between S and the leaf-set.

Let $p(s)$ denote the path of the leaf v associated with the sample point s and let $|p(s)|$ denote its length. Then

$$M_T(S) = \max_s |p(s)|$$

is the depth of T.

Lemma 2.1.1 $\Sigma_{s \in S} 2^{-|p(s)|} = 1$ *for every reasonable algorithm.*

Proof. True for $|S| = 1$. A straightforward induction on $|S|$ proves the general case. $\square$

Lemma 2.1.1 is well known in the binary tree literature. The proofs are included here for completeness.

A group testing algorithm T for the sample space S is called *admissible* if there does not exist another algorithm T' for S such that

$$|p(s)| \geq |p'(s)| \quad \text{for all } s \in S$$

with at least one strict inequality true, where $p'(s)$ is the path of s in T'.

Theorem 2.1.2 *A group testing algorithm is admissible if and only if it is reasonable.*

Proof. It is obvious that "reasonable" is necessary. To show sufficiency, suppose to the contrary that T is an inadmissible reasonable algorithm, i.e., there exists T' such that

$$|p(s)| \geq |p'(s)| \quad \text{for all } s \in S$$

with at least one strict inequality true. Then

$$\Sigma_{s \in S} 2^{-|p'(s)|} > \Sigma_{s \in S} 2^{-|p(s)|} = 1 ,$$

hence T' is not reasonable. We have an infinite sequence of inadmissible $T \to T' \to T'' \to \cdots$, with $\Sigma_{s \in S} 2^{-|p'(s)|}$ strictly increasing, contradicting the finiteness of the number of algorithms. Therefore, T is admissible when T is reasonable. □

From now on only admissible, or reasonable, algorithms are considered in the volume. The word "algorithm" implies an admissible algorithm.

Since $M(n, n) = M(0, n) = 0$, whenever the (d, n) problem is studied, it is understood that $0 < d < n$. Hu, Hwang and Wang [3] proved some basic inequalities about the M function which are reported in this section.

Corollary 2.1.3 $M(d, n) \leq M(d, n + 1).$

Proof. Add an imaginary good new item I_{n+1} to the item set. Then each sample point in $S(d, n)$ is augmented to a sample point in $S(d, n+1)$ since I_{n+1} of the former can only be good.

Note that adding a good item to any group does not affect the test outcome. Therefore, no additional piece of good item is actually needed; an imaginary piece of good item will do. □

Let $M(m; d, n)$ denote the minimum number of tests necessary to identify the d defectives among n items when a particular subset of m items is known to be contaminated.

Theorem 2.1.4 $M(m; d, n) \geq 1 + M(d - 1, n - 1)$ *for $m \geq 2$ and $0 < d < n$.*

Proof. By Lemma 1.2.2

$$M(m; d, n) \geq M(2; d, n) \quad \text{for } m \geq 2 .$$

Let T be an algorithm for the $(2; d, n)$ problem, and let $M_T(2; d, n) = k$, i.e., k is the maximum path length of a leaf in T. Let I_1 and I_2 denote the two items in the contaminated group.

Claim. Every path of length k in T includes at least one test that contains either I_1 or I_2.

Proof of claim. Suppose to the contrary that for some leaf v the path $p(v)$ has length k and involves no test containing I_1 or I_2. Since no test on $p(v)$ can distinguish I_1 from I_2, and since $\{I_1, I_2\}$ is a contaminated group, I_1 and I_2 must both be defective in the sample point $s(v)$. Let u be the sibling node of v. Then u is also a leaf since v has maximum path length. Since $p(u)$ and $p(v)$ have the same set of tests, I_1 and I_2 must also be both defective in the sample point $s(u)$. Since $s(u) \neq s(v)$, there exist indices i and j such that I_i is defective and I_j is good in the sample point $s(u)$, while I_i is good and I_j is defective in $s(v)$. Let w denote the parent node of u and v; thus $S(w) = \{s(u), s(v)\}$. Then no test on $p(w)$ can be of the form $G \cup \{I_j\}$, where G, possibly empty, contains only items classified as good in $s(u)$, since such a test must yield a positive outcome for $s(v)$ and a negative outcome for $s(u)$, and hence would have separated $s(u)$ from $s(v)$. Define s to be the sample point identical to $s(u)$ except that I_2 is good and both I_i and I_j are defective. Then s can be distinguished from $s(u)$ only by a test containing I_2, which by assumption does not exist on $p(w)$, or by a test of the form $G \cup \{I_j\}$, whose existence has also been ruled out. Thus $s \in S(w)$, and u and v cannot both be leaves, a contradiction that completes the proof of the claim.

If a path involves only I_2, we may change I_2 to I_1 by symmetry. Let z be the first node on the path incorporating this change. Then I_1 and I_2 should be interchanged in the above subtree rooted at z. One may assume that every path of length k in T involves a test that contains I_1. Add an imaginary defective to the $(d-1, n-1)$ problem and label it I_1, and map the $n-1$ items of the $(d-1, n-1)$ problem one-to-one to the items of the (d, n) problem except I_1. Then the modified T can be used to solve the $(d-1, n-1)$ problem except that every test containing I_1 is skipped since the positive outcome is predictable. But each path of length k in T contains such a test. Hence the maximum path length in applying T to the $(d-1, n-1)$ problem is $k-1$, i.e.,

$$M_T(2; d, n) \geq 1 + M_T(d-1, n-1) .$$

Since T is arbitrary, the proof is complete.   □

Lemma 2.1.5 $M(d, n) \leq n - 1$.

Proof. The individual testing algorithm needs only $n-1$ tests since the state of the last item can be deduced by knowing the states of the other items and knowing d. □

Corollary 2.1.6 $M(n-1, n) = n - 1$.

Proof. Trivially true for $n = 1$. For $n \geq 2$

$$M(n-1, n) = M(n; n-1, n) \geq 1 + M(n-2, n-1) \geq n-1 + M(0,1) = n-1 .$$

□

Theorem 2.1.7 $M(d,n) \geq 1 + M(d-1, n-1) \geq M(d-1, n)$ *for* $0 < d < n$.

Proof. By noting

$$M(d,n) = M(n; d, n) ,$$

the first inequality follows from Theorem 2.1.4. The second inequality is trivially true for $d = 1$. The general case is proved by using the induction assumption

$$M(d,n) \geq M(d-1, n) .$$

True for $d = 1$. For $d > 1$, let T be the algorithm which first tests a single item and then uses a minimax algorithm for the remaining problem. Then

$$
\begin{aligned}
M(d-1, n) & \leq & M_T(d-1, n) \\
& = & 1 + \max\{M(d-1, n-1), \ M(d-2, n-1)\} \\
& = & 1 + M(d-1, n-1) .
\end{aligned}
$$

$\square$

Sorting version of Theorem 2.1.7 is still open.

Lemma 2.1.8 *Suppose that* $n - d > 1$. *Then* $M(d,n) = n-1$ *implies* $M(d, n-1) = n - 2$.

Proof. Suppose to the contrary that $M(d, n-1) \neq n - 2$. By Lemma 2.1.5, this is equivalent to assuming $M(d, n-1) < n-2$. Let T denote an algorithm for the (d, n) problem which first tests a single item and then uses a minimax algorithm for the remaining problem. Then

$$
\begin{aligned}
M(d, n) & \leq & M_T(d, n) \\
& = & 1 + \max\{M(d, n-1), M(d-1, n-1)\} \\
& = & 1 + M(d, n-1) \quad \text{by Theorem 2.1.7} \\
& < & n - 1,
\end{aligned}
$$

a contradiction to the assumption of the lemma. $\square$

Theorem 2.1.9 $M(d,n) = M(d-1, n)$ *implies* $M(d,n) = n - 1$.

Proof. Suppose $n - d = 1$. Then Theorem 2.1.9 follows from Corollary 2.1.6. The general case is proved by induction on $n-d$. Note that $M(d,n) = M(d-1, n)$ implies

$$M(d,n) = 1 + M(d-1, n-1)$$

by Theorem 2.1.7. Let T be a minimax algorithm for the (d, n) problem. Suppose that T first tests a group of m items. If $m > 1$, then

$$
\begin{aligned}
M_T(d, n) &\geq 1 + M(m; d, n) \\
&\geq 2 + M(d - 1, n - 1) \quad \text{by Theorem 2.1.4,}
\end{aligned}
$$

a contradiction to what has just been shown. Therefore $m = 1$ and

$$
\begin{aligned}
M(d, n) &= 1 + \max\{M(d, n - 1), M(d - 1, n - 1)\} \\
&= 1 + M(d, n - 1)
\end{aligned}
$$

by Theorem 2.1.7 and the fact that $d < n - 1$. It follows that

$$
M(d - 1, n - 1) = M(d, n - 1).
$$

Hence

$$
M(d - 1, n - 1) = n - 2
$$

by induction. Therefore

$$
M(d, n) = 1 + M(d - 1, n - 1) = n - 1 \ .
$$

$\square$

Lemma 2.1.10 *Suppose $M(d, n) < n - 1$. Then*

$$
M(d, n) \geq 2l + M(d - l, n - l) \text{ for } 0 < l \leq d < n \ .
$$

Proof. By Corollary 2.1.6 and Theorem 2.1.7, $M(d, n) < n - 1$ implies $n - d > 1$. First consider the case $l = 1$.

Let T be a minimax algorithm for the (d, n) problem which first tests a set of m items. If $m > 1$, then Lemma 2.1.10 is an immediate consequence of Theorem 2.1.4. Therefore assume $m = 1$. Suppose to the contrary that

$$
M_T(d, n) < 2 + M(d - 1, n - 1) \ .
$$

Then

$$
\begin{aligned}
1 + M(d - 1, n - 1) &\geq M_T(d, n) \\
&= 1 + \max\{M(d, n - 1), M(d - 1, n - 1)\} \\
&= 1 + M(d, n - 1)
\end{aligned}
$$

by Theorem 2.1.7. Therefore

$$
M(d - 1, n - 1) = M(d, n - 1) = n - 2
$$

by Theorem 2.1.9. Consequently,

$$
M(d, n) = 1 + M(d, n - 1) = n - 1 \ ,
$$

a contradiction to the assumptions of the lemma. Thus Lemma 2.1.10 is true for $l = 1$. The general case is proved by a straightforward induction argument (on l). $\square$

Corollary 2.1.11 $M(d,n) \geq \min\{n-1, 2l + \lceil \log \binom{n-l}{d-l} \rceil\}$ for $0 < l \leq d < n$.

Hwang, Song and Du [10] proved that $M(\bar{d}, n)$ is at most one more than $M(d,n)$, by first proving the following crucial lemma.

Let T denote a procedure for the (d,n) problem. Let v be a terminal node of T and $s \in S(v)$. Partition the d defectives in s into two categories, the *fixed items* and the *free items*. $x \in s$ is a fixed item if there exists a group tested in $H(v)$ such that the group does not contain any other element of s; otherwise, x is a free item. A free item is identified as defective through the identification of $n - d$ good items.

Lemma 2.1.12 *Suppose that v is a terminal node with $f \geq 1$ free items. Let u be the sibling node of v. Then u is the root of a subtree whose maximum path length is at least $f - 1$.*

Proof. Let G denote the last group tested before v. Since whenever $n - d$ good items are identified the (d,n) problem is necessarily solved, free items can be identified only at the last test. Therefore $f \geq 1$ implies that v corresponds to the negative outcome of G. Hence G cannot contain any item of s for $s \in S(v)$.

Let y denote a free item of s and $x \in G$. Then $(s \setminus \{y\}) \cup \{x\} \in S(u)$. To see this, note that any test group containing y must contain another element of s, or y would be a fixed item. Therefore changing y from defective to good does not change the outcome of any test in $H(v)$. Furthermore $(s \setminus \{y\}) \cup \{x\}$ is consistent with the contaminated outcome of G, hence it is in $S(u)$.

Let S_x denote the family $\{(s \setminus \{y\}) \cup \{x\} \mid y \in s \text{ and } y \text{ is free }\}$. Then $M(S(u)) \geq M(S_x) = |S_x| - 1 = f - 1$ by Lemma 1.2.2 and Corollary 2.1.6. □

Theorem 2.1.13 *For each procedure T of the (d,n) problem, there exists a procedure T' for the $(\bar{d}, n)$ problem such that*

$$M_T(d,n) + 1 \geq M_{T'}(\bar{d}, n) .$$

Proof. Let T' be obtained from T by adding a subtree T_v to each terminal node v having a positive number of free items (see Figure 2.2). T_v is the tree obtained by testing the free items one by one. Since free items are the only items at v whose states are uncertain when (d,n) is changed to $(\bar{d}, n)$, T' is a procedure for the $(\bar{d}, n)$ problem. From Lemma 2.1.12, the sibling node of v is the root of a subtree with maximum path length at least $f - 1$ where f is the number of free items of s_v. The theorem follows immediately. □

Corollary 2.1.14 $M(d,n) + 1 \geq M(\bar{d}, n) \geq M(d, n+1)$.

Proof. The first inequality follows from the theorem. The second inequality follows from the observation that the $(d, n+1)$ problem can be solved by any procedure for the $(\bar{d}, n)$ problem, provided one of the $n+1$ items is put aside. But the nature of the item put aside can be deduced with certainty once the natures of the other n items are known. □

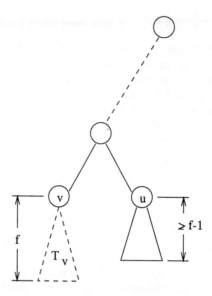

Figure 2.2: From tree T to tree T'.

2.2   The Structure of Group Testing

The information lower bound is usually not achievable. For example, consider a set of six items containing exactly two defectives. Then $\lceil \log |S| \rceil = \lceil \log \binom{6}{2} \rceil = 4$. If a subset of one item is tested, the split is 10 (negative) and 5 (positive); it is 6 and 9 for a subset of two, 3 and 12 for a subset of three, and 1 and 14 for a subset of four. By Theorem 1.3.1, at least four more tests are required.

The reason that information lower bound cannot be achieved in general for group testing is that the split of $S(u)$ at an internal node u is not arbitrary, but must be realizable by a group test. Therefore it is of importance to study which types of splitting are permissible in group testing. The rest of this section reports work done by Hwang, Lin and Mallows [9].

While a group testing algorithm certainly performs the tests in the order starting from the root of the tree proceeding to the leaves, the analysis is often more convenient if started from the leaves (that is the way the Huffman tree - a minimum weighted binary tree - is constructed). Thus instead of asking what splits are permissible, the question becomes: for two children nodes x, y of u, what types of $S(x)$ and $S(y)$ are permitted to merge into $S(u)$.

Let N denote a set of n items, D the defective set and $S_0 = \{D_1, \cdots, D_k\}$ the initial sample space. Without loss of generality assume $\cup_{i=1}^{k} D_i = N$, for any item not in $\cup_{i=1}^{k} D_i$ can immediately be identified as good and deleted from N. A subset

S_i of S_0 is said to be *realizable* if there exists a group testing tree $T(A)$ for S_0 and a node u of T such that $S(u) = S_i$. Let $\pi = (S_1, \cdots, S_m)$ be a *partition* of S_0, i.e., $S_i \cap S_j = \emptyset$ for all $i \neq j$ and $\cup_{i=1}^m S_i = S_0$. The partition π is said to be *realizable* if there exists a group testing tree T for S_0 and a set of m nodes $(u_1, \cdots, u_m)$ of T such that $S(u_i) = S_i$ for $1 \leq i \leq m$. Define $\| S \| = \cup_{D_i \in S} D_i$, $\overline{\| S \|} = N \backslash \| S \|$, the complement of $\| S \|$, and $\hat{S} = \{A \mid A \subseteq \| S \|, A \supseteq \text{ some } D_i\}$, the closure of S. Furthermore, in a partition $\pi = (S_1, \cdots, S_m)$ of S_0, S_i and S_j are said to be *separable* if there exists an $I \subseteq N$ such that $I \cap D = \emptyset$ for all $D \in S_i$, and $I \cap D \neq \emptyset$ for all $D \in S_j$ (or vice versa).

Given π, define a directed graph G_π by taking each S_i as a node, and a directed edge from S_i to S_j ($S_i \to S_j$), $i \neq j$, if and only if there exist $A_i \in \hat{S}_i$, $A_j \in \hat{S}_j$ such that $A_i \subseteq A_j$, i.e., there exists $D \in S_i$ such that $D \subseteq \| S_j \|$.

Theorem 2.2.1 *The following statements are equivalent:*
(i) S_i and S_j are not separable.
(ii) $S_i \to S_j \to S_i$ in G_π.
(iii) $\hat{S}_i \cap \hat{S}_j \neq \emptyset$.

Proof: By showing (i) $\Rightarrow$ (ii) $\Rightarrow$ (iii) $\Rightarrow$ (i).

(i) $\Rightarrow$ (ii): It is first shown that if $S_i \not\to S_j$, then $I = \overline{\| S_j \|} \cap \| S_i \| \neq \emptyset$ and I separates S_i, S_j. Clearly, if $I = \emptyset$, then $\| S_i \| \subseteq \| S_j \|$; since $\| S_i \| \in \hat{S}_i$ and $\| S_j \| \in \hat{S}_j$, it follows that $S_i \to S_j$, a contradiction. Thus $I \neq \emptyset$. Also, $I \cap D = \emptyset$ for all $D \in S_j$ since $I \subseteq \overline{\| S_j \|}$. Furthermore, if there is a $D \in S_i$ such that $I \cap D = \emptyset$, then from the definition of I, $\overline{\| S_j \|} \cap \| S_i \| \cap D = \overline{\| S_j \|} \cap D = \emptyset$ and hence $D \subseteq \| S_j \| \in \hat{S}_j$. This implies $S_i \to S_j$, again a contradiction. Therefore $I \cap D \neq \emptyset$ for all $D \in S_i$ and I separates S_i, S_j. The proof is similar if $S_j \not\to S_i$.

(ii) $\Rightarrow$ (iii): Suppose $S_i \to S_j \to S_i$. Let $A_i, A_i' \in \hat{S}_i$ and $A_j, A_j' \in \hat{S}_j$ such that $A_i \subseteq A_j$ and $A_i' \supseteq A_j'$. Furthermore, let $u = \| S_i \| \cap \| S_j \|$. Then $u \neq \emptyset$. Since $A_i \subseteq A_j \subseteq \| S_j \|$, $A_i \subseteq \| S_i \| \cap \| S_j \| = u \subseteq \| S_i \|$ and thus $u \in \hat{S}_i$. A similar argument shows $u \in \hat{S}_j$. Therefore $\hat{S}_i \cap \hat{S}_j \neq \emptyset$.

(iii) $\Rightarrow$ (i): Suppose $w \in \hat{S}_i \cap \hat{S}_j$ ($w \neq \emptyset$) but S_i and S_j are separable. Let $I \subseteq N$ be a subset such that $I \cap D_i \neq \emptyset$ for all $D_i \in S_i$ and $I \cap D_j = \emptyset$ for all $D_j \in S_j$. But $w \in \hat{S}_i \Rightarrow$ there exists a $D_i \in S_i$ such that $D_i \subseteq w$, hence $I \cap w \supseteq I \cap D_i \neq \emptyset$. On the other hand $w \in \hat{S}_j \Rightarrow w \subseteq \| S_j \| \Rightarrow I \cap w = \emptyset$, a contradiction. Therefore, S_i and S_j are not separable. $\qquad\square$

Theorem 2.2.2 *π is realizable if and only if G_π does not contain a directed cycle.*

Proof. Suppose G_π has a cycle C. Let π' be a partition of S_0 obtained by merging two (separable) sets S_i and S_j in π. From Theorem 2.2.1, G_π cannot contain the cycle $S_i \to S_j \to S_i$ for otherwise S_i and S_j are not separable, therefore not mergeable. Since every edge in G_π except those between S_i and S_j is preserved in $G_{\pi'}$, $G_{\pi'}$ must contain a cycle C'. By repeating this argument, eventually one obtains a partition with no two parts separable. Therefore π is not realizable.

Next assume that G_π contains no cycle. The graph G_π induces a partial ordering on the S_i's with $S_i < S_j$ if and only if $S_i \to S_j$. Let S_j be a minimal element in this ordering. Then $I = \| S_j \|$ separates S_j from all other S_i's. Let $G_{\pi'}$ be obtained from G_π by deleting the node S_j and its edges. Then clearly, $G_{\pi'}$ contains no cycle. Therefore the above argument can be repeated to find a set of tests which separate one S_i at a time. $\qquad\square$

Unfortunately, local conditions, i.e., conditions on S_i and S_j alone, are not sufficient to tell whether a pair is validly mergeable or not. (S_i and S_j is *validly mergeable* if merging S_i and S_j preserves the realizability of the partition.) Theorem 2.2.1 provides some local necessary conditions while the following corollaries to Theorem 2.2.2 provide more such conditions as well as some sufficient conditions.

Corollary 2.2.3 *Let M be the set of S_i's which are maximal under the partial ordering induced by G_π. (If $|M| = 1$, add to $M = \{S_i\}$ an element S_j such that $S_j < S_i$ and $S_j \not< S_k$ for all other S_k.) Then every pair in M is validly mergeable.*

Corollary 2.2.4 *Let π be realizable. Then the pair S_i, S_j is validly mergeable if there does not exist some other S_k such that either $S_i \to S_k$ or $S_j \to S_k$.*

Corollary 2.2.5 *S_i and S_j are not validly mergeable if there exists another S_k such that either $S_i \to S_k \to S_j$ or vice versa.*

Corollary 2.2.6 *Let π be the partition of S_0 in which every S_i consists of just a single element. Then π is realizable.*

Let $S \subset S_0$ ($S \neq \emptyset$) and let $\pi = \{S, S_1, S_2, \cdots, S_m\}$ be the partition of S_0 where each S_i consists of a single element D_i. The following theorem shows a connection between the realization of S and the realization of π.

Theorem 2.2.7 *The following statements are equivalent:*
(i) S is realizable.
(ii) $\hat{S} \cap S_0 = S$.
(iii) π is realizable.

Proof. We show (i) $\Rightarrow$ (ii) $\Rightarrow$ (iii) $\Rightarrow$ (i).

(i) $\Rightarrow$ (ii): Since $S \subseteq S_0$, clearly $\hat{S} \cap S_0 \supseteq S$. So only $\hat{S} \cap S_0 \subseteq S$ needs to be shown. Let $D \in \hat{S} \cap S_0$, then $D \in \hat{S}$ and hence there is some $D' \in S$ such that $D' \subseteq D \subseteq \| S \|$. Suppose $D \notin S$. Then $D = S_i$, for some i. But $D \in \hat{S}$ implies $S_i \to S$ and $D' \subseteq D$ implies $S \to S_i$. Hence S is not realizable by Theorem 2.2.2.

(ii) $\Rightarrow$ (iii): If π is not realizable, then G_π contains a directed cycle. Since each S_i is a single element, $\hat{S}_i = S_i$ and hence any directed cycle must contain S, say $S_1 \rightarrow S_2 \rightarrow \cdots \rightarrow S_k \rightarrow S \rightarrow S_1$. But $S_1 \rightarrow S_2 \rightarrow \cdots \rightarrow S_k \rightarrow S$ implies $S_1 \rightarrow S$ since S_i's are single elements. By Theorem 2.2.1, $S \rightarrow S_1 \rightarrow S$ implies $\hat{S} \cap \hat{S}_1 = \hat{S} \cap \{D_1\} \neq \emptyset$. This implies $D_1 \in \hat{S} \cap S_0$. Since $D_1 \notin S$, $\hat{S} \cap S_0 \neq S$.

(iii) $\Rightarrow$ (i): Trivially true by using the definition of realizability. $\square$

2.3 Li's s-Stage Algorithm

Li [12] extended a 2-stage algorithm of Dorfman [2] (for PGT) to s stages. At stage 1 the n items are arbitrarily divided into g_1 groups of k_1 (some possibly $k_1 - 1$) items. Each of these groups is tested and items in pure groups are identified as good and removed. Items in contaminated groups are pooled together and arbitrarily redivided into g_2 groups of k_2 (some possibly $k_2 - 1$) items; thus entering stage 2. In general, at stage i, $2 \leq i \leq s$, items from the contaminated groups of stage $i - 1$ are pooled and arbitrarily divided into g_i groups of k_i (some possibly $k_i - 1$) items, and a test is performed on each such group. k_s is set to be 1; thus every item is identified at stage s. Let t_s denote the number of tests required by Li's s-stage algorithm.

Note that $s = 1$ corresponds to the *individual testing algorithm*, i.e., testing the items one by one. Thus $t_1 = n$. Next consider $s = 2$. For easier analysis, assume that n is divisible by k_1. Then

$$t_2 = g_1 + g_2 \leq \frac{n}{k_1} + dk_1 \ .$$

Ignoring the constraint that k_1 is an integer, the upper bound is minimized by setting $k_1 = \sqrt{n/d}$ (using straightforward calculus). This gives $g_1 = \sqrt{nd}$ and $t_2 \leq 2\sqrt{nd}$.

Now consider the general s case.

$$t_s = \sum_{i=1}^{s} g_i \leq \frac{n}{k_1} + \frac{dk_1}{k_2} + \cdots + \frac{dk_{s-2}}{k_{s-1}} + dk_{s-1} \ .$$

Again, ignoring the integral constraints, then the upper bound is minimized by

$$k_i = \left(\frac{n}{d}\right)^{\frac{s-i}{s}} \ , \quad 1 \leq i \leq s - 1 \ .$$

This gives

$$g_i \leq d \left(\frac{n}{d}\right)^{\frac{1}{s}}$$

and

$$t_s \leq sd \left(\frac{n}{d}\right)^{\frac{1}{s}} \ .$$

The first derivative of the above upper bound with respect to a continuous s is

$$d \left(\frac{n}{d}\right)^{\frac{1}{s}} \left(1 - \frac{s \ln \frac{n}{d}}{s^2}\right) ,$$

which has a unique root $s = \ln\left(\frac{n}{d}\right)$. It is easily verified that $s = \ln\left(\frac{n}{d}\right)$ is the unique maximum of the upper bound. Hence

$$t_s \leq sd \left(\frac{n}{d}\right)^{\frac{1}{s}} \leq ed \, \ln\left(\frac{n}{d}\right) = \frac{e}{\log e} d \log\left(\frac{n}{d}\right) ,$$

where $e \cong 2.718$. Since $sd\left(\frac{n}{d}\right)^{\frac{1}{s}}$ is not concave in s, one cannot conclude that the integer s which maximizes the function is either $\lfloor \ln\left(\frac{n}{d}\right) \rfloor$ or $\lceil \ln\left(\frac{n}{d}\right) \rceil$. Li gave numerical solutions for such s for given values of n/d.

To execute the algorithm, one needs to compute the optimal s and k_i for $i = 1, \cdots, s$. Each k_i can be computed in constant time. Approximating the optimal s by the ceiling or floor function of $\log(n/d)$, then Li's s-stage algorithm runs in $O(\log(n/d))$ time.

Li's s-stage algorithm can be easily adapted to be a parallel algorithm. Define $n' = \lceil n/p \rceil$. Apply Li's algorithm to the (d, n') problem except that the g_i groups at stage i, $i = 1, \ldots, s$, are partitioned into $\lceil g_i/p \rceil$ classes and groups in the same class are tested in the same round. Then the number of rounds with p processors is about the same as $M_{Li}(d, n')$.

We now show the surprising result that Li's s-stage algorithm can be implemented as a 3-bin algorithm. The three bins are labeled "queue," "good item" and "new queue." At the beginning of stage i, items which have been identified as good are in the good-item bin, and all other items are in the queue bin. Items in the queue bin are tested in groups of size k_i (some possibly $k_i - 1$) as according to Li's s-stage algorithm. Items in groups tested negative are thrown into the good-item bin, and items in groups tested positive are thrown into the new-queue bin. At the end of stage i, the queue bin is emptied and changes labels with the new-queue bin to start the next stage. Of course, at stage s, each group is of size one and the items thrown into the new-queue bin are all defectives.

2.4 Hwang's Generalized Binary Splitting Algorithm

It is well known that one can identify a defective from a contaminated group of n items in $\lceil \log n \rceil$ tests through *binary splitting*. Namely, partition the n items into two disjoint groups such that neither group has size exceeding $2^{\lceil \log n \rceil - 1}$. Test one such group, the outcome indicates either the tested group or the other one is contaminated. Apply binary splitting on the new contaminated group. A recursive argument shows that in $\lceil \log n \rceil$ tests a contaminated group of size 1 can be obtained, i.e., a defective is identified. A special binary splitting method is the *halving method* which partitions the two groups as evenly as possible.

By applying binary splitting d times, one can identify the d defectives in the (d, n) problem in at most $d\lceil \log n \rceil$ tests. Hwang [7] suggested a way to coordinate the d applications of binary splitting such that the total number of tests can be reduced. The idea is, roughly, that there exists in average a defective in every n/d items. Instead of catching a contaminated group of size about half of the original group, which is the spirit of binary splitting, one could expect to catch a much smaller contaminated group and thus to identify a defective therein in fewer number of tests. The following is his *generalized binary splitting* algorithm G:

Algorithm G

Step 1. If $n \leq 2d - 2$, test the n items individually. If $n \geq 2d - 1$, set $l = n - d + 1$. Define $\alpha = \lfloor \log(l/d) \rfloor$.

Step 2. If $n > 2d - 2$, test a group of size 2^α. If the outcome is negative, the 2^α items in the group are identified as good. Set $n := n - 2^\alpha$ and go to Step 1. If the outcome is positive, use binary splitting to identify one defective and an unspecified number, say x, of good items. Set $n := n - 1 - x$ and $d := d - 1$. Go to Step 1.

Theorem 2.4.1

$$M_G(d, n) = \begin{cases} n & \text{for } n - 1 \leq 2d - 2, \\ (\alpha + 2)d + p - 1 & \text{for } n \geq 2d - 1, \end{cases}$$

where $p < d$ is a non-negative integer uniquely defined in $l = 2^\alpha d + 2^\alpha p + \theta$, $0 \leq \theta < 2^\alpha$.

Proof. The case $n \leq 2d - 2$ is true due to Step 1. For $2d - 1 \leq n \leq 3d - 2$, α must be 0 and G is reduced to individual testing. Furthermore, $\theta = 0$ and $p = l - d = n - 2d + 1$. Thus

$$(\alpha + 2)d + p - 1 = 2d + n - 2d + 1 - 1 = n = M_G(d, n) \ .$$

For $d = 1$, then $l = n - d + 1 = n$. It is easily verified that except for $n = 2^\alpha$, G is reduced to binary splitting and

$$(\alpha + 2)d + p - 1 = \alpha + 1 = \lfloor \log n \rfloor + 1 = \lceil \log n \rceil = M_G(1, n) \ .$$

For $n = 2^\alpha$, G spends one more test than binary splitting (by testing the whole set first) and

$$(\alpha + 2)d + p - 1 = 1 + \lceil \log n \rceil = M_G(1, n) \ .$$

For the general case $d \geq 2$ and $n \geq 3d - 1$ Theorem 2.4.1 is proved by induction on $d + n$. From Step 2

$$M_G(d, n) = \max\{1 + M_G(d, n - 2^\alpha), 1 + \alpha + M_G(d - 1, n - 1)\}.$$

For $n' = n - 2^\alpha$ and $d' = d$,

$$l' \;=\; n' - d' + 1 = n - 2^\alpha - d + 1 = l - 2^\alpha$$

$$= \begin{cases} 2^\alpha d + 2^\alpha(p - 1) + \theta & \text{for } p \geq 1 \\ 2^{\alpha-1}d + 2^{\alpha-1}(d - 2) + \theta & \text{for } p = 0, \theta < 2^{\alpha-1} \\ 2^{\alpha-1}d + 2^{\alpha-1}(d - 1) + (\theta - 2^{\alpha-1}) & \text{for } p = 0, \theta \geq 2^{\alpha-1}. \end{cases}$$

Hence by induction

$$M_G(d, n - 2^\alpha) = \begin{cases} (\alpha + 2)d + (p - 1) - 1 & \text{for } p \geq 1 \\ (\alpha + 1)d + (d - 2) - 1 & \text{for } p = 0, \theta < 2^{\alpha-1} \\ (\alpha + 1)d + (d - 1) - 1 & \text{for } p = 0, \theta \geq 2^{\alpha-1}. \end{cases}$$

Consequently

$$1 + M_G(d, n - 2^\alpha) = \begin{cases} (\alpha + 2)d + p - 2 & \text{for } p = 0, \theta < 2^{\alpha-1} \\ (\alpha + 2)d + p - 1 & \text{otherwise.} \end{cases}$$

For $d' = d - 1$ and $n' = n - 1$,

$$l' = n' - d' + 1 = l \;=\; \begin{cases} 2^\alpha(d - 1) + 2^\alpha(p + 1) + \theta & \text{for } p \leq d - 3 \\ 2^{\alpha+1}(d - 1) + \theta & \text{for } p = d - 2 \\ 2^{\alpha+1}(d - 1) + 2^\alpha + \theta & \text{for } p = d - 1. \end{cases}$$

Hence by induction

$$M_G(d - 1, n - 1) = \begin{cases} (\alpha + 2)(d - 1) + (p + 1) - 1 & \text{for } p \leq d - 3 \\ (\alpha + 3)(d - 1) - 1 & \text{for } d - 2 \leq p \leq d - 1. \end{cases}$$

Consequently,

$$1 + \alpha + M_G(d - 1, n - 1) = \begin{cases} (\alpha + 2)d + p - 2 & \text{for } p = d - 1 \\ (\alpha + 2)d + p - 1 & \text{otherwise.} \end{cases}$$

Since for $d \geq 2$, $p = 0$ and $p = d - 1$ are mutually exclusive,

$$\begin{aligned} M_G(d, n) &= \max\{1 + M_G(d, n - 2^\alpha), 1 + \alpha + M_G(d - 1, n - 1)\} \\ &= (\alpha + 2)d + p - 1. \end{aligned}$$

$\square$

For n/d large, $M_G(d,n) \to d \log(n/d)$ which compares favorably either with the $d \log n$ tests of binary splitting, or the upper bound $(e/\log e)d \log(n/d)$ of Li's s stage algorithm. In fact, $M_G(d,n)$ is not too far away from the information lower bound $\lceil \log \binom{n}{d} \rceil$.

Corollary 2.4.2 $M_G(d,n) - \lceil \log \binom{n}{d} \rceil \leq d - 1$ for $d \geq 2$.

Proof.

$$\binom{n}{d} = \binom{l+d-1}{d} > \frac{l^d}{d!} = \frac{(2^\alpha d + 2^\alpha p + \theta)^d}{d!}$$

$$\geq \frac{[2^\alpha d(1+p/d)]^d}{d!} \geq 2^{(\alpha+1)d+p-1},$$

since $\frac{d^d}{d!} \geq 2^{d-1}$ and $(1 + \frac{p}{d})^d \geq 2^p$. □

To execute G, one needs to compute α for each set of updated n and d. Since it takes constant time to compute α, the generalized binary splitting algorithm can be solved in $O(d \log(n/d))$ time.

2.5   The Nested Class

Sobel and Groll [14] introduced a class of simple and efficient algorithms for PGT, called the *nested class*. A nested algorithm can be described by the following rules:

1. There is no restriction on the test group until a group is tested to be contaminated. Mark this group the *current contaminated group* and denote it by C.

2. The next test must be on a group, say G, which is a proper subset of C. If G is contaminated, then G replaces C as the current contaminated group. Otherwise, items in G are classified as good and $C \backslash G$ replaces C as the current contaminated group.

3. If the current contaminated group is of size one, identify the item in the group as defective. Test any group of unidentified items, if any.

Note that the generalized binary splitting algorithm is in the nested class.

Due to Lemma 2.7.1, a simple set of recursive equations can now describe the number of tests required by a minimax nested algorithm. Let $H(d,n)$ denote that number and let $F(m;d,n)$ denote the same except for the existence of a current contaminated group of size m.

$$H(d,n) = \min_{1 \leq m < n} \max\{H(d,n-m),\ F(m;d,n)\},$$

$$F(m;d,n) = \min_{1 \leq k < m} \max\{F(m-k;d,n-k), F(k;d,n)\},$$

with the boundary conditions

$$H(d,d) \;=\; H(0,n) = 0 \,,$$
$$F(1;d,n) \;=\; H(d-1,n-1) \,.$$

Since the recursive equations have three parameters d, n, m, and each equation compares $O(m)$ values where the range of m is n, a brute force solution requires $O(n^3 d)$ time. However, a careful analysis can significantly cut down the time complexity.

Define a *line algorithm* as one which orders the unclassified items linearly and always tests a group at the top of the order. It is easily verified that a line algorithm identifies the items in order except

1. A good item may be identified together with a sequence of items up to the first defective after it.

2. When only one unidentified defective is left, then the order of identification is from both ends towards the defective (this is because once a contaminated group is identified, all other items can be deduced to be good).

Lemma 2.5.1 *Every nested algorithm can be implemented as a line algorithm.*

Proof. By Lemma 2.7.1 all unidentified items belong to two equivalent classes, those in the current contaminated group and those not. Since items in an equivalent class are indistinguishable, they can be arbitrarily ordered and any test involving items in this equivalent class can be assumed to be applied to a group at the top of the order.

At the beginning, items in a (d, n) problem are in one equivalent class. Thus they can be linearly ordered. The first test is then on a group at the top of the order. If this group is pure, then items in this group are deleted from the linear order. Except for updating n, the situation is unchanged and the next test is still taken from the top of the order. If the first group is contaminated, then items in the contaminated group again constitute an equivalent class. Without loss of generality, assume that the linear order of this class is same as the original order. Then the next test, taken from the top of the smaller order, is also from the top of the original order. Lemma 2.5.1 is proved by a repeated use of this argument.   □

The following lemma demonstrates some monotonicity properties of $H(d, n)$ and $F(m; d, n)$.

Lemma 2.5.2 $H(d, n)$ *is nondecreasing in n and d. $F(m; d, n)$ is nondecreasing in m, n and d.*

Proof. That $H(d, n)$ and $F(m; d, n)$ are nondecreasing in n follows from Lemma 2.2.1 and the trick of adding an imaginary good item. That $F(m; d, n)$ is increasing in m also follows from Lemma 2.2.1.

$H(d,n) \geq H(d-1,n)$ obviously for $d=1$. For $d \geq 2$, consider testing one item in the $(d-1,n)$ problem. Then

$$
\begin{aligned}
H(d-1,n) &\leq 1 + \max\{H(d-1,n-1), H(d-2,n-1)\} \\
&= 1 + H(d-1,n-1) \text{ by induction.}
\end{aligned}
$$

Suppose now that a minimax algorithm for the (d,n) problem first tests m items. Then for $d < n$,

$$
\begin{aligned}
H(d,n) &= 1 + \max\{H(d,n-m), F(m;d,n)\} \\
&\geq 1 + F(m;d,n) \\
&\geq 1 + F(1;d,n) \\
&= 1 + H(d-1,n-1) \\
&\geq H(d-1,n) \ .
\end{aligned}
$$

Finally, for $m=1$ and $d \geq 2$,

$$
\begin{aligned}
F(1;d,n) &= H(d-1,n-1) \\
&\geq H(d-2,n-1) \\
&= F(1;d-1,n) \ .
\end{aligned}
$$

For general $m > 1$

$$
\begin{aligned}
F(m;d,n) &= 1 + \min_{1 \leq k < m} \max\{F(m-k;d,n-k), F(k;d,n)\} \\
&\geq 1 + \min_{1 \leq k < m} \max\{F(m-k;d-1,n-k), F(k;d-1,n)\} \text{ by induction} \\
&= F(m;d-1,n) \ .
\end{aligned}
$$

$\square$

Define $f_d(t)$ as the maximum n such that

$$H(d,n) \leq t.$$

By Lemma 2.5.2, $H(d,n)$ is nondecreasing in n. Thus the specification of $f_d(t)$ is equivalent to the specification of $H(d,n)$.

While binary splitting can identify a defective among n items in $\lceil \log n \rceil$ tests, one would also like to identify as many good items as possible in the process when identifying one defective is a subroutine in a bigger problem. Chang, Hwang and Weng [1] gave the following result.

Lemma 2.5.3 *There exists an algorithm which can identify a defective among n items in at most $k \equiv \lceil \log n \rceil$ tests. Furthermore, if $\lceil \log n \rceil$ tests are actually used, then at least $2^k - n$ good items are also identified.*

Proof. Lemma 2.5.3 is trivially true for $k = 1$. The general case is proved by induction on k. Consider two cases:

1. $n - 2^{k-1} > 2^{k-2}$. Test a group of $n - 2^{k-1}$ items. If the outcome is negative, then $n - 2^{k-1} \geq 2^k - n$ good items are identified, while a defective can be identified from the remaining 2^{k-1} items in $k - 1$ tests by binary splitting. If the outcome is positive, then by induction, at least $2^{k-1} - (n - 2^{k-1}) = 2^k - n$ good items are identified along with a defective if $k - 1$ more tests are used.

2. $n - 2^{k-1} \leq 2^{k-2}$. Test a group of 2^{k-2} items. If the outcome is negative, then 2^{k-2} good items are already identified and by induction another $2^{k-1} - (n - 2^{k-2})$ good items will be identified in the remaining $n - 2^{k-2}$ items along with a defective if $k - 1$ more tests are used. If the outcome is positive, then a defective can be identified in the 2^{k-2} items in $k - 2$ tests and a total of $k - 1$ tests are used.

□

From the proof it is also clear that the guaranteed identification of $2^k - n$ good items is the best possible. Let $l(i, t)$ denote the maximum number of items in a contaminated group such that a line algorithm can identify a defective in either $t - 1$ tests, or t tests with at most i items unidentified.

Corollary 2.5.4

$$l(i, t) = \begin{cases} \lfloor \frac{2^t + i}{2} \rfloor & \text{for } 0 \leq i \leq 2^t, \\ 2^t & \text{for } i > 2^t. \end{cases}$$

Let $f_d(t)$ denote the largest n such that $M(d, t) \leq t$ over all line algorithms.

Theorem 2.5.5 *For* $d \geq 2$, $f_d(t) = f_d(t-1) + l(f_{d-1}(t') - f_d(t-1), t - 1 - t')$, *where* t' *is defined in*

$$f_{d-1}(t') \geq f_d(t-1) > f_{d-1}(t'-1).$$

Proof. Suppose that $f_d(t-1) < n \leq f_d(t)$. It is easier to present the algorithm by reversing the order of the line. The first test must be on a group not fewer than $n - f_d(t-1)$ items for otherwise a negative outcome would leave too many items for the remaining $t - 1$ tests. On the other hand there is no need to test more than $n - f_d(t-1)$ items since only the case of a positive outcome is of concern and by Lemma 2.5.2, the fewer items in the contaminated group the better.

For the time being, assume that $f_{d-1}(t'+1) \geq f_d(t)$. Under this assumption, if the first defective lies among the first $n - f_{d-1}(t')$ items, then after its identification the remaining items need $t' + 1$ further tests. Therefore only $t - 2 - t'$ tests are available to identify the first defective. Otherwise, the remaining items can be identified by

t' tests and one more test is available to identify the first defective. Therefore, the maximum value of doable n is

$$n - f_d(t-1) = l(f_{d-1}(t') - f_d(t-1), t-1-t') .$$

The proof of $f_{d-1}(t'+1) \geq f_d(t)$ is very involved. The reader is referred to [8] which proved the same for the corresponding R^*-minimax merging algorithm (see Section 2.6).   □

By noting $f_1(t) = 2^t$, $f_2(t)$ has a closed-form solution.

Corollary 2.5.6

$$f_2(t) = \begin{cases} 2^{\frac{t}{2}} + \lfloor \frac{2^{\frac{t}{2}-1}+2}{3} \rfloor & \text{for t even and } \geq 4, \\ 2^{\frac{t-1}{2}} + \lfloor \frac{2^{\frac{t-1}{2}}+2}{3} \rfloor & \text{for t odd and } \geq 3. \end{cases}$$

The recursive equation for $f_d(t)$ can be solved in $O(td)$ time. Since the generalized binary splitting algorithm is in the nested class, $H(d,n)$ cannot exceed $M_G(d,n)$, which is of the order $d \log(n/d)$. Therefore, $f_x(y)$ for $x \leq d$ and $y \leq d \log(n/d)$ can be computed in $O(d^2 \log(n/d))$ time, a reduction by a factor of $n^3/d \log(n/d)$ from the brute force method.

For given n and d, compute $f_x(y)$ for all $x \leq d$ and $y \leq d \log(n/d)$. A minimax nested algorithm is defined by the following procedure (assume that unidentified items form a line):

Step 1. Find t such that $f_d(t) < n \leq f_d(t+1)$.

Step 2. Test a group of $n - f_d(t)$ items.

Step 3. If the group is pure, set $n := f_d(t)$ and go back to Step 1.

Step 4. If the group is contaminated, use the algorithm given in Lemma 2.5.3 to identify the first defective, say the ith-item. Set $n := n - i$ and $d := d - 1$ and go back to Step 1.

Step 1 requires $O(t)$ time and the other steps all take constant time for each test. Therefore, once the f values are available, the minimax nested procedure can be carried out in $O(t^2) = O(d^2(\log(n/d))^2)$ time.

All nested algorithms are 4-bin algorithms. Intuitively, one expects the minimax nested algorithm to be a minimax 4-bin algorithm. But this involves proving that the following type of tests can be excluded from a minimax algorithm : Suppose a contaminated group C exists. Test a group G which is not a subset of C. When G is also contaminated, throw G into the bins containing C and throw $C \setminus G$ into the other bin containing unidentified items. Note that the last move loses information on finding C contaminated. But it is hard to relate this to nonminimaxity.

For nested algorithms Hwang [6] gave an interesting result which is stated here without proof.

Theorem 2.5.7 $F(m; d, n+1) = F(m; \bar{d}, n)$.

Corollary 2.5.8 $H(d, n+1) = H(\bar{d}, n)$.

This is stronger than Theorem 2.1.13.

2.6 (d, n) Algorithms and Merging Algorithms

A problem seemingly unrelated to the group testing problem is the *merging* problem which has been studied extensively in the computer science literature (see [11], for example). Consider two linearly ordered sets

$$A_d = \{a_1 < a_2 < \cdots < a_d\},$$
$$B_g = \{b_1 < b_2 < \cdots < b_g\}.$$

Assuming a_i and b_j are all distinct, the problem is to merge A_d with B_g into a single linearly ordered set

$$U_{d+g} = \{u_1 < u_2 < \cdots < u_{d+g}\}$$

by means of a sequence of pairwise comparisons between elements of A_d and elements of B_g. Hwang [5] compared the two problems and established some relationships between them whereby algorithms for solving one problem may be converted to similar algorithms for solving the other problem. In particular, he showed that a class of merging algorithms well studied in the merging literature can be converted to a class of corresponding (d, n) algorithms.

The problem of merging A_d with B_g can also be viewed as the problem of determining which elements in U_{d+g} are elements of A_d. Interpreting elements of A_d as defectives and elements of B_g as good items, then the sample space of A_d in U_{d+g} is exactly the same as that of the d defectives in $I = \{I_1, \cdots, I_n\}$, where $n = d + g$. Furthermore, both the merging problem and the (d, n) problem are to determine the one sample point from the sample space $S(d, n)$. Clearly, a merging algorithm can also be represented by a binary tree:

(i) A sequence of comparisons is represented by a directed path from the root to a node. Each internal node is associated with a comparison while the two outgoing links of the node denote the two possible outcomes.

(ii) Each node is also associated with the event whose sample points are consistent with the outcomes of the sequence of comparisons made along the path preceding the node.

A merging algorithm and a (d, n) algorithm are said to be mutually *convertible* if they can be represented by the same rooted binary tree.

Though a comparison and a test serve the same function of partitioning the sample space into two smaller subspaces, the sets of realizable partitions induced by each of them are quite different. In general, a comparison of a_i versus b_j answers the question: Are there at least i of the $i + j - 1$ smallest elements of U_{d+g} elements of A_d? On the other hand, a group test on $X \subseteq I$ answers the question: Is there at least one defective in X? However, if $i = 1$ or d, then the comparison a_i versus b_j can be seen to correspond to a group test on $X = (I_1, I_2, \cdots, I_j)$ or $X = (I_{j+d}, I_{j+1+d}, \cdots, I_{g+d})$ respectively in the sense that there is a one-to-one correspondence between each of the two possible outcomes in the two problems such that the resulting situations again have isomorphic sample spaces. This is made explicit in the following table: It is

Merging	(d, n) problem
Comparison a_1 vs. b_j	Group test on $X = (I_1, I_2, \ldots, I_j)$
$a_1 > b_j$	X pure
$a_1 < b_j$	X contaminated
Comparison a_d vs. b_j	Group test on $X = (I_{j+d}, \ldots, I_{g+d})$
$a_d < b_j$	X pure
$a_d > b_j$	X contaminated

easily seen that if $i \neq 1$ or d, then a comparison of a_i versus b_j doesn't correspond to a group test. Thus

Theorem 2.6.1 *A necessary and sufficient condition that a merging algorithm is convertible to a (d, n) algorithm is that a comparison of a_i versus b_j is allowed only if a_i is one of the two extreme elements among the set of undetermined elements of A_d.*

Corollary 2.6.2 *All merging algorithms for $d = 2$ are convertible to (d, n) algorithms.*

In [8], a procedure r to merge A_d with B_g is defined to be an R-class algorithm, i.e., $r \in R(d, g)$ if it satisfies the following requirements:

(i) The first comparison made by r must involve at least one of the four extreme elements a_1, a_d, b_1, b_g.

(ii) Suppose the first comparison is a_d versus b_j for some j. If $a_d < b_j$, then an algorithm $r' \in R(d, j - 1)$ is used to merge A_d with B_{j-1}. If $a_d > b_j$, then a sequence of comparisons (if needed) involving a_d are used to merge a_d into B_g, i.e. to establish $b_i < a_d < b_{i+1}$ for some i, $j \leq i \leq g(b_{g+1} = \infty)$. Subsequently, an algorithm $r'' \in R(d - 1, i)$ is used to merge A_{d-1} with B_i. If the first comparison involves an extreme element other than a_d, then a scheme similar to the above-mentioned one would be used.

Some R-class procedures which have been well analyzed are the tape merge, binary insertion, generalized binary insertion (see [11]) and the R-minimax [8] algorithms. The first three merging algorithms are respectively convertible to individual testing, binary splitting and generalized binary splitting (d, n) algorithms. The R-minimax algorithm $\bar{r}$ is a recursively defined R-class procedure such that $M_{\bar{r}}(d, g) \leq M_r(d, g)$ for all $r \in R(d, g)$.

Not every R-class merging algorithm is convertible to a (d, n) algorithm since a comparison may involve the extreme elements of the B-set but not the extreme elements of the A-set, hence violating the condition in Theorem 2.6.1. However, the subclass of merging algorithms $R^\star \subset R$ which use only comparisons involving the extreme elements of the A-set are certainly convertible. Furthermore, every $r \in R(d, g)$ can be modified to be an $r^\star \in R^\star(d, g)$ by using tape merge to complete the remaining problem whenever a comparison not involving the extreme elements of the A-set comes up in r.

Note that most of the good R-class merging algorithms always merge an extreme element of the current shorter set into the current longer set. Consider such an algorithm $r(d, g)$. If $d \geq g$ to start with, then the corresponding $r^\star(d, g)$ will be the tape merge which in turn yields the individual testing (d, n) algorithm. But individual testing is indeed minimax [4] for this case. If $d < g$, then $r^\star(d, g)$ will mimic $r(d, g)$ until at some stage the starting shorter set A becomes the current longer set. At this time, $r(d, g)$ will merge an extreme element of the B-set while $r^\star(d, g)$ will shift to tape merge for the remaining problem.

Many R-class algorithms, like tape merge, generalized binary, and R-minimax, have the property that the starting shorter set cannot become the longer set without passing a stage where the two sets are of equal length. Hence, they can be modified to become an $R^\star$ algorithm without increasing their maximum numbers of tests since tape merge is indeed minimax in the required situation. Let $R^\star$-minimax be the $R^\star$ algorithm modified from the R-minimax algorithm. From the above discussion, we have proved

Theorem 2.6.3 $M_{R^\star\text{-}minimax}(d, n) = M_{R\text{-}minimax}(d, n)$ *for all d and n.*

Theorem 2.6.4 *The $R^\star$-class merging algorithms and the nested algorithms are mutually convertible.*

Proof. It has been shown that every $R^\star$-class merging algorithm is convertible to a (d, n) algorithm. Clearly, that resultant (d, n) algorithm is a nested algorithm. Therefore, it suffices to prove that every nested algorithm is convertible to a merging algorithm of $R^\star$-class.

Let $I = \{I_1, I_2, \cdots, I_n\}$ be the set of items. Without loss of generality, assume that the first test is on the group $G = \{I_1, \cdots, I_k\}$ for some $k \leq n$. If G is pure, relabel the unclassified items so that the current I has $n - k$ items and repeat the procedure. If G is contaminated, then the next group to be tested must be a subset of G. Again without loss of generality, assume that the group to be tested is $\{I_1, \cdots, I_{k'}\}$ for some $k' < k$. Proceeding like this, every group being tested consists of the first i items in the sequence of unclassified items for some i. Clearly each such test corresponds to a comparison of a_1 vs. b_i. The proof is complete.

Corollary 2.6.5 *The (d, n) algorithm which is obtained by converting the $R^\star$-minimax merging algorithm is a minimax nested algorithm (whose required number of tests is given in Theorem 2.5.5).*

2.7 Number of Group Testing Algorithms

One interesting problem is to count the number of group testing algorithms for S. This is the total number of binary trees with $|S|$ leaves (labeled by members of S) which satisfy the group testing structure. While this problem remains open, Moon and Sobel [13] counted for a class of algorithms when the sample space S is the power set of n items.

Call a group *pure* if it contains no defective, and *contaminated* otherwise. A group testing algorithm is *nested* if whenever a contaminated group is known, the next group to be tested must be a proper subset of the contaminated group. (A more detailed definition is given in Sec. 2.3.) Sobel and Groll [14] proved

Lemma 2.7.1 *Let U be the set of unclassified items and suppose that $C \subset U$ is tested to be contaminated. Furthermore, suppose $C' \subset C$ is then tested to be contaminated. Then items in $C \backslash C'$ can be mixed with items in $U \backslash C$ without losing any information.*

Proof. Since C' being contaminated implies C being contaminated, the sample space given both C and C' being contaminated is the same as only C' being contaminated. But under the latter case, items in $C \backslash C'$ and $U \backslash C$ are indistinguishable. □

Thus under a nested algorithm, at any stage the set of unclassified items is characterized by two parameters m and n, where $m \geq 0$ is the number of items in a contaminated group and n is the total number of unclassified items. Let $f(m, n)$ denote the number of nested algorithms when the sample space is characterized by such m and n. By using the "nested" property, Moon and Sobel obtained

$$
\begin{aligned}
f(0,0) &= 1 \\
f(0,n) &= \Sigma_{k=1}^{n} f(0, n-k) f(k, n) \quad \text{for } n \geq 1, \\
f(1,n) &= f(0, n-1) \quad \text{for } n \geq 1, \\
f(m,n) &= \Sigma_{k=1}^{m-1} f(m-k, n-k) f(k, n) \quad \text{for } n \geq m \geq 1,
\end{aligned}
$$

where k is the size of the group to be tested. Recall that the Catalan numbers

$$
C_k = \frac{1}{k} \binom{2k-2}{k-1}
$$

satisfy the recurrence relation

$$C_k = \Sigma_{i=1}^{k-1} C_i C_{k-i}$$

for $k \geq 2$. Moon and Sobel gave

Theorem 2.7.2

$$
\begin{aligned}
f(0,n) &= C_{n+1}\Pi_{i=1}^{n-1} f(0,i) & \text{for } n \geq 2, \\
f(m,n) &= C_m \Pi_{i=1}^{m} f(0,n-i) & \text{for } 1 \leq m \leq n .
\end{aligned}
$$

Proof. Theorem 2.7.2 is easily verified for $f(0,2)$ and $f(1,n)$. The general case is proved by induction

$$
\begin{aligned}
f(0,n) &= \Sigma_{k=1}^{n} f(0,n-1) f(k,n) \\
&= \Sigma_{k=1}^{n} \left(C_{n-k+1}\Pi_{i=1}^{n-k-1} f(0,i) \right) \left(C_k \Pi_{i=1}^{k} f(0,n-i) \right) \\
&= C_{n+1}\Pi_{i=1}^{n-1} f(0,i) . \\
f(m,n) &= \Sigma_{k=1}^{m-1} f(m-k,n-k) f(k,n) \\
&= \Sigma_{k=1}^{m-1} \left(C_{m-k}\Pi_{i=1}^{m-k} f(0,n-k-i) \right) \left(C_k \Pi_{i=1}^{k} f(0,n-i) \right) \\
&= C_m \Pi_{i=1}^{m} f(0,n-i) . \quad \Box
\end{aligned}
$$

Define $F(n) = f(0,n)$. The following recurrence relations follow readily from Theorem 2.7.2 and the definition of the Catalan numbers.

Corollary 2.7.3 *If $n \geq 1$, then*

$$F(n) = \frac{C_{n+1}}{C_n} F^2(n-1) = \frac{2(2n-1)}{n+1} F^2(n-1) .$$

Corollary 2.7.4 *If $n \geq 2$, then*

$$F(n) = C_{n+1} C_n C_{n-1}^2 C_{n-2}^4 \cdots C_2^{2^{n-2}} .$$

Corollary 2.7.5 *If $n \geq 1$, then*

$$F(n) = 4^{2^n - 1}\Pi_{i=1}^{n} \left\{ 1 - \frac{3}{2(i+1)} \right\}^{2^{n-i}} .$$

The first few values of $F(n)$ are

n	1	2	3	4	5	6
$F(n)$	1	2	10	280	235,220	173,859,840,000

The limiting behavior of $F(n)$ can be derived from the formula in Corollary 1.4.5.

Corollary 2.7.6

$$\lim_{n\to\infty}\{F(n)\}^{2^{-n}} = 4\Pi_{i=1}^{\infty}\left\{1 - \frac{3}{2(i+1)}\right\}^{2^{-i}} = 1.526753\cdots.$$

More generally, it can be shown that

$$F(n) = \frac{1}{4}\alpha^{2^n}\left\{1 + \frac{3/2}{n} + o\left(\frac{1}{n}\right)\right\}$$

as $n \to \infty$, where $\alpha = 1.526753\cdots$; in particular, $F(n) > \frac{1}{4}\alpha^{2^n}$ for $n \geq 1$.

The proof of this is omitted.

References

[1] X. M. Chang, F. K. Hwang and J. F. Weng, Group testing with two and three defectives, *Ann. N.Y. Acad. Sci.* Vol. 576, Ed. M. F. Capobianco, M. Guan, D. F. Hsu and F. Tian, (New York, 1989) 86-96.

[2] R. Dorfman, The detection of defective members of large populations, *Ann. Math. Statist.* 14 (1943) 436-440.

[3] M. C. Hu, F. K. Hwang and J. K. Wang, A boundary problem for group testing, *SIAM J. Alg. Disc. Methods* 2 (1981) 81-87.

[4] F. K. Hwang, A minimax procedure on group testing problems, *Tamkang J. Math.* 2 (1971) 39-44.

[5] F. K. Hwang, Hypergeometric group testing procedures and merging procedures, *Bull. Inst. Math. Acad. Sinica* 5 (1977) 335-343.

[6] F. K. Hwang, A note on hypergeometric group testing procedures, *SIAM J. Appl. Math.* 34 (1978) 371-375.

[7] F. K. Hwang, A method for detecting all defective members in a population by group testing, *J. Amer. Statist. Assoc.* 67 (1972) 605-608.

[8] F. K. Hwang and D. N. Deutsch, A class of merging algorithms, *J. Assoc. Comput. Math.* 20 (1973) 148-159.

[9] F. K. Hwang, S. Lin and C. L. Mallows, Some realizability theorems group testing, *SIAM J. Appl. Math.* 17 (1979) 396-400.

[10] F. K. Hwang, T. T. Song and D. Z. Du, Hypergeometric and generalized hyper-geometric group testing, *SIAM J. Alg. Disc. Methods* 2 (1981), 426-428.

[11] D. E. Knuth, *The Art of Computer Programming*, Vol. 3, (Addison-Wesley, Reading, Mass. 1972).

[12] C. H. Li, A sequential method for screening experimental variables, *J. Amer. Statist. Assoc.* 57 (1962) 455-477.

[13] J. W. Moon and M. Sobel, Enumerating a class of nested group testing procedures, *J. Combin. Theory*, Series B 23 (1977) 184-188.

[14] M. Sobel and P. A. Groll, Group testing to eliminate efficiently all defectives in a binomial sample, *Bell System Tech. J.* 38 (1959) 1179-1252.

3

Sequential Algorithms for Special Cases

When d is very small or very large, more is known about $M(d,n)$. $M(1,n) = \lceil \log n \rceil$ by Theorem 1.2.1, and by using binary splitting. Surprisingly, $M(2,n)$ and $M(3,n)$ are still open problems, although "almost" minimax algorithms are known. On the other hand one expects individual testing to be minimax when n/d is small. It is known that the threshold value for this ratio lies between $21/8$ and 3, and was conjectured to be 3.

3.1 Two Disjoint Sets Each Containing Exactly One Defective

Chang and Hwang [1], [2] studied the CGT problem of identifying two defectives in $A = \{A_1, \ldots, A_m\}$ and $B = \{B_1, \ldots, B_n\}$ where A and B are disjoint and each contains exactly one defective. At first, it seems that one cannot do better than working on the two disjoint sets separately. The following example shows that intuition is not always reliable for this problem.

Example 3.1. Let $A = \{A_1, A_2, A_3\}$ and $B = \{B_1, B_2, B_3, B_4, B_5\}$. If one identifies the defectives in A and B separately, then it takes $\lceil \log 3 \rceil + \lceil \log 5 \rceil = 2 + 3 = 5$ tests. However, the following algorithm shows that the two defectives can be identified in 4 tests.

Step 1. Test $\{A_1, B_1\}$. If the outcome is negative, then A has two items and B has four items left. Binary splitting will identify the two defectives in $\log 2 + \log 4 = 3$ more tests. Therefore, it suffices to consider the positive outcome.

Step 2. Test B_1. If the outcome is negative, then A_1 must be defective. The defective in the four remaining items of B can be identified in 2 more tests. If the outcome is positive, then the defective in the three items of A can be identified in 2 more tests.

Note that there are $3 \times 5 = 15$ samples $\{A_i, B_j\}$. Since $\lceil \log 15 \rceil = 4$, one certainly cannot do better than 4 tests.

In general, the sample space is $A \times B$ which will also be denoted by $m \times n$ if $\mid A \mid = m$ and $\mid B \mid = n$. Does there always exist an algorithm to identify the two defectives in $A \times B$ in $\lceil \log mn \rceil$ tests? Chang and Hwang [2] answered in the affirmative.

A sample space is said to be *A-distinct* if no two samples in it share the same A-item A_j. Suppose S is a sample space with

$$\mid S \mid = 2^r + 2^{r-1} + \cdots + 2^{r-p} + q \,,$$

where $2^{r-p-1} \geq q > 0$. An algorithm T for S is called *A-sharp* if it satisfies the following conditions:

(i) T solves S in $r + 1$ tests.

(ii) Let $v(i)$ be the ith node on the *all-positive path* of T, the path where every outcome is positive. Let $v'(i)$ be the child-node of $v(i)$ with the negative outcome. Then $\mid S(v'(i)) \mid = 2^{r-i}$ for $i = 0, 1, \ldots, p$.

(iii) $\mid S(v(p+1)) \mid = q$ and $S(v(p+1))$ is A-distinct.

If $\mid S \mid = 2^r$, then the above conditions are replaced by the single condition.

(i') T solves S in r tests.

Lemma 3.1.1 *There exists an A-sharp algorithm for any A-distinct sample space.*

Proof. Ignore the B-items in the A-distinct sample space. Since the A-items are all distinct, there is no restriction on the partitions. It is easily verified that there exists a binary splitting algorithm which is A-sharp.   □

For m fixed, define n_k to be the largest integer such that $mn_k \leq 2^k$. Clearly, there exists a k for which $n_k = 1$.

Theorem 3.1.2 $M(m \times n_k) = k$ *for all* $n_k \geq 1$. *Furthermore, if* n_k *is odd, then there exists an A-sharp algorithm for the sample space* $m \times n_k$.

Proof. By the definition of n_k and Theorem 1.2.1, $M(m \times n_k) \geq k$. Therefore it suffices to prove $M(m \times n_k) \leq k$. If m is even, test half of A and use induction. So, it suffices to consider odd m.

The sample space $m \times 1$ is A-distinct. Therefore there exists an A-sharp algorithm by Lemma 3.1.1. For general $n_k > 1$, Theorem 3.1.2 is proved by induction on n_k.

Note that

$$2^{k-2} < mn_{k-1} \leq 2^{k-1} < m(n_{k-1} + 1)$$

implies
$$2^{k-1} < m(2n_{k-1}) \le 2^k < m(2n_{k-1} + 2) .$$

Therefore n_k is either $2n_{k-1}$ or $2n_{k-1} + 1$. In the former case test half of the set B and use induction on the remaining $(m \times n_{k-1})$-problem. In the latter case, let r be the largest integer such that
$$n_k = 2^r n_{k-r} + 1 .$$

Then $r \ge 1$ and n_{k-r} is necessarily odd. Let
$$mn_{k-r} = 2^{k-r-1} + 2^{k-r-2} + \cdots + 2^{k-r-p} + q ,$$

where
$$0 < q \le 2^{k-r-p-1} .$$

Then
$$
\begin{aligned}
mn_k &= m(2^r n_{k-r} + 1) \\
&= 2^{k-1} + 2^{k-2} + \cdots + 2^{k-p} + 2^r q + m .
\end{aligned}
$$

Let T be an A-sharp algorithm for the $(m \times n_{k-r})$-problem. The existence of T is assured by the induction hypothesis. Let v be the node on the all-positive path of T associated with q samples. Let J be the set of j such that $(A_i, B_j) \in S(v)$ for some A_i. For $j \in J$, let L_j denote a set consisting of those A_i's such that $(A_i, B_j) \in S(v)$. Since $S(v)$ is A-distinct, the L_j's are disjoint.

An A-sharp algorithm is now given for the $(m \times n_k)$-problem. For notational convenience, write n for n_{k-r} and n' for n_k. Then B will refer to the set of n items and B' to the set of n' items. Partition $B' - \{B_{n'}\}$ into n groups of 2^r items $G_1, \cdots, G_n$. Consider T truncated at the node v; i.e., delete the subtree rooted at v from T. Let T' be an algorithm for the $(m \times n')$-problem where T' is obtained from T by replacing each item B_j in a test by the group G_j and adding $B_{n'}$ to every group tested on the all-defective path. Then each terminal node of T', except the node v' corresponding with v, will be associated with a set of solutions $(A_i \times G_j)$ for some i and j. Since the only uncertainty is on G_j and $|G_j| = 2^r$, r more tests suffice.

Therefore, it suffices to give an A-sharp algorithm for the sample space
$$S(v') = \{\cup_{j \in J}(L_j \times G_j)\} \cup (A \times B_{n'}) ,$$

with $|S(v')| = 2^r q + m$. Let $G_{j1}, \cdots, G_{j2^r}$ denote the 2^r items in G_j. Define
$$T_1 = \{\cup_{j \in J} G_{j1}\} \cup R ,$$

where R is a subset of A-items not in any of the L_j, $j \in J$, with $|R| = 2^r q + m - 2^{k-p-1} - q$. Note that there are a total of $m - q$ A-items not in any of the L_j. It is now proved that $m - q \ge |R| > 0$. The former inequality follows immediately from the fact that
$$2^r q \le 2^r 2^{k-r-p-1} = 2^{k-p-1} .$$

Furthermore, since

$$2^{k-1} < m(n_{k-1} + 1) = m(2^{r-1}n_{k-r} + 1)$$
$$= 2^{k-2} + 2^{k-3} + \cdots + 2^{k-p-1} + 2^{r-1}q + m ,$$

it follows that

$$2^{r-1}q + m > 2^{k-p-1} ,$$

or

$$\mid R \mid > 2^{r-1}q - q \geq 0 .$$

Test T_1 at $S(v')$. Let S_g and S_d denote the partition of $S(v')$ according as to whether the outcome of T_1 is negative or positive. Then

$$S_d = \{\cup_{j \in J}(L_j \times G_{j1})\} \cup (R \times B_{n'}),$$

with

$$\mid S_d \mid = q + 2^r q + m - 2^{k-p-1} - q$$
$$= 2^r q + m - 2^{k-p-1} ,$$

and

$$S_g = \left\{\cup_{w=2}^{2^r} \cup_{j \in J} (L_j \times G_{jw})\right\} \cup (\{A \setminus R\} \times B_{n'}) ,$$

with $\mid S_g \mid = \mid S(v') \mid - \mid S_d \mid = 2^{k-p-1}$. Since S_d is A-distinct, there exists an A-sharp algorithm for S_d by Lemma 3.1.1. It remains to be shown that S_g can be done in $k - p - 1$ tests.

Note that S_g can also be represented as

$$S_g = \{\cup_{j \in J}(L_j \times \{G_j \setminus \{G_{j1}\} \cup \{B_{n'}\}\})\} \cup (\{(A \setminus R) \setminus \cup_{j \in J}L_j\} \times B_{n'}) .$$

Since $\mid G_j \setminus \{G_{j1}\} \cup \{B_{n'}\} \mid = 2^r$, $\mid (A \setminus R) \setminus \cup_{j \in J}L_j \mid$ must also be a multiple of 2^r. Partition $A - R - \{\cup_{j \in J}L_j\}$ into 2^r subsets of equal size, $H_1, \cdots, H_{2^r}$. Define

$$T_w = \{\cup_{j \in J}G_{jw}\} \cup H_w \quad \text{for } w = 2, 3, \cdots, 2^r.$$

Then the T_w's are disjoint. By testing a sequence of proper combinations of T_w's, it is easily seen that in r tests S_g can be partitioned into 2^r subsets consisting of

$$S_w = \{\cup_{j \in J}(L_j \times G_{jw})\} \cup (H_w \times B_{n'}) , \quad w = 2, \cdots, 2^r ,$$

and

$$S_1 = S_g \setminus \left\{\cup_{w=2}^{2^r} S_w\right\} .$$

Furthermore, S_w is A-distinct and $\mid S_w \mid = 2^{k-p-r-1}$ for each $w = 1, \cdots, 2^r$. Therefore each S_w can be solved in $k - p - r - 1$ more tests by Lemma 3.1.1. This shows that the algorithm just described for $S(v')$ is A-sharp. Therefore, the algorithm T' plus the extension on v' as described is A-sharp. $\square$

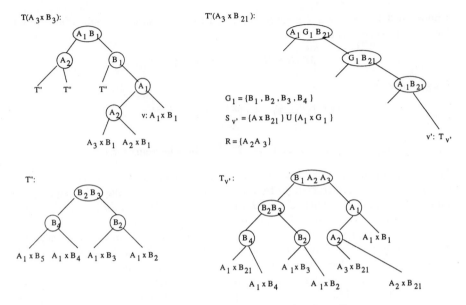

Figure 3.1: An A-sharp algorithm for $A_3 \times B_{21}$.

Corollary 3.1.3 $M(m \times n) = \lceil \log mn \rceil$ *for all m and n.*

The corollary follows from Theorem 3.1.2 by way of the easily verifiable fact that $M(m \times n)$ is monotone nondecreasing in n.

It can be easily verified that if the $m \times n$ model is changed to A and B each containing "at least" one defective and the problem is to identify one defective from each of A and B. Then Corollary 3.1.3 remains true. Denote the new problem by $\bar{m} \times \bar{n}$. Then

Corollary 3.1.4 $M(\bar{m} \times \bar{n}) = \lceil \log mn \rceil$ *for all m and n.*

Ruszinko [12] studied the line version, i.e., A and B are ordered sets and a test group must consist of items from the top of the two orders. He showed that for $m = 11$ and $n = (2^{10k} - 1)/11$ (which is an integer by Fermat's theorem), the first test group must consist of 8 items from A and 2^{10k-4} items from B. But no second test can split the remaining samples into two parts both of sizes not exceeding 2^{10k-2}. He also proved

Theorem 3.1.5 *If* $\log m + \log n - \lfloor \log m \rfloor - \lfloor \log n \rfloor \geq 0.8$, *then* $\lceil \log mn \rceil$ *suffice.*

Weng and Hwang [14] considered the case of k disjoint sets.

Theorem 3.1.6 *Suppose that set S_i has $2^{2^i}+1$ items containing exactly one defective for $i = 0, 1, \cdots, m$. Then*

$$M(S_0 \times S_1 \times \cdots \times S_m) = 2^{m+1} .$$

Proof. Since

$$
\begin{aligned}
\Pi_{i=0}^m (2^{2^i} + 1) &= 2^{2^{m+1}-1} + 2^{2^{m+1}-2} + \cdots + 2^1 + 2^0 \\
&= 2^{2^{m+1}} - 1 , \\
M(S_0 \times S_1 \times \cdots \times S_m) &\geq 2^{m+1} \qquad \text{by Theorem 1.2.1} .
\end{aligned}
$$

The reverse inequality is proved by giving an algorithm which requires only 2^{m+1} tests. Let I_i be an arbitrary item from S_i, $i = 0, 1, \cdots, m$. Consider the sequence of subsets $J_1, \cdots, J_{2^{m+1}-1}$, where $J_{2^k} = \{I_k\}$ for $k = 0, 1, \cdots, m$ and $J_{2^k+j} = \{I_k\} \cup J_j$ for $1 \leq j < 2^k$. It is easily proved by induction that $\sum_{I_i \in J_j} 2^i = j$ for $1 \leq j \leq 2^{m+1} - 1$.

The actual testing of groups is done in the reverse order of J_j until either a negative outcome is obtained or J_1 is tested positive. Note that a subset is tested only when all subsets containing it have been tested. Therefore $J_{2^{m+1}-1}, \cdots, J_{j+1}$ all tested positive and J_j negative imply that items in J_j are good and items in $\{I_0, I_1, \cdots, I_m\} \backslash J_j$ are defective. Thus the $(S_0 \times S_1 \times \cdots \times S_m)$ problem is reduced to the $(\Pi_{I_i \in J_j}(S_i \backslash \{I_i\}))$ problem. The total number of tests is

$$2^{m+1} - j + \sum_{I_i \in J_j} 2^i = 2^{m+1} .$$

If $J_{2^{m+1}-1}, \cdots, J_1$ all tested positive, then each I_i, $0 \leq i \leq m$, has been identified as a defective through individual testing. Therefore all defectives are identified while the total number of tests is simply $2^{m+1} - 1$.   □

3.2 An Application to Locating Electrical Shorts

A prevalent type of fault in the manufacture of electrical circuits is the presence of a short circuit ("short") between two nets of a circuit. Short testing constitutes a significant part of the manufacturing process. Several fault patterns can be described as variations or combination of these types of faults. Applications of short testing ranges from printed circuit board testing and circuit testing to functional testing.

Short testing procedures can have two different objectives; a *detecting* procedure aims simply to detect the presence of a short, while a *locating* procedure identifies the shorted pairs of nets. A short detector in common use is an apparatus involving two connecting leads which, when connected respectively to two nets or groups of nets, can detect, but not locate, the presence of a short between these nets or groups of nets. An obvious way to use this device for short location is the so called n-square testing, which checks each pair of nets separately. If the circuit has n nets to start with, then this location procedure requires $\binom{n}{2}$ tests.

Figure 3.2: A short detector.

Garey, Johnson, and So [7] proposed a procedure for detecting shorts between nets in printed circuit boards. They showed that no more than 5, 8, or 12 tests (depending on the particular assumptions) will ever be required, independent of the number of nets. However, it is not a locating procedure, and their assumptions allow only shorts occurring vertically or horizontally, not diagonally.

Skilling [13] proposed a clever locating procedure much more efficient than the n-square testing. In his method each net is tested individually against all other nets, collectively. Thus after n tests one obtains all the shorted nets, though not knowing to which other nets they are shorted. If there are d shorted nets, then $\binom{d}{2}$ more tests are required to determine which of these are shorted to which others. Thus the total number of tests is $n + \binom{d}{2}$, which can be significantly less than $\binom{n}{2}$ for n much larger than d.

Chen and Hwang [1] proposed a locating procedure, based on Theorem 3.1.2, which requires approximately $2(d+1)\log n$ tests. Consider a circuit board with n nets. Without loss of generality assume $n = 2^a$. This testing process can be mathematically described as follows: Let $[\sum_{i=1}^{k}(a_i \times b_i)]$ denote the configuration where there exist $2k$ disjoint sets with $a_1, b_1, \cdots, a_k, b_k$ nets such that there exists a shorted pair between the nets in a_i and the nets in b_i for at least one i. Let $[\sum_{i=1}^{k} a_i]$ denote the configuration where there exist k disjoint sets with $a_1, \cdots, a_k$ nets such that no shorted pair exists between the a_i nets and the a_j nets for any i and j.

Lemma 3.2.1 *A shorted pair can be located in the configuration* $[a \times b]$ *in* $\lceil \log ab \rceil$ *tests.*

Proof. It suffices to show that any group testing algorithm T for the $(a \times b)$ problem studied in Sec. 3.1 can be converted to a short-locating algorithm T' for the $[a \times b]$ configuration. Consider a one-to-one mapping between the a items (denote the set by A) and the a nets (denote the set by A'), and similarly, between the b items of the set B and the b nets of the set B'. Whenever T tests a group $G_1 \cup G_2$, $G_1 \subseteq A$ and $G_2 \subseteq B$, T' will connect nets $\bar{G}_1$ to one lead and nets $\bar{G}_2$ to the other lead, where $\bar{G}_i$, $i = 1, 2$, is the complementary set of G_i with respect to A or B. A negative (positive) outcome on the group $G_1 \cup G_2$ corresponds to a presence (an absence) of short between nets on the two leads. Clearly, this correspondence preserves the partition of the sample space. Hence T and T' have the same binary tree representation. Lemma

3.2.1 now follows from Theorem 3.1.2. □

Define the *halving procedure* H for the short testing problem as follows. For the configuration $[\sum_{i=1}^{k} a_i]$ split each set of a_i nets into half (as closely as possible); connect one half to one lead and the other half to the other lead. When no short is present, move into the configuration $[\sum_{i=1}^{2k} a_i']$ where each a_i splits into a_i' and a_{i+k}'. When a short is present, move into the configuration $[\sum_{i=1}^{k} \lfloor a_i/2 \rfloor \times \lceil a_i/2 \rceil]$. Use binary splitting on the k pairs to locate one pair $\lfloor a_i/2 \rfloor \times \lceil a_i/2 \rceil$ that contains a short in $\lfloor \log k \rfloor$ tests. By Lemma 3.2.1 a shorted pair from the configuration $[\lfloor a_i/2 \rfloor \times \lceil a_i/2 \rceil]$ can be located.

Lemma 3.2.2 *The halving procedure H can locate a shorted pair in n nets in $2\lceil \log n \rceil - 1$ tests, or ascertain the nonexistence of a shorted pair in $\lceil \log n \rceil$ tests.*

Proof. Since the starting configuration is $[n]$, it is clear that all configurations of the form $[\sum_{i=1}^{k} a_i]$ H encounters has k a power of 2 and each $a_i \leq 2^{\alpha - \log k}$ where $\alpha \equiv \lceil \log n \rceil$. Consequently, all the $[\sum_{i=1}^{k} a_i \times b_i]$ configurations H encounters also have k a power of 2 and each $a_i b_i \leq 2^{2(\alpha - \log k - 1)}$. Suppose that the first time that the configuration of the form $[\sum_{i=1}^{k} a_i \times b_i]$ is obtained is when $k = 2^m$. Then $m + 1$ tests have been used. In another m tests a pair $a \times b$ which contains a shorted pair is obtained. Finally, the shorted pair is located in $2\lceil \log n \rceil - 2m - 2$ more tests. Adding up the tests yields $2\lceil \log n \rceil - 1$. If after $\lceil \log n \rceil$ tests the configuration $[\sum_{i=1}^{2\alpha} a_i]$ with each $a_i \leq 1$ is obtained, then clearly no shorted pair exists. □

Now consider two modes of operation, R and $\bar{R}$, depending on whether a located short is immediately repaired or not. An important difference is that a newly detected short cannot be a previously located short under mode R.

Theorem 3.2.3 *If the n nets contain d shorted pairs, d unknown, then $d + 1$ runs of H will locate all shorted pairs in at most $(2d + 1)\lceil \log n \rceil - d$ tests under mode R.*

In practice, if it is known that no shorted pair exists between a set of $\sum_{i=1}^{k} a_i$ nets and a set of $\sum_{i=1}^{k} b_i$ nets in a run, then the test can certainly be skipped in all later runs.

Corollary 3.2.4 *At most $(2d + 1)\lceil \log n \rceil$ tests are required if mode R is replaced by mode $\bar{R}$.*

Proof. After H located a shorted pair (x, y), remove y and test x against the other $n-2$ nets. If a short is detected, then locate another shorted pair in $1 + \log(n-2) \leq 2\lceil \log n \rceil$ tests by Corollary 3.1.4. If no short is detected, then (x, y) is the only shorted pair involving x. Remove x and apply H to the other $n - 1$ nets (y is put back). Thus the detection of each shorted pair may consume one extra test. □

TABLE 3.1

A COMPARISON OF THREE METHODS

	n-square	Skilling method					Procedure H (mode R)				
n	method	$d=0$	$d=2$	$d=4$	$d=6$	$d=8$	$d=0$	$d=2$	$d=4$	$d=6$	$d=8$
64	2016	64	65	70	79	92	6	28	50	72	94
128	8128	128	129	134	143	156	7	33	59	85	111
256	32640	256	257	262	271	284	8	38	68	98	128
512	130816	512	513	518	527	540	9	43	77	111	145
1024	523776	1024	1025	1030	1039	1052	10	48	86	124	162
2048	2096128	2048	2049	2054	2063	2076	11	53	95	137	179

Skilling [13] compared the number of tests required by his method with the n-square method for $n = 64, 128, \cdots, 2048$ and $d = 0, 2, \cdots, 8$. Table 3.1 adds the corresponding numbers for H into the comparison.

Thus procedure H can save significant numbers of tests over Skilling's method for practical values of n and d. Note that all three compared procedures do not assume the knowledge of d.

Previous discussions assumed no restriction on the number of nets that can be included in a test. However, in practice, this is sometimes not the case. Therefore, in order to have practical implementation of the proposed algorithm, the algorithm needs to be modified to accommodate hardware restrictions. The original analysis given in [1] contains some errors. The following is a revised account.

Theorem 3.2.5 *Suppose that at most l nets can be included in one of the two groups. Then there exists a procedure for mode R which requires at most $\lceil n/l \rceil + \lceil n/2l \rceil \lceil \log l \rceil + d \lceil 2 \log l \rceil + d + \binom{d}{2}$ tests.*

Proof. Partition the n nets into $\lceil n/l \rceil$ units where each unit has l nets except possibly one unit has fewer. Suppose that there exists k between-unit shorted pairs and $d - k$ within-unit shorted pairs. First, use the Skilling procedure on the units to locate the k (at most) pairs of units containing between-unit shorted pairs in $\lceil n/l \rceil + \binom{k}{2}$ tests. Note that in the Skilling procedure one group always contains a single unit, hence no more than l nets. For each of k unit-pairs, use the procedure in Lemma 3.2.1 to locate a shorted pair in $\lceil \log l^2 \rceil$ tests. Repair the pair and test the same unit-pair again to see if another shorted-pair exists. If it does, repeat the same procedure. Thus each between-unit shorted pair can be located in $\lceil 2 \log l \rceil + 1$ tests.

To locate the within-unit shorted pair, merge any two units. The choice of merging units is not unique, but all possible choices have the same testing complexity. Apply the procedure H to the merged unit with the first test pitting one unit against the other skipped. Note that the procedure H on $2l$ nets puts at most l nets in a group. Let k_i denote the number of shorted pairs in the ith merged unit, $i = 1, \cdots, \lceil n/2l \rceil$. By Theorem 3.2.3 all $\sum_{i=1}^{\lceil n/2l \rceil} k_i = d - k$ shorted pairs can be located in

$$\sum_{i=1}^{\lceil n/2l \rceil} \{(2k_i + 1)\lceil \log 2l \rceil - k_i - 1\}$$
$$= (2d - 2k + \lceil n/2l \rceil)\lceil \log 2l \rceil - d + k - \lceil n/2l \rceil$$

tests. Thus the total number of tests is

$$\lceil n/l \rceil + \binom{k}{2} + k(\lceil 2\log l \rceil + 1) + (2d - 2k + \lceil n/2l \rceil)\lceil \log 2l \rceil - d + k - \lceil n/2l \rceil$$
$$= \lceil n/l \rceil + \binom{k}{2} + k(\lceil 2\log l \rceil + 1) + (2d - 2k + \lceil n/2l \rceil)\lceil \log l \rceil + d - k$$

which achieves the maximum

$$\lceil n/l \rceil + d\lceil 2\log l \rceil + \lceil n/2l \rceil \lceil \log l \rceil + d + \binom{d}{2}$$

at $k = d$. Theorem 3.2.5 follows immediately.   □

Corollary 3.2.6 *At most d more tests are needed if mode R is replaced by mode $\bar{R}$.*

Let $n = 1024$ in the following table for numbers of tests with various values of d and l.

TABLE 3.2
PROCEDURE H UNDER CONSTRAINT

$d \backslash l$	1	2	4	8	16	32	64	128	256	512
0	1024	768	512	320	192	112	64	36	20	11
2	1027	775	523	335	211	135	91	67	55	50
4	1034	786	538	354	234	162	122	102	94	93
6	1045	801	557	377	261	193	157	141	137	140
8	1160	820	580	404	292	228	196	184	184	191

Note that procedure H requires a slightly greater number of tests than Skilling's method for $l = 1$. Also note that for d large the number of tests is not necessarily decreasing in l. This suggests two things. First, the benefit of having larger l is decreasing. Second, for l large one may not want to use the full capacity. It is clear that $l > n/2$ is never needed since one can always apply the capacity constraint to the smaller group of nets. Therefore $l = 512$ corresponds to the case of no capacity constraint. A discrepancy of one test between $l = 512$ and $n = 1024$ for procedure H in Table 3.2 is due to a slight difference in analysis.

3.3   The 2-Defective Case

Let $n_t(d)$ denote the largest n such that the (d, n) problem can be solved in t tests. Since $M(d, n)$ is nondecreasing in d for $d < n$ (Theorem 1.5.5), a complete solution of $n_t(d)$ is equivalent to a complete solution of $M(d, n)$. While $n_t(1) = 2^t$ is easily obtained by binary splitting, the solution of $n_t(2)$ is surprisingly hard and remains open. In this section bounds on $n_t(2)$ are studied.

For $t \geq 1$ let i_t denote the integer such that

$$\binom{i_t}{2} < 2^t < \binom{i_t + 1}{2}.$$

Since no integer i is a solution of $\binom{i}{2} = 2^t$ for $t \geq 1$, no ambiguity arises from the definition of i_t. By the information lower bound (Theorem 1.2.1), i_t is clearly an upper bound of $n_t(2)$. Chang, Hwang and Lin [3] showed that $i_t - 1$ is also an upper bound of $n_t(2)$. First some lemmas.

Lemma 3.3.1 $i_t = \lfloor 2^{\frac{t+1}{2}} - \frac{1}{2} \rfloor + 1$.

Proof. It suffices to prove

$$\binom{\lfloor 2^{\frac{t+1}{2}} - \frac{1}{2} \rfloor + 1}{2} < 2^t < \binom{\lfloor 2^{\frac{t+1}{2}} - \frac{1}{2} \rfloor + 2}{2}.$$

Since

$$\lfloor 2^{\frac{t+1}{2}} - \frac{1}{2} \rfloor + 1 < 2^{\frac{t+1}{2}} + \frac{1}{2} < \lfloor 2^{\frac{t+1}{2}} - \frac{1}{2} \rfloor + 2,$$

$$\binom{\lfloor 2^{\frac{t+1}{2}} - \frac{1}{2} \rfloor + 1}{2} < \frac{\left(2^{\frac{t+1}{2}} + \frac{1}{2}\right)\left(2^{\frac{t+1}{2}} - \frac{1}{2}\right)}{2} = 2^t - \frac{1}{8} < \binom{\lfloor 2^{\frac{t+1}{2}} - \frac{1}{2} \rfloor + 2}{2}.$$

By noting that no integer i is a solution of $\binom{i}{2} = 2^t$, it follows

$$\binom{\lfloor 2^{\frac{t+1}{2}} - \frac{1}{2} \rfloor + 1}{2} < 2^t < \binom{\lfloor 2^{\frac{t+1}{2}} - \frac{1}{2} \rfloor + 2}{2}. \quad \square$$

Lemma 3.3.2 $\binom{i_{t+1}}{2} - \binom{i_{t-1}}{2} > 2^t$.

Proof. For t even, $i_{t+1} = 2^{\frac{t+2}{2}}$. Therefore

$$\binom{i_{t+1}}{2} - \binom{i_t - 1}{2} = \frac{1}{2}\left\{2^{\frac{t+2}{2}}\left(2^{\frac{t+2}{2}} - 1\right) - (i_t - 1)(i_t - 2)\right\}$$

$$= \frac{1}{2}\left\{2^{t+2} - 2^{\frac{t+2}{2}} - (i_t - 1)i_t + 2(i_t - 1)\right\}$$

$$= \left[2^{t+1} - \binom{i_t}{2}\right] + \left[(i_t - 1) - 2^{\frac{t}{2}}\right] > 2^t,$$

since

$$2^{t+1} - \binom{i_t}{2} > 2^{t+1} - 2^t = 2^t$$

and

$$i_t - 1 \geq 2^{\frac{t}{2}}$$

is easily verified.

For t odd, $i_t = 2^{\frac{t+1}{2}}$. $t = 1$ and 3 can be directly verified. Assume $t \geq 5$. Therefore

$$\binom{i_{t+1}}{2} - \binom{i_t - 1}{2} = \frac{1}{2}\left\{(i_{t+1} - 1)i_{t+1} - (2^{\frac{t+1}{2}} - 1)(2^{\frac{t+1}{2}} - 2)\right\}$$

$$= \frac{1}{2}\left\{(i_{t+1} + 1)i_{t+1} - 2(i_{t+1} - 1) - 2^{t+1} + 3 \cdot 2^{\frac{t+1}{2}} - 4\right\}$$

$$= \left\{\binom{i_{t+1} + 1}{2} - 2^t\right\} + \left\{3 \cdot 2^{\frac{t-1}{2}} - (i_{t+1} + 1)\right\} > 2^t,$$

since

$$\binom{i_{t+1} + 1}{2} - 2^t > 2^{t+1} - 2^t = 2^t$$

and

$$\binom{3 \cdot 2^{\frac{t-1}{2}}}{2} > 2^{t+1} \text{ implies } 3 \cdot 2^{\frac{t-1}{2}} \geq i_{t+1} + 1.$$

□

Theorem 3.3.3 $n_t(2) \leq i_t - 1$ *for* $t \geq 4$.

Proof. It is easily verified that $n_4 = 5 = i_4 - 1$. The general case is proved by induction on t. Consider an arbitrary algorithm T. It will be shown that $M_T(2, i_t) > t$.

Suppose that the first test of T is on a set of m items. If $m < i_t - (i_{t-1} - 1)$, consider the negative outcome. Then the problem is reduced to the $(2, i_t - m)$ problem. Since $i_t - m > i_{t-1} - 1$, at least t more tests are needed by the induction hypothesis. If $m \geq i_t - (i_{t-1} - 1)$, consider the positive outcome. The set of samples after the first test has cardinality

$$\binom{i_t}{2} - \binom{i_t - m}{2} \geq \binom{i_t}{2} - \binom{i_{t-1} - 1}{2} > 2^{t-1} \text{ by Lemma 3.3.2}.$$

Thus again, at least t more tests are needed. $\square$

Chang, Hwang and Lin also gave a lower bound for $n_t(2)$, which was later improved by Chang, Hwang and Weng [4]. Algorithm of the latter is reported here.

Theorem 3.3.4 *There exists an algorithm c such that the $(2, c_t)$ problem can be solved in t tests where $c_t = n_t(2)$ for $t \le 11$ and*

$$c_t = \begin{cases} 89 \cdot 2^{k-6} & \text{for } t = 2k \ge 12 \\ 63 \cdot 2^{k-5} & \text{for } t = 2k+1 \ge 13 \ . \end{cases}$$

Proof. Constructions for $c_t, t \le 11$, were given in [4] and will not be repeated here. These c_t equal $i_t - 1$ for $t \ge 4$ or i_t for $t \le 3$, hence equal $n_t(2)$ by Theorems 3.3.3 and 1.2.1. For $t \ge 12$, there exists a generic algorithm as follows:

1. Test a group of $c_t - c_{t-1}$ items. If the outcome is negative, follow the c_{t-1} construction.

2. If the outcome of the first test is positive, next test a group of m items from the untested group (with c_{t-1} items) where

$$m = \begin{cases} 39 \cdot 2^{k-6} & \text{for } t = 2k, \\ 55 \cdot 2^{k-6} & \text{for } t = 2k+1. \end{cases}$$

If the outcome is positive, the problem is reduced to the $(c_t - c_{t-1}) \times m$ problem. Since

$$(c_t - c_{t-1})m = \begin{cases} (26 \cdot 2^{k-6})(39 \cdot 2^{k-6}) < 2^{2k-2} & \text{for } t = 2k, \\ (37 \cdot 2^{k-6})(55 \cdot 2^{k-6}) < 2^{2k-1} & \text{for } t = 2k+1, \end{cases}$$

by Corollary 3.1.3, $t - 2$ more tests suffice.

3. If the outcome of the second test is negative, next test a group of $\lfloor m/2 \rfloor$ items from the untested group (with $c_{t-1} - m$ items). If the outcome is positive, the problem is reduced to the $(c_t - c_{t-1}) \times \lfloor m/2 \rfloor$ problem. Since

$$(c_t - c_{t-1})\lfloor \frac{m}{2} \rfloor \le \frac{1}{2}(c_t - c_{t-1})m < 2^{t-3} \ ,$$

$t - 3$ more tests suffice. If the outcome is negative, a total of

$$c_t - m - \lfloor \frac{m}{2} \rfloor \le \begin{cases} 89 \cdot 2^{k-6} - 39 \cdot 2^{k-6} - 19 \cdot 2^{k-6} = 31 \cdot 2^{k-6} < c_{t-3} & \text{for } t = 2k, \\ 63 \cdot 2^{k-5} - 55 \cdot 2^{k-6} - 27 \cdot 2^{k-6} = 44 \cdot 2^{k-6} < c_{t-3} & \text{for } t = 2k+1 \end{cases}$$

items is left; hence $t - 3$ more tests suffice. $\square$

Corollary 3.3.5 $c_t/n_t(2) > 0.983$.

Proof. For $t \leq 11$, $c_t/n_t(2) = 1$. For $t \geq 12$ substituting $i_t - 1$ for $n_t(2)$,

$$\frac{c_t}{n_t} > \begin{cases} \frac{89 \cdot 2^{k-6}}{2^{k+1/2}} = \frac{89}{64\sqrt{2}} > 0.983 & \text{for } t = 2k, \\ \frac{63 \cdot 2^{k-5}}{2^{k+1}} = \frac{63}{64} > 0.984 & \text{for } t = 2k+1. \end{cases}$$

$\square$

    Chang, Hwang and Weng also gave an improvement of the algorithm c. Let w be the algorithm resulting from the selection of the largest m satisfying

$$(w_t - w_{t-1})m \leq 2^{t-2} ,$$

$$(w_t - w_{t-1})\lfloor \frac{m}{2} \rfloor \leq 2^{t-3} ,$$

$$w_t - m - \lfloor \frac{m}{2} \rfloor \leq w_{t-3} .$$

Clearly, the largest m is

$$m = \lfloor \frac{2^{t-2}}{w_t - w_{t-1}} \rfloor ,$$

and w_t can be recursively computed as the largest integer satisfying

$$w_{t-3} \geq w_t - \lfloor \frac{2^{t-2}}{w_t - w_{t-1}} \rfloor - \lfloor \frac{2^{t-3}}{w_t - w_{t-1}} \rfloor .$$

Let u_t denote the bound $i_t - 1 = \lfloor 2^{(t+1)/2} - 1/2 \rfloor$.

Theorem 3.3.6 $w_t/u_t \to p^*$ *as* $t \to \infty$ *where*

$$p^* = \left(\frac{3}{4(5 - 3\sqrt{2})} \right)^{1/2} > 0.995 .$$

Proof. It suffices to show that for any positive $p < p^*$ there exist t_p and q, where q depends on p and t_p but not on t, such that

$$\frac{w_t}{u_t} > \frac{w_t}{2^{(t+1)/2}} \geq p - \frac{q}{2^{(t+1)/2}} \qquad \text{if } t \geq t_p .$$

Relax the inequality defining w_t to

$$w_{t-3} \geq w_t - \left(\frac{2^{t-2}}{w_t - w_{t-1}} - 1 \right) - \left(\frac{2^{t-3}}{w_t - w_{t-1}} - 1 \right)$$

or equivalently,

$$(w_t - w_{t-1})(w_t - w_{t-3} + 2) - 3 \cdot 2^{t-3} \leq 0 .$$

Though this relaxation may decrease w_t, it doesn't affect the asymptotic result.

Define

$$a_1 = \frac{5 - 3\sqrt{2}}{2}p^2 - \frac{3}{8},$$

$$a_2 = \left(\frac{8\sqrt{2} - 7}{2} + \frac{12\sqrt{2} - 9}{4}p\right)p,$$

$$a_3 = 3 + 6p + \frac{9p^2}{4} - \frac{18\sqrt{2} - 15}{4}pq,$$

$$a_4 = -\left(\frac{15}{2} + \frac{27p}{4}\right)q,$$

$$a_5 = \frac{9}{2}q^2$$

and

$$a_3' = 3 + 6p + \frac{9p^2}{4}.$$

Note that $a_1 < 0$ for $p < p^\star$. Furthermore, there exists a t_p large enough such that for all $t \geq t_p$,

$$a_1 2^t + a_2 2^{t/2} + a_3' < 0.$$

Also note that t_p is determined independent of q. Let

$$q = 2^{(t_p+1)/2}p.$$

Then it is easily verified

$$\frac{w_t}{u_t} > 0 > p - \frac{q}{2^{(t+1)/2}} \quad \text{for } t < t_p.$$

The proof that

$$\frac{w_t}{u_t} \geq p - \frac{q}{2^{(t+1)/2}} \quad \text{for } t \geq t_p$$

is by induction on t. It will be shown that

$$y = \left(p - \frac{q}{2^{(t+1)/2}}\right)u_t + 1$$

satisfies the inequality

$$(y - w_{t-1})(y - w_{t-3} + 2) - 3 \cdot 2^{t-3} \leq 0.$$

Since w_t is the largest integral solution of the relaxed inequality,

$$w_t \geq y > \left(p - \frac{q}{2^{(t+1)/2}}\right)u^t.$$

For easier writing define $r = 2^{t/2}$. Then $u_t \leq \sqrt{2}r$, $u_{t-1} \geq r - 3/2$ and $u_{t-3} \geq r/2 - 3/2$. Hence

$$\left[\left(p - \frac{q}{2^{(t+1)/2}}\right)u_t + 1 - w_{t-1}\right]\left[\left(p - \frac{q}{2^{(t+1)/2}}\right)u_t + 1 - w_{t-3} + 2\right] - 3 \cdot 2^{t-3}$$

$$\leq \left[\left(p - \frac{q}{\sqrt{2}r}\right)\sqrt{2}r + 1 - \left(p - \frac{q}{r}\right)\left(r - \frac{3}{2}\right)\right]$$

$$\cdot \left[\left(p - \frac{p}{\sqrt{2}r}\right)\sqrt{2}r + 3 - \left(p - \frac{2q}{r}\right)\left(\frac{4}{2} - \frac{3}{2}\right)\right] - \frac{3}{8}r^2$$

$$= \left[(\sqrt{2} - 1)pr + 1 + \frac{3p}{2} - \frac{3q}{2}q^{-1}\right] \cdot \left[\left(\sqrt{2} - \frac{1}{2}\right)pr + 3 + \frac{3p}{2} - 3q_{r-1}\right] - \frac{3}{8}r^2$$

$$= a_1r^2 - a_2r + a_3 + a_4r^{-1} + a_5r^{-2}.$$

Since $q \geq 0$,

$$a_1r^2 + a_2r + a_3 \leq a_1r^2 + a_2r + a_3' < 0 \quad \text{for } t \geq t_p.$$

Furthermore,

$$a_4r^{-1} + a_5r^{-2} = -a_4r^{-2}\left(\frac{a_5}{-a_4} - r\right)$$

$$= a_4r^{-2}\left(\frac{18q}{30 + 27p} - r\right)$$

$$= a_4r^{-2}\left(\frac{18 \cdot 2^{(t_p+1)/2}p}{30 + 27p} - r\right) \leq 0,$$

since

$$\frac{18\sqrt{2}p}{30 + 27p} < 1 \quad \text{and} \quad 2^{t_p/2} \leq r \quad \text{for } t \geq t_p.$$

Hence the inequality concerning y is proved.   □

3.4   The 3-Defective Case

Chang, Hwang and Weng [4] gave the following result.

Theorem 3.4.1 *There exists an algorithm k such that the $(3, h_t)$ problem can be solved in t tests where*

$$h_t = \begin{cases} t + 1 & \text{for } t \leq 7, \\ h_{3k+1} + 2^{k-1} & \text{for } t = 3k + 2 \geq 8, \\ c_{2k} + 2^{k-2} + 1 & \text{for } t = 3k \geq 9, \\ \lfloor (c_{2k+1} + c_{2k})/2 \rfloor + 3 \cdot 2^{k-3} + 1 & \text{for } t = 3k + 1 \geq 10, \end{cases}$$

except $h_{12} = 26$, $h_{13} = 32$, $h_{14} = 40$ and $h_{15} = 52$, where c_t are given in Theorem 3.3.4.

Proof. For $t \leq 7$ let h be the individual testing algorithm. For $t = 3k + 2 \geq 8$ let h be the following algorithm:

First test a group of 2^{k-1} items. If the outcome is negative, the number of remaining items is

$$h_{3k+2} - 2^{k-1} = h_{3k+1} \ .$$

Hence $3k + 1$ more tests suffice. If the outcome is positive, identify a defective in the contaminated group in $k - 1$ more tests. The number of remaining items is at most

$$h_{3k+2} - 1 \leq 108 \cdot 2^{k-6} + 3 \cdot 2^{k-3} + 2^{k-1} = 41 \cdot 2^{k-4} < c_{2k+2} \ .$$

The total number of tests is at most

$$1 + k - 1 + 2k + 2 = 3k + 2 \ .$$

For $t = 3k$ let h be the following algorithm:

1. First test a group of $3 \cdot 2^{k-3}$ items. If the outcome is negative, the number of remaining items is

$$
\begin{aligned}
h_{3k} - 3 \cdot 2^{k-3} &= 89 \cdot 2^{k-6} + 2^{k-2} + 1 - 3 \cdot 2^{k-1} = 81 \cdot 2^{k-6} + 1 \\
&\leq \lfloor 107 \cdot 2^{k-7} \rfloor + 3 \cdot 2^{k-4} + 1 + 2^{k-2} \leq h_{3k-1} \ .
\end{aligned}
$$

Hence $3k - 1$ more tests suffice.

2. If the outcome of the first test is positive, next test a group of 2^{k-2} items consisting of 2^{k-3} items from each of the following two groups; the contaminated (with $3 \cdot 2^{k-3}$ items) group and the untested (with $h_{3k} - 3 \cdot 2^{k-3}$ items) group. If the outcome is negative, the size of the contaminated group is reduced to 2^{k-2}. Identify a defective therein in $k - 2$ tests, the number of remaining items is at most

$$h_{3k} - 2^{k-2} - 1 \ \leq \ c_{2k} \qquad \text{for } k \leq 5 \ ,$$

$$= \ c_{2k} \qquad \text{for } k \geq 6 \ .$$

The total number of tests is at most

$$2 + k - 2 + 2k = 3k \ .$$

3. If the outcome of the second test is positive, then the unidentified items are divided into four sets A, B, C, D of sizes $2^{k-2}, 2^{k-3}, 2^{k-3}$ and $h_{3k} - 2^{k-1}$ such that $A \cup B$ and $B \cup C$ each contains a defective. Next test the set A. If the outcome is negative, then B must contain a defective. Identify it in $k - 3$ tests. The number of remaining items is at most

$$2^{k-3} - 1 + 2^{k-3} + h_{3k} - 2^{k-1} = h_{3k} - 2^{k-2} - 1 \ ,$$

which has been shown to be at most c_{2k}. The total number of tests is at most

$$3 + k - 3 + 2k = 3k .$$

If the outcome is positive, then identify a defective in each of A and $B \cup C$ in $k - 2$ tests. The number of remaining items is at most

$$h_{3k} - 2 = c_{2k} + 2^{k-2} - 1 = 89 \cdot 2^{k-6} + 2^{k-2} - 1 < 2^{k+1} .$$

Hence $k + 1$ more tests identify the last defective. The total number of tests is at most

$$3 + k - 2 + k - 2 + k + 1 = 3k .$$

Finally, for $t = 3k + 1 \geq 10$, let h be the following algorithm:

First test a group of $h_{3k+1} - h_{3k}$ items. If the outcome is negative, there are h_{3k} items left and the problem can be solved in $3k$ more tests. If the outcome is positive, the contaminated group contains

$$h_{3k+1} - h_{3k} \;=\; \left\lfloor \frac{c_{2k+1} - c_{2k}}{2} \right\rfloor + 2^{k-3}$$

$$= \begin{cases} \left\lfloor \frac{63-44}{2} \right\rfloor + 2^2 & \text{for } k = 5 , \\[2mm] \left\lfloor \frac{37 \cdot 2^{k-6}}{2} \right\rfloor + 2^{k-3} & \text{for } k \geq 6 . \end{cases}$$

It is easily verified that

$$2^{k-2} < h_{3k+1} - h_{3k} < 2^{k-1} .$$

By Lemma 2.3.3, a defective can be identified from the contaminated group either in $k - 2$ tests, or in $k - 1$ tests with at least

$$2^{k-1} - (h_{3k+1} - h_{3k})$$

good items also identified. In the first case, the number of remaining items is at most $h_{3k+1} - 1$ which can be verified to be $\leq c_{2k+2}$ for all $k \geq 3$. In the second case, the number of remaining items is

$$h_{3k+1} - 1 - [2^{k-1} - (h_{3k+1} - k_{3k})]$$

$$= \; 2h_{3k+1} - h_{3k} - 2^{k-1} - 1$$

$$\leq \; c_{2k+1} + c_{2k} + 3 \cdot 2^{k-2} + 2 - c_{2k} - 2^{k-1} - 1 = c_{2k+1} .$$

In either case the total number of tests is easily verified to be $3k + 1$.   □

Let $v_t = \lfloor 6^{1/3} 2^{t/3} \rfloor + 1$. Since

$$\binom{v_t + 1}{3} > 2^t ,$$

v_t is an upper bound for $n_t(3)$.

Corollary 3.4.2 *There exists a t^* large enough such that $h_t/v_t > 0.885$ for all $t > t^*$.*

Proof. As $t \to \infty$,

$$\frac{h_{3k}}{v_{3k}} \to \frac{105 \cdot 2^{k-6}}{6^{1/3} 2^k} = \frac{105}{64 \cdot 6^{1/3}} > 0.902 \,,$$

$$\frac{h_{3k+1}}{v_{3k+1}} \to \frac{263 \cdot 2^{k-7}}{6^{1/3} 2^{k+1/3}} > 0.896 \,,$$

$$\frac{h_{3k+2}}{v_{3k+2}} \to \frac{327 \cdot 2^{k-7}}{6^{1/3} 2^{k+2/3}} > 0.885 \,.$$

□

3.5 When is Individual Testing Minimax?

The individual testing algorithm for the (d, n) problem requires $n - 1$ tests since the nature of the last item can be deduced. D. Newman conjectured and Hwang [9] proved that individual testing is minimax if $d < n \le 2d$. Later, Hu, Hwang and Wang [8] strengthened that result to $d < n \le \lfloor (5d + 1)/2 \rfloor$. They also conjectured that individual testing is minimax if $d < n \le 3d$. If the conjecture is true, the bound $3d$ is sharp since Hu, Hwang and Wang proved

Theorem 3.5.1 $M(d, n) < n - 1$ for $n > 3d$.

Proof. It suffices to prove Theorem 3.5.1 for $M(d, 3d + 1)$ due to Lemma 1.5.7. For $d = 1$, $M(1, 4) = 2 < 4 - 1$ by binary splitting. The general case is proved by induction on d.

Let T be a nested (line) algorithm which always tests a group of two items (unless only one is left) if no contaminated group exists. When a contaminated group of two items exists, T identifies a defective in it by another test. In the case that the item in the contaminated group being tested is good, then a good item is identified at no additional cost. All other good items are identified in pairs except that those good items appearing after the last defective are identified by deduction without testing. Note that T has at most $3d$ tests since the d defectives require $2d$ tests and another d tests identify $2d$ good items. As the number of good items is odd, one of them will either be identified for free or is the last item for which no test is needed (since it appears after the last defective).

Suppose that T takes $3d$ tests. Then before the last defective is identified, at least $2d$ good items must have been identified. If the last defective is identified with a free good item, then no more good item appears after the last defective; otherwise, at most one good item appears after. In either case, before the last two tests which identify the last defective, at most two items, one good and one defective, are unidentified. By testing one of them the nature of the other item is deduced. Thus only $3d - 1$ tests are needed.   □

The latest progress towards proving the $n \leq 3d$ conjecture is a result by Du and Hwang [6] which shows that individual testing is minimax for $n \leq \lfloor 21d/8 \rfloor$.

Consider the following minimization problem. Let m and n be relatively prime positive integers, l an integer satisfying $0 \leq l \leq m + n - 2$, and λ a positive number. Define $l_1 = \lfloor m(l+1)/(m+n) \rfloor$. The problem is to locate the minimum of

$$F(k) = \binom{(m+n)k + l}{mk + l_1} \lambda^k$$

over the non-negative integers $k = 0, 1, 2, \cdots$.

Let $l_2 = \lfloor n(l+1)/(m+n) \rfloor$. Since m and n are relatively prime and $l+1 < m+n$, neither $m(l+1)/(m+n)$ nor $n(l+1)/(m+n)$ can be an integer. Therefore

$$\frac{m(l+1)}{m+n} - 1 < l_1 < \frac{m(l+1)}{m+n} \ , \quad \frac{n(l+1)}{m+n} - 1 < l_2 < \frac{n(l+1)}{m+n} \ .$$

Adding up, one obtains

$$l - 1 < l_1 + l_2 < l + 1 \ ,$$

or $l_1 + l_2 = l$.

Define

$$f(x) = \frac{\lambda \Pi_{i=0}^{m+n-1}[(m+n)(x+1) + l - i]}{\Pi_{i=0}^{m-1}[m(x+1) + l_1 - i] \Pi_{i=0}^{n-1}[n(x+1) + l_2 - i]}$$

for real $x \geq 0$. Then

$$f(k) = \frac{F(k+1)}{F(k)} \quad \text{for } k = 0, 1, 2, \cdots .$$

If $f(x) = 1$ has no non-negative solution, then $F(k)$ is either monotone increasing or monotone decreasing. If $f(x) = 1$ has a unique non-negative solution x^0, then $F(k)$ has a minimum k^0 which is either $\lfloor x^0 \rfloor$ or $\lceil x^0 \rceil$. Of course, since solving $f(x) = 1$ is equivalent to solving a polynomial of degree $m + n - 1$, one would not expect in general that $f(x) = 1$ would have so few solutions. However, Du and Hwang gave an interesting and novel method to show that indeed $f(x) = 1$ has at most one non-negative solution.

Define $M = \max\{(m + l_1)/m, (n + l_2)/n\}$ and

$$c = \frac{m^m n^n}{(m+n)^{m+n}\lambda} \ .$$

Theorem 3.5.2 *If $c > 1$ or $c \leq 2(l+1)/(m+n+2(l+1))$, $f(x) = 1$ has no non-negative solution. If $1 \geq c > 1 - 1/2M$, $f(x) = 1$ has a unique non-negative solution, lying in the interval $(1/2(1-c) - M, c/2(1-c) - (l+1)/(m+n))$. If $1 - 1/2M \geq c > 2(l+1)/m+n+2(l+1)$, $f(x) = 1$ either has no non-negative solution or has a unique one, lying in the interval $[0, c/2(1-c) - (l+1)/(m+n)]$.*

Proof. See [6]. □

Theorem 3.5.3 $M(d,n) = n - 1$ *for* $n \leq \frac{21}{8}d$.

Proof. Since $M(d,n)$ is nondecreasing in n (Corollary 1.5.2), it suffices to prove Theorem 3.5.3 for $n = \lfloor \frac{21}{8}d \rfloor$. The proof is decomposed into eight cases.

Case (i). $d = 8k$. Then $n = \lfloor \frac{21}{8}d \rfloor = 21k$. Set $t = 4k$. Then $n - t = 17k$. $d - t = 4k$, $n - 2t - 2 = 13k - 2$. The inequality $\binom{17k}{4k} > 2^{13k-2}$ is proved by showing that

$$\min_k \binom{17k}{4k}/2^{13k-2} > 1 .$$

Theorem 3.5.3 then follows from Corollary 1.5.10 by setting $l = t$.

Define

$$F(k) = \binom{17k}{4k}/2^{13k} .$$

Then $m = 4$, $n = 13$, $l = l_1 = 0$, $\lambda = 2^{-13}$. Compute

$$M = \max\left(\frac{m+l_1}{m}, \frac{n+l_2}{n}\right) = 1 ,$$

$$1 > c = \frac{m^n n^n}{(m+n)^{m+n}\lambda} = 0.7677 > 1 - \frac{M}{2} = 0.5 .$$

Therefore, from Theorem 3.5.2, $f(k) = 1$ has a unique non-negative solution in the interval $(1.15, 2.59)$. Namely, $F(k)$, and hence $\binom{17k}{4k}/2^{13k-2}$ attains a minimum at $k = 2$. Thus we have

$$\min_k \binom{17k}{4k}/2^{13k-2} = \binom{34}{8}/2^{24} = 1.08 > 1 .$$

As the proofs for the other seven cases are analogous to case (i) but with different parameter values, only the values of the parameters are given in each case without further details. K^0 will always denote the value of k that minimizes $\binom{n-t}{d-t}/2^{n-2t-2}$.

Case (ii). $d = 8k + 1$, $n = 21k + 2$, $t = 4k + 1$, $1.08 < K^0 < 2.54$.

$$\min_k \binom{17k+1}{4k}/2^{13k-2} = \binom{35}{8}/2^{24} = 1.40 > 1 .$$

Case (iii). $d = 8k + 2$, $n = 21k + 5$, $t = 4k + 2$, $0.92 < K^0 < 2.42$.

$$\min_k \binom{17k+3}{4}/2^{13k-1} = \min\left\{\binom{20}{4}/2^{12} = 1.18 \; , \; \binom{37}{8}/2^{25} = 1.15\right\} > 1 \; .$$

Case (iv). $d = 8k + 3$, $n = 21k + 7$, $t = 4k + 2$, $0.84 < K^0 < 2.30$.

$$\min_k \binom{17k+5}{4k+1}/2^{13k+1} = \min\left\{\binom{22}{5}/2^{14} = 1.60 \; , \; \binom{39}{9}/2^{27} = 1.58\right\} > 1 \; .$$

Case (v). $d = 8k + 4$, $n = 21k + 10$, $t = 4k + 3$, $0.69 < K^0 < 2.18$.

$$\min_k \binom{17k+7}{4k+1}/2^{13k+2} = \min\left\{\binom{24}{5}/2^{15} = 1.29 \; , \; \binom{41}{9}/2^{28} = 1.30\right\} > 1 \; .$$

Case (vi). $d = 8k + 5$, $n = 21k + 13$, $t = 4k + 3$, $0.54 < K^0 < 2.01$.

$$\min_k \binom{17k+10}{4k+2}/2^{13k+5} = \min\left\{\binom{27}{6}/2^{18} = 1.13, \binom{44}{10}/2^{31} = 1.16\right\} > 1 \; .$$

Case (vii). $d = 8k + 6$, $n = 21k + 15$, $t = 4k + 3$, $0.40 < K^0 < 1.88$.

$$\min_k \binom{17k+12}{4k+3}/2^{13k+7} = \binom{29}{7}/2^{30} = 1.48 > 1 \; .$$

Case (viii). $d = 8k + 7$, $n = 21k + 18$, $t = 4k + 4$, $0.31 < K^0 < 1.77$.

$$\min_k \binom{17k+14}{4k+3}/2^{13k+8} = \binom{31}{7}/2^{21} = 1.25 > 1 \; .$$

$\square$

Recently, Riccio and Colbourn [11] gave an asymptotic result.

Theorem 3.5.4 *If $c < \log_{3/2} 3 \sim 2.7095$, then for all d large enough, $M(d, cn) = n - 1$.*

3.6   Identifying a Single Defective with Parallel Tests

Karp, Upfal and Wigderson [10] studied the problem of identifying a single defective from the sample space $S(\bar{n}, n) \setminus S(0, n)$, with p processors. Let $t(n, p)$ denote the minimax number of rounds of tests required. They proved

Theorem 3.6.1 *For all n and p*

$$t(n, p) = \lceil \log_{p+1} n \rceil.$$

Proof. The inequality $t(n,p) \leq \lceil \log_{p+1} n \rceil$ is obtained by construction. Partition the n items into $p+1$ groups as evenly as possible and use the p processors to test the first p groups. Either a group is tested to be contaminated, or one concludes that the untested group is. Apply the same to the singled-out contaminated group and repeat the partition and testing until a contaminated group of size one is identified. Clearly, at most $\lceil \log_{p+1} n \rceil$ rounds of tests are required.

The inequality $t(n,p) \geq \log_{p+1} n$ is obtained by an oracle argument. Note that a complete description of the information available to the algorithm at any point of its execution is a set consisting of known contaminated groups and a known pure group. Without loss of generality, assume that items in the pure group are not involved in any future tests. Let m_i denote the size of a smallest contaminated group before the round-i tests. Then $m_1 = n$ since the set of all n items constitutes a contaminated group. Whenever $m_i = 1$, a defective is identified and the algorithm ends. The role of the oracle is to choose outcomes of the tests so that the reduction of m at each round is controlled.

Suppose that $Q_1, \cdots, Q_p$ are the p tests at round i (some could be vacuous) and $m_i > 1$. It suffices to prove that $m_{i+1} \geq m_i/(p+1)$. The oracle imposes a negative outcome for each Q_j with $|Q_j| < m_i/(p+1)$ and updates all Q_k to $Q_k \setminus Q_j$. Note that a negative outcome on Q_j is consistent with the test history since otherwise Q_j would be a known contaminated group with a size smaller than

$$m_i - x \frac{m_i}{p+1}, \quad 0 \leq x \leq p$$

which is the size of the smallest such group after x updates of Q_k. The oracle also imposes a positive outcome on each Q_j with $|Q_j| \geq m_i/(p+1)$. Again such an outcome is consistent since it agrees with the sample that all items not in the known pure group are defectives. This particular sample also confirms that at any given time the smallest known contaminated group is among those Q_j's, the updated ones and the newly added ones. These outcomes of Q_j's are determined in the following order:

Let Q denote the set of Q_j's just tested.

Step 1. If Q is empty, stop. Otherwise, let Q_1 be the smallest Q_j in Q.

Step 2. If $|Q_1| < \frac{m}{p} + 1$, let Q_1 be pure. Set $Q_j := Q_j \setminus Q_1$ for all j.

Step 3. If $|Q_1| \geq \frac{m}{p} + 1$, let Q_1 be contaminated. Set $Q = Q - \{Q_1\}$. Go to Step 1.

It is easily verified that the size of an existing Q_j after the round-i tests is at least

$$|Q_j| - p \frac{m_i}{p+1} \geq \frac{m_i}{p+1},$$

and the size of a newly added Q_j is at most $m_i/(p+1)$. Since $t(n,p)$ is an integer, Theorem 3.6.1 follows. □

Karp, Upfal and Wigderson motivated their study of $t(n, p)$ by showing that it is a lower bound of the time complexities of the two problems of finding maximal and maximum independent sets in a graph.

References

[1] G. J. Chang and F. K. Hwang, A group testing problem, *SIAM J. Alg. Disc. Methods* 1 (1980) 21-24.

[2] G. J. Chang and F. K. Hwang, A group testing problem on two disjoint sets, *SIAM J. Alg. Disc. Methods* 2 (1981) 35-38.

[3] G. J. Chang, F. K. Hwang and S. Lin, Group testing with two defectives, *Disc. Appl. Math.* 4 (1982) 97-102.

[4] X. M. Chang, F. K. Hwang and J. F. Weng, Group testing with two and three defectives, in *Graph Theory and Its Applications: East and West*, ed. M. F. Capobianco, M. Guan, D. F. Hsu and T. Tian, (The New York Academy of Sciences, New York, 1989) 86-96.

[5] C. C. Chen and F. K. Hwang, Detecting and locating electrical shorts using group testing, *IEEE Trans. Circuits Syst.* 36 (1989) 1113-1116.

[6] D. Z. Du and F. K. Hwang, Minimizing a combinatorial function, *SIAM J. Alg. Disc. Methods* 3 (1982) 523-528.

[7] M. R. Garey, D. S. Johnson and H. C. So, An application of graph coloring to printed circuit testing, *IEEE Trans. Circuits Syst.* 23 (1976) 591-599.

[8] M. C. Hu, F. K. Hwang, J. K. Wang, A boundary problem for group testing, *SIAM J. Alg. Disc. Methods* 2 (1981) 81-87.

[9] F. K. Hwang, A minimax procedure on group testing problems, *Tamkang J. Math.* 2 (1971) 39-44.

[10] R. M. Karp, E. Upfal and A. Wigderson, The complexity of parallel search, *J. Comput. Syst. Sci.* 36 (1988) 225-253.

[11] L. Riccio and C.J. Colbourn, Sharper bounds in adaptive group testing, *Taiwanese J Math.* to appear.

[12] M. Ruszinkó, On a 2-dimensional search problem, *J. Statist. Plan. and Infern.* 37 (1993) 371-383.

[13] J. K. Skilling, Method of electrical short testing and the like, *US Patent* 4342959, Aug. 3, 1982.

[14] J. F. Weng and F. K. Hwang, An optimal group testing algorithm for k disjoint sets, *Oper. Res. Lett.* 13 (1993) 43-44.

4

Competitive Group Testing

In the previous chapters, the number of defectives or an upper bound of it was generally assumed to be known (except in Sec. 3.2). However, in practice, one may have no information about it. Probably, one only knows the existence of defectives and nothing else. How effective can group testing still be in this situation? We discuss this problem in this chapter.

4.1 The First Competitiveness

For convenience, assume that no information on defectiveness is known. In fact, knowing the existence of defectives may save at most one test. It doesn't affect the results in this chapter. Let us start our discussion with an example. Consider a tree

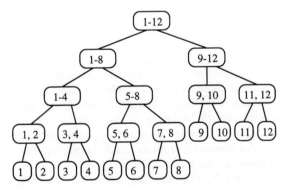

Figure 4.1: Tree T.

T as shown in Figure 4.1. An ordering of nodes of T is given as follows: (1) The root is the first one. It is followed by nodes at the second level, then nodes at the third level and so on. (2) Nodes at the same level are ordered left to right. The search along this ordering is called *breadth-first search*. Based on breadth-first search, an algorithm for 12 items is designed as follows:

> *input items 1, 2, $\cdots$, 12*
> **repeat**
>> *find an untested node X of T by breadth-first search;*
>>   *test X;*
>> **if** X *is pure*
>>> **then** *prune all descendants of X from T;*
> **until** *T has no untested node.*

If the input sample contains only one defective, say 7, then the algorithm tests 9 nodes of T as shown in Figure 4.2. If the input sample contains six defectives 1, 3, 5, 7, 9 and 11, then the algorithm tests all nodes of T in Figure 1. This example

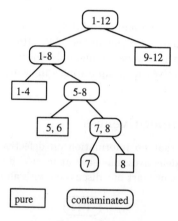

Figure 4.2: Only 7 is defective.

tells us that although no information is known about defectives, group testing can still save tests if the input contains a small number of defectives. But, if the number of defectives in the input is too large, then group testing may take more tests than individual testing does. So, the behavior of an algorithm depends on the number of defectives in the input. Motivated by study of on-line algorithms [7, 9] and the above situation, Du and Hwang [3] proposed the following criterion for group testing algorithms with unknown d, the number of defectives.

For an algorithm α, let $N_\alpha(s)$ denote the number of tests used by the algorithm α on the sample s. Define $M_\alpha(d \mid n) = \max_{s \in S(d,n)} N_\alpha(s)$ where $S(d,n)$ is the set of samples of n items containing d defectives. An algorithm α is called a *c-competitive* algorithm if there exists a constant a such that for $0 \le d < n$, $M_\alpha(d \mid n) \le c \cdot M(d,n) + a$. Note that the case $d = n$ is excluded in the definition because $M(n,n) = 0$ and for any algorithm α, $M_\alpha(n \mid n) \ge n$. A c-competitive algorithm for a constant c is simply called a competitive algorithm while c is called the *competitive ratio* of the algorithm.

To establish competitiveness of an algorithm, a lower bound for $M(d, n)$ is usually needed. The following lemma is quite useful.

Lemma 4.1.1 *For $0 < d < \rho n$,*

$$M(d, n) \geq d(\log \frac{n}{d} + \log(e\sqrt{1 - \rho})) - 0.5 \log d - 0.5 \log(1 - \rho) - 1.567.$$

Proof. Note that the information lower bound is $\lceil \log \binom{n}{d} \rceil$ for $M(d, n)$. Since $n/d < (n - i)/(d - i)$ for $0 < i < d$, $M(d, n) \geq d\log(n/d)$. Now, the following estimation is obtained by using Stirling's formula $n! = \sqrt{2\pi n} \left(\frac{n}{e}\right)^n e^{\frac{\epsilon}{12n}}$ $(0 < \epsilon < 1)$ [8].

$$
\begin{aligned}
\binom{n}{d} &\geq \sqrt{\frac{n}{2\pi d(n - d)}} (\frac{n}{d})^d (\frac{n}{n - d})^{n-d} \exp(-\frac{1}{12d} - \frac{1}{12(n - d)}) \\
&> \frac{1}{\sqrt{d}} (\frac{n}{d})^d [(1 + \frac{d}{n - d})^{(n-d)/d+0.5}]^d (\frac{n}{n - d})^{-0.5d+0.5} \frac{1}{\sqrt{2\pi}} \exp(-\frac{1}{6}) \\
&> \frac{1}{\sqrt{d}} (\frac{n}{d})^d (e\sqrt{1 - \rho})^d (1 - \rho)^{-0.5} 2^{-1.567}.
\end{aligned}
$$

Thus,

$$M(d, n) > d(\log \frac{n}{d} + \log(e\sqrt{1 - \rho})) - 0.5 \log d - 0.5 \log(1 - \rho) - 1.567.$$

$\square$

For convenience, assume that the value of the function $d \log \frac{n}{d}$ at $d = 0$ is 0 because $\lim_{d \to 0} d \log \frac{n}{d} = 0$. Clearly, with this assumption, the lower bound in Lemma 4.1.1 also holds for $d = 0$.

Du and Hwang [2] showed that for $d/n \geq 8/21$, $M(d, n) = n - 1$ (Theorem 3.5.3). Applying the above result to the case of $\rho = 8/21$, the following is obtained.

Corollary 4.1.2 *For $0 \leq d < (8/21)n$,*

$$M(d, n) \geq d(\log \frac{n}{d} + 1.096) - 0.5 \log d - 1.222.$$

4.2 Bisecting

Let S be a set of n items. The principle of the bisecting algorithm is that at each step, if a contaminated subset X of S is discovered, then bisect the set X and test the resulting two subsets X' and X''. How one bisects will affect the competitive ratio. A better way is to choose X' to contain $2^{\lceil \log |X| \rceil - 1}$ items and $X'' = X \setminus X'$ where $|X|$ denotes the number of elements in X.

Let G be a bin for good items and D a bin for defectives. Let Test(X) denote the event that a test on set X is performed. The following is a bisecting algorithm.

Algorithm A1:
>   *input S;*
> $G \leftarrow \emptyset;$
> $D \leftarrow \emptyset;$
>   *TEST(S);*
>   **if** *S is pure*
>   **then** $G \leftarrow S$ *and* $Q \leftarrow \emptyset$
>   **else** $Q \leftarrow \{S\};$
>   **repeat**
>   *pop the frontier element X of queue Q;*
>   *bisect X into X' and $X'';$*
>   *TEST(X');*
>   **if** X' *is contaminated* **then** *TEST(X'');*
>   *{if X' is pure, then it is known that X'' is contaminated.}*
>   **for** $Y \leftarrow X'$ *and* X'' **do begin**
>   **if** *Y is pure* **then** $G \leftarrow G \cup Y;$
>   **if** *Y is a contaminated singleton* **then** $D \leftarrow D \cup Y;$
>   **if** *Y is contaminated but not a singleton*
>   **then** *push Y into the queue Q*
>   **end-for;**
>   **until** $Q = \emptyset$
> **end-algorithm.**

Algorithm A1 is a variation of the algorithm demonstrated in the example in the last section. Instead of pruning a tree, algorithm A1 builds up a binary tree T during the computation. However, these two algorithms end with the same tree T provided that they bisect every set in the same way. Let T^* be the binary tree T at the end of the computation. Then all tested sets are nodes of T^*. For the algorithm in the last section, every node of T^* is a tested set. However, for algorithm A1, some nodes such as X''''s may not be tested sets. In the following, an upper bound of the number of nodes of T^* is established. This means that the analysis below does not take advantage of possible saving of A1. The analysis holds for both algorithms.

Lemma 4.2.1 $M_{A1}(d \mid n) \leq 2n - 1$ *for any d.*

Proof. A binary tree is a rooted tree with property that each *internal node* has exactly two sons. A node is said to be on the kth level of the tree if the path from the root to the node has length $k - 1$. So, the root is on the first level. Let i be the number of nodes in a binary tree and j the number of internal nodes in the tree. It is well-known that $i = 2j + 1$.

Consider the binary tree T^*. Note that each leaf of T^* must identify at least one distinct item. So, T^* has at most n leaves. It follows that T^* has at most $2n - 1$

nodes. Therefore, $M_{A1}(d \mid n) \leq 2n - 1$. $\qquad\square$

Note that if $d/n \geq 8/21$, then $M(d, n) = n - 1$. Hence $M_{A1}(d \mid n) \leq 2M(d, n) + 1$ for $d/n \geq 8/21$. In the next three lemmas, another upper bound for $M_{A1}(d \mid n)$ is shown, which is useful in the case that $d/n < 8/21$.

The following lemma is an important tool for the analysis.

Lemma 4.2.2 *Let $d = d' + d''$ and $n = n' + n''$ where $d' \geq 0, d'' \geq 0, n' > 0$ and $n'' > 0$. Then*

$$d' \log \frac{n'}{d'} + d'' \log \frac{n''}{d''} \leq d \log \frac{n}{d}.$$

Proof. Note that $\frac{d^2}{dx^2}(-x \log x) = -\frac{1}{x \ln 2} < 0$ for $x > 0$. So, $-x \log x$ is a concave function. Thus,

$$
\begin{aligned}
& d' \log \frac{n'}{d'} + d'' \log \frac{n''}{d''} \\
= \; & n(\frac{n'}{n} \frac{d'}{n'} \log \frac{n'}{d'} + \frac{n''}{n} \frac{d''}{n''} \log \frac{n''}{d''}) \\
\leq \; & n(\frac{d}{n} \log \frac{n}{d}) \\
= \; & d \log \frac{n}{d}.
\end{aligned}
$$

$\qquad\square$

Clearly, when n is a power of 2, the analysis would be relatively easy. So, this case is analyzed first.

Lemma 4.2.3 *Let n be a power of 2. Then for $1 \leq d \leq n$*

$$M_{A1}(d \mid n) \leq 2d(\log \frac{n}{d} + 1) - 1.$$

Proof. Consider a binary tree T^*. Clearly, every internal node must be contaminated and there exist exactly d contaminated leaves. Next, count how many contaminated nodes the tree can have. Denote $u = \log n$, $v = \lceil \log d \rceil$ and $v' = v - \log d$. Then tree T^* has $u + 1$ levels. The ith level contains 2^{i-1} nodes. Note that each level has at most d contaminated nodes and the $(v + 1)$st level is the first one which has at least d nodes. Thus, the number of contaminated nodes is at most

$$
\begin{aligned}
& \sum_{i=1}^{v} 2^{i-1} + (u - v + 1)d \\
= \; & 2^v - 1 + d(\log \frac{n}{d} + 1 - v') \\
= \; & -1 + d(\log \frac{n}{d} + 1 - v' + 2^{v'}) \\
\leq \; & -1 + d(\log \frac{n}{d} + 2).
\end{aligned}
$$

The last inequality sign holds since $f(v') = -v' + 2^{v'}$ is a convex function of v' and v' is between 0 and 1. Thus, T^* has at most $-1 + d(\log(n/d) + 1)$ internal nodes and hence at most $2d(\log(n/d) + 1) - 1$ nodes.   □

According to the method of bisecting, each level of tree T^* contains at most one node which is of size not a power of 2. This property plays an important role in the following.

Lemma 4.2.4 *For $0 \le d \le n$*

$$M_{A1}(d \mid n) \le 2d(\log \frac{n}{d} + 1) + 1.$$

Proof. It is proved by induction on n. For $n = 1$, it is trivial. For $n > 1$, let S be the set of n items. Note that for $d = 0$ only one test is enough so that the lemma holds obviously. Next, assume $d > 0$ and consider two cases according to S' and S'' obtained by bisecting S.

Case 1. S' is contaminated. Since the number of items in S' is a power of 2, algorithm A1 spends at most $2d'(\log \frac{|S'|}{d'} + 1) - 1$ tests on S' where d' is the number of defectives in S'. Let d'' be the number of defectives in S''. By the induction hypothesis, algorithm A1 spends at most $2d''(\log \frac{|S''|}{d''} + 1) + 1$ tests. Adding the test on S, the total number of tests is at most

$$2d'(\log \frac{|S'|}{d'} + 1) + 2d''(\log \frac{|S''|}{d''} + 1) + 1$$
$$\le 2d(\log \frac{n}{d} + 1) + 1.$$

Case 2. S' is pure. In this case, algorithm A1 spends a test on S' and at most $2d(\log \frac{|S''|}{d} + 1) + 1$ tests on S''. So, adding the test on S, the total number of tests is at most

$$2 + 2d(\log \frac{|S''|}{d} + 1) + 1$$
$$\le 2d(\log \frac{2|S''|}{d} + 1) + 1$$
$$\le 2d(\log \frac{n}{d} + 1) + 1.$$

□

Based on the above estimation, the following is obtained.

Theorem 4.2.5 $M_{A1}(d \mid n) \le 2M(d, n) + 5$ *for $0 \le d \le n - 1$.*

Proof. By the remark that was made after the proof of Lemma 4.2.1, it suffices to consider the case that $d/n < 8/21$. In this case, by Corollary 4.1.2,

$$M(d,n) > d(\log \frac{n}{d} + 1.096) - 0.5 \log d - 1.222.$$

Thus, by Lemma 4.2.4,

$$M_{A1}(d \mid n) \leq 2M(d,n) + 2(0.5 \log d + 1.722 - 0.096d).$$

Denote $h(d) = 0.5 \log d - 0.096d$. Note that $h'(d) = 0.5/(d \ln 2) - 0.096$. So, $h(d)$ is decreasing for $d \geq 8$ and is increasing for $d \leq 7$. Since d is an integer, $h(d) \leq \max(h(7), h(8)) \leq 0.74$. Therefore, $M_{A1}(d \mid n) \leq 2M(d,n) + 5$. □

The competitiveness of the bisecting algorithm was first proved by Du and Hwang [3]. They presented a bisecting algorithm with competitive ratio 2.75. The above improvement was made by Du, Xue, Sun and Cheng [5].

4.3 Doubling

Bar-Noy, Hwang, Kessler and Kutten [1] proposed another idea to design a competitive group testing algorithm. Their basic idea was as follows. Because d, the number of defectives, is unknown, the algorithm tries to estimate the value of d. If d is small, the algorithm would like to find large pure sets while if d is large the algorithm would like to find small contaminated sets. To have this behavior, the algorithm uses a doubling strategy. It tests disjoint sets of sizes $1, 2, \cdots, 2^i$ until a contaminated set is found. Namely, the first i sets are pure and the last set is contaminated. So, the algorithm identifies $1 + 2 + \cdots + 2^{i-1} = 2^i - 1$ good items and a contaminated set of size 2^i with $i + 1$ tests. Next, the algorithm identifies a defective from the contaminated set by a binary search, which takes i tests. Thus, totally, the algorithm spends $2i + 1$ tests and identifies 2^i items.

Note that if $d = 0$, then the doubling process would take $\lceil \log |S| \rceil$ tests instead of one. Thus a test on S is inserted at the beginning to take care of this case. The following is a formal description of the doubling algorithm A2.

First, introduce a function *DIG* which identifies a defective from a contaminated set X with $\lceil \log |X| \rceil$ tests.

function *DIG(X);*
    $Y \leftarrow X;$
   repeat
       $Y' \leftarrow \lceil |Y|/2 \rceil$ *items from* $Y;$
       TEST(Y');
       if Y' *is contaminated*
          then $Y \leftarrow Y'$

          else $Y \leftarrow Y \setminus Y'$;
   until Y *is a singleton;*
   $DIG \leftarrow Y$;
end-function;

The following is the main body of the algorithm.

Algorithm A2:
   input S;
   $D \leftarrow \emptyset$;
   $G \leftarrow \emptyset$;
   while $S \neq \emptyset$ **do**
      $TEST(S)$;
      if S *is pure*
         then $G \leftarrow G \cup S$
             $S \leftarrow \emptyset$;
      $k \leftarrow 1$;
      $X \leftarrow \emptyset$;
      repeat
         $X \leftarrow \min(k, |S|)$ *items from S;*
         $TEST(X)$;
         if X *is pure*
            then $G \leftarrow G \cup X$
               $k \leftarrow 2k$
               $S \leftarrow S \setminus X$;
      until X *is contaminated;*
      $S \leftarrow S \setminus DIG(X)$;
      $D \leftarrow D \cup DIG(X)$;
   end-while;
end-algorithm.

Bar-Noy, Hwang, Kessler and Kutten [1] commented that A2 is a 2.16-competitive algorithm. We now show that it is 2-competitive by a more careful analysis.

Lemma 4.3.1 *For $0 \leq d \leq n$, $M_{A2}(d \mid n) \leq 2n - 1$.*

Proof. We prove it by induction on d. For $d = 0$, it is trivial that $M_{A2}(0 \mid n) = 1 \leq 2n - 1$. For $d > 0$, algorithm A2 first identifies $2^i - 1$ good items and one defective with at most $2i + 2$ tests for some $i \geq 0$. By the induction hypothesis, the rest of items are identified by using at most $2(n - 2^i) - 1$ tests. Thus, we have

$$M_{A2}(d \mid n) \leq 2(n - 2^i) - 1 + 2i + 2 \leq 2n - 1.$$

$\square$

Lemma 4.3.2 *For* $1 \leq d \leq n$, $M_{A2}(d \mid n) \leq 2d(\log \frac{n}{d} + 1)$.

Proof. We prove it by induction on d. For $d = 1$, algorithm A2 first identifies $2^i - 1$ good items and one defective with $2i+1$ tests and then identifies the remaining $n - 2^i$ good items with one test. Clearly, $i \leq \log n$. Therefore, the lemma holds. For $d > 1$, algorithm A2 first identifies $2^i - 1$ good items and one defective with at most $2i + 2$ tests for some $i \geq 0$. By the induction hypothesis, the remaining $n - 2^i$ items are identified with at most $2(d-1)(\log \frac{n-2^i}{d-1} + 1)$ tests. Thus, the total number of tests is at most

$$2(\log 2^i + 1) + 2(d-1)(\log \frac{n - 2^i}{d - 1} + 1)$$
$$\leq 2d(\log \frac{n}{d} + 1) \quad \text{(by Lemma 4.2.2)}.$$

$\square$

Theorem 4.3.3 *For* $1 \leq d \leq n - 1$, $M_{A2}(d \mid n) \leq 2M(d, n) + 4$.

Proof. Similar to the proof of Theorem 4.2.5. $\square$

4.4   Jumping

In their original paper, Bar-Noy, Hwang, Kessler and Kutten employed a trick on testing three items in their doubling algorithm. Du, Xue, Sun and Cheng [5] extended this technique and obtained a 1.65-competitive algorithm. This section is contributed to this algorithm. The basic idea is explained in Figure 4.3. Instead of climbing stairs

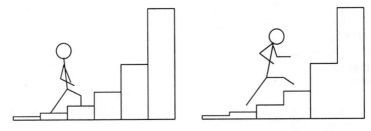

Figure 4.3: Doubling and jumping.

one by one in the doubling process, the jumping algorithm skips every other stair; that is, instead of testing disjoint sets of size $1, \cdots, 2^i$ the algorithm tests disjoint sets of size $1+2$, $4+8$, $\cdots$, $2^i + 2^{i+1}$ for even i until a contaminated set is found. In this way, the algorithm identifies $2^i - 1$ good items with $i/2$ tests instead of i tests. However, it finds a contaminated set of size $3 \cdot 2^i$ instead of 2^i, which requires one more test on a subset of size 2^i in order to reduce the contaminated set either to size 2^i or to size 2^{i+1} with 2^i identified good items.

Let us first describe a procedure for three items, which is a modification of a procedure in [1]. The input for this procedure is a contaminated set of three items. With two tests, the procedure identifies either two defectives or at least one good item and one defective.

Procedure *3-TEST*($\{x, y, z\}$);
    TEST(x);
    TEST(y);
    if *x is defective*
        then $D \leftarrow D \cup \{x\}$
        else $G \leftarrow G \cup \{x\}$;
    if *y is defective*
        then $D \leftarrow D \cup \{y\}$
        else $G \leftarrow G \cup \{x\}$;
    if *x and y are both good*
        then $S \leftarrow S \setminus \{x, y, z\}$
                $D \leftarrow D \cup \{z\}$
        else $S \leftarrow S \setminus \{x, y\}$;
end-procedure;

An extension of the above procedure is as follows. The input is a contaminated set of $3 \cdot 2^k$ items ($k > 0$). The procedure first identifies either a contaminated set of size 2^k or a pure set of size 2^k and a contaminated set of size 2^{k+1} and then identifies a defective from the resultant contaminated set.

Procedure *BIG-3-TEST(X)*;
    $X' \leftarrow \min(2^k, |X|)$ *items from X*;
    TEST(X');
    if *X' is contaminated*
        then $X \leftarrow X'$
        else $X \leftarrow X \setminus X'$
                $G \leftarrow G \cup X'$
                $S \leftarrow S \setminus X'$;
    $X \leftarrow X \setminus DIG(X)$;
    $D \leftarrow D \cup DIG(X)$;
    $S \leftarrow S \setminus DIG(X)$;
end-procedure;

The following is the main body of the algorithm.

Algorithm A3;
    input S;
    $D \leftarrow \emptyset$;

```
G ← ∅;
while |S| ≥ 3 do
    k ← 0;
    repeat{jumping process}
        X ← min(2^k + 2^{k+1}, |S|) items from S;
        TEST(X);
        if X is pure
            then G ← G ∪ X
                 S ← S \ X
                 k ← k + 2;
        if k = 10
            then TEST(S)
                 if S is pure
                     then G ← G ∪ S
                          S ← ∅;
    until S = ∅ or X is contaminated;
    if X is contaminated then
        if k = 0 then 3-TEST(X);
        if k > 0 then BIG-3-TEST(X);
end-while;
while S ≠ ∅ do
    x ← an item from S;
    TEST(x);
    if x is good then G ← G ∪ {x};
    if x is defective then D ← D ∪ {x};
    S ← S \ {x};
end-while;
end-algorithm.
```

Next, algorithm A3 is analyzed in the way similar to that for algorithm A2 in the last section.

Lemma 4.4.1 *For $0 \le d \le n$,*

$$M_{A3}(d \mid n) \le 1.65d(\log \frac{n}{d} + 1.031) + 6.$$

Proof. It is proved by induction on d. For $d = 0$, since the algorithm will test S when $k = 10$, it takes at most six tests to find out that S is pure. Thus, $M_{A3}(0 \mid n) \le 6$.

For $d > 0$, suppose that the first time that the computation exits the jumping process is with $k = i$. So, a contaminated set X of size at most $2^i + 2^{i+1}$ (i is even) and $2^i - 1$ good items are found with $i/2 + 1$ tests. Next, consider three cases.

Case 1. $i = 0$. Procedure 3-TEST identifies either two defectives in two tests or at least one good item and one defective in two tests. Applying the induction hypothesis to the remaining $n-2$ items, in the former subcase, the total number of tests is at most

$$3 + 1.65(d-2)(\log \frac{n-2}{d-2} + 1.031) + 6$$

$$= 1.5 \cdot 2(\log \frac{2}{2} + 1) + 1.65(d-2)(\log \frac{n-2}{d-2} + 1.031) + 6$$

$$\leq 1.65d(\log \frac{n}{d} + 1.031) + 6.$$

In the latter subcase, the total number of tests is at most

$$3 + 1.65(d-1)(\log \frac{n-2}{d-1} + 1.031) + 6$$

$$= 1.5(\log \frac{2}{1} + 1) + 1.65(d-1)(\log \frac{n-2}{d-1} + 1.031) + 6$$

$$\leq 1.65d(\log \frac{n}{d} + 1.031) + 6.$$

Case 2. $2 \leq i \leq 8$. Procedure BIG-3-TEST identifies either one defective with at most $i+1$ tests or one defective and 2^i good items with at most $i+2$ tests. In the former subcase, the total number of identified items is 2^i and the total number of tests for identifying them is at most

$$(i/2+1) + (i+1) \leq 1.65(\log 2^i + 1.031).$$

In the latter subcase, the total number of identified items is 2^{i+1} and the total number of tests for identifying them is at most

$$(i/2+1) + (i+2) \leq 1.50(\log 2^{i+1} + 1).$$

Applying the induction hypothesis to the remaining unidentified items and using Lemma 4.2.2, the upper bound $1.65d(\log \frac{n}{d} + 1.031) + 6$ is obtained for the total number of tests.

Case 3. $i \geq 10$. This case is similar to Case 2. The difference is that the algorithm spends one more test on S when $k = 10$. So, there are two subcases corresponding to the two subcases in Case 2. In the former subcase, the total number of tests for identifying $2^i - 1$ good items and one defective is at most

$$(i/2+1) + (i+2) \leq 1.65(\log 2^i + 1.031);$$

in the latter subcase, the total number of tests for identifying 2^{i+1} good items and one defective is at most

$$(i/2+1) + (i+3) \leq 1.65(\log 2^{i+1} + 1.031).$$

The proof is completed by applying the induction hypothesis to the left unidentified items and using Lemma 4.2.2.   □

Lemma 4.4.2 *For $0 \le d \le n$, $M_{A3}(d \mid n) \le 1.5n$.*

Proof. It is proved by induction on d. For $d = 0$, the algorithm needs one test when $n \le 3$, two tests when $4 \le n \le 15$ and at most five tests when $n > 16$, so that $M_{A3}(0 \mid n) \le 1.5n$. For $d > 0$, suppose that the first time that the algorithm leaves the jumping process is when $k = i$. So, a contaminated set X of size at most $2^i + 2^{i+1}$ (i is even) and $2^i - 1$ good items are found with $i/2 + 1$ tests. Next, the proof follows the idea of the proof of the last lemma to verify that in each case, the number of tests is at most one and a half times the number of identified items.

Case 1. $i = 0$. Two items are identified with three tests.

Case 2. $2 \le i \le 8$. Either 2^i items are identified with $1.5i + 2$ tests or 2^{i+1} items are identified with $1.5i + 3$ tests. Since $i \ge 2$, $1.5i + 2 \le 1.5 \cdot 2^i$ and $1.5i + 3 \le 1.5 \cdot 2^{i+1}$.

Case 3. $i \ge 10$. Either 2^i items are identified with $1.5i + 3$ tests or 2^{i+1} items are identified with $1.5i + 4$ tests. Since $i \ge 10$, $1.5i + 3 \le 1.5 \cdot 2^i$ and $1.5i + 4 \le 1.5 \cdot 2^{i+1}$.

The proof is completed by applying the induction hypothesis to the remaining unidentified items and adding the bound to the inequalities in the above. $\square$

Theorem 4.4.3 *For $1 \le d \le n - 1$, $M_{A3}(d \mid n) < 1.65 M(d, n) + 10$.*

Proof. If $d/n \ge 8/21$, then $M(d, n) = n - 1$. The theorem then follows by Lemma 4.4.2; if $d/n < 8/21$, then by Lemma 4.4.1 and Corollary 4.1.2,

$$M_{A3}(d \mid n) \le 1.65 M(d, n) + 6 + 1.65(0.5 \log d - 0.065d + 1.222).$$

Denote $h(d) = 0.5 \log d - 0.065d$. Then $h(d)$ increases for $d \le 11$ and decreases for $d \ge 12$. Thus, $h(d) \le \max(h(11), h(12)) < 2.237$. Hence, $M_{A3}(d \mid n) \le 1.65 M(d, n) + 10$. $\square$

By modifying algorithm A3, the competitive ratio could be further improved to approach 1.5. The modification can be done through studying the competitive group testing on small number of items. For example, instead of procedure 3-TEST, using a procedure for testing 12 items, the competitive ratio can be decreased to be less than 1.6. However, it certainly requires a new technique in order to push the competitive ratio down under 1.5.

4.5 The Second Competitiveness

A number of papers (see Chapter 3) have appeared in studying group testing algorithms for $1 \le d \le 3$. In those papers, the following number was studied

$$n(d, k) = \max\{n \mid M(d, n) \le k\} \quad \text{for } d \ge 1.$$

Motivated by this situation, Du and Park [4] defined the second competitiveness as follows.

Consider an algorithm α. Define $n_\alpha(d \mid k) = \max\{n \mid M_\alpha(d \mid n) \leq k\}$ for $d \geq 1$. An algorithm α is called a *strongly c-competitive* algorithm if there exists a constant a such that for every $d \geq 1$ and $k \geq 1$, $n(d, k) \leq c \cdot n_\alpha(d \mid k) + a$. Note that $d = 0$ is excluded because $\max\{n \mid M(0, n) \leq k\} = \infty$ for any $k \geq 1$. A strongly competitive algorithm is a strongly c-competitive algorithm for some constant c.

Theorem 4.5.1 *Every strongly competitive algorithm α satisfies the following:*
(1) There exists a constant c' such that for $1 \leq d \leq n - 1$,

$$M_\alpha(d \mid n) \leq c' M(d, n).$$

(2) For $d \geq 1$,

$$\lim_{n \to \infty} \frac{M_\alpha(d \mid n)}{M(d, n)} = 1.$$

Before proving this theorem, a lemma is given.

Lemma 4.5.2 *For $0 \leq d \leq n$,*

$$d \log \frac{n}{d} \leq M(d, n) \leq d \log \frac{n}{d} + (1 + \log e)d.$$

Proof. Since $\binom{n}{d} \geq \left(\frac{n}{d}\right)^d$, the first inequality follows from the information lower bound. To prove the second inequality, first note that $M(0, n) = M(n, n) = 0$, $M(1, n) = \lceil \log n \rceil$, and for $n \leq \frac{21}{8}d$, $M(d, n) = n - 1$. So, the inequality holds trivially for $d = 0, 1$ and $d \geq \frac{8}{21}n$. Next, consider $2 \leq d < \frac{8}{21}n$. From the proof of Corollary 2.2.2,

$$M(d, n) \leq M_G(d, n) \leq \log \binom{n}{d} + d - 1.$$

Moreover, for $2 \leq d < \frac{8}{21}n$,

$$\binom{n}{d} \leq \sqrt{\frac{n}{2\pi d(n - d)}} \left(\frac{n}{d}\right)^d \left(1 + \frac{d}{n - d}\right)^{n-d} \exp\left(\frac{1}{12n}\right)$$

$$\leq \sqrt{\frac{21}{52\pi}} \left(\frac{n}{d}\right)^d \exp\left(d + \frac{1}{36}\right)$$

$$\leq \left(\frac{n}{d}\right)^d e^d .$$

Thus,

$$M(d, n) \leq d \log \frac{n}{d} + (1 + \log e)d.$$

$\square$

Now, Theorem 4.5.1 is ready to be proved.

Proof of Theorem 4.5.1. Let $n(d, k) \leq c \cdot n_\alpha(d \mid k) + a$. Without loss of generality, assume that c and a are positive integers (otherwise, one may use two positive integers bigger than c and a instead of c and a). From the above inequality, it follows that

$$M_\alpha(d \mid n) = \min\{k \mid n_\alpha(d \mid k) \geq n\}$$
$$\leq \min\{k \mid (n(d, k) - a)/c \geq n\} = M(d, cn + a).$$

Thus, for $d \geq 1$,

$$1 \leq \frac{M_\alpha(d \mid n)}{M(d, n)} \leq \frac{M(d, cn + a)}{M(d, n)} \leq \frac{d \log \frac{cn + a}{d} + (1 + \log e)d}{d \log \frac{n}{d}}.$$

Clearly, the right hand side is bounded by a constant. So, α is a competitive algorithm. Moreover, the right hand side approaches one as n goes to infinity. Therefore $\lim_{n \to \infty} M_\alpha(d \mid n)/M(d, n) = 1$. □

The inverse of the above theorem is not true. The next theorem gives a sufficient condition for strong competitiveness.

Theorem 4.5.3 *If for algorithm α there exists a constant c such that for $1 \leq d \leq n - 1$,*

$$M_\alpha(d \mid n) \leq d \log \frac{n}{d} + cd,$$

then α is strongly competitive.

Proof. Note that

$$n_\alpha(d \mid k) = \max\{n \mid M_\alpha(d \mid n) \leq k\}$$
$$\geq \max\{n \mid d \log \frac{n}{d} + cd \leq k\}$$
$$\geq d2^{\frac{k}{d} - c} - 1$$

and

$$n(d, k) = \max\{n \mid M(d, n) \leq k\}$$
$$\leq \max\{n \mid d \log \frac{n}{d} \leq k\}$$
$$\leq d2^{\frac{k}{d}}.$$

Thus,

$$n(d, k) \leq 2^c(n_\alpha(d \mid n) + 1).$$

□

4.6   Digging

Note that if both X and X' are contaminated sets with $X' \subset X$, then the information from the test on X' renders the information from the test on X useless (Lemma 1.4.1). Thus, in the bisecting algorithm, a lot of tests produce no information for the final result. This observation suggests the following improvement: Once a contaminated set is found, a defective is identified from the set. This will be called *digging*, which results in a strongly competitive algorithm as follows. (The procedure DIG for digging a defective has been introduced in Sec. 4.3.)

Algorithm A4:
        input S;
        $G \leftarrow \emptyset$;{*the bin of good items*}
        $D \leftarrow \emptyset$;{*the bin of defectives*}
        $Q \leftarrow \{S\}$;
        repeat
                pop the frontier element X from queue Q;
                TEST(X);
                if X *is pure*
                        then $G \leftarrow G \cup X$
                        else begin
                                $Y \leftarrow DIG(X)$;
                                $X \leftarrow X \setminus Y$;
                                $D \leftarrow D \cup Y$;
                                bisect X into X' and X";
                                if $X' \neq \emptyset$ **then** *push X' into queue Q;*
                                if $X'' \neq \emptyset$ **then** *push X" into queue Q;*
                        end-else
        until $Q = \emptyset$.
end-algorithm.

The following is an analysis for algorithm A4.

Lemma 4.6.1 *Let n be a power of 2. Then for $0 \leq d \leq n$.*

$$M_{A4}(d \mid n) \leq d \log \frac{n}{d+1} + 4d - \log(d+1) + 1.$$

Proof. Let $n = 2^u$, $v = \lfloor \log(d+1) \rfloor$ and $v' = \log(d+1) - v$. Note that a defective detected from a set of size k by function DIG needs $\lceil \log k \rceil$ tests. By the definition of algorithm A4, it is not hard to see that function DIG applies to at most one set of size n, at most two sets of sizes between $1 + n/4$ and $n/2$, ..., and in general, at most 2^i sets of sizes between $1 + n/2^i$ and $n/2^{i-1}$. Thus, the number of tests consumed by function DIG is at most

$$
\begin{aligned}
&u + 2(u-1) + \cdots + 2^{v-1}(u-v+1) + (d - 2^v + 1)(u-v) \\
={}& u(2^v - 1) - (v2^v - 2^{v+1} + 2) + (d - 2^v + 1)(u-v) \\
={}& ud - v(d+1) + 2^{v+1} - 2 \\
={}& d(u - v - v') + v'd - v + 2^{v+1} - 2 \\
={}& d(u - v - v') + (v' + 2^{1-v'})(d+1) - 2 - \log(d+1) \\
\leq{}& d \log \frac{n}{d+1} + 2d - \log(d+1).
\end{aligned}
$$

The last inequality holds because $v' + 2^{1-v'} \leq 2$ for $0 \leq v' < 1$. In fact, $v' + 2^{1-v'}$ is a convex function with minimum value 2 at $v' = 0$ and $v' = 1$.

Now, consider tree T^* which is built up by a bisecting process, that is, the node set of T^* consists of S and all sets X' and X'' appearing in the computation, and node X is the father of the two sons X' and X'' iff X' and X'' are obtained by bisecting X after identifying a defective. Clearly, every internal node is a contaminated set from which a defective is identified. Thus, T^* has at most d internal nodes. It follows that the total number of nodes of T^* is at most $2d+1$. Therefore,

$$
M_{A4}(d \mid n) \leq d \log \frac{n}{d} + 4d - \log(d+1) + 1.
$$

$\square$

Lemma 4.6.2 *For* $1 \leq d \leq n$,

$$
M_{A4}(d \mid n) \leq d(\log \frac{n}{d} + 4).
$$

Proof. It is proved by induction on d. For $d = 1$, the algorithm identifies the only defective with $\lceil \log n \rceil + 3$ tests which is clearly bounded by $\log n + 4$. For $d > 1$, the algorithm identifies the first defective with $\lceil \log n \rceil + 1$ tests, and bisects the remaining $n - 1$ items into two sets S' and S'' of sizes n' and n'' where $n' = 2^{u-1}$ and $u = \lceil \log(n-1) \rceil$. Suppose that S' and S'' contain d' and d'' defectives, respectively. So, $d' + d'' + 1 = d$ and $n' + n'' + 1 = n$. Then by Lemma 4.6.1, the number of tests for identifying items in S' is at most

$$
d'(\log \frac{n'}{d'+1} + 4) - \log(d'+1) + 1.
$$

Next, consider two cases.

Case 1. $n \neq 2^u + 1$. Then $u = \lceil \log n \rceil$. If $d'' = 0$, then the algorithm uses one test to detect S''. If $d'' > 0$, then use the induction hypothesis on S''. In either situation, the number of tests for identifying items in S'' is at most

$$
d''(\log \frac{n''}{d''} + 4) + 1.
$$

Thus, the total number of tests is at most

$$u + 3 + d'(\log \frac{n'}{d'+1} + 4) - \log(d'+1) + d''(\log \frac{n''}{d''} + 4)$$

$$\leq (d'+1)(\log \frac{n'}{d'+1} + 4) + d''(\log \frac{n''}{d''} + 4)$$

$$\leq d(\log \frac{n-1}{d} + 4) \quad \text{(by Lemma 4.2.2)}$$

$$\leq d(\log \frac{n}{d} + 4).$$

Case 2. $n = 2^u + 1$. Then $u + 1 = \lceil \log n \rceil$ and $n'' = n' = 2^{u-1}$. If $d'' = 0$, then the total number of tests is at most

$$u + 4 + d'(\log \frac{n'}{d'+1} + 4) - \log(d'+1)$$

$$\leq 1 + d(\log \frac{n'}{d} + 4)$$

$$\leq d(\log \frac{n}{d} + 4).$$

If $d'' > 0$, then apply the induction hypothesis to S''. It is easy to see that the total number of tests has the same upper bound as that in Case 1. □

Theorem 4.6.3 *Algorithm A4 is strongly competitive.*

Proof. It follows immediately from Lemma 4.6.2 and Theorem 4.5.3. □

4.7   Tight Bound

Du and Hwang [3] conjectured that there exists a method A of bisecting such that

$$M_A(d \mid n) \leq 2M(d, n) + 1$$

for $0 \leq d \leq n-1$. Since for any method A of bisecting, $M_A(n-1 \mid n) = 2M(n-1, n)+1$ and $M_A(1 \mid n) = 2M(1, n) + 1$, this bound is tight. Du, Xue, Sun, and Cheng [5] showed that the bisecting method $A1$ in Section 4.2 actually meets the requirement.

Theorem 4.7.1 *For $0 \leq d \leq n - 1$,*

$$M_{A1}(d \mid n) \leq 2M(d, n) + 1.$$

The proof of this result involves a more accurate analysis on the upper bound of $M_{A1}(d \mid n)$. Such techniques can also be applied to other algorithms to yield tighter bounds. In this section, the main idea of their proof is introduced.

By the remark that we made after the proof of Lemma 4.2.1, it suffices to consider the case that $d/n < 8/21$. In this case, by Corollary 4.1.2,

$$M(d,n) > d(\log \frac{n}{d} + 1.096) - 0.5 \log d - 1.222.$$

Thus, by Lemma 4.2.4,

$$M_{A1}(d \mid n) \leq 2M(d,n) + 1 + 2(0.5 \log d + 1.222 - 0.096d).$$

Denote $h(d) = 0.5 \log d - 0.096d$. Note that $h'(d) = (0.5/\ln 2)d - 0.096$. So, $h(d)$ is decreasing for $d \geq 8$. To obtain the tight bound, one needs $h(d) \leq -1.222$. This yields $d \geq 41$. Therefore, for $d \geq 41$, $M_{A1}(d \mid n) \leq 2M(d,n) + 1$.

Next, consider $1 \leq d \leq 41$. Define

$$f(n,d) = \frac{\binom{n}{d}\sqrt{2}}{\left(\frac{n}{d}\right)^d 2^d}.$$

If $f(n,d) > 1$, then by Lemma 4.2.4 and the information lower bound for $M(d,n)$, it is easy to see that

$$M_{A1}(d \mid n) < 2M(d,n) + 2.$$

Since both sides of the inequality are integers,

$$M_{A1}(d \mid n) \leq 2M(d,n) + 1.$$

In order to find when $f(n,d) > \sqrt{2}$, consider the following ratio

$$\frac{f(n,d+1)}{f(n,d)} = \frac{n-d}{2n}(1 + \frac{1}{d})^d.$$

It is easy to see that

$$\frac{n-d}{2n} \cdot e > \frac{f(n,d+1)}{f(n,d)} > \frac{n-d}{2n}(\frac{d}{d+1})^{1/2} \cdot e.$$

Thus,

Lemma 4.7.2 *For $d/n \geq 1 - 2/e$, $f(n,d)$ is decreasing with respect to d. For $d/n \leq 1 - (2/e)\sqrt{(d+1)/d}$, $f(n,d)$ is increasing with respect to d.*

This lemma indicates the behavior of the function $f(n,d)$ with respect to d. Next, study the function with respect to n. Consider

$$g(n,d) = \frac{f(n+1,d)}{f(n,d)} = \frac{\frac{n+1}{n-d+1}}{(\frac{n+1}{n})^d}.$$

Note that

$$\frac{g(n, d+1)}{g(n, d)} = \frac{n(n-d+1)}{(n+1)(n-d)} \geq 1$$

because

$$n(n-d+1) - (n+1)(n-d) = d.$$

Moreover, $g(n, 1) = 1$. Thus, for $d \geq 1$, $g(n, d) \geq 1$. Therefore, the following theorem holds.

Lemma 4.7.3 *For* $d \geq 1$, $f(n, d)$ *is increasing in* n.

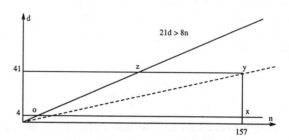

Figure 4.4: Pairs of n and d.

From Lemmas 4.7.2 and 4.7.3, it can be seen that if $f(n^*, d^*) > 1$, then for every $n \geq n^*$ and $(1 - \frac{2}{e}\sqrt{\frac{d}{d-1}})n + 1 \geq d \geq d^*$, $f(n, d) > 1$. Note that $f(157, 5) > 1$ and $(1 - \frac{2}{e}\sqrt{\frac{40}{41}}) \cdot 157 + 1 > 41$. By Lemma 4.7.2, $f(157, d) > 1$ for $5 \leq d \leq 40$. Furthermore, by Lemma 4.7.3, $f(n, d) > 1$ for $n \geq 157$ and $5 \leq d \leq 40$. (See Figure 4.4.) Unfortunately, the above argument does not help in the case of $d \leq 4$. In fact, it is easy to prove that in this case $f(n, d) < 1$. Actually, one needs a more accurate upper bound of $M_{A1}(d \mid n)$ for $1 \leq d \leq 4$.

By the definition of algorithm A1, it is easy to find the following recursive formulas for computing $M_{A1}(d \mid n)$.

$$M_{A1}(d \mid n) = \max_{0 \leq d' \leq d} \{1 + M_{A1}(d' \mid n') + M_{A1}(d'' \mid n'')\} (d \geq 1)$$
$$M_{A1}(0 \mid n) = 1.$$

where $n' = 2^{\lceil \log n \rceil - 1}$, $n'' = n - n'$ and $d'' = d - d'$. From these formulas, the following lemmas can be obtained.

Lemma 4.7.4

$$M_{A1}(1 \mid 2^u) = 2u + 1 \quad \text{for } u \geq 0,$$
$$M_{A1}(2 \mid 2^u) = 4u - 1 \quad \text{for } u \geq 1,$$
$$M_{A1}(3 \mid 2^u) = 6u - 5 \quad \text{for } u \geq 2,$$
$$M_{A1}(4 \mid 2^u) = 8u - 9 \quad \text{for } u \geq 2.$$

Proof. The proof is by induction on u. It is easy to check each equation for the initial value of u. For the induction step, the recursive formula is employed to yield the following.

$$
\begin{aligned}
M_{A1}(1 \mid 2^u) &= 1 + M_{A1}(1 \mid 2^{u-1}) + M_{A1}(0 \mid 2^{u-1}) \\
&= 1 + 2(u-1) + 1 + 1 = 2u + 1. \\
M_{A1}(2 \mid 2^u) &= \max(1 + M_{A1}(2 \mid 2^{u-1}), 1 + 2M_{A1}(1 \mid 2^{u-1})) \\
&= \max(4u - 4, 4u - 1) = 4u - 1. \\
M_{A1}(3 \mid 2^u) &= \max(1 + M_{A1}(3 \mid 2^{u-1}), 1 + M_{A1}(1 \mid 2^{u-1}) + M_{A1}(2 \mid 2^{u-1})) \\
&= \max(6u - 10, 6u - 5) = 6u - 5. \\
M_{A1}(4 \mid 2^u) &= \max_{0 \le d' \le 4}(M_{A1}(d' \mid 2^{u-1}) + M_{A1}(4 - d' \mid 2^{u-1})) \\
&= \max(8u - 17, 8u - 11, 8u - 9) = 8u - 9.
\end{aligned}
$$

$\square$

Lemma 4.7.5 *Let* $u + 1 = \lceil \log n \rceil$, $v = \lceil \log(n - 2^u) \rceil$, *and* $w = \lceil \log(n - 2^u - 2^{v-1}) \rceil$. *Then*

$$
\begin{aligned}
M_{A1}(1 \mid n) &\le 2(u+1) + 1, \\
M_{A1}(2 \mid n) &\le \max(4u + 1, 2(u + v + 1) + 1), \\
M_{A1}(3 \mid n) &\le \max(6u - 3, 4u + 2v + 1), \\
M_{A1}(4 \mid n) &\le \max(8u - 7, 6u + 2v - 3, 4u + 4v - 3, 4u + 2v + 2w + 1).
\end{aligned}
$$

Proof. Use the recursive formula and note that $M_{A1}(d \mid n - 2^u) \le M_{A1}(d \mid 2^v)$. $\square$

Now, Theorem 4.7.1 for $1 \le d \le 4$ is proved as follows. Note that u and v are defined the same as those in Lemma 4.7.5.

For $d = 1$, $M_{A1}(1 \mid n) \le 2(u+1) + 1 = 2M(1, n) + 1$.

For $d = 2$, if $v < u$, then $M_{A1}(2 \mid n) \le 4u + 1$ and

$$
M(2, n) \ge \lceil \log \binom{n}{2} \rceil \ge \lceil \log \frac{(2^u + 1)2^u}{2} \rceil = 2u.
$$

So, $M_{A1}(2 \mid n) \le 2M(2, n) + 1$. If $u = v$, then $M_{A1}(2 \mid n) \le 2(2u + 1) + 1$ and

$$
\begin{aligned}
\lceil \log \binom{n}{2} \rceil &\ge \lceil \log \frac{(2^u + 2^{u-1} + 1)(2^u + 2^{u-1})}{2} \rceil \\
&\ge \lceil \log(2^{2u} + 2^{2u-3}) \rceil \\
&= 2u + 1.
\end{aligned}
$$

Thus, Theorem 4.7.1 holds.

For $d = 3$ and $u = 1$, it is trivial. Next, consider $d = 3$ and $u \geq 2$. If $v < u$, then $M_{A1}(3 \mid n) \leq 2(3u - 2) + 1$ and

$$
\begin{aligned}
\lceil \log \binom{n}{3} \rceil &\geq \lceil \log \frac{(2^u + 1)2^u(2^u - 1)}{6} \rceil \\
&\geq \lceil \log((2^u + 1)2^{2u-3}) \rceil \\
&\geq 3u - 2.
\end{aligned}
$$

Thus, Theorem 4.7.1 holds. If $u = v$, then $M_{A1}(3 \mid n) \leq 6u + 1$ and

$$
\begin{aligned}
\lceil \log \binom{n}{3} \rceil &\geq \lceil \log \frac{(2^u + 2^{u-1} + 1)(2^u + 2^{u-1})(2^u + 2^{u-1} - 1)}{6} \rceil \\
&\geq \lceil \log((2^{2u+1} + 2^{2u-2} - 1)2^{u-2}) \rceil \\
&\geq 3u.
\end{aligned}
$$

For $d = 4$, it is trivial to verify Theorem 4.7.1 in the cases of $u = 1$ and $u = 2$. Next, consider $u \geq 3$. If $v < u$ and $w < u - 1$, then $M_{A1}(4 \mid n) \leq 2(4u - 3) + 1$ and

$$
\begin{aligned}
\lceil \log \binom{n}{4} \rceil &\geq \lceil \log \frac{(2^u + 1)2^u(2^u - 1)(2^u - 2)}{8 \cdot 3} \rceil \\
&= \lceil \log \frac{(2^{3u} - 2^{2u} - 2^{u-1} + 1)2^{u-2}}{3} \rceil \\
&\geq 4u - 3.
\end{aligned}
$$

Thus, Theorem 4.7.1 holds. If $u = v$ and $w < u - 1$, then $M_{A1}(4 \mid n) \leq 2(4u - 2) + 1$ and

$$
\lceil \log \binom{n}{4} \rceil
$$

$$
\begin{aligned}
&\geq \lceil \log \frac{(2^u + 2^{u-1} + 1)(2^u + 2^{u-1})(2^u + 2^{u-1} - 1)(2^u + 2^{u-1} - 2)}{8 \cdot 3} \rceil \\
&\geq \lceil \log \frac{((2^u + 2^{u-1})^2 - 1)((2^u + 2^{u-1} - 1)^2 - 1)}{3 \cdot 8} \rceil \\
&\geq \lceil \log \frac{2^{2u+1} + 2^{2u-2} - 1}{3} \cdot \frac{2^{2u+1} + 2^{2u-2} - 2^u - 2^{u-1}}{8} \rceil \\
&\geq \lceil \log((2^{2u-1} + 1)2^{2u-2}) \rceil \\
&\geq 4u - 2.
\end{aligned}
$$

So, Theorem 4.7.1 holds. If $w = u - 1$, then it must be the case $u = v$ and $M_{A1}(4 \mid n) \leq 2(4u - 1) + 1$. Note that $n \geq 2^u + 2^{u-1} + 2^{u-2} + 1$. Thus,

$$
\lceil \log \binom{n}{4} \rceil
$$

$$\geq \left\lceil \log \frac{((2^u + 2^{u-1} + 2^{u-2})^2 - 1)((2^u + 2^{u-1} + 2^{u-2} - 1)^2 - 1)}{3 \cdot 8} \right\rceil$$

$$\geq \left\lceil \log \frac{2^{2u+1} + 2^{2u} + 2^{2u-4} - 1}{3} \cdot \frac{2^{2u+1} + 2^{2u-4}}{8} \right\rceil$$

$$\geq \lceil \log((2^{2u} + 1)2^{2u-2}) \rceil$$

$$\geq 4u - 1.$$

Therefore, Theorem 4.7.1 holds.

Finally, for finitely many pairs of (n, d) located in polygon $oxyz$ as shown in Figure 4.4, compute $M_{A1}(d \mid n)$ by the recursive formula. Also compute a lower bound of $M(d, n)$ by the following formula

$$\ell(d, n) = \min\{n - 1, \max_{0 \leq k < d}[\lceil \log \binom{n-k}{d-k} \rceil + 2k]\}.$$

(This lower bound is in Lemma 1.5.9.) Comparing the two computation results, one finds that $M_{A1}(d \mid n) \leq 2\ell(d, n) + 1$. (The details can be found in [5].) This completes the proof of Theorem 4.7.1.

References

[1] A. Bar-Noy, F.K. Hwang, I. Kessler, and S. Kutten, Competitive group testing in high speed networks, *Discrete Applied Mathematics* 52 (1994) 29-38.

[2] D.Z. Du and F.K. Hwang, Minimizing a combinatorial function, *SIAM J. Alg. Disc. Method* 3 (1982) 523-528.

[3] D.Z. Du and F.K. Hwang, Competitive group testing, in L.A. McGeoch and D.D. Sleator (ed.) *On-Line Algorithm*, DIMACS Series in Discrete Mathematics and Theoretical Computer Science, Vol. 7 (AMS & ACM, 1992) 125-134. (Also in *Discrete Applied Mathematics* 45 (1993) 221-232.)

[4] D.Z. Du and H. Park, On competitive algorithms for group testing, *SIAM J. Computing* 23 (1994) 1019-1025.

[5] D.Z. Du, G.-L. Xue, S.-Z. Sun, and S.-W. Cheng, Modifications of competitive group testing, *SIAM J. Computing* 23 (1994) 82-96.

[6] M.C. Hu, F.K. Hwang and J.K. Wang, A boundary problem for group testing, *SIAM J. Alg. Disc. Method* 2 (1981) 81-87.

[7] M.S. Manasse, L.A. McGeoch, and D.D. Sleator, Competitive algorithms for on-line problems, *Proceedings of 20th STOC*, (1988) 322-333.

[8] E. M. Palmer, *Graphical Evolution: An Introduction to the Theory of Random Graphs*, (John Willy & Sons, New York, 1985).

[9] D.D. Sleator and R.E. Tarjan, Amortized efficiency of list update and paging rules, *Communications of ACM*, 28 (1985) 202-208.

5

Unreliable Tests

In the previous chapters, all tests are reliable, i.e., the test outcomes are error-free. In this chapter, we will shift our attention to unreliable tests, i.e., each test may make an error with a certain possibility.

5.1 Ulam's Problem

Stanislaw M. Ulam (1909-1984) is one of the great mathematicians in the twentieth century. In his autobiography "*Adventures of a Mathematician*" [23], he wrote the following.

" Someone thinks of a number between one and one million (which is just less than 2^{20}). Another person is allowed to ask up to twenty questions, to each of which the first person is supposed to answer only yes or no. Obviously the number can be guessed by asking first: Is the number in the first half-million? and then again reduce the reservoir of numbers in the next question by one-half, and so on. Finally the number is obtained in less than $\log_2(1,000,000)$ questions. Now suppose one were allowed to lie once or twice, then how many questions would one need to get the right answer? One clearly needs more than n questions for guessing one of the 2^n objects because one does not know when the lie was told. This problem is not solved in general."

Ulam's problem is a group testing problem with one defective and at most one or two erroneous tests. In general, more defectives and more errors may be considered. Suppose there are n items with d defectives and at most r errors are allowed. For any algorithm α identifying all defectives with such unreliable tests, let $N_\alpha^r(\sigma \mid d, n)$ denote the number of unreliable tests performed by α on sample σ and let

$$M_\alpha^r(d, n) = \max_{\sigma \in S(d,n)} N_\alpha^r(\sigma \mid d, n)$$
$$M^r(d, n) = \min_\alpha M_\alpha^r(d, n).$$

Ulam's problem is equivalent to finding $M^1(1, 10^6)$ and $M^2(1, 10^6)$.

Rivest, Meyer, Kleitman, Winklmann, and Spencer [19] and Spencer [21] showed that $25 \leq M^1(1, 10^6) \leq 26$. Pelc [12] determined $M^1(1, 10^6) = 25$ by proving the following result.

Theorem 5.1.1

$$M^1(1, n) = \begin{cases} \min\{k \mid n(k+1) \leq 2^k\} & \text{if n is even,} \\ \min\{k \mid n(k+1) + (k-1) \leq 2^k\} & \text{if n is odd.} \end{cases}$$

Pelc's proof uses a weight function introduced by Berlekamp [2].

A *history* of group testing is a sequence of tests together with outcomes. Associated with a history, a *state* is a couple (a, b) of natural numbers. The first number a is the number of items which, if defective, satisfy all test-outcomes. (The set of such items is called the *truth-set*.) The second number b is the number of items which, if defective, satisfy all but one test-outcomes. (The set of all items of this type is called the *lie-set*.) For example, consider items $\{1, 2, 3, 4, 5\}$ and a history $T(1, 2) = 0, T(2, 3, 4) = 1, T(2, 4, 5) = 1$. Then the state (a, b) associated with this history is determined as follows:

$$\begin{aligned} a &= |\{3, 4, 5\} \cap \{2, 3, 4\} \cap \{2, 4, 5\}| = |\{4\}| = 1 \\ b &= |(\{3, 4, 5\} \cap \{2, 3, 4\} \cap \{1, 3\}) \cup (\{3, 4, 5\} \cap \{1, 5\} \cap \{2, 4, 5\}) \\ &\quad \cup (\{1, 2\} \cap \{2, 3, 4\} \cap \{2, 4, 5\})| \\ &= |\{3, 5, 2\}| = 3. \end{aligned}$$

For a certain k, to look at whether k tests are enough or not, one introduces the weight of a state (a, b) obtained from a history of j tests as follows.

$$w_{k-j}(a, b) = a(k - j + 1) + b.$$

This definition is interpreted by Spencer [21] as the number of possibilities that the remaining $k - j$ tests lie or not. In fact, if an item in the truth-set is defective, then the remaining $k - j$ tests can have exactly one lie or none at all so that $k - j + 1$ possibilities exist; if an item in the lie-set is defective, then the remaining $k - j$ tests cannot lie so that only one possibility exists.

When a new test is performed at a state (a, b), it yields two new states (a_1, b_1) and (a_2, b_2) corresponding to the two outcomes of the test. An important property of the weight is that

$$w_j(a, b) = w_{j-1}(a_1, b_1) + w_{j-1}(a_2, b_2),$$

i.e. the total weight is invariant. The proof of this equation is quite easy. In fact, suppose that the test is on a set containing x items in the truth-set and y items in the lie-set. Then the state corresponding to the positive outcome is $(x, y + a - x)$ and the state corresponding to the negative outcome is $(a - x, b - y + x)$. Thus, the total weight of the two states is

$$
\begin{aligned}
& w_{j-1}(x, y + a - x) + w_{j-1}(a - x, b - y + x) \\
=\ & xj + y + a - x + (a - x)j + b - y + x \\
=\ & a(j + 1) + b \\
=\ & w_j(a, b).
\end{aligned}
$$

Using this weight function, Pelc first proved the following three lemmas before proving Theorem 5.1.1.

Lemma 5.1.2 *For even n, if $n(k + 1) > 2^k$, then $M^1(1, n) > k$. For odd n, if $n(k + 1) + (k - 1) > 2^k$, then $M^1(1, n) > k$.*

Proof. First, consider even n. Suppose to the contrary that there exists an algorithm α identifying the defective within k tests. Let α be represented by a binary tree. Consider a path from the root to a leaf; each node has weight not smaller than that of its sibling. Suppose that the length of the path is $k - j$ (≥ 0). Since the root is in the state $(n, 0)$ with weight $n(k + 1) > 2^k$, the leaf has weight more than 2^j. Note that the state of a leaf must be $(1, 0)$ with weight $j + 1$ or $(0, 1)$ with weight 1. Thus, either

$$
j + 1 > 2^j
$$

or

$$
1 > 2^j.
$$

Both inequalities are impossible.

Next, consider odd n. Suppose to the contrary that there exists an algorithm α identifying the defective within k tests. Note that the first test must yield states (a_1, b_1) and (a_2, b_2) with weights satisfying

$$
\max(w_{k-1}(a_1, b_1), w_{k-1}(a_2, b_2)) \geq \frac{n + 1}{2} k + \frac{n - 1}{2} \geq 2^{k-1}.
$$

Then an argument similar to the case of even n results in a contradiction. $\qquad\square$

Clearly, Lemma 5.1.2 means that for even n

$$
M^1(1, n) \geq \min\{k \mid n(k + 1) \leq 2^k\}
$$

and for odd n

$$
M^1(1, n) \geq \min\{k \mid n(k + 1) + (k - 1) \leq 2^k\}.
$$

To prove the inequality in the other direction of inequalities, the following two lemmas are needed. Define

$$
ch(a, b) = \min\{k \mid w_k(a, b) \leq 2^k\}.
$$

Lemma 5.1.3 *Let b be a natural number and $k = ch(1, b)$. Then there exists an algorithm identifying the defective, starting from the state $(1, b)$, in k more tests.*

Lemma 5.1.4 *Let (a, b) be a state such that $b \geq a - 1 \geq 1$. Then there exists a test which yields states (a_1, b_1) and (a_2, b_2) such that*

1. $\lfloor \frac{a}{2} \rfloor \leq a_1 \leq \lfloor \frac{a+1}{2} \rfloor, \lfloor \frac{a}{2} \rfloor \leq a_2 \leq \lfloor \frac{a+1}{2} \rfloor$;

2. $b_1 \geq a_1 - 1, b_2 \geq a_2 - 1$;

3. $ch(a_1, b_1), ch(a_2, b_2) \leq ch(a, b) - 1$.

The following explains how to prove Theorem 5.1.1 by using these two lemmas and also gives the proofs of two lemmas.

Proof of Theorem 5.1.1. It suffices to prove that for even n, if $n(k+1) \leq 2^k$, then there exists an algorithm identifying the defective in k tests; for odd n, if $n(k+1) + (k-1) \leq 2^k$, then there exists an algorithm identifying the defective in k tests.

First, consider even n. Let $n = 2a$. Select the first test on a set of a items, which yields state (a, a) with $ch(a, a) \leq k - 1$. If $a = 1$, then by Lemma 5.1.3, the defective can be identified by $k - 1$ more tests. If $a > 1$, then the state (a, a) satisfies the assumption of Lemma 5.1.4. Note that Conditions 1 and 2 guarantee that Lemma 5.1.4 can be applied repeatedly until a state $(1, b)$ is reached after $t \leq \lfloor a \rfloor + 1$ tests. Condition 3 guarantees $ch(1, b) \leq k - 1 - t$ for every state $(1, b)$ that is reached. By Lemma 5.1.3, the defective can be identified by $k - 1 - t$ more tests. So the total number of tests for identifying the defective is at most $1 + t + (k - 1 - t) = k$.

For odd n, let $n = 2a + 1$. Select the first test on a set of $a + 1$ items, which yields states $(a+1, a)$ and $(a, a+1)$. Note that $w_{k-1}(a, a+1) = ak+a+1 \leq w_{k-1}(a, a+1) = (a+1)k + a = (n(k+1) + (k-1))/2 \leq 2^{k-1}$. So,

$$ch(a, a+1) \leq k - 1, ch(a+1, a) \leq k - 1.$$

The rest is similar to that in the case of even n.   □

Proof of Lemma 5.1.3. It is proved by induction on b. For $b = 0$, $ch(1, 0) = 1$, so the lemma holds trivially. In the induction step, consider two cases.

Case 1. $b < k$. The test on the truth-set yields states $(1, 0)$ and $(0, 1 + b)$ with

$$w_{k-1}(1, 0) \geq w_{k-1}(0, 1 + b).$$

The state $(1, 0)$ is always a leaf and

$$w_{k-1}(0, 1 + b) \leq 2^{k-1}.$$

It follows that $k - 1$ tests are enough to identify the defective starting from the state $(0, 1 + b)$, because the truth-set being empty implies that the remaining $k - 1$ tests will not make any error.

Case 2. $b \geq k$. Let $x = \lfloor (n - k + 1)/2 \rfloor$. Then the test on the set consisting of the unique element in the truth-set and x elements in the lie-set yields states $(1, x)$ and $(0, b + 1 - x)$. Note that

$$|w_{k-1}(1, x) - w_{k-1}(0, b + 1 - x)| = |k - b - 1 + 2x| \leq 1$$
$$w_{k-1}(1, x) + w_{k-1}(0, b + 1 - x) = w_k(1, b) \leq 2^k.$$

It follows that

$$w_{k-1}(1, x) \leq 2^{k-1}, w_{k-1}(0, b + 1 - x) \leq 2^{k-1}.$$

So, $ch(1, x) \leq k - 1$ and $ch(0, b + 1 - x) \leq k - 1$. By the induction hypothesis, $k - 1$ tests are enough to identify the defective from the state $(1, x)$. Moreover, it is clear that $k - 1$ tests are also enough to identify the defective, starting from the state $(0, b + 1 - x)$. Therefore, a total of k tests are enough to identify the defective, starting from the state $(1, b)$.   □

Proof of Lemma 5.1.4. First, consider the case of $b = a - 1 \geq 1$. Let $\ell = ch(a, b)$.

If a is even, then $a = 2c$ and $b = 2c - 1$. The test on the set consisting of c elements in the truth-set and c elements in the lie-set yields states $(c, 2c)$ and $(c, 2c - 1)$. Clearly, Conditions 1 and 2 are satisfied. Condition 3 follows from the fact that $w_{\ell-1}(c, 2c) - w_{\ell-1}(c, 2c - 1) = 1$.

If a is odd, then $a = 2c + 1$ and $b = 2c$. First, assume $a > 5$. The test on the set consisting of $c + 1$ elements from the truth-set and $c - \lfloor \ell/2 \rfloor$ elements from the lie-set yields states $(c + 1, 2c - \lfloor \ell/2 \rfloor)$ and $(c, 2c + \lfloor \ell/2 \rfloor + 1)$. Condition 1 is clearly satisfied. To prove Condition 2, note that for $a \geq 6$,

$$a(a + 1) + (a - 1) \leq 2^a.$$

Hence, $\ell = ch(a, a - 1) \leq a$, which implies that

$$2c - \lfloor \ell/2 \rfloor \geq c;$$

that is, Condition 2 is satisfied. For Condition 3, it suffices to notice that

$$|w_{\ell-1}(c + 1, 2c - \lfloor \ell/2 \rfloor) - w_{\ell-1}(c, 2c + \lfloor \ell/2 \rfloor + 1)|$$
$$= |\ell - 2\lfloor \ell/2 \rfloor - 1| \leq 1.$$

Next, consider $a \leq 5$. Since $b = a - 1 \geq 1$, there are only two states $(3, 2)$ and $(5, 4)$. For the state $(3, 2)$, the test on two elements in the truth-set yields states $(2, 1)$ and $(1, 4)$ satisfying Conditions 1, 2, and 3. For the state $(5,4)$, the test on three elements of the truth-set yields states $(3,2)$ and $(2,7)$ satisfying Conditions 1, 2, and 3.

Now, consider $b > a - 1 \geq 1$. Denote $x = b - a + 1$, $m = ch(a, b)$, and $\ell = ch(a, a - 1)$. By the above proved case, there exists a test on a set of s elements from the truth-set and t elements from the lie-set which, starting from the state

$(a, a-1)$, yields states (a_1, b_1) and (a_2, b_2) satisfying Conditions 1, 2, and 3. Let $v_i = w_{m-1}(a_i, b_i)$. Then $v_1, v_2 \leq 2^m$, $w_m(a, a-1) = v_1+v_2$, and $w_m(a, b) = v_1+v_2+x$.

Denote $y = \min(x, 2^{m-1} - v_1)$. For the state (a, b), the test on a set of s elements from the truth-set and $t+y$ elements from the lie-set yields states $(a_1, b_1 + y)$ and $(a_2, b_2 + x - y)$. Clearly, Conditions 1 and 2 are satisfied for them. Moreover,

$$w_{m-1}(a_1, b_1 + y) = v_1 + y \leq 2^{m-1}$$

and

$$w_{m-1}(a_2, b_2 + x - y) = v_2 + x - y = \max(v_2, v_1 + v_2 + x - 2^{m-1})$$
$$= \max(v_2, w_m(a, b) - 2^{m-1}) \leq 2^{m-1}.$$

This completes the proof of Lemma 5.1.4.   □

When r errors are allowed, each state is described by a $(r+1)$-tuple $(t_0, t_1, \cdots, t_r)$ where t_i is the size of A_i, the set of items each of which, if defective, satisfies all but i tests in the history.

Czyzowicz, Mundici, and Pelc [6, 7] determined $M^2(1, 2^m)$ by using the weight function

$$w_k(a, b, c) = F(k)a + (k+1)b + c,$$

where

$$F(k) = \frac{k^2 + k + 2}{2}.$$

Their result is that

$$M^2(1, 2^m) = \min\{k \mid k^2 + k + 1 \leq 2^{k-m+1}\}.$$

From this, they were able to show that

$$M^2(1, 10^6) = 29.$$

Guzicki [9] determined $M^2(1, n)$ completely. The result that he obtained is as follows.

Theorem 5.1.5 *Let*

$$ch(a, b, c) = \min\{k \mid w_k(a, b, c) \leq 2^k\}.$$

Denote $k = ch(n, 0, 0)$. *Then*

$$k \leq M^2(1, n) \leq k+1.$$

Moreover, if $k \geq 14$, *then* $M^2(1, n) = k$ *if and only if the following conditions hold.*

Case 1. $n = 4m$. Then $n \cdot F(k) \leq 2^k$.

Case 2. $n = 4m + 1$. Then

        if $k = 4\ell$ then
$$(m+1)F(k-2) + (2m - \ell + 1) + m + \ell - 1 \leq 2^{k-2},$$

        if $k = 4\ell + 1$ then
$$mF(k-2) + (2m + \ell + 1)(k - 1) + m - \ell \leq 2^{k-1},$$

        if $k = 4\ell + 2$ then
$$mF(k-2) + (2m + \ell + 1)(k - 1) + m - \ell \leq 2^{k-2},$$

        if $k = 4\ell + 3$ then
$$(2m + 1)F(k - 1) + 2mk \leq 2^{k-1}.$$

Case 3. $n = 4m + 2$. Then

        if $k = 4\ell$ then
$$mF(k-2) + (2m + \ell + 1)(k - 1) + n - \ell + 1 \leq 2^{k-2},$$

        if $k = 4\ell + 1$ then $nF(k) \leq 2^k$,

        if $k = 4\ell + 2$ then
$$(m+1)F(k-2) + (2m - \ell + 2)(k - 1) + m + \ell \leq 2^{k-2},$$

        if $k = 4\ell + 3$ then
$$mF(k-2) + (2m + \ell + 2)(k - 1) + m - \ell \leq 2^{k-2}.$$

Case 4. $n = 4n + 3$. Then

        if $k = 2\ell$ then
$$(2m + 2)F(k - 1) + (2m + 1)k \leq 2^{k-1},$$

        if $k = 2\ell + 1$ then
$$(m + 1)F(k - 2) + (2m + 2)(k - 1) + m \leq 2^{k-2}.$$

Negro and Sereno [10] proved that

$$M^3(1, 10^6) = 33.$$

In general, it seems pretty hard to give an explicit formula for $M^r(1, n)$ when $r \geq 3$. From the work of Pelc [13] and Guzicki [10], it can be seen that the formula for $M^1(1, n)$ depends on the outcome of the first test and the formula for $M^2(1, n)$ depends on the outcomes of the first and second tests. We conjecture that the formula for $M^r(1, n)$ depends on the outcomes of the first r tests.

5.2 General Lower and Upper Bounds

For $r \geq 3$, determining $M^r(1, n)$ is not easy. So, it is worth giving lower bounds and upper bounds.

For a state $(t_0, t_1, \cdots, t_r)$, testing a set consisting of s_i elements in A_i for all i will yield two states $(s_0, s_1 + t_0 - s_0, s_2 + t_1 - s_1, \cdots, s_r + t_{r-1} - s_{r-1})$ and $(t_0 - s_0, t_1 - s_1 + s_0, t_2 - s_2 + s_1, \cdots, t_r - s_r + s_{r-1})$. Consider the problem of whether the unique defective can be identified in k tests or not. Define the weight of a state $(t_0, t_1, \cdots, t_r)$

as follows:

$$w_m(t_0, t_1, \cdots, t_r) = \sum_{i=0}^{r} t_i \left(\binom{m}{r-i} \right)$$

where m is the number of remaining tests and

$$\left(\binom{m}{k} \right) = \sum_{j=0}^{k} \binom{m}{j}.$$

Note that

$$\left(\binom{m-1}{k-1} \right) + \left(\binom{m-1}{k} \right) = \left(\binom{m}{k} \right).$$

It is easy to verify that

$$
\begin{aligned}
&w_m(t_0, t_1, \cdots, t_r) \\
=\ &w_{m-1}(s_0, s_1 + t_0 - s_0, s_2 + t_1 - s_1, \cdots, s_r + t_{r-1} - s_{r-1}) \\
&+ w_{m-1}(t_0 - s_0, t_1 - s_1 + s_0, t_2 - s_2 + s_1, \cdots, t_r - s_r + s_{r-1}).
\end{aligned}
$$

The following result is a generalization of Lemma 5.1.2.

Theorem 5.2.1 *For even* n,

$$M^r(1, n) \geq \min\{k \mid n \left(\binom{k}{r} \right) \leq 2^k\}$$

and for odd n,

$$M^r(1, n) \geq \min\{k \mid \frac{n+1}{2} \left(\binom{k-1}{r} \right) + \frac{n-1}{2} \left(\binom{k-1}{1} \right) \leq 2^{k-1}\}.$$

Proof. First, consider even n. Suppose to the contrary that there exists an algorithm α identifying the defective in k tests with

$$n \left(\binom{k}{r} \right) > 2^k.$$

Representing α by a binary tree, select a path from the root to a leaf such that each node has a weight not smaller than that of its sibling. Suppose that the length of the path is $k - j$ (≥ 0). Since the root is in the state $(n, 0, \cdots, 0)$ with weight $n(\binom{k}{r}) > 2^k$, the leaf has weight more than 2^j. Note that every leaf must be in a state of type $(0, \cdots, 0, 1, 0, \cdots, 0)$. Thus,

$$\left(\binom{j}{r-i} \right) > 2^j$$

for some i, $0 \leq i \leq r$, which is impossible. In the case of odd n, the proof is similar. $\square$

To obtain a better upper bound, one needs to divide the weight function evenly. However, as r increases, the difficulty of doing that increases rapidly. Rivest et al.[19] found an interesting way to get around this trouble. They put n items at $\frac{1}{n}, \frac{2}{n}, \cdots$, 1 in the interval $(0, 1]$ and use the question "Is $x > c$?" corresponding to a test on the set of items located in $(c, 1]$ where x is the location of the unique defective item. Then they proved that there exists a c to divide a continuous version of the weight function evenly. In this way, they proved the following upper bound.

Theorem 5.2.2

$$M^r(1, n) \leq \min\{k + r \mid n \left(\binom{k}{r} \right) \leq 2^k\}.$$

A detailed proof of this result will be given after the following lemma.

Lemma 5.2.3 *For any two natural numbers k and r, let $\epsilon(k, r)$ denote the smallest ϵ such that k "Yes-No" questions about an unknown $x \in (0, 1]$, up to r of which may receive erroneous answers, are sufficient in the worst case to determine a subset A of $(0, 1]$ with $x \in A$ and $|A| \leq \epsilon$. Then*

$$\epsilon(k, r) = \left(\binom{k}{r} \right) \cdot 2^{-k}.$$

Moreover, this smallest ϵ can be achieved by a strategy using only comparisons "Is $x \leq c$?".

Proof. At the stage that q questions remain, the state of knowledge of the questioner can be represented by an $(r + 1)$-tuple $(A_0, A_1, \cdots, A_r)$ where A_i is the set of points satisfying all but i answers. Consider the weight function

$$w_k(A_0, A_1, \cdots, A_r) = \sum_{i=0}^{r} |A_i| \left(\binom{k}{r-i} \right),$$

where $|A_i|$ is the total length of A_i. Note that any "Yes-No" question is equivalent to a question "Is $x \in T$?" for some set $T \subseteq (0, 1]$. So, it suffices to consider the question of the latter type. For the question "Is $x \in T$?", a "Yes"-answer results in a state $(A'_0, A'_1, \cdots, A'_r)$ with

$$A'_0 = A_0 \cap T$$

and

$$A_i = (A_i \cap T) \cup (A_{i-1} \setminus T) \text{ for } 1 \leq i \leq r$$

and a "No"-answer results in a state $(A''_0, A''_1, \cdots, A''_r)$ with

$$A''_0 = A_0 \setminus T$$

and

$$A_i'' = (A_i \setminus T) \cup (A_{i-1} \cap T).$$

Clearly,

$$w_k(A_0, A_1, \cdots, A_r) = w_{k-1}(A_0', A_1', \cdots, A_r') + w_{k-1}(A_0'', A_1'', \cdots, A_r'').$$

Thus, each test can reduce the weight by at most a half. Note that

$$w_k((0, 1], \emptyset, \cdots, \emptyset) = \left(\binom{k}{r} \right)$$

and

$$w_0(A_0, A_1, \cdots, A_r) = |A_0| + |A_1| + \cdots + |A_r| = \epsilon(k, r).$$

Thus,

$$\epsilon(k, r) \geq \left(\binom{k}{r} \right) 2^{-k}.$$

The above analysis also shows that the best questioning strategy is to choose the next question "Is $x \in T$?" such that the two resultant weights are equal. Any such strategy would make $\epsilon(k, r)$ achieve $(\binom{k}{r}) 2^{-k}$. This can be done with a comparison "Is $x \leq c$?". In fact, $w_{k-1}(A_0', A_1', \cdots, A_r')$ and $w_{k-1}(A_0'', A_1'', \cdots, A_r'')$ are continuous functions of c. Moreover, for $c = 0$,

$$\begin{aligned}
& w_{k-1}(A_0', A_1', \cdots, A_r') \\
= \; & w_{k-1}(\emptyset, A_0, \cdots, A_{r-1}) \\
= \; & \sum_{i=0}^{r-1} |A_i| \left(\binom{k-1}{r-i-1} \right) \\
= \; & \sum_{i=0}^{r} |A_i| \left(\binom{k-1}{r-i} \right) \\
= \; & w_{k-1}(A_0, A_1, \cdots, A_r) \\
= \; & w_{k-1}(A_0'', A_1'', \cdots, A_r'')
\end{aligned}$$

and similarly, for $c = 1$,

$$w_{k-1}(A_0', A_1', \cdots, A_r') \geq w_{k-1}(A_0'', A_1'', \cdots, A_r'').$$

Thus, there exists c such that the two weights are equal.   □

Proof of Theorem 5.2.2. Place n items at $\frac{1}{n}, \frac{2}{n}, \cdots, 1$, respectively. Consider the optimal comparison strategy for the continuous problem as described in the proof of Lemma 5.2.3. Let $(A_0, A_1, \cdots, A_r)$ be the final state. We will show that r additional comparison questions suffice to reduce the set $\cup_{i=0}^r A_r$ to a single interval. Since this interval has length at most $\epsilon(k,r)$, it contains at most one item if $\epsilon(k,r) \leq \frac{1}{n}$. (Note: the interval is always in the form $(a,b]$.) This means that

$$M^r(1,n) \leq \min\{k+r \mid n\left(\binom{k}{r}\right) \leq 2^{-k}\}.$$

Now, we show how to reduce $\cup_{i=0}^r A_r$ to a single interval. Suppose that the questions "Is $x \leq c'_u$?" for $u = 1, \cdots, k'$ where $c'_1 \leq c'_2 \leq \cdots \leq c'_{k'}$ received the "Yes"-answer and the questions "Is $x \leq c''_v$?" for $v = 1, \cdots, k''$ where $c''_1 \geq c''_2 \geq \cdots \geq c''_{k''}$ received the "No"-answer. For convenience, define $c'_u = 1$ for $u > k'$ and $c''_v = 0$ for $v > k''$. Then $\cup_{i=0}^r A_i \subseteq (c''_r, c'_r]$. For $y \in (c'_{r+1}, c''_{r+1}]$, $y \notin \cup_{i=0}^r A_i$ if and only if there exists u such that $c'_u < y \leq c''_{r+1-u}$. It follows that

$$\begin{aligned}
\cup_{i=0}^r A_i &= (c''_{r+1}, c'_{r+1}] \setminus (\cup_{c'_u \leq c''_{r+1-u}} (c'_u, c''_{r+1-u}]) \\
&= \cup_{c'_u < c''_{r+2-u}} (c'_u, c''_{r+1-u}].
\end{aligned}$$

(See Figure 5.1.) Clearly, each interval of $\cup_{i=0}^r A_i$ contains at least one of the following

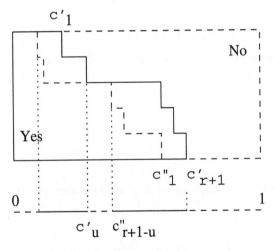

Figure 5.1: The set $\cup_{i=1}^r A_i$.

intervals

$$(c'_u, c''_{r+2-u}] \text{ for } c'_u < c''_{r+2-u} \text{ and } 1 \leq u \leq r+1.$$

There are at most $r+1$ intervals in this list. Choose the next question "Is $x \leq c$?" such that c is located between two intervals of $\cup_{i=0}^r A_i$. Note that any answer for this question will reduce by at least one the number of intervals in the above list. Thus, at most r questions would suffice to reduce $\cup_{i=0}^r A_i$ to a single interval. $\square$

Consider an algorithm α for identifying the unique defective from n items with at most r lies. When α is represented by a binary tree, every leaf is associated with the identified defective and each edge is labeled by a test outcome 0 or 1, representing 'pure' and 'contaminated' respectively. Then each path from the root to a leaf gives a binary string to the item labeling the leaf. This code has the property that for any two different items, their binary strings differ in at least $2r + 1$ bits. Thus, α corresponds to a r-error correcting prefix code of n objects, and vice versa.

The error-correcting code is an important subject in coding theory. Pelc [14] compared Ulam's problem with coding theory and raised the following problems: What is the minimum number of "Yes-No" questions sufficient to find an unknown $x \in \{1, \cdots, n\}$ or to detect errors, if up to k errors are possible? What is the minimum number of "Yes-No" questions sufficient to find an unknown $x \in \{1, \cdots, n\}$ or to determine the number of lies if up to r lies are possible? For the first problem, he gave a complete answer: the number is $\lceil \log n \rceil + k$. For the second problem, he obtained the answer for $k = 2$ and left the problem open for $k \geq 3$.

Pelc [13] studied a constrained group testing problem with a lie. We will discuss it in Chapter 11.

5.3 Linearly Bounded Lies (1)

Lies are said to be *linearly bounded* if each initial sequence of m tests contains at most qm lies for a constant q $(0 < q < 1)$. So, an item can be identified to be good (or defective) if and only if in an initial sequence of m tests, the item is identified to be good (or defective) for more than qm times. From the upper bound in Theorem 5.2.2, Pelc [15] was able to derive the following.

Theorem 5.3.1 *If $0 \leq q < \frac{1}{3}$, there exists a constant c such that for $k \geq c \log n$, $M^{qk}(1, n) \leq k$.*

The proof of this theorem is based on a well-known inequality on $\left(\binom{m}{j}\right)$.

Lemma 5.3.2 *For $j \leq m/2$,*

$$\left(\binom{m}{j}\right) \leq (\frac{m}{j})^j (\frac{m}{m-j})^{m-j} = 2^{mH(j/m)}$$

where $H(x) = -x \log x - (1-x) \log(1-x)$.

Proof. It is proved by induction on m. The initial case $m = 1$ is trivial. In the induction step, if $j = m/2$, then $H(k/m) = 1$ and hence $\left(\binom{m}{j}\right) \leq 2^m = 2^{mH(j/m)}$; if $j \leq (m-1)/2$, then

$$\left(\binom{m}{j}\right)$$

$$\leq \binom{m-1}{0} + \sum_{i=1}^{j} \left(\binom{m-1}{i-1} + \binom{m-1}{i} \right)$$

$$= \sum_{i=0}^{j} \binom{m-1}{i} + \sum_{i=0}^{j-1} \binom{m-1}{i}$$

$$= (\frac{m-1}{j})^j (\frac{m-1}{m-j-1})^{m-1-j} + (\frac{m-1}{j-1})^{j-1} (\frac{m-1}{m-j})^{m-j}$$

$$= (\frac{m}{j})^j (\frac{m}{m-j})^{m-j} [\frac{j}{m} \frac{(1+\frac{1}{j-1})^{j-1}}{(1+\frac{1}{m-1})^{m-1}} + \frac{m-j}{m} \frac{(1+\frac{1}{m-j-1})^{m-j-1}}{(1+\frac{1}{m-1})^{m-1}}]$$

$$\leq (\frac{m}{j})^j (\frac{m}{m-j})^{m-j}.$$

$\square$

Proof of Theorem 5.3.1. By Theorem 5.2.2 and Lemma 5.3.2,

$$M^{qk}(1,n) \leq \min\{k \mid \frac{n}{2^{(1-q)k}} \left(\binom{(1-q)k}{qk} \right) \leq 1\}$$

$$\leq \min\{k \mid 2^{(1-q)k(H(q/(1-q))-1)} n \leq 1\}$$

$$\leq k$$

for $k \geq c \log n$ where $c = \log \frac{1}{(1-q)(1-H(q/(1-q)))}$. $\square$

Theorem 5.3.1 means that for $q < 1/3$, the defective can be identified through $O(\log n)$ tests. It was a major open problem in [15] whether for $1/3 \leq q < 1/2$, the unique defective can be identified through $O(\log n)$ tests or not. Aslam-Dhagat [1] solved this problem by providing a positive answer. We will exhibit their solution in the next two sections. Before doing so, we introduce some results of Spencer and Winkler [22] in this section which are helpful for understanding the nature of the problem.

Spencer and Winkler [22] considered three versions of linearly bounded lies in a game with two players, "Paul" and "Carole". Paul is the questioner and Carole is the answerer. The game proceeds as follows: Carole thinks of an item x from a set of n items; Paul tries to determine x. For fixed k and q, a winning strategy for Paul is an algorithm by which he can identify x with at most k questions if Carole follows a certain rule. The following are three rules which give three versions of the game.

(A) For each question of Paul, Carole has to answer immediately. In addition, every initial sequence of k' of Carole's answers contains at most $k'q$ lies.

(B) For each question of Paul, Carole has to answer immediately. In addition, of k answers, Carole can lie at most kq times.

(C) Carole can wait until Paul submits all k questions and then she gives k answers which contain at most kq lies.

Note that any "Yes-No" question is equivalent to a question "Is $x \in T$?" for some subset T of items. It is easy to see that the first version is equivalent to the linearly-bounded-lie model defined at the beginning of this section. They proved the following for it.

Theorem 5.3.3 *If $q \geq \frac{1}{2}$ and $n \geq 3$, then there does not exist a strategy to identify an unknown x from $\{1, \cdots, n\}$ under the condition that the possible lies are linearly bounded with ratio q, i.e., there does not exist a winning strategy for Paul in the first version of the game.*

Proof. Carole chooses two items, say 1 and 2, one of which is the unknown x. Then she uses the following strategy.

(1) If Paul asks a question "Is $x \in T$?" where T contains exactly one of items 1 and 2, then Carole gives an answer by alternately assuming

a . 1 is the unknown x,

b . 2 is the unknown x.

(2) If (1) does not occur, then Carole always tells the truth.

A crucial fact is that if $n \geq 3$, then Paul must ask a question such that (2) occurs in order to find that the unknown x is not an item other than 1 and 2. Thus, both conclusions (a) and (b) are compatible with at least one half of the answers. This means that Paul cannot distinguish (a) from (b).   □

Theorem 5.3.3 was also discovered by Frazier [8].

For the second version, there exists a winning strategy for Paul if and only if there exists a natural number k such that $M^{qk}(1, n) \leq k$. Theorem 5.3.1 says that if $0 \leq q < \frac{1}{3}$, then such a k exists. Spencer and Winkler also proved the following negative result.

Theorem 5.3.4 *Let $q \geq \frac{1}{3}$ and $n \geq 5$. Then there does not exist k such that $M^{qk}(1, n) \leq k$, i.e., there does not exist a winning strategy for Paul in the second version of the game.*

Proof. Let $A_i(t)$ be the set of items satisfying all but i answers at time t (i.e., $t - 1$ questions have been answered and Paul is asking the tth question). Place $A_0(t)$, $A_1(t)$, $\cdots$ on a line. Then naturally, an ordering is assigned to all items. Each answer of Carole will move some items from A_i to A_{i+1}. All items in A_i for $i > kq$ are considered as removed items while the others are remaining items. Consider the following strategy of Carole.

(1) As long as $|A_0(t)| \geq 3$, Carole makes sure that no more than $\lfloor |A_0(t)|/2 \rfloor$ items move from A_0.

(2) As long as at least three items remain, Carole never moves the first three items at the same time.

(3) If only two items remain, Carole never moves two items at the same time.

Let i_1, i_2, and i_3 be three indices such that the first three items at time t are in A_{i_1}, A_{i_2}, and A_{i_3}, respectively. Define

$$f(t) = i_1 + i_2 + \min(i_3, \lfloor qk \rfloor + 1).$$

Then

$$f(t+1) \le f(t) + 1 \quad \text{for } 1 \le t \le qk.$$

Since $n \ge 5$, $|A_0(2)| \ge 3$. Thus, $f(1) = f(2) = 0$. Suppose to the contrary that Paul has a winning strategy. Then at the end of the game, the first item must be in $A_{\lfloor qk \rfloor}$ and the second item has just been removed, i.e., it has just moved to $A_{\lfloor qk \rfloor + 1}$. So, for some $k' \le k$, $f(k'+1) = 3\lfloor qk \rfloor + 2$. Thus,

$$3\lfloor qk \rfloor + 2 = f(k'+1) \le 1 + f(k') \le \cdots \le k' - 1 + f(2) \le k - 1,$$

that is,

$$k \ge 3(\lfloor qk \rfloor + 1) > 3qk,$$

contradicting $q \ge \frac{1}{3}$. $\square$

The third version of the game is equivalent to the nonadaptive CGT with one defective and linearly bounded lies. (In this case, since all answers are given at the same time, the concept of the initial sequence is useless.) For this version, Spencer and Winkler proved the following.

Theorem 5.3.5 *In the third version of the game, Paul wins with $O(\log n)$ questions if $q < \frac{1}{4}$; Paul has no winning strategy if $q > \frac{1}{4}$; when $q = \frac{1}{4}$, Paul wins with $\Omega(n)$ questions.*

From Theorems 5.3.3 and 5.3.4, one can understand that for $\frac{1}{3} \le q < \frac{1}{2}$, a winning strategy of Paul for the first version of the game has to use the on-line boundary (at most qt lies at time t) to obtain a truth outcome. How many times does Paul have to use it? Aslam and Dhagat [1] gave a three-stage strategy. In the first stage, Paul can use it only once to remove all but $O(\log n)$ items. In the second stage, Paul also needs to use it only once to remove all but $O(1)$ items. In the last stage, Paul needs to use it $O(1)$ times. Thus, totally, Paul needs to use the on-line boundary for only a constant number of times. What is the minimum number? It is an interesting open question.

When there is no deterministic winning strategy for Paul, probabilistic algorithms may be useful. Pelc [15] proved that for $\frac{1}{3} \le q < \frac{1}{2}$, Paul can still win the second version of the game with any fixed reliability $p < 1$ by using $O(\log^2 n)$ questions.

5.4   The Chip Game

Aslam and Dhagat [1] proposed a different approach to establish the upper bound
for $M^r(1, n)$. The advantage of their approach is in the implementation. No weight
function needs to be computed in their algorithm. However, in the approach of Rivest
et al. or others, the weight function is involved and a lot of computation is required.
How can Aslam and Dhagat eliminate the weight function? Here is a little explanation
before introducing their method. From the use of the weight function, it is easy to
know that the new test should be chosen to divide the current weight as evenly as
possible. One way to do this is to choose the new test on a set consisting of nearly
half of the elements from A_i for all i. This strategy is obtained by keeping the weight
in mind, but not depending on the weight. For a simple description of their strategy,
Aslam and Dhagat [1] used a chip game formulation.

The chip game is played on a unidimensional board with levels from 0 upward
(see Figure 5.2). There are two players, a chooser Paul and a pusher Carole. At the

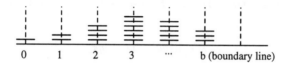

Figure 5.2: Chip Game

beginning all chips are on level 0. Each chip represents an item. (Chips and items will
not be distinguished in the rest of this chapter.) So, they are labeled by $1, 2, \cdots, n$.
At each step, the chooser Paul divides $\{1, 2, \cdots, n\}$ into two disjoint subsets. Then
the pusher Carole picks one of these two subsets and pushes every chip in this subset
to the next level. There is a boundary line at some level. Every chip that passes
over the boundary line can be removed by Paul. To win, Paul must remove all but
one chip from the board. The location of the boundary line is based on how many
errors are allowed. For up to r errors, the boundary line is set at level r. When r is
a function of the number of tests, the boundary line has to be updated at each step.
For example, if lies are linearly bounded, i.e., $r = qk$ at step k, then the boundary
line should be placed at level $\lfloor qdm \rfloor$ at step k. So, it is updated by moving it forward
one more level approximately every $1/(rd)$ steps.

Group testing for one defective can be explained as a chip game in the following
way: A test corresponds to a step of the chip game. When Paul divides $\{1, 2, \cdots, n\}$
into two subsets, it means that the test is on one of these two subsets. (It does not
matter which subset is tested because the test outcome is the same: one subset is pure
and the other is contaminated.) The test outcome corresponds to the choice of Carole.
The subset pushed by Carole is the pure subset. From the above correspondence, it
is easy to see that each chip at level i is contained in pure subsets i times. If it is
defective, then i lies have been made. So, the chips at level i form exactly A_i, the

set of items each of which, if defective, satisfies all but exactly i test outcomes in the test history. The following table summarizes the above description.

group testing with one defective	the chip game
the test subset and its complement	two subsets obtained by Paul's division
the pure subset	the subset pushed by Carole
the items in the set A_i	the chips at level i
the state	the sequence of the number of chips at each level

Aslam and Dhagat's approach can be extended to more defectives. In the generalized chip game, the chip board and players are the same as before. At the beginning all chips are also at level 0. However, at each step, the chooser Paul divides $\{1, 2, \cdots, n\}$ into $d+1$ disjoint subsets instead of two subsets. The pusher Carole picks one of the $d+1$ subsets and pushes every chip in the chosen subset to the next level. To win, Paul must eliminate all but d chips from the board.

The generalized chip game corresponds to a certain type of group testing algorithms. At each step, Carole's choice corresponds to the testing in the following way: Sequentially test d of the $d+1$ sets determined by Paul. If a test outcome is negative, then push the tested set and move to the next step; if all test outcomes are positive, then push the $(d+1)$th group.

Let $h_m(i)$ denote the number of chips at level i after m steps. Consider a strategy for Paul as follows: At each step, first label all chips on the board, one level followed by another level, with natural numbers starting from 1. Then choose the ith group consisting of chips with labels congruent to i modulo $d+1$. According to this strategy, at step $m+1$, each group contains chips at the ith level of sizes between $\lfloor h_m(i)/(d+1)\rfloor$ and $\lceil h_m(i)/(d+1)\rceil$.

Denote

$$b_m(i) = \frac{nd^{m-i}}{(d+1)^m}\binom{m}{i}$$

and

$$\Delta_m(i) = h_m(i) - b_m(i).$$

The normalized binomial coefficient $b_m(i)$ is used to approximate $h_m(i)$. In fact, to find out how many chips are left on the board, one needs to estimate $\sum_{i=0}^{r} h_m(i)$. However, this sum is hard to determine exactly. As a replacement, an upper bound will be given to $\sum_{i\leq\lfloor qkd\rfloor}\Delta_m(I)$. The following results are generalizations of those in [1].

Lemma 5.4.1 $(\forall m \geq 0)\ \Delta_m(0) \leq d.$

Proof. This is proved by induction on m. For $m = 0$, $h_0(0) = n = b_0(i)$ and hence $\Delta_0(0) = 0$. Assume $\Delta_{m-1}(0) \leq 1$. Then

$$
\begin{aligned}
h_m(0) &\leq h_{m-1}(0) - \lfloor \frac{h_{m-1}(0)}{d+1} \rfloor \\
&\leq \frac{h_{m-1}(0)d}{d+1} + \frac{d}{d+1} \\
&= \frac{(b_{m-1}(0) + \Delta_m(0))d}{d+1} + \frac{d}{d+1} \\
&\leq b_m(0) + d.
\end{aligned}
$$

Thus, $\Delta_m(0) = h_m(0) - b_m(0) \leq d$.   □

Lemma 5.4.2 $(\forall m \geq 0)$ $\sum_{i=0}^{m} \Delta_m(i) = 0$.

Proof. It follows immediately from the fact that $\sum_{i=0}^{m} h_m(i) = n = \sum_{i=0}^{m} b_m(i)$.

Lemma 5.4.3 $\sum_{i=0}^{j-1} b_{m-1}(i) + \frac{b_{m-1}(j)d}{d+1} = \sum_{i=0}^{j} b_m(i)$.

Proof. Note that $\binom{m-1}{i-1} + \binom{m-1}{i} = \binom{m}{i}$.

$$
\begin{aligned}
&\sum_{i=0}^{j-1} b_{m-1}(i) + \frac{b_{m-1}(j)d}{d+1} \\
=& \sum_{i=0}^{j-1} \frac{d^{m-1-i}}{(d+1)^{m-1}} \binom{m-1}{i} + \frac{d^{m-j}}{(d+1)^m} \binom{m-1}{j} \\
=& \frac{n}{(d+1)^m} [\sum_{i=0}^{j-1} (d+1)d^{m-1-i} \binom{m-1}{i} + d^{m-j} \binom{m-1}{j}] \\
=& \frac{n}{(d+1)^m} [d^m \binom{m-1}{0} + d^{m-1}[\binom{m-1}{0} + \binom{m-1}{1}] + \cdots \\
&+ d^{m-j}[\binom{m-1}{j-1} + \binom{m-1}{j}]] \\
=& \frac{n}{(d+1)^m} [d^m \binom{m}{0} + d^{m-1} \binom{m}{1} + \cdots + d^{m-j} \binom{m}{j}] \\
=& \sum_{i=0}^{m} b_m(i).
\end{aligned}
$$

□

Lemma 5.4.4 *For all $m \geq 0$ and $j \leq m$, $\sum_{i=0}^{j} \Delta_m(i) \leq (j+1)d$.*

Proof. This is proved by induction on m. The case $m = 0$ is trivial because $\Delta_0(0) = 0$. In the induction step, for $j = 0$ and $j = m$, the lemma follows from Lemmas 5.4.1 and 5.4.2. For $0 < j < m$, note that

$$
\begin{aligned}
\sum_{i=0}^{j} h_m(i) &\leq \sum_{i=0}^{j} h_{m-1}(i) - \left\lfloor \frac{h_{m-1}(j)}{d+1} \right\rfloor \\
&\leq \sum_{i=0}^{j-1} h_{m-1}(i) + \frac{h_{m-1}(j)d}{d+1} + \frac{d}{d+1} \\
&= \sum_{i=0}^{j-1} b_{m-1}(i) + \frac{b_{m-1}(j)d}{d+1} \\
&\quad + \sum_{i=0}^{j-1} \Delta_{m-1}(i) + \frac{\Delta_{m-1}(j)d}{d+1} + \frac{d}{d+1} \\
&= \sum_{i=0}^{j} b_m(i) + \sum_{i=0}^{j-1} \Delta_{m-1}(i) + \frac{\Delta_{m-1}(j)d}{d+1} + \frac{d}{d+1}.
\end{aligned}
$$

If $\Delta_{m-1}(j) \leq d$, then

$$
\begin{aligned}
&\sum_{i=0}^{j-1} \Delta_{m-1}(i) + \frac{\Delta_{m-1}(j)d}{d+1} + \frac{d}{d+1} \\
&\leq \sum_{i=0}^{j-1} \Delta_{m-1}(i) + d \\
&\leq (j+1)d.
\end{aligned}
$$

If $\Delta_{m-1}(i) > d$, then

$$
\begin{aligned}
&\sum_{i=0}^{j-1} \Delta_{m-1}(i) + \frac{\Delta_{m-1}(j)d}{d+1} + \frac{d}{d+1} \\
&\leq \sum_{i=0}^{j} \Delta_{m-1}(i) \\
&\leq (j+1)d.
\end{aligned}
$$

Therefore,

$$
\begin{aligned}
\sum_{i=0}^{j} \Delta_m(i) &= \sum_{m}^{j} h_m(i) - \sum_{i=0}^{j} b_m(i) \\
&\leq \sum_{m-1}^{j-1} \Delta_{m-1}(i) + \frac{\Delta_{m-1}(j)d}{d+1} + \frac{d}{d+1} \\
&\leq (j+1)d.
\end{aligned}
$$

$\square$

Theorem 5.4.5 *After m steps in the chip game, there are at most*

$$d(r+1) + \frac{n}{(d+1)^m} \cdot \sum_{i=0}^{r} d^{m-i}\binom{m}{i}$$

chips left at levels from 0 to r.

Proof. It follows immediately from Lemmas 5.4.4.   □

If m satisfies

$$n \cdot \sum_{i=0}^{r} d^{m-i}\binom{m}{i} < (d+1)^m,$$

then after m steps, there are only $d(r+1)$ chips left at levels from 0 to r. Suppose that there are at most r errors. Then all chips not at levels from 0 to r can be removed. By Lemma 5.3.2,

$$\sum_{i=0}^{r} d^{m-i}\binom{m}{i} \le (d2^{H(r/m)})^m.$$

Choose $m = \max(4dr, 1 + \lfloor \frac{\log n}{\log \frac{d+1}{d} - H(\frac{1}{4d})} \rfloor) = O(\log n)$. Note that $\log \frac{d}{d+1} > H(\frac{1}{4d})$. So,

$$n(d2^{H(r/m)})^m \le n(d2^{H(1/4d)})^m < (d+1)^m,$$

that is, for this chosen m, after m steps, there are at most $d(r+1)$ chips left on the board. Since at each step, at least one chip is pushed up unless there are only d chips left on the board, $dr(r+1)$ steps are enough to remove the other dr good chips. Therefore, it follows

Corollary 5.4.6 *Let r, d and n be natural numbers with $d \le n$. Then*

$$M^r(d,n) \le dr(r+1) + \min\{m \mid n \cdot \sum_{i=0}^{r} d^{m-i}\binom{m}{i} < (1+\frac{1}{d})^m\}.$$

Furthermore, if r is a constant, then $M^r(d,n) = O(\log n)$.

When $d = 1$, the upper bound in this corollary is weaker than that in Theorem 5.2.2. We conjecture that

$$M^r(d,n) \le dr + \min\{m \mid n \cdot \sum_{i=0}^{r} d^{m-i}\binom{m}{i} \le (1+\frac{1}{d})^m\}$$

and for any r and d, there exists an n such that the equality sign holds.

Finally, a remark should be made that in the above results, the boundary is used only at the end of the game, i.e., all identified chips are removed according to the last boundary line.

5.5 Linearly Bounded Lies (2)

In Theorem 5.4.5, set $r = qdm$ and $m = \lceil \frac{\log \frac{n}{d}}{\log \frac{d+1}{d} - H(qd)} \rceil$ $(= O(\log n)$ when $\log \frac{d+1}{d} > H(qd))$. Then the following is obtained.

Theorem 5.5.1 *Suppose that $\log \frac{d+1}{d} > H(qd)$ and $q < \frac{1}{2d}$. Then with the strategy provided in the last section, the chooser can remove all but $O(\log n)$ chips from the board within $O(\log n)$ steps.*

Based on this result, the following theorem will be proved in this section.

Theorem 5.5.2 *Suppose $H(qd) < \log \frac{d+1}{d}$. Then there exists an algorithm identifying all d defectives from n items in $O(\log n)$ tests with linearly bounded errors in proportion to q.*

The algorithm consists of three stages. In the first stage, it corresponds to the chip game described in the last section, which achieves the result stated in Theorem 5.5.1. In order to remove the remaining $O(\log n)$ good chips, two more stages are used; they are similar to those introduced in [1]. In the second stage, all but $O(1)$ chips on the board will be removed in $O(\log n)$ tests. In the third stage, all but d chips on the board will be removed in $O(\log n)$ tests. The details are as follows.

Suppose that there are $c_1 \log n$ chips left on the board with the boundary line at level $c_2 \log n$. Let us still use the chip game language to describe the algorithm at the second stage. At the beginning of the second stage, Paul moves some chips to the left such that each level contains at most $d + 1$ chips and then continues to form groups in the same way as that in the first stage. In order to get such an initial state for the second stage, Paul may need to add $\lceil (c_1 \log n)/(d+1) \rceil$ levels below level 0. An equivalent treatment is to relabel the levels such that the first level is still level 0 and the boundary line is at level $c_2 \log n + \lceil (c_1 \log n)/(d+1) \rceil (= c_3 \log n)$. In the following, the latter way is used. The next lemma states an invariant property of the second stage.

Lemma 5.5.3 *The property that each level on the board contains at most $d+1$ chips is invariant during the second stage.*

Proof. At each step, a level receives at most one chip from the previous level. If this level contains exactly $d + 1$ chips at the beginning of the step, then it must have a chip going to the next level. Thus, at the end of the step, each level still contains at most $d + 1$ chips. $\qquad\square$

Choose $k = \lceil 2/(1 - (d+1)dq) \rceil$. It will be shown that Paul removes all but $(d+1)k$ chips on the board in $O(\log n)$ steps. To do so, define the level weight of the board to be the sum of level numbers where its $(d + 1)k$ leftmost chips are located.

Lemma 5.5.4 *After each step, the level weight of the board increases by at least $k-1$.*

Proof. Among $(d+1)k$ leftmost chips there are at least k pushed up at each step. Of those k chips there are at least $k - 1$ chips which remain in the set of $(d+1)k$ leftmost chips after the step. Thus, the level weight of the board increases by at least $k - 1$. □

Theorem 5.5.5 *If $q(d+1)d < 1$, then at the second stage, Paul removes all but $(d+1)k$ chips from the board in $O(\log n)$ steps.*

Proof. Let S be the number of steps taken during the second stage. Let W be the level weight of the board at the end of the second stage. Note that initially the level weight of the board is non-negative. By Lemma 5.5.4, $W \geq S(k-1)$. Moreover, the boundary line at the end of the second stage is $c_3 \log n + \lfloor qdS \rfloor$. Thus, $W \leq (d+1)k(c_3 \log n + qdS)$. Combining the two inequalities, one obtains

$$S \leq \frac{(d+1)kc_3 \log n}{k - 1 - q(d+1)dk}.$$

So, $S = O(\log n)$. □

Note that the generalized chip game corresponds to a certain type of testing method. Since a testing method of a different type is used at the third stage, it is convenient to use the original terminology of group testing except the chip board stays. Suppose that there are c chips left on the board after the second stage and meanwhile the boundary line is at level $b = O(\log n)$.

First, choose an algorithm α for identifying d defectives from c items. Then perform α with *brute force* in the following way: For each test of α, repeat the test until either the number of negative outcomes or the number of positive outcomes exceeds the boundary line.

Let x_i denote the number of repetitions for the ith test. Suppose that the boundary line is moved to level b_i with brute force on the ith test. Then $(1 - q)x_i \leq 1 + b_{i-1} + \lfloor qx_i \rfloor$. Thus,

$$x_i \leq \frac{1 + b_{i-1}}{1 - 2q}$$

and

$$
\begin{aligned}
1 + b_i &\leq 1 + b_{i-1} + \lfloor qx_i \rfloor \\
&\leq \frac{(1 + b_{i-1})(1 - q)}{1 - 2q} \\
&\leq (1 + b)\left(\frac{1 - q}{1 - 2q}\right)^i.
\end{aligned}
$$

Consequently,

$$x_i \leq \frac{1+b}{1-2q}(\frac{1-q}{1-2q})^{i-1}$$

and

$$\sum_{i=1}^{m} x_i \leq (\frac{1+b}{q})((\frac{1-q}{1-2q})^m - 1) = O(\log n)$$

where m is the number of reliable tests for identifying d defectives from c items, which is a constant.

Finally, the proof of Theorem 5.5.2 is completed by an analysis of the three stages and noting

$$H(qd) < \log \frac{d+1}{d} \Rightarrow q < \frac{1}{d(d+1)}.$$

In fact,

$$H(qd) \leq \log \frac{d+1}{d} \leq \frac{1}{d+1} \log(d+1) + \frac{d}{d+1} \log \frac{d+1}{d} = H(\frac{1}{d+1})$$

and $H(x)$ is increasing when $x \leq \frac{1}{2}$.   □

Note that the number of reliable tests for identifying d defectives from n items is at most $d \log \frac{n}{d} + d$ by Lemma 7.5.2. Thus, the number of linearly bounded unreliable tests for identifying d defective ones from n items is at most

$$\sum_{i=1}^{\lfloor d \log \frac{n}{d} + d \rfloor} x_i$$

$$\leq \frac{1}{q}((\frac{1-q}{1-2q})^{d(\log \frac{n}{d}+1)} - 1)$$

for $q < 1/2$. For $H(qd) \geq \log \frac{d+1}{d}$ and $q < \frac{1}{2}$, it is still an open problem whether or not there exists an algorithm identifying all d defective ones from n items by using at most $O(\log n)$ tests with linearly bounded errors in proportion q.

Theorem 5.5.2 for $d = 1$ is exactly the result obtained by Aslam and Dhagat [1].

Corollary 5.5.6 *Suppose $q < 1/2$. Then there exists an algorithm identifying the unique defective from n items within $O(\log n)$ tests with linearly bounded errors in proportion q.*

Pelc [15] also studied the following model: Each test makes an error with probability q. This model is called the *known error probability* model which is different from the linearly bounded error model. In fact, in the former, n tests may have more than qn errors. (Exactly k errors exist with probability $\binom{n}{k}q^k(1-q)^{n-k}$.) But, in the latter, n tests cannot have more than qn errors. Since in the known error probability model, the number of errors has no upper bound, no item can be identified definitely. So, the reliability of the identification has to be introduced. An algorithm has *reliability* p if each item can be identified to be a good (or defective) item with probability p. Pelc [15] also proposed the following open question. With error probability $q < \frac{1}{2}$, can the unique defective be identified with $O(\log n)$ questions for every reliability p? This question can be answered positively by using the result of Aslam and Dhagat and an argument of Pelc.

In fact, let r_k be the number of errors in a sequence of k answers. By Chebyshev's inequality,

$$Prob(|\frac{r_k}{k} - q| \geq \epsilon) \leq \frac{q(1-q)}{k\epsilon^2}$$

for any $\epsilon > 0$. Let $\epsilon = (\frac{1}{2} - q)/2$. Then $q + \epsilon < \frac{1}{2}$ and $r_k \leq (q + \epsilon)k$. Thus,

$$Prob(r_k \leq (q + \epsilon)k) \geq Prob(|\frac{r_k}{k} - q| < \epsilon) \geq 1 - \frac{c}{k}$$

where $c = 16p(1-q)/(1-2q)^2$.

This means that for any fixed reliability p, the number of errors in a sequence of $k > (1-p)/c$ answers can be bounded by $(q + \epsilon)k < \frac{1}{2}k$. Note that in the proof of Theorem 5.5.2, the first stage has $O(\log n)$ steps and needs to identify items only at the end of the stage. Thus, when n is sufficiently large such that the number of steps in the first stage becomes more than $(1-p)/c$, every identification would take place after step $\lceil (1-p)/c \rceil$. This means that every item is identified with reliability p. Thus, Paul's $O(\log n)$ winning strategy for the linearly bounded error model also gives an algorithm with reliability p for the known error probability model. Thus, we have

Theorem 5.5.7 *With error probability $q < 1/2$, the unique defective can be identified in $O(\log n)$ tests for any reliability p.*

For nonadaptive testing, does a similar result exist? It is an open problem.

Finally, it is worth mentioning that Brylawski [4] and Schalkwijk [20] pointed out that the search with linearly bounded lies is equivalent to the problem of optimal block coding for a noisy channel with a noiseless and delayless feedback channel.

5.6   Other Restrictions on Lies

In Sec. 5.2, to obtain an upper bound for $M^k(1, n)$, we studied the problem of identifying an unknown point from a continuous domain $(0, 1]$. In this section, we will discuss this kind of problem with a general restriction on lies. When all tested objects form a continuous domain (such as a segment, a polygon, etc.), it is impossible to identify an unknown point exactly from the domain. Hence, the task is to identify the unknown point with a given accuracy ϵ, i.e., to determine a set of measure at most ϵ such that the set contains the unknown. Let $\mu(A)$ denote the measure of set A.

What is the smallest ϵ such that k tests with at most r lies can in the worst case determine a set A with $\mu(A) \leq \epsilon$? Lemma 5.2.3 has given the answer. However, there is a very interesting generalization of Lemma 5.2.3, which was given by Ravikumar and Lakshmanan [18].

Consider a test history H of k tests. Denote an erroneous test by 1 and a correct test by 0. Then the lie pattern of H can be described by a binary string. The restriction on lies can be represented by a set R of binary strings. For example, if R consists of all strings having at most r 1's, then the restriction is that at most r lies are possible. They proved the following.

Theorem 5.6.1 *Let k be a natural number and R a restriction on lies. Let $\epsilon(k, R)$ denote the smallest ϵ such that k "Yes-No" questions about an unknown $x \in (0, 1]$, with restriction R on lies, are sufficient in the worst case to determine a subset A of $(0, 1]$ with $x \in A$ and $\mu(A) \leq \epsilon$. Then*

$$\epsilon(k, R) = |R \cap \{0, 1\}^k| \cdot 2^{-k}$$

where $\{0, 1\}^k$ is the set of all binary strings of length k. Moreover, this smallest ϵ can be achieved by a strategy using only comparisons "Is $x \leq c$?".

Actually, the lower bound can be stated more generally.

Theorem 5.6.2 *Let k be a natural number and R a restriction on lies. Let $\epsilon_D(k, R)$ denote the smallest ϵ such that k "Yes-No" questions about an unknown $x \in D$, with restriction R on lies, are sufficient in the worst case to determine a subset A of D with $x \in A$ and $\mu(A) \leq \epsilon$. Then*

$$\epsilon_D(k, R) \geq |R \cap \{0, 1\}^k| \cdot 2^{-k}\mu(D).$$

Proof. Consider an algorithm with k tests, which can be represented by a binary tree of depth k. Suppose that lie patterns in $R \cap \{0, 1\}^k$ are linearly ordered. Let S_{ij} denote subsets of D such that $x \in S_{ij}$ if and only if the choice of x and the jth lie pattern lead to the ith leaf of the binary tree. For any fixed lie pattern $y_j \in R$, the sets S_{ij}, $i = 1, 2, \ldots, 2^k$ form a partition of D. That is,

$$S_{ij} \cap S_{i'j} = \emptyset \quad \text{for } i \neq i' \text{ and } \cup_{i=1}^{2^k} S_{ij} = D.$$

In addition,

$$S_{ij} \cap S_{ij'} = \emptyset \quad \text{for } j \neq j'.$$

Since one does not know which lie pattern appears, the set of uncertainty after k tests is $D_k(i) = \cup_{y_j \in R \cap \{0,1\}^k} S_{ij}$ if the testing process leads to the ith leaf. Therefore, the worst case value of the measure of the set of uncertainty is

$$\max_i \mu(D_k(i)).$$

Note that

$$\sum_i \mu(D_k(i)) = \sum_i \sum_j \mu(S_{ij}) = \sum_j \sum_i \mu(S_{ij}) = \sum_j \mu(D) = \mu(D)|R \cap \{0,1\}^k|.$$

Therefore,

$$\max_i \mu(D_k(i)) \geq 2^{-k}|R \cap \{0,1\}^k|\mu(D).$$

□

De Bonis, Gargano, and Vaccaro [3] considered more than one unknown point. Suppose that there are d unknown points in $(0,1]$. Then the search space becomes

$$D = \{(x_1,\ldots,x_d) \mid x_1,\ldots,x_d \in (0,1]\}.$$

Each test consists of a question "Is $\{x_1,\ldots,x_d\} \cap T = \emptyset$?" on a subset T of $(0,1]$. Let $\epsilon_d(k,r)$ denote the smallest ϵ such that k "Yes-No" questions about an unknown $x \in D$, with at most r lies, are sufficient in the worst case to determine a subset A of D with $x \in A$ and $\mu(A) \leq \epsilon$. By Theorem 5.6.2,

$$\epsilon_d(k,r) \geq \left(\binom{k}{r}\right) \cdot 2^{-k}\mu(D) = \frac{\left(\binom{k}{r}\right)}{2^k d!}.$$

They further proved the following.

Theorem 5.6.3 $\epsilon_2(k,r) = \left(\binom{k}{r}\right) 2^{-(k+1)}$.

They also obtained a similar result for parity testing, i.e., each test consists of a question "Does T contain exactly one of $x_1, \ldots, x_d$?" on a subset T of $(0,1]$.

In Sec. 5.2, Lemma 5.2.3 was used to obtain an upper bound for the discrete version of the problem. Could Theorem 5.6.1 be used to obtain a similar result to Theorem 5.2.2? Czyzowicz, Lakshmanan, and Pelc [5] gave a kind of negative answer. For each string p, let R_p be the set of binary strings which do not contain p as a substring. Then they proved that

Theorem 5.6.4 *Identifying an unknown x from $\{1,\ldots,n\}$ by "Yes-No"-queries with restriction R_p on lies is possible if and only if p is one of the following* 0, 1, 01, *and* 10.

Compared with Theorem 5.6.1, how should one understand this result? Applying Theorem 5.6.1 to the interval $(0,n]$, with a certain number of tests, the set of uncertainty can have very small measure. However, this set may have too many connected components distributed "evenly" in $(0,n]$ so that none of 1, ..., n can be excluded. In this case, identifying x is impossible.

Czyzowicz, Lakshmanan, and Pelc [5] also obtained optimal strategies for the four possible cases. In fact, for $p=0,1$, it is trivial and for $p=01,10$, the result is stated in the following.

Theorem 5.6.5 *The depth of the optimal binary search tree for finding x in $\{1, \ldots, n\}$ with restriction R_{10} on lies is*

$$M^{R_{10}}(1,n) = \begin{cases} \min\{t \mid (t+1)n \le 2^t\}, & \text{if } n \text{ is even,} \\ \min\{t \mid (t+1)n + (t-1) \le 2^t\}, & \text{if } n \text{ is odd.} \end{cases}$$

The same result holds for restriction R_{01}.

Rivest *et al.* [19] introduced another model of erroneous response. It is supposed that the answer "Yes" is always true and lies occur only in "No"-answers. This is called the *half-lie* model. In the half-lie model, not every lie pattern leads to a well-defined testing. In fact, if the forbidden lie pattern p ends with a 0, then a conflict may result when the testing gives different outcomes according to the half-lie model and to the forbidden lie pattern. To see this, consider $q = 1$, i.e., every test outcome is erroneous. Now, if the query is "Is $x \in \emptyset$?", the erroneous response is "Yes", which is always supposed to be true in the half-lie model, a contradiction. For the forbidden lie pattern p with a 1 at the end, Czyzowicz, Lakshmanan, and Pelc [5] proved the following.

Theorem 5.6.6 *In the half-lie model, search with restriction R_p is feasible for every p ending with a 1.*

References

[1] J.A. Aslam and A. Dhagat, Searching in presence of linearly bounded errors, *Proceedings of 23rd STOC*, 1991, pp. 486-493.

[2] E.R. Berlekamp, Block for the binary symmetric channel with noiseless delayless feedback, in *Error-Correcting Codes*, (Wiley, New York, 1968) 61-85.

[3] A. De Bonis, L. Gargano, and U. Vaccaro, Group testing with unreliable tests, manuscript.

[4] T.H. Brylawski, The mathematics of watergate, Unpublished manuscript.

[5] J. Czyzowicz, K. B. Lakshmanan, A. Pelc, Searching with a forbidden lie pattern in responses, *Information Processing Letters* 37 (1991) 127-132.

[6] J. Czyzowicz, D. Mundici, and A. Pelc, Solution of Ulam's problem on binary search with two lies, *J. Combin. Theory* A49 (1988) 384-388.

[7] J. Czyzowicz, D. Mundici, and A. Pelc, Ulam's searching game with lies, *J. Combin. Theory* A52 (1989) 62-76.

[8] M. Frazier, Searching with a nonconstant number of lies, manuscript.

[9] W. Guzicki, Ulam's searching game with two lies, *J. Combin. Theory* A54 (1990) 1-19.

[10] A. Negro and M. Sereno, Solution of Ulam's problem on binary search with three lies, *J. Combin. Theory* A59 (1992) 149-154.

[11] A. Negro and M. Sereno, An Ulam's searching game with three lies, *Advances in Mathematics*

[12] A. Pelc, Solution of Ulam's problem on searching with a lie, *J. Combin. Theory* A44 (1987) 129-140.

[13] A. Pelc, Prefix search with a lie, *J. Combin. Theory* A48 (1988) 165-173.

[14] A. Pelc, Detecting errors in searching games, *J. Combin. Theory* A51 (1989) 43-54.

[15] A. Pelc, Searching with known error probability, *Theoretical Computer Science* 63 (1989) 185-202.

[16] A. Pelc, Detecting a counterfeit coin with unreliable weighings, *Ars Combin.* 27 (1989) 181-192.

[17] B. Ravikumar, K. Ganesan, and K.B. Lakshmanan, On selecting the largest element in spite of erroneous information, *Proceedings of ICALP '87*, 99-89.

[18] B. Ravikumar and K.B. Lakshmanan, Coping with known patterns of lies in a search game, *Theoretical Computer Science*, 33 (1984) 85-94.

[19] R.L. Rivest, A.R. Meyer, D.J. Kleitman, K. Winklmann, and J. Spencer, Coping with errors in binary search procedures, *J. Computer and System Sciences* 20 (1980) 396-404.

[20] J.P. Schalkwijk, A class of simple and optimal strategies for block coding on the binary symmetric channel with noiseless feedback, in *IEEE Trans. Information Theory* 17:3 (1971) 283-287.

[21] J. Spencer, Guess a number–with lying, *Math. Mag.* 57 (1984) 105-108.

[22] J. Spencer and P. Winkler, Three thresholds for a liar, Preprint, 1990.

[23] S.M. Ulam, *Adventures of a Mathematician*, (Scribner's New York 1976).

6

Complexity Issues

From previous chapters, one probably gets the impression that it is very hard to find the optimal solution of CGT when d, the number of defectives, is more than one. In this chapter, this impression will be formalized through studying the complexity of CGT.

6.1 General Notions

In this section, we give a very brief introduction to some important concepts in computational complexity theory.

The computation model for the study of computational complexity is the Turing machine as shown in Figure 6.1, which consists of three parts, a tape, a head, and a finite control. There are two important complexity measures, *time* and *space*. The time is the number of moves of the Turing machine. The space is the number of cells, on the tape, which have been visited by the head during the computation.

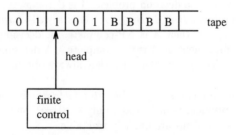

Figure 6.1: A Turing machine.

A problem is called a *decision* problem if its answer is "Yes" or "No". In the study of computational complexity, an optimization problem is usually formulated as a decision problem. For example, the prototype group testing problem of CGT is equivalent to the following decision problem.

The Decision Version of the Prototype Group Testing Problem: Given n items and two integers d and k ($0 < d, k < n$), determine whether $M(d,n) \geq k$ or not.

When a Turing machine computes a decision problem, both the time and the space are functions of the input size. If they are bounded by a polynomial, we say that they are polynomial time and polynomial space, respectively.

There exist two types of Turing machines, *deterministic* TM and *nondeterministic* TM. They differ with respect to the function of the finite control. The interested reader may refer to [6] for details.

The following are three of the most important complexity classes.

P: A decision problem belongs to P if it can be computed by a polynomial-time deterministic TM.

NP: A decision problem belongs to NP if it can be computed by a polynomial-time nondeterministic TM.

PSPACE: A decision problem belongs to PSPACE if it can be computed by a polynomial-space deterministic (or nondeterministic) TM.

It is well-known that P $\subseteq$ NP $\subseteq$ PSPACE. However, no one knows so far whether the above inclusions are proper or not.

A decision problem A is *polynomial-time many-one reducible* to a decision problem B, denoted by $A \leq_m^p B$, if there is a polynomial-time computable mapping f from instances of A to instances of B such that A has the Yes-answer on x if and only if B has the Yes-answer on $f(x)$.

For a complexity class $\mathcal{C}$, a decision problem A is $\mathcal{C}$-*complete* if (1) A is in $\mathcal{C}$ and (2) for any decision problem $B \in \mathcal{C}$, $B \leq_m^p A$. It is a well-known fact that if B is NP-complete and $B \leq_m^p A$, then A is NP-complete. A decision problem A is *co-NP-complete* if the complement of A is NP-complete. (A decision problem B is the *complement* of another decision problem A if they always obtain different answers on the same input.)

Usually, a decision problem is said to be *intractable* if it is not in P. It is known that an NP-complete problem is in P if and only if NP=P. Most people believe NP $\neq$ P, i.e., NP-complete problems are unlikely tractable.

To establish the intractability of a problem, a popular approach is to show the completeness of the problem in a class which is unlikely to be equal to P. For example, many problems have been proved to be NP-complete, including the problem of finding the maximum bipartite subgraph in a given graph [5].

The following is a well-known NP-complete problem.

The Decision Version of Vertex-Cover: Given a graph $G = (V, E)$ and an integer $k \leq |V|$, determine whether there is a set $V' \subseteq V$ of size k such that each edge $e \in E$ is incident to at least one $v \in V'$.

Some completeness results exhibited in the later sections will be based on a reduction from this problem. Please note that for simplicity, one used to use Vertex-Cover to mean the decision version of Vertex-Cover in the study of computational complexity.

6.2   The Prototype Group Testing Problem is in PSPACE

Although one believes that the prototype group testing problem is intractable, no formal proof has appeared at this moment. The computational complexity of the prototype group testing problem is a long-standing open problem. Du and Ko [2] considered the general combinatorial search problem as follows.

CSP: Given a domain D and an integer k, determine whether there is a decision tree of height $\leq k$ of which each path uniquely determines an object in D. Here, each internal node of the decision tree corresponds to a Yes-No query and the left and the right sons of the internal node are the queries following the two answers, respectively (unless they are leaves). Leaves are sample points consistent with the answers to the previous queries.

They proved the following.

Theorem 6.2.1 *CSP belongs to PSPACE.*

Proof. For given D and k, one may guess nondeterministically a decision tree of height k in the depth-first-ordering and verify that for each of its paths, there is only one sample point, in D, consistent with the queries and answers of this path. Note that at any step of the computation, this algorithm needs only $O(k)$ space to store one path of the decision tree, although the complete tree contains about 2^k nodes. □

Clearly, the prototype group testing problem is a special case of the CSP. It is worth mentioning that the input size of the prototype group testing problem is considered to be $n \log n + \log d + \log k$. In fact, the names of n items need at least $n \log n$ spaces. For the prototype group testing problem, the domain D has $\binom{n}{d}$ sample points. However, they can be easily enumerated using a small amount of space.

Because the instance of the prototype group testing problem has too simple a structure, it is hard to do the reduction to it from other complete problems. This is the main difficulty in proving the intractability of the prototype group testing problem.

It was proved in [4] that if the input to a problem is defined by two integers, then the problem cannot be PSPACE-complete unless P=PSPACE. Thus, to obtain any completeness results on the prototype group testing problem, it is necessary to reformulate the problem by adding a more complex structure to the problem instance. A typical approach to this is to treat the problem as a special case of a more general problem with instances in more general forms. For example, Even and Tarjan [3] extended the game Hex to general graphs and showed that the latter is PSPACE-complete, while the complexity of the original game Hex remains open. Du and Ko [2] added a test history to the input of the prototype group testing problem. A *history* of the prototype group testing problem is a finite sequence of tests together with outcomes.

GPP (Generalized Prototype Group Testing Problem): Given n items, a test history, and two integers d and k ($0 < d, k < n$), determine whether or not there exists a decision tree of height $\leq k$ of which each path uniquely determines a sample point in $S(d, n)$ where $S(d, n)$ consists of all sample points each consisting of exactly d defectives from n items.

Du and Ko [2] conjectured that the GPP is PSPACE-complete. It is still open at this moment. They also considered the following related problems:

Consistency: Given a history H, determine whether or not there exists a sample consistent with the history.

Determinacy: Given a finite sequence of queries, determine whether for any two samples, there exists a query in the sequence which receives different answers from the two samples.

It is clear that the above two problems are closely related to CSP. We will exhibit some results on these two problems in the next three sections.

6.3   Consistency

Let GT_k denote CGT with $(k+1)$-nary test outcomes, i.e., the outcomes are $0, 1, \cdots, k-1$ and k^+. To give a more precise description of the consistency problem, let us introduce some notations. For a sample S, let $\mathcal{R}_S(T)$ denote the result of a test T. Thus, in the problem GT_k,

$$\mathcal{R}_S(T) = \begin{cases} i, & \text{if } |S \cap T| = i < k, \\ k, & \text{if } |S \cap T| \geq k. \end{cases}$$

Consistency-GT_k: Given two integers n and d and a history $H = \{(T_i, a_i) \mid i = 1, \cdots, m$, with $T_i \subseteq N, a_j \in \{0, \cdots, k\}$ for $i = 1, \cdots, m\}$, determine whether the set $C = \{S \in S(d, n) \mid \mathcal{R}_S(T_i) = a_i$ for $i = 1, \cdots, m\}$ is nonempty.

Du and Ko [2] proved the following.

Theorem 6.3.1 *For all $k \geq 1$, Consistency-GT_k is NP-complete.*

Proof. It is trivial that Consistency-GT_k is in NP. Thus, it is sufficient to reduce an NP-complete problem to Consistency-GT_k. The reduction consists of two parts. In the first part, it is proved that a well-known NP-complete problem, Vertex-Cover, is polynomial-time reducible to Consistency-GT_1. In the second part, Consistency-GT_1 is polynomially reduced to Consistency-GT_k.

Let (G, k) be a given instance of Vertex-Cover, where $G = (V, E)$ is a graph with vertex set $V = \{v_1, \cdots, v_p\}$ and the edge set $E = \{e_1, \cdots, e_q\}$, and k is an integer less than or equal to n. Define an instance $(n, d, H = \{(T_j, a_j) \mid j = 1, \cdots, m\})$ of Consistency-GT_1 as follows.

$$n = p; m = q; d = k;$$
$$\text{for each } j = 1, \cdots, m, \text{ let } T_j = \{i \mid v_i = e_j\} \text{ and } a_j = 1.$$

For each $V' \subseteq V$, define a set $S_{V'} \in S(d, n)$ by $S_{V'} = \{i \mid v_i \in V'\}$. Then this is a one-to-one correspondence between subsets of V of size k and sets in $S(d, n)$. Furthermore, V' is a vertex-cover of E if and only if $S_{V'} \cap T_j \neq \emptyset$ for all $j = 1, \cdots, m$. This shows that the mapping from (G, k) to (n, d, H) is a reduction from Vertex-Cover to Consistency-GT_1.

For the second part, let $(n, d, H = \{(T_j, a_j) \mid j = 1, \cdots, m\})$ be an instance of Consistency-GT_1. Define an instance $(n', d', H' = \{(T'_j, a'_j) \mid j = 1, \cdots, m\})$ of Consistency-GT_k $(k > 1)$ as follows:

$$n' = n + k - 1; m' = m + k - 1; d' = d + k - 1;$$
$$\text{for each } j = 1, \cdots, m,$$
$$\text{if } a_j = 0 \text{ then let } T'_j = T_j \text{ and } a'_j = 0,$$
$$\text{if } a_j = 1 \text{ then let } T'_j = T_j \cup \{n+1, \cdots, n+k-1\} \text{ and } a'_j = k;$$
$$\text{for each } j = m+1, \cdots, m+k-1, \text{ let } T'_j = \{n+j-m\} \text{ and } a'_j = 1.$$

Assume that (n, d, H) is consistent for Model GT_1 and $S \in S(d, n)$ satisfies the condition that for all $j = 1, \cdots, m$, $S \cap T_j \neq \emptyset$ if and only if $a_j = 1$. Define

$$S' = S \cup \{m+1, \cdots, m+k-1\}.$$

Then, $S \in S(d', n')$. Moreover, for all $j = 1, \cdots, m$,

$$\text{if } a_j = 0, \text{ then } |S' \cap T'_j| = |S \cap T_j| = 0 = a'_j, \text{ and}$$
$$\text{if } a_j = 1, \text{ then } |S' \cap T'_j| = |S \cap T_j| + (k-1) \geq k = a'_j;$$

and for all $j = m+1, \cdots, m+k-1$,

$$|S' \cap T'_j| = 1 = a'_j.$$

Thus, (n', d', H') is consistent for Model GT_k.

Conversely, if (n', d', H') is consistent for Model GT_k, then there is a set

$$S' \subseteq \{1, \cdots, m + k - 1\}$$

such that $\mathcal{R}_{S'}(T_j) = a'_j$ for $j = 1, \cdots, m + k - 1$. Let $S = S' \cap \{1, \cdots, m\}$. It is claimed that $S \cap T_j = \emptyset$ if and only if $a_j = 0$ for all $j = 1, \cdots, m$.

First, if $a_j = 0$, then $T'_j = T_j$ and $a'_j = 0$. So, $S' \cap T'_j = \emptyset$. Next, if $a_j = 1$, then $\mathcal{R}_{S'}(T'_j) = a'_j = k$ implies $|S' \cap T'_j| \geq k$. Since

$$|S' \cap \{n+1, \cdots, n+k-1\}| \leq k-1, |S \cap T_j| = |S' \cap T'_j \cap \{1, \cdots, n\}| \geq 1.$$

This completes the proof.   □

6.4 Determinacy

For Model GT_k, the precise description of the determinacy problem is as follows.

Determinacy-GT_k: Given two integers n and d and a set $Q = \{T_i \mid i = 1, \cdots, m\}$, with $T_i \subseteq N$, for $i = 1, \cdots, m\}$, determine whether, for any two sets S_1, S_2 in $S(d, n)$, $S_1 \neq S_2$ implies $\mathcal{R}_{S_1}(T_j) \neq \mathcal{R}_{S_2}(T_j)$ for some $j = 1, \cdots, m$.

The following result was proved by Yang and Du [7].

Theorem 6.4.1 *For all $k \geq 1$, Determinacy-GT_k is co-NP-complete.*

Proof. It is easy to see that Determinacy-GT_k belongs to co-NP. One shows that Vertex-Cover is polynomial-time reducible to the complement of Determinacy-GT_k.

Let $G = (V, E)$ and an integer h $(0 < h < |V| - 1)$ form an instance of Vertex-Cover. Assume $V = \{1, 2, \cdots, m\}$. Every edge e is represented by a subset of two elements of V. For convenience, assume that G has no isolated vertices. Define an instance (n, d, Q) of Determinacy-GT_k as follows:

$$n = m + k + 1, d = k + h,$$
$$Q = \{X_i \mid i = 1, 2, \cdots, m + k - 1\} \cup \{T_e \mid e \in E\}$$

where

$$X_i = \{i\} \text{ for } i = 1, 2, \cdots, m + k - 1,$$
$$T_e = e \cup \{m+1, m+2, \cdots, m+k\} \text{ for } e \in E.$$

First, assume that G has a vertex-cover Y with $|Y| = h$. Define two sets

$$S_1 = Y \cup \{m+1, m+2, \cdots, m+k\}$$
$$S_2 = Y \cup \{m+1, m+2, \cdots, m+k-1, m+k+1\}.$$

Obviously, $|S_1| = |S_2| = d$, $S_1 \neq S_2$, and

$$\mathcal{R}_{S_1}(X_i) = \mathcal{R}_{S_2}(X_i) \text{ for } i = 1, 2, \cdots, m+k-1,$$
$$\mathcal{R}_{S_1}(T_e) = \mathcal{R}_{S_2}(T_e) \text{ for } e \in E.$$

Hence, (n, d, Q) is not determinant.

Conversely, assume that (n, d, Q) is not determinant. Then there exists $S_1, S_2 \in S(d, n)$, $S_1 \neq S_2$, such that for all $T \in Q$, $\mathcal{R}_{S_1}(T) = \mathcal{R}_{S_2}(T)$. From $\mathcal{R}_{S_1}(X_i) = \mathcal{R}_{S_2}(X_i)$, it follows that $i \notin S_1 \setminus S_2$ and $i \notin S_2 \setminus S_1$ for all $i = 1, 2, \cdots, m+k-1$. Hence, $S_1 \setminus S_2 = \{m+k\}$ and $S_2 \setminus S_1 = \{m+k+1\}$. This implies that for any $e \in E$, $|S_1 \cap T_e| = |S_2 \cap T_e| + 1$. Furthermore, since $\mathcal{R}_{S_1}(T_e) = \mathcal{R}_{S_2}(T_e)$,

$$|S_2 \cap T_e| \geq k \;\; \forall e \in E,$$
$$S_2 \cap e \neq \emptyset.$$

Next, it is shown that

$$\{m+1, m+2, \cdots, m+k-1\} \subset S_2.$$

Assume that

$$\{m+1, m+2, \cdots, m+k-1\} \not\subset S_2.$$

Then

$$|S_2 \cap \{m+1, m+2, \cdots, m+k-1\}| = k-2 \text{ and } e \subset S_2 \;\; \forall e \in E.$$

Because G has no isolated vertices, $V \subseteq S_2$. Thus,

$$m + k - 2 = |S_2| - 1 = d - 1 = k + h - 1,$$

which implies that $m - 1 \leq h$. Since $h < |V| - 1 = m - 1$, there is a contradiction. Hence, $\{m+1, m+2, \cdots, m+k-1\} \subset S_2$. Define $Y = S_2 \setminus \{m+1, m+2, \cdots, m+k-1\}$, then $|Y| \leq d - k = h$. Since $S_2 \cap e \neq \emptyset$, $Y \cap e \neq \emptyset$ $\forall e \in E$. So Y is a vertex-cover of G with $|Y| \leq h$.

If G has i isolated vertices, then let G' be a graph obtained from G by deleting these i isolated vertices and let $h' = h - i$. Applying the above argument to G' and h', then Vertex-Cover is polynomial-time reducible to Determinacy-GT_k. $\qquad\square$

6.5   On Sample Space $S(n)$

In Chapter 4, we considered a model in which the number of defectives is unknown. In this case, the sample space is $S(n)$ consisting of all subsets of $\{1, 2, \cdots, n\}$, the set of n items. For this sample space, there are some interesting positive results on the corresponding consistency and determinacy problems. Let GT_k' denote the problem with the sample space $S(n)$ and $(k+1)$-nary test outcomes. The precise descriptions for the two problems are as follows.

Consistency-GT'_k: Given an integer n and a history $H = \{(T_i, a_i) \mid i = 1, \cdots, m$, with $T_i \subseteq N$, $a_j \in \{0, \cdots, k\}$ for $i = 1, \cdots, m\}$, determine whether the set $C = \{s \in S(n) \mid \mathcal{R}_s(T_i) = a_i$ for $i = 1, \cdots, m\}$ is nonempty.

Determinacy-GT'_k: Given an integer n and a set $Q = \{T_i \mid i = 1, \cdots, m$, with $T_i \subseteq N$, for $i = 1, \cdots, m\}$, determine whether, for any two sets S_1, S_2 in $S(n)$, $S_1 \neq S_2$ implies $\mathcal{R}_{S_1}(T_j) \neq \mathcal{R}_{S_2}(T_j)$ for some $j = 1, \cdots, m$.

In the following, some positive results obtained in [2] and [7] are reported.

Theorem 6.5.1 *Consistency-GT'_1 is polynomial-time solvable.*

Proof. Let an instance $(n, H = \{(T_j, a_j) \mid j = 1, \cdots, m\})$ of Consistency-GT'_1 be given, where for each $j = 1, \cdots, m$, $T_j \in S(n)$ and $a_j \in \{0, 1\}$. Define

$$I = \{j \mid 1 \leq j \leq m, a_j = 0\} \text{ and } J = \{j \mid 1 \leq j \leq m, a_j = 1\}.$$

Also let $X = \cup_{j \in I} T_j$ and $Y = \{1, \cdots, n\} \setminus X$. Then it is easy to check that H is consistent iff for each $j \in J, T_j \cap Y \neq \emptyset$. This characterization provides a polynomial-time algorithm for Consistency-GT'_1. $\square$

Theorem 6.5.2 *For $k = 1, 2$, Determinacy-GT'_k is polynomial-time solvable.*

The following is a characterization which provides a polynomial-time algorithm for determinacy-GT'_1.

Lemma 6.5.3 *Let (n, Q) be an instance of Determinacy-GT'_1. Then (n, Q) is determinant if and only if for every $i = 1, \cdots, n$, the singleton set $\{i\}$ is in Q.*

Proof. The backward direction is obvious, because the set $\{i\}$ distinguishes between two sets S_1 and S_2 whenever $i \in S_1 \setminus S_2$.

For the forward direction, consider two sets $S_1 = \{1, \cdots, n\}$ and $S_2 = S_1 \setminus \{i\}$. Then the only set T that can distinguish between S_1 and S_2 is $T = \{i\}$ so that $\mathcal{R}_{S_1}(T) = 1$ and $\mathcal{R}_{S_2}(T) = 0$. $\square$

The next three lemmas give characterizations of Determinacy-GT'_2.

Lemma 6.5.4 *Let (n, Q) be an instance of Determinacy-GT'_k. If (n, Q) is not determinant, then there exist S_1 and S_2 in $S(n)$ such that*
   (1) $S_1 \neq S_2$,
   (2) $S_1 \cup S_2 = \{1, \cdots, n\}$, *and*
   (3) *for all $T \in Q$, $\mathcal{R}_{S_1}(T) = \mathcal{R}_{S_2}(T)$.*

Proof. Since (n, Q) is not determinant, there exist S_1' and S_2' in $S(n)$ such that for all $T \in Q$, $\mathcal{R}_{S_1'}(T) = \mathcal{R}_{S_2'}(T)$. Let $S_i = S_i' \cup (N \setminus (S_1' \cup S_2'))$ for $i = 1, 2$. Then

$$\mathcal{R}_{S_i}(T) = \min\{k, \mathcal{R}_{S_i'}(T) + |T \cap (N \setminus (S_1' \cup S_2'))|\}.$$

Thus, $\mathcal{R}_{S_1'}(T) = \mathcal{R}_{S_2'}(T)$ implies $\mathcal{R}_{S_1}(T) = \mathcal{R}_{S_2}(T)$. $\qquad\square$

Lemma 6.5.5 *Let (n, Q) be an instance of Determinacy-GT_2'. Then (n, Q) is not determinant if and only if there exist Y_1, Y_2 in $S(n)$ such that $Y_1 \cap Y_2 = \emptyset$, $Y_1 \cup Y_2 \neq \emptyset$, and for every $T \in Q$, the following holds:*
  (1) *If $|T| \leq 2$, then $|Y_1 \cap T| = |Y_2 \cap T|$.*
  (2) *If $|T| \geq 3$, then $|Y_1 \cap T| \leq |T| - 2$ and $|T \cap Y_2| \leq |T| - 2$.*

Proof. Assume that (n, Q) is not determinant. By Lemma 6.5.4, there exist S_1, S_2 in $S(n)$ such that $S_1 \neq S_2$, $S_1 \cup S_2 = N$, and $\mathcal{R}_{S_1}(T) = \mathcal{R}_{S_2}(T)$ for all $T \in Q$. Define $Y_1 = S_1 \setminus S_2 = N \setminus S_2$, $Y_2 = S_2 \setminus S_1 = N \setminus S_1$. If $|T| \leq 2$, then $|S_1 \cap T| = |S_2 \cap T|$. So

$$
\begin{aligned}
|Y_1 \cap T| &= |S_1 \cap T| - |T \cap S_1 \cap S_2| \\
&= \mathcal{R}_{S_1}(T) - |T \cap S_1 \cap S_2| \\
&= \mathcal{R}_{S_2}(T) - |T \cap S_1 \cap S_2| \\
&= |S_2 \cap T| - |T \cap S_2 \cap S_2| \\
&= |Y_2 \cap T|.
\end{aligned}
$$

If $|T| \geq 3$, then $|S_1 \cap T| \geq 2$ or $|S_2 \cap T| \geq 2$. Assume, without loss of generality, that $|S_1 \cap T| \geq 2$. Then $\mathcal{R}_{S_2}(T) = \mathcal{R}_{S_1}(T) = 2$. Thus, $|S_2 \cap T| \geq 2$. Therefore,

$$|Y_i \cap T| \leq |T| - 2 \text{ for } i = 1, 2.$$

Conversely, assume that there exist Y_1, Y_2 in $S(n)$ such that $Y_1 \cap Y_2 = \emptyset$, $Y_1 \cup Y_2 \neq \emptyset$, and (1) and (2) hold. Define $S_i = N \setminus Y_i$ for $i = 1, 2$. Then $S_1 \neq S_2$ and $\mathcal{R}_{S_1}(T) = \mathcal{R}_{S_2}(T)$ for all $T \in Q$. $\qquad\square$

Let (n, Q) be an instance of Determinacy-GT_2'. Define a graph $G(Q) = (N, E)$ by setting $E = \{T \in Q \mid |T| = 2\}$. A graph $G = (V, E)$ is *bicolorable* if its vertices can be marked by two colors such that no edge has both its endpoints colored the same. A set of vertices with the same color is called a *monochromatic* set. For a connected bicolorable graph, there is only one way to divide its vertices into two monochromatic sets.

Lemma 6.5.6 *Let (n, Q) be an instance of Determinacy-GT_2'. Then (n, Q) is not determinant if and only if $G(Q)$ has a connected component that is bicolorable and its monochromatic vertex subsets Y_1 and Y_2 satisfy the following conditions.*
  (1) *If $T \in Q$ with $|T| = 1$, then $T \cap (Y_1 \cup Y_2) = \emptyset$.*
  (2) *If $T \in Q$ with $|T| \geq 3$, then $|T \cap Y_i| \leq |T| - 2$ for $i = 1, 2$.*

Proof. Assume that $G(Q)$ has a connected component that is bicolorable; the monochromatic vertex subsets Y_1 and Y_2 of the connected component satisfy the conditions (1) and (2). Then by Lemma 6.5.5, (n, Q) is not determinant. Conversely, assume that (n, Q) is not determinant. Then there exist Y_1 and Y_2 satisfying the conditions in Lemma 6.5.5. For any $T \in E$, since $|Y_i \cap T| = 0$ or 1 for $i = 1, 2$, either $T \cap (Y_1 \cup Y_2) = \emptyset$ or $T \subset Y_1 \cup Y_2$. Hence, the subgraph $G(Q)|_{Y_1 \cup Y_2}$ induced by $Y_1 \cup Y_2$ is a union of some connected components of $G(Q)$. Moreover, for each edge T of $G(Q)|_{Y_1 \cup Y_2}$, one must have $|T \cap Y_1| = |T \cap Y_2| = 1$. Thus, $G(Q)|_{Y_1 \cup Y_2}$ is bicolorable. Consider a connected component of $G(Q)|_{Y_1 \cup Y_2}$. Its two monochromatic vertex subsets must be subsets of Y_1 and Y_2, respectively, and hence satisfy the conditions (1) and (2). □

Proof of Theorem 6.5.2. By Lemma 6.5.3, it is easy to see that Determinacy-GT'_1 is polynomial-time solvable. A graph is bicolorable if and only if it contains no odd cycle, the latter holds if and only if there exists no odd cycle in a basis of cycles. Hence, the bicoloring of a graph can be determined in polynomial-time. If a connected graph is bicolorable, then its vertex set can be uniquely partitioned into two disjoint monochromatic subsets. By Lemma 6.5.6, Determinacy-GT'_2 is polynomial-time solvable. □

The following negative result and its proof can also be found in [2] and [7].

Theorem 6.5.7 *For $k \geq 2$, Consistency-GT'_k is NP-complete and for $k \geq 3$, Determinacy-GT'_k is co-NP-complete.*

A polynomial-time solvable special case for Determinacy-GT'_3 was discovered by Yang and Du [7].

Theorem 6.5.8 *Let (n, Q) be an instance of Determinacy-GT'_3. If (n, Q) does not contain a test of three items, then it can be determined in polynomial-time whether (n, Q) is determinant or not.*

To prove this result, the following lemma is needed.

Lemma 6.5.9 *Let (n, Q) be an instance of Determinacy-GT'_3. Then (n, Q) is not determinant if and only if there exist Y_1, Y_2 in $S(n)$, $Y_1 \cap Y_2 = \emptyset$, $Y_1 \cup Y_2 \neq \emptyset$, such that for any $T \in Q$, the following conditions hold:*
  (1) *If $|T| \leq 3$, then $|Y_1 \cap T| = |Y_2 \cap T|$.*
  (2) *If $|T| = 4$, then $|Y_1 \cap T| = |Y_2 \cap T|$ or $|T \cap (Y_1 \cup Y_2)| = 1$.*
  (3) *If $|T| \geq 5$, then $|Y_i \cap T| \leq |T| - 3$ for $i = 1, 2$.*

Proof. Assume that (n, Q) is not determinant. By Lemma 6.5.4, there exist S_1 and S_2 in $S(n)$ such that $S_1 \neq S_2$, $S_1 \cup S_2 = N$, and $\mathcal{R}_{S_1}(T) = \mathcal{R}_{S_2}(T)$ for $T \in Q$. Define

$Y_1 = S_1 \setminus S_2 = N \setminus S_2$ and $Y_2 = S_2 \setminus S_1 = N \setminus S_1$. If $|T| \leq 3$, then

$$
\begin{aligned}
|Y_1 \cap T| &= |S_2 \cap T| - |T \cap S_1 \cap S_2| \\
&= \mathcal{R}_{S_1}(T) - |T \cap S_1 \cap S_2| \\
&= \mathcal{R}_{S_2}(T) - |T \cap S_1 \cap S_2| \\
&= |S_2 \cap T| - |T \cap S_1 \cap S_2| \\
&= |Y_2 \cap T|.
\end{aligned}
$$

If $|T| = 4$ and $|Y_1 \cap T| \neq |Y_2 \cap T|$, then $|S_1 \cap T| \neq |S_2 \cap T|$. Thus, $\mathcal{R}_{S_1}(T) = \mathcal{R}_{S_2}(T)$ implies $|S_i \cap T| \geq 3$ for $i = 1, 2$. Hence, $|Y_i \cap T| \leq 1$. Furthermore, $|Y_1 \cap T| = 0$ (or 1) if and only if $|Y_2 \cap T| = 1$ (or 0). Therefore, $|T \cap (Y_1 \cup Y_2)| = 1$. If $|T| \geq 5$, then the proof is similar to the case $|T| \geq 4$ in the proof of Lemma 6.5.5.

Conversely, assume that there exist Y_1 and Y_2 satisfying the conditions in the lemma. Define $S_1 = N \setminus Y_2$ and $S_2 = N \setminus Y_1$. Then it is easy to verify that $S_1 \neq S_2$ and $\mathcal{R}_{S_1}(T) = \mathcal{R}_{S_2}(T)$ for $T \in Q$. □

Let (n, Q) be an instance of Determinacy-GT_3' such that Q contains no set of size 3. Define the graph $G(Q)$ as before. Assume that the bicolorable connected components of $G(Q)$ are $G_1, G_2, \ldots, G_m$ and the monochromatic vertex subsets of G_i are X_i and Z_i. The following is an algorithm for testing the determinacy property of (n, Q).

Algorithm: Initially, let
$$
R := N \setminus \cup_{i=1}^{m}(X_i \cup Z_i).
$$
For $i = 1, 2, \ldots, m$, carry out the following steps in the ith iteration. If the algorithm does not stop within the first m iterations, then (n, Q) is determinant.

Step 1. Let $Y := X_i$ and $Y' := Z_i$.

Step 2. If Y and Y' satisfy the condition that
    (1) for $T \in Q$ with $|T| = 1$, $T \cap (Y \cup Y') = \emptyset$,
    (2) for $T \in Q$ with $|T| = 4$, $|Y \cap T| = |Y' \cap T|$ or $|(Y \cup Y') \cap T| = 1$, and
    (3) for $T \in Q$ with $|T| \geq 5$, $|Y \cap T| \leq |T| - 3$ and $|Y' \cap T| \leq |T| - 3$,
    then the algorithm stops and concludes that (n, Q) is not determinant; else, it goes to the next step.

Step 3. If Y and Y' do not satisfy (1) or (3), then let $R := R \cup X_i \cup Z_i$ and go to the $(i + 1)$th iteration.

If Y and Y' satisfy (1) and (3), but do not satisfy (2), then there exists $T \in Q$ with $|T| = 4$ such that either

$$
|T \cap Y| \geq 2 \text{ and } |T \cap Y'| \leq 1 \tag{6.1}
$$

or

$$|T \cap Y| \leq 1 \text{ and } |T \cap Y'| \geq 2. \tag{6.2}$$

If $T \subseteq Y \cup Y'$, then let $R := R \cup X_i \cup Z_i$ and go to the $(i+1)$th iteration; else, choose $x \in T \setminus (Y \cup Y')$.

If $x \in R$, then let $R := R \cup X_i \cup Z_i$ and go to the $(i+1)$th iteration; else, x must be a vertex of G_j for some $j = 1, 2, \cdots, m$.

If

$$|T \cap Y| \geq 2 \text{ and } |T \cap Y'| \leq 1,$$

then let

> $Y :=$ the union of Y and the monochromatic vertex subset that does not contain x;
>
> $Y' :=$ the union of Y and the monochromatic vertex subset that contains x.

If

$$|T \cap Y| \leq 1 \text{ and } |T \cap Y'| \geq 2,$$

then let

> $Y :=$ the union of Y and the monochromatic vertex subset that contains x;
>
> $Y' :=$ the union of Y and the monochromatic vertex subset that does not contain x.

Go to Step 2.

To show the correctness of the algorithm, assume that Y_1 and Y_2 satisfy Lemma 6.5.9. Note that for $T \in Q$ with $|T| = 2$, $|T \cap Y_1| = |T \cap Y_2|$. So, $G(Q)|_{Y_1 \cup Y_2}$ is the union of some bicolorable connected components of $G(Q)$. Let G_{i^*} be the connected component of $G(Q)|_{Y_1 \cup Y_2}$ with the smallest index. It will be proved that the algorithm stops not later than the i^*th iteration and hence concludes that (n, Q) is not determinant. To prove it, the following two lemmas will be used.

Lemma 6.5.10 *At the i^*th iteration, $Y \subseteq Y_1$, $Y' \subseteq Y_2$ (or $Y \subseteq Y_2$, $Y' \subseteq Y_1$).*

Proof. If $Y = X_{i^*}$, $Y' = Z_{i^*}$, then obviously $Y \subseteq Y_1$ and $Y' \subseteq Y_2$. In the following, it is shown that the lemma remains true when Y and Y' are redefined in Step 3. For convenience, let $\bar{Y}$ and $\bar{Y}'$ denote the redefined Y and Y'. It suffices to prove that $Y \subseteq Y_1$ and $Y' \subseteq Y_2$ imply $\bar{Y} \subseteq Y_1$ and $\bar{Y}' \subseteq Y_2$. If (6.1) occurs, then $Y \subseteq Y_1$, $|T| = 4$, and $|Y_1 \cap T| \geq 2$. By Lemma 6.5.9, $|Y_1 \cap T| = |Y_2 \cap T| = 2$. Hence, $(T \setminus (Y \cup Y')) \subseteq Y_2$, $x \in Y_2$. Thus, $\bar{Y} \subseteq Y_1$ and $\bar{Y}' \subseteq Y_2$. If (6.2) occurs, then the argument is similar. $\square$

Lemma 6.5.11 *The algorithm cannot go to the $(i^* + 1)th$ iteration from the i^*th iteration.*

Proof. For contradiction, assume that the algorithm goes to the $(i^* + 1)$th iteration from the i^*th iteration, then one of the following occurs.

(a) Y and Y' do not satisfy the conditions (1) and (3) in Step 2.

(b) Y and Y' do not satisfy the condition (2) with T and $T \subseteq Y \cup Y'$.

(c) $(T \setminus (Y \cup Y')) \cap R \neq \emptyset$ holds.

If (a) occurs, then by Lemma 6.5.10, Y_1 and Y_2 do not satisfy the condition (1) or (3) in Lemma 6.5.9. If (b) occurs, then $T \subseteq Y \cup Y'$. By Lemma 6.5.10, one may assume $Y \subseteq Y_1$ and $Y' \subseteq Y_2$. Thus, $|Y \cap T| = |Y_1 \cap T|$ and $|Y' \cap T| = |Y_2 \cap T|$. Hence, Y_1 and Y_2 do not satisfy the condition (2) in Lemma 6.5.9. Therefore, (a) and (b) cannot occur. Next, suppose (c) occurs. Note that $|T| = 4$. By Lemma 6.5.10, $|T \cap (Y_1 \cup Y_2)| \geq |T \cap (Y \cup Y')| \geq 2$. Since Y_1 and Y_2 satisfy the conditions in Lemma 6.5.9, $|T \cap Y_1| = |T \cap Y_2|$. Moreover, $\max(|T \cap Y_1|, |T \cap Y_2|) \geq \max(|T \cap Y|, |T \cap Y'|) \geq 2$. Hence $|T \cap Y_1| = |T \cap Y_2| = 2$. Thus, $T \subseteq Y_1 \cup Y_2$. (c) implies $R \cap (Y_1 \cup Y_2) \neq \emptyset$. However, during the computation of the i^*th iteration,

$$R = N \setminus \cup_{h=i^*}^{m} (X_h \cup Z_h);$$

and by the assumption on G_{i^*},

$$Y_1 \cup Y_2 \subseteq \cup_{h=i^*}^{m} (X_h \cup Z_h),$$

contradicting $R \cap (Y_1 \cup Y_2) \neq \emptyset$.   □

Proof of Theorem 6.5.8. If (n, Q) is not determinant, then by Lemma 6.5.11 the algorithm must stop before or at the i^*th iteration. Note that the loop at each iteration must be finite since each time the computation goes from Step 3 to Step 2, the number of vertices in $Y \cup Y'$ increases. Therefore, the algorithm must stop at the place where it concludes that (n, Q) is not determinant.

If (n, Q) is determinant, then it suffices to prove that the computation must pass the m iterations. For contradiction, suppose that the computation stops in the ith iteration. Then there exist Y and Y' which satisfy the conditions (1), (2), and (3) in Step 3. It follows that Y and Y' satisfy the conditions in Lemma 6.5.9. Hence, (n, Q) is not determinant, a contradiction.   □

6.6   Learning by Examples

Computational learning theory is an important area in computer science [1]. "Learning by examples" has been a rapidly developing direction in this area during the past 10 years. The problem that has been studied in this direction can be described as follows: Suppose there is an unknown boolean function which belongs to a certain family. When values are assigned to the variables, the function value is returned.

The problem is how to identify the unknown function by using a small number of assignments.

The prototype group testing problem can also be seen as a special case of this problem. To see this, let $\mathcal{F} = \{x_{i_1} + \cdots + x_{i_d} \mid 1 \leq i_1 < \cdots < i_d \leq n\}$. Suppose that the unknown function f is chosen from $\mathcal{F}$. For each assignment a, let $T(a)$ be the set of indices i such that the variable x_i is assigned 1 under the assignment a. Then the following correspondence holds.

$f(x) = x_{i_1} + \cdots + x_{i_d}$	$i_1, \cdots, i_d$ are defectives.
$f(a) = 1$	$T(a)$ is contaminated.
$f(a) = 0$	$T(a)$ is pure.

Thus, learning the unknown function from $\mathcal{F}$ by examples is exactly the (d, n) prototype group testing problem.

However, in learning theory, if the unknown function can be learned by polynomially many assignments with respect to n, then this problem is considered to be an easy problem. The (d, n) prototype group testing problem can be solved with at most $d(\log_2 \frac{n}{d} + 1)$ tests. Thus, from the viewpoint of learning, it is an easy problem. However, the prototype group testing problem is indeed a hard problem if finding the optimal strategy is the goal.

References

[1] D. Angluin, Computational learning theory: survey and selected bibliography, *Proceedings of 24th STOC*, 1992, 351-369.

[2] D.-Z. Du and K.-I Ko, Some completeness results on decision trees and group testing, *SIAM Algebraic and Discrete Methods*, 8 (1987) 762-777.

[3] S. Even and R.E. Tarjan, A combinatorial problem which is complete in polynomial space, *J. Assoc. Comput. Mach.*, 23 (1976) 710-719.

[4] S. Fortune, A note on sparse complete sets, *SIAM J. Comput.*, 8 (1979) 431-433.

[5] M.R. Garey and D.S. Johnson, *Computers and Intractability*, (W.H. Freeman, San Francisco, 1979).

[6] J.E. Hopcroft and J.D. Ullman, *Introduction to Automata Theory, Languages, and Computation*, (Addison-Wesley, Reading, Mass., 1979).

[7] F. Yang and D.-Z. Du, The complexity of determinacy problem on group testing, *Discrete Applied Mathematics*, 28 (1990) 71-81.

Part II
Nonadaptive Group Testing Algorithms

7

Deterministic Designs
and Superimposed Codes

A group testing algorithm is *nonadaptive* if all tests must be specified without knowing the outcomes of other tests. The necessity of nonadaptive algorithms can occur in two different scenarios. The first comes from a time constraint: all tests must be conducted simultaneously. The second comes from a cost constraint: the cost of obtaining information on other tests could be prohibitive. A mathematical study of nonadaptive CGT algorithms does not distinguish these two causes.

A seemingly unrelated problem is the construction of superimposed codes first studied by Kautz and Singleton for retrieving files. The thing that unifies non-adaptive CGT algorithms and superimposed codes is that both use the same matrix representation where the constraints are imposed on the unions of any d or up to d columns.

7.1 The Matrix Representation

Consider a $t \times n$ 0-1 matrix M where R_i and C_j denote row i and column j. $R_i(C_j)$ will be viewed as a set of column (row) indices corresponding to the 1-entries. M will be called *d-separable* ($\bar{d}$-separable) if the unions, or Boolean sums, of d columns (up to d columns) are all distinct. M will be called *d-disjunct* if the union of any d columns does not contain any other column. Note that d-disjunct also implies that the union of any up to d columns does not contain any other column.

These definitions are now explained in terms of nonadaptive CGT algorithms and superimposed codes, respectively. A $t \times n$ d-separable matrix generates a nonadaptive (d, n) algorithm with t tests by associating the columns with items, the rows with tests, and interpreting a 1-entry in cell (i, j) as the containment, and the 0-entry as a noncontainment, of item j in test i. A set of d columns will be referred to as a sample, if they are associated with d defectives. The union of d columns in a sample corresponds to the set of tests (those rows with a "1" entry in the union) which give positive outcomes given that sample. Thus the d-separable property implies that each sample in $S(d, n)$ induces a different set of tests with positive outcomes. By matching the sets of positive tests with the samples in $S(d, n)$, the d defectives can be identified. Similarly, the $\bar{d}$-separable property implies that samples in $S(\bar{d}, n)$ are distinguishable.

A d-disjunct matrix also corresponds to a nonadaptive $(\bar{d}, n)$ algorithm, but with an additional property which allows the defectives to be identified easily. To see this let s denote a set of columns constituting a sample. Define

$$P(s) = \cup_{j \in s} C_j .$$

$P(s)$ can be interpreted as the set of tests with positive outcomes under the sample s.

An item contained in a test group with a negative outcome can certainly be identified as good. In a nonadaptive algorithm represented by a d-disjunct matrix, all other items can be identified as defectives. This is because the columns associated with these items are contained in $P(s)$, and thus must be defectives or the matrix is not d-disjunct. Consequently one does not have to look up a table mapping sets of contaminated groups to samples in $S(d, n)$ or $S(\bar{d}, n)$. This represents a reduction of time complexity from $O(n^d)$ to $O(d)$. Another desirable property first observed by Schultz [29] is that if after the deletion of all items from groups with negative outcomes, the number of remaining items is more than d, then the false assumption of $s \in S(\bar{d}, n)$ is automatically detected.

A $t \times n$ $\bar{d}$-separable matrix also generates a binary superimposed code with n code words of length t. The $\bar{d}$-separable property allows the transmitter to superimpose up to d code words into one supercode word (with the same length) and transmit. The receiver is still able to uniquely decode the supercode word back to the original code words if the channel is errorless. A d-separable matrix achieves the same except that a supercode word always consists of d original code words. The disjunct property again allows easier decoding by noting that the components of a supercode code are exactly those code words which are contained in the supercode word.

Kautz and Singleton [20] were the first to study superimposed codes. They indicated applications of superimposed codes in file retrieval, data communication and design of magnetic memory.

Although nonadaptive CGT algorithms and superimposed codes have the same mathematical representation, the respective problems have different focuses. For the former, one wants to minimize the number t of tests for a given number n of items. For the latter one wants to maximize the number n of codewords for a given number t of alphabets. Of course these two focuses are really the two sides of the same problem. For $\bar{d}$-separable or d-disjunct, both applications want to maximize d.

7.2   Basic Relations and Bounds

Kautz and Singleton proved the following two lemmas.

Lemma 7.2.1 *If a matrix is d-separable, then it is k-separable for every $1 \leq k \leq d < n$.*

Proof. Suppose that M is d-separable but not k-separable for some $1 \leq k < d < n$. Namely, there exist two distinct samples s and s' each consisting of k columns such that $P(s) = P(s')$. Let C_x be a column in neither s nor s'. Then

$$C_x \cup P(s) = C_x \cup P(s') .$$

Adding a total of $d - k$ such columns C_x to both s and s' yields two distinct samples s_d and s'_d each consisting of d columns such that $P(s_d) = P(s'_d)$. Hence M is not d-separable. If there are only $\ell < d - k$ such columns C_x, then select $d - k - \ell$ pairs of columns (C_y, C_z) such that C_y is in s but not in s' and C_z is in s' but not in s. Then

$$C_z \cup P(s) = P(s) = P(s') = C_y \cup P(s') .$$

Therefore these pairs can substitute for the missing C_x. Since M is d-separable, a total of $d - k$ C_x and (C_y, C_z) can always be found to yield two distinct s_d and s'_d each consisting of d columns. □

The following result shows that d-disjunct is stronger than $\bar{d}$-separable.

Lemma 7.2.2 *d-disjunct implies $\bar{d}$-separable.*

Proof. Suppose that M is not $\bar{d}$-separable, i.e., there exist a set K of k columns and another set K' of k' columns, $1 \leq k$, $k' \leq d$, such that $P(K) = P(K')$. Let C_j be a column in $K' \setminus K$. Then $C_j \subseteq P(K)$ and M is not k-disjunct, hence not d-disjunct. □

It is clear that $\bar{d}$-separable implies d-separable, hence d-disjunct implies d-separable. Saha and Sinha [28] proved that the latter implication holds even if after the deletion of an arbitrary row from the d-disjunct matrix. Huang and Hwang [16] gave a result which strengthens both the result of Saha and Sinha and Lemma 7.2.2.

Lemma 7.2.3 *Deleting any row R_i from a d-disjunct matrix M yields a d-separable matrix M_i.*

Proof. Let $s, s' \in S(\bar{d}, n)$. Then $P(s)$ and $P(s')$ must differ in at least 2 rows or one would contain the other. Hence, they are different even after the deletion of a row. □

Kautz and Singleton also proved the following two lemmas.

Lemma 7.2.4 *$(\overline{d+1})$-separable implies d-disjunct.*

Proof. Suppose that M is $(\overline{d+1})$-separable but not d-disjunct, i.e., there exists a sample s of d columns such that $P(s)$ contains another column C_j not in s. Then

$$P(s) = C_j \cup P(s),$$

a contradiction to the assumption that M is $(\overline{d+1})$-separable. □

From Lemmas 7.2.2 and 7.2.4 any property held by a $\bar{d}$-separable matrix also holds for a d-disjunct matrix, and any property held for a d-disjunct matrix also holds for a $\overline{d+1}$-separable matrix. In the rest of the chapter, we will state the result either for d-disjunct or for $\bar{d}$-separable, whichever is a stronger statement, but not for both.

Figure 7.1 summarizes the relations between these properties.

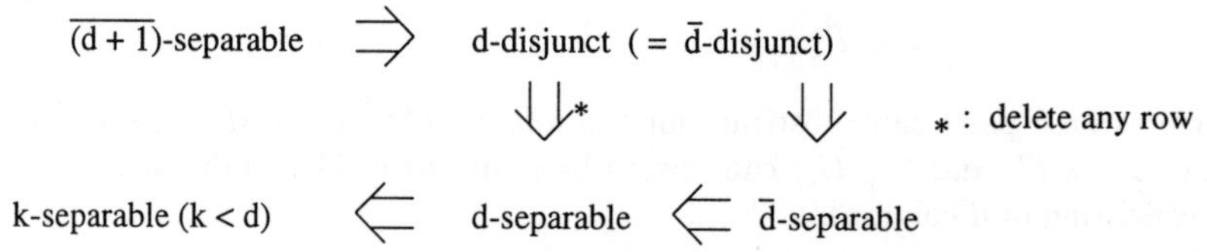

$(\overline{d+1})$-separable $\implies$ d-disjunct ($= \bar{d}$-disjunct)

$\Downarrow_*$ $\Downarrow$ $*$: delete any row

k-separable (k < d) $\impliedby$ d-separable $\impliedby$ $\bar{d}$-separable

Figure 7.1: An ordering among properties.

Lemma 7.2.5 *If M is a d-separable matrix, then $|P(s)| \geq d - 1$ for $s \in S(d,n)$.*

Proof. Suppose to the contrary that $|P(s)| < d - 1$ for some $s \in S(d, n)$. For each $j \in s$ let t_j denote the number of rows intersecting C_j but not any other column of s. Note that except for one column every $j \in s$ must intersect some rows of $P(s)$ or j cannot be identified as a member of s. Furthermore, $|P(s)| < d$ implies that there exist at least two indices $i(1)$ and $i(2)$ such that $t_{i(1)} = t_{i(2)} = 0$. Let $s_1 = s \backslash i(1)$ and $s_2 = s \backslash i(2)$. Then $P(s_1) = P(s_2)$, so M is not a $(d-1)$-separable matrix, a contradiction to Lemma 7.2.1. □

Corollary 7.2.6

$$\binom{n}{d} \leq \sum_{j=d-1}^{t} \binom{t}{j}.$$

Proof. The RHS of the inequality gives the total number of ways of selecting distinct $P(s)$. □

Kautz and Singleton gave a stronger inequality

$$\sum_{i=1}^{d} \binom{n}{i} \leq \sum_{j=d}^{t} \binom{t}{j}$$

for a $\bar{d}$-separable matrix. Unfortunately, their result is incorrect. An $n \times n$ identity matrix is certainly $\bar{n}$-separable, but does not observe the inequality for $d > n/2$.

Let w_j, called the *weight*, denote the number of 1-entries in C_j. For a given 0-1 matrix let $r(w)$ denote the number of columns with weight w. A subset of $\{1, \cdots, t\}$ is called *private* if it is contained in one unique column. A column containing a private singleton subset is called *isolated*; in other words, there exists a row intersecting only this column. Note that there exist at most t isolated columns. Dyachkov and Rykov [6] proved

Lemma 7.2.7 *Any column of a d-disjunct matrix with weight $\leq d$ is isolated and consequently*

$$\sum_{w=1}^{d} r(w) \leq t .$$

Proof. Suppose to the contrary that C_j is not isolated and $w_j \leq d$. Then C_j is contained in a union of at most d columns and M cannot be d-disjunct.   □

For a given set P of parameters, let $t(P)$ denote the minimum number of rows in a matrix satisfying P and let $n(P)$ denote the maximum number of columns in a matrix satisfying P. For example, $t(d, n)$ denotes the minimum number of rows for a d-disjunct matrix with n columns. Bassalygo (see [7]) proved

Lemma 7.2.8 $t(d, n) \geq w + t(d - 1, n - 1)$.

Proof. Suppose that the d-disjunct matrix M has a column C with weight w. Delete C and the w rows which intersect C and let the resultant matrix be M'. Then M' is a $(d - 1)$-disjunct matrix. If it were not, say, there exists a column C_i' contained in a union of $P(s')$ of $d - 1$ columns in M'. Then C_i must be in $P(s)$ where s consists of C and the same $d - 1$ columns in M, contradicting the assumption that M is d-disjunct. □

Theorem 7.2.9 $t(d, n) \geq \min \left\{ \binom{d+2}{2}, n \right\}$ *for a d-disjunct matrix.*

Proof. Theorem 7.2.9 is trivially true for $n = 1$. The general case is proved by induction on n.

If M has a column of weight $w \geq d + 1$, then from Lemma 7.2.8

$$t(d, n) \geq d + 1 + \min \left\{ \binom{d+1}{2}, n - 1 \right\}$$

$$\geq \min \left\{ \binom{d+2}{2}, n \right\} .$$

If M does not have such a column, then from Lemma 7.2.7,

$$t(d, n) \geq \sum_{w=1}^{d} r(w) = n \geq \min \left\{ \binom{d+2}{2}, n \right\} .$$

□

Corollary 7.2.10 *For $\binom{d+2}{2} \geq n$, $t(d,n) = n$.*

Proof. $t(d,n) \geq n$ from Theorem 7.2.9. $t(d,n) \leq n$ since the $n \times n$ identity matrix is d-disjunct. $\qquad\Box$

Define $v = \lceil w/d \rceil$. Erdös, Frankl, and Füredi [10] proved

Lemma 7.2.11 *Let M be a $t \times n$ d-disjunct matrix. Then*

$$r(w) \leq \frac{\binom{t}{v}}{\binom{w-1}{v-1}}.$$

Proof. Let C be a column of M and let $F(C)$ be the family of nonprivate v-subsets of C ($u \in F(C)$ implies the existence of a column C' of M, $C' \neq C$, such that $u \subseteq C'$). Let $u_1, \ldots, u_d \in F(C)$. Then clearly, $\cup_{i=1}^{d} u_i \neq C$ or M would not be d-disjunct. By a result of Frankl (Lemma 1 in [12]), any family of v-subsets satisfying the above property has at most $\binom{w-1}{v}$ members. Therefore C must contain at least

$$\binom{w}{v} - \binom{w-1}{v} = \binom{w-1}{v-1}$$

v-subsets not contained in any other column of M. Since there are only $\binom{t}{v}$ distinct v-subsets, Lemma 7.2.11 follows immediately. $\qquad\Box$

By summing over $r(w)$ over w and using the Stirling formula for factorials, they obtained

Theorem 7.2.12 $t(d,n) > d(1 + o(1)) \ln n$.

Dyachkov and Rykov [6] obtained a better lower bound by a more elaborate analysis.

Let

$$h(u) = -u \log u - (1-u) \log(1-u)$$

be the binary entropy function and define

$$f_d(v) = h(v/d) - vh(1/d) .$$

Also define $K_1 = 1$ and for $d \geq 2$, K_d is uniquely defined as

$$K_d = [\max f_d(v)]^{-1} ,$$

where the maximum is taken over all v satisfying

$$0 < v \leq 1 - K_{d-1}/K_d .$$

Theorem 7.2.13 *For d fixed and n → ∞*

$$t(d, n) \geq K_d \, (1 + o(1)) \log n .$$

Proof. (sketch) For $d = 1$, Theorem 7.2.13 follows from Corollary 7.2.6. For $d \geq 2$ Theorem 7.2.13 follows from verifying that

$$K_{d-1} \leq \lim_{n\to\infty} \frac{t(d-1, n)}{\log n} \quad \text{implies}$$

$$K_d \leq \lim_{n\to\infty} \frac{t(d, n)}{\log n} .$$

□

Dyachkov and Rykov computed $K_2 = 3.106$, $K_3 = 5.018$, $K_4 = 7.120$, $K_5 = 9.466$ and $K_6 = 12.048$. They also showed $K_d \to \frac{d^2}{2 \log d}(1 + o(1))$ as $d \to \infty$.

Note that Lemma 7.2.11, i.e., $r(w) \leq \binom{t}{v} / \binom{w-1}{v-1}$, can also be written as (ignoring integrality)

$$n(d, t, w) \leq d \binom{t}{w/d} / \binom{w}{w/d}.$$

As a complete proof of Theorem 7.2.13 is complicated, we will show a result of Ruszinkó [26] with a slightly smaller coefficient, but a much simpler proof.

Theorem 7.2.14 $\frac{\log n(d,t)}{t} \leq 8 \cdot \frac{\log d}{d^2}$.

Proof. Suppose that $d^2 \mid t$ and t/d is even. Let M be a t-row d-disjunct w-matrix. Suppose that at each step we throw away a column with (current) weight $> 2t/d$, along with the rows it intersects. By Lemma 7.2.8, the remaining matrix is $(d-1)$-disjunct. Suppose that in q steps, p rows are deleted. Then

$$
\begin{aligned}
n(d, t) &\leq \sum_{w=1}^{2t/d} n(d - q, t - p, w) + q \\
&\leq \sum_{w=1}^{2t/d} n(d/2, t, w) + d/2 \\
&\leq \sum_{w=1}^{2t/d} \frac{d \binom{t}{2w/d}}{2 \binom{w}{2w/d}} + d/2 \\
&\leq \sum_{w=1}^{2t/d} \frac{d}{2} \binom{t}{2w/d} \leq t \binom{t}{4t/d^2}.
\end{aligned}
$$

Using $\binom{n}{cn} \leq 2^{nh(c)} \cdot n^k$ where k is a constant,

$$
\begin{aligned}
\log n(d,t) &\leq \log t + k \log t + t \cdot h(4/d^2) \\
&= o(t) + t\left(\frac{4}{d^2} \cdot \log \frac{d^2}{4} + (1 - \frac{4}{d^2}) \log \frac{d^2}{d^2 - 4}\right) \\
&= o(t) + t\left(8\frac{\log d}{d^2} - \frac{8}{d^2} + \frac{1}{d^2} \log(1 + \frac{d^2}{d^2 - 4})^{d^2 - 4}\right) \\
&= o(t) + t\left(8\frac{\log d}{d^2} - \frac{8}{d^2} + \frac{4 \log e}{d^2}\right) \\
&\leq o(t) + \frac{8t \log d}{d^2}.
\end{aligned}
$$

$\square$

Dyachkov, Rykov and Rashad [8] obtained an asymptotic upper bound of $t(d, n)$.

Theorem 7.2.15 *For d constant and $n \to \infty$*

$$
t(d, n) \leq \frac{d}{A_d}(1 + o(1)) \log n ,
$$

where

$$
A_d = \max_{0 \leq q \leq 1} \max_{0 \leq Q \leq 1} \left\{ -(1 - Q) \log(1 - q^d) + d\left[Q \log \frac{q}{Q} + (1 - Q) \log \frac{1 - q}{1 - Q}\right] \right\} .
$$

They also showed that

$$
A_d \to \frac{1}{d \log e}(1 + o(1)) \text{ as } d \to \infty .
$$

For d-separable, the asymptotic A_d is two times the above and $k_d > d$ for $d \geq 11$ (private communication from Dyachkov and Rykov).

7.3   Constant Weight Matrices

Kautz and Singleton introduced some intermediate parameters to get better bounds. Let λ_{ij} denote the dot product of C_i with C_j, i.e., the number of rows that both C_i and C_j have a 1-entry (we also say C_i and C_j intersect λ_{ij} times). Define

$$
\underline{w} = \min_j w_j (\bar{w} = \max_j w_j)
$$

and

$$
\bar{\lambda} = \max_{i,j} \lambda_{ij} .
$$

Let M be a $t \times n$ matrix with the parameters $\underline{w}$ and $\bar{\lambda}$. Then any $(\bar{\lambda}+1)$-subset of the underlying t-set can be in at most one column. Thus

$$\sum_{j=1}^{n} \binom{w_j}{\bar{\lambda}+1} \leq \binom{t}{\bar{\lambda}+1} .$$

The case $w_j = w$ for all j, was first obtained by Johnson [18] as follows:

Lemma 7.3.1 *For a matrix with constant weight w*

$$n \leq \frac{\binom{t}{\bar{\lambda}+1}}{\binom{w}{\bar{\lambda}+1}} .$$

Lemma 7.3.2 *Let M be a $t \times n$ matrix with parameters $\underline{w}$ and $\bar{\lambda}$. Then M is d-disjunct with $d = \lfloor (\underline{w} - 1)/\bar{\lambda} \rfloor$.*

Proof. C_j has at most $d\bar{\lambda} < \underline{w} \leq w_j$ intersections with the union of any d columns. Hence C_j cannot be in that union. $\qquad\square$

Define $t'(w, \bar{\lambda}, n)$ as the minimum t for a $t \times n$ matrix with constant column weight w and maximum number of intersections $\bar{\lambda}$ (between two columns). Johnson also showed that

$$t(w - \bar{\lambda}) \geq n(w^2 - t\bar{\lambda}) .$$

Nguyen and Zeisel [22] used this Johnson bound to prove

Theorem 7.3.3 *A $t \times n$ constant weight d-disjunct matrix with $d = \lfloor (w - 1)/\bar{\lambda} \rfloor$ exists only if $dw < 2t$.*

Proof. Define $\alpha = dw/t$. By Lemma 7.3.2, $\bar{\lambda} \leq \lfloor (w - 1)/d \rfloor$. Thus

$$w^2 - t\bar{\lambda} \geq \left(\frac{\alpha t}{d}\right)^2 - t\left\lfloor \frac{w-1}{d} \right\rfloor \geq \left(\frac{\alpha t}{d}\right)^2 - \frac{tw}{d} \geq \left(\frac{\alpha t}{d}\right)^2 - \frac{\alpha t^2}{d^2}$$

$$= \frac{\alpha t^2}{d^2}(\alpha - 1) > 0 \quad for \ \alpha > 1 .$$

The Johnson bound can be written as

$$n \leq \frac{t(w - \bar{\lambda})}{w^2 - t\bar{\lambda}},$$

which is increasing in $\bar{\lambda}$. Therefore setting $\bar{\lambda} = w/d$, it follows that

$$n \leq \frac{t\left(\frac{\alpha t}{d} - \frac{\alpha t}{d^2}\right)}{\frac{\alpha t^2}{d^2}(\alpha - 1)} = \frac{d - 1}{\alpha - 1} .$$

Since $n > d - 1$, necessarily, $\alpha < 2$. $\qquad\square$

Corollary 7.3.4 *Suppose that d is fixed and* $n \to \infty$ *in a constant weight d-disjunct matrix. Then* $t \geq dw$.

Proof. For fixed d and $\alpha = dw/t \geq 1$, $n \leq \frac{d-1}{\alpha - 1}$ cannot be satisfied with $n \to \infty$.

Nguyen and Zeisel used Lemma 7.3.1 to obtain a better asymptotic lower bound of t than the one given in Corollary 7.2.13.

Theorem 7.3.5 *For* $d \gg 1$ *and* $n \to \infty$,

$$t(d, n) \geq \frac{d^2 \log\ n}{\alpha\ \log d} \ , \ \text{where } \alpha = dw/t < 1 \ .$$

Proof. From the Stirling formula it is easily verified that for any sequence k_n where $\lim_{n \to \infty} k_n/n = q < 1$,

$$\lim_{n \to \infty} \frac{1}{n} \log \binom{n}{k_n} = h(q) \ .$$

Using this fact and Lemma 7.3.1,

$$t(d, n) \geq \frac{d^2 \log\ n}{\alpha \log \frac{d}{\alpha} - (d^2 - \alpha) \log(1 - \frac{\alpha}{d}) + \alpha(d - 1) \log(1 - \frac{1}{d})} \ .$$

Theorem 7.3.5 follows by noting $d \gg 1$. $\qquad\qquad\qquad\qquad\qquad\qquad\qquad\qquad$ □

Setting $\lambda = 1$ in the Johnson bound, then

$$t \geq \frac{nw^2}{n + w - 1} \geq \frac{n(d + 1)^2}{n + d} > \min\{n, d^2\}$$

since if $n \leq d^2$, then

$$\frac{n(d + 1)^2}{n + d} \geq \frac{n(d + 1)^2}{d^2 + d} > n$$

and if $n \geq d^2$, then

$$\frac{n(d + 1)^2}{n + d} = \frac{(d + 1)^2}{1 + d/n} \geq \frac{(d + 1)^2}{1 + \frac{1}{d}} > d^2 \ .$$

Define

$$m_0 = \max\left\{ \binom{n}{d}, \min\{n, d^2\} \right\} \ .$$

Dyachkov and Rykov [7] used the above results and known bounds of the binomial coefficients in a variation of Lemma 7.2.11 to prove

Theorem 7.3.6 *Let d, n, m_0 be given integers such that $3 \leq d < n$, $1/d + 1/n \leq 1/2$ and*

$$\frac{1/d + 1/n}{d} + \frac{1}{m_0} < \frac{1}{ed + 1} \ .$$

Then

$$t \geq F(d, n, m_0) \equiv \left\lceil \frac{\log n + \frac{1}{2}\log(\pi/4)}{h(1/d + 1/n)/(d + 1/m_0) - (1/d + 1/n)h(1/d)} \right\rceil \ .$$

Theorem 7.3.6 can be used to improve m_0. For $k \geq 1$ define

$$m_k = \max\{m_{k-1}, \ F(d, n, m_{k-1})\}.$$

Let k_0 be the smallest k satisfying $m_k = m_{k-1}$. Then $m_{k_0} \geq m_0$ is a lower bound of $t'(w, \lambda, n)$.

Corollary 7.3.7 *For d constant and $n \to \infty$, the asymptotic inequality*

$$t \geq (h(1/d^2) - h(1/d)/d)(1 + o(1)) \log n$$

holds.

Applying the inequality $h(u) \leq u\log(e/u)$, one can verify

$$h(1/d^2) - \frac{h(1/d)}{d} \geq \frac{d^2}{\log(de)} \ .$$

Dyachkov and Rykov recently claimed (private communication) a stronger result

$$t \geq \frac{1}{h(q_d)}(1 + o(1)) \log n \ ,$$

where $q_d = \frac{1}{2}\frac{-\sqrt{d(d-1)}}{2d-1}$.
They showed that

$$\frac{1}{h(q_d)} \to \frac{8d^2}{\log d}(1 + o(1)) \quad \text{as } d \to \infty \ .$$

To obtain an upper bound of $t(d, n)$, Erdös, Frankel and Füredi [10] proved

Theorem 7.3.8 $n \geq \binom{t}{v}/\binom{w}{v}^2$.

Proof. Let N be a maximal set of t-vectors with constant weight $w = d(v-1)+1$ such that any two columns intersect at most $v-1$ places. Then N is d-disjunct. Thus for any t-vector V there exists a vector $U \in N$ such that $|U \cap V| \geq v$ (if $V \in N$, set $U = V$; if not, then U exists due to the maximality of N). Hence,

$$\binom{t}{w} \leq \sum_{U \in N} |\{V \in N \mid |U \cap V| \geq v\}| \leq |N| \binom{w}{v}\binom{t-v}{w-v},$$

or

$$|N| \geq \binom{t}{w} / \left[\binom{w}{v}\binom{t-v}{w-v}\right] = \binom{t}{v} / \binom{w}{v}^2.$$

$\square$

For a special set of w, they showed that the lower bound of n approaches the upper bound. Let $S(T, K, V)$ denote a Steiner T-design in which every T-tuple of a base set with V elements appears exactly once in a block (with constant size K).

Theorem 7.3.9 *Let* $w = d(v-1)+1+x$, *where* $0 \leq x < d$. *Then for* t *large enough,*

$$(1 - o(1))\binom{t-x}{v} / \binom{w-x}{v} \leq n \leq \binom{t-x}{v} / \binom{w-x}{v}$$

holds for (a) $x = 0, 1$, *(b)* $x < d/(2v^2)$, *(c)* $v = 2$, $x < \lceil 2d/3 \rceil$. *Furthermore, the second inequality becomes equality if and only if a Steiner system* $S(w-x, v, t-x)$ *exists.*

Corollary 7.3.10 *Let* w *and* x *be such that* n *is approximately* $\binom{t}{v} / \binom{w}{v}$. *Then*

$$t(d, n) = O(d^2 \log(n/d)).$$

Proof. Choose $w = t/(kd)$ for some positive number k. Then $v = w/d = t/(kd^2)$. Using the approximation

$$\binom{t}{\lambda t} \sim \frac{2^{th(\lambda)}}{c\sqrt{t}},$$

when c is a constant and $0 < \lambda < 1$, we obtain

$$\frac{\binom{t}{v}}{\binom{w}{v}} \sim \frac{\frac{2^{th(1/(kd^2))}}{\sqrt{t}}}{\frac{2^{wh(1/d)}}{\sqrt{w}}} = 2^{t[h(1/(kd^2)) - h(1/d)/(kd)]}\sqrt{kd}.$$

Thus,

$$t \sim \frac{\log n}{h(1/(kd^2)) - h(1/d)/(kd)} \sim \frac{\log n}{(1/(kd^2)) \log(kd^2) - (1/d) \log d/(kd)} \sim \frac{kd^2 \log n}{\log d}.$$

$\square$

7.4   General Constructions

An *equireplicated pairwise balanced design* (EPBD) is a family of t subsets, called blocks, of an underlying set $N = \{1, \cdots, n\}$ such that every element of N occurs in exactly r subsets and every pair of elements of N occurs together in exactly λ subsets. When all blocks have the same cardinality, an EPBD becomes a *balanced incomplete block design* (BIBD) which is a well-studied subject in experimental designs and combinatorial designs. Bush, Federer, Pesotan and Raghavarao [2] proved

Lemma 7.4.1 *An EPBD yields a $t \times n$ d-disjunct matrix if $r > d\lambda$.*

Proof. The incidence matrix of an EPBD, i.e., where the rows are the blocks and the columns are the elements of the underlying set, yields a d-disjunct matrix by Lemma 7.3.2. □

Kautz and Singleton pointed out that EPBDs do not yield useful d-disjunct matrices since $t \geq n$ by the Fisher's inequality. In both nonadaptive CGT and superimposed code applications, the goal is to have small t and large n, hence the d-disjunct matrix generated by an EPBD is inferior to the $n \times n$ identity matrix. Kautz and Singleton also noted that the only BIBD which can lead to an interesting d-disjunct matrix M is when $\lambda = 1$, because M^T (transpose) has the property $\lambda^T = 0$ or 1. From Lemma 7.3.2, where the constant weight is k, M^T is a $(k-1)$-disjunct matrix.

Thus it seems that the combinatorial designs which yield interesting d-disjunct matrices are those with nonconstant λ. The following result is a generalization of Lemma 7.3.2 towards that direction.

An (n, b) design T is simply a family B of b blocks of the set $N = \{1, \cdots, n\}$. For K a subset of N, let r_K denote the number of blocks in T intersecting all columns of K. Let $r_i(l, k)$ $(r_i(-l, k))$ denote an upper (lower) bound for the sum of the l largest (smallest) $r_{\{i\} \cup K}$ over all k-subset K.

Theorem 7.4.2 *If for every $i \in N$ and every d-subset D not containing i,*

$$r_{\{i\}} + \sum_{j=1}^{d} (-1)^j r_i((-1)^{j+1} \binom{d}{j}, j) > 0 ,$$

then T is a d-disjunct matrix.

Proof. Let D denote a given d-subset of N and let D_j, $0 \leq j \leq d$, denote an arbitrary j-subset of D. Using the inclusion-exclusion principle,

$$\sum_{j=0}^{d} (-1)^j \sum_{D_j} r_{\{i\} \cup D_j} \geq r_{\{i\}} + \sum_{j=1}^{d} (-1)^j r_i((-1)^{j+1} \binom{d}{j}, j) > 0 ,$$

is the number of blocks having an 1-entry in $P(\{i\})$ but not in $P(D)$. Therefore D does not contain i. Since the above inequality holds for any D, T is a d-disjunct matrix by Lemma 7.3.8.   □

A *t-design* is a (n, b) design where every block is of a constant size k and every t-tuple occurs in a constant number λ_t of blocks. It is well known that a t-design is also a j-design for $1 \leq j \leq t - 1$. In fact λ_j can be computed as

$$\lambda_j = \frac{\binom{n-j}{t-j}}{\binom{k-j}{t-j}} \lambda_t .$$

Note that the inclusion-exclusion formula yields a lower bound if truncated to end at a negative term. Saha, Pesotan and Raktoc [27] obtained

Corollary 7.4.3 *A t-design B yields a d-disjunct matrix if*

$$\sum_{j=0}^{t^\star} (-1)^j \binom{d}{j} \frac{\binom{n-1-j}{t-1-j}}{\binom{k-1-j}{t-1-j}} > 0 ,$$

where

$$t^\star = \begin{cases} d & \text{if } t-1 \geq d \\ t-1 & \text{if } t-1 \text{ is odd and } < d , \\ t-2 & \text{if } t-1 \text{ is even and } < d . \end{cases}$$

Unfortunately, a t-design as a 2-design is an EPBD. So again $t \geq n$ and the constructed d-disjunct matrix is not interesting.

An *m-associate partially balanced incomplete block design* (PBIBD) is otherwise a 2-design except that the number of subsets containing two elements i and j belongs to a set $\{\lambda_{21} > \lambda_{22} > \cdots > \lambda_{2m}\}$. A PBIBD is *group divisible* if the elements can be partitioned into groups of constant size such that an intergroup pair gets λ_{21} and an intragroup pair gets λ_{22}. By truncation at λ_{21}, Saha, Pesotan and Raktoc proved

Corollary 7.4.4 *A 2-associate PBIBD B yields a d-disjunct matrix if*

$$\lambda_1 - d\lambda_{21} > 0 .$$

The following is an example of using Corollary 7.4.4 to obtain a 2-disjunct matrix with fewer tests than the number of items.

Example 7.1 Let B be the 2-associated PBIBD consisting of the subsets:

$$B_1 = \{1, 2, 3, 4\}, \quad B_2 = \{5, 6, 7, 8\}, \quad B_3 = \{9, 10, 11, 12\} \quad B_4 = \{13, 14, 15, 16\},$$

$$B_5 = \{1, 5, 9, 13\}, \quad B_6 = \{2, 6, 10, 14\}, \quad B_7 = \{3, 7, 11, 15\}, \quad B_8 = \{4, 8, 12, 16\},$$

$$B_9 = \{1, 6, 11, 16\}, \quad B_{10} = \{2, 7, 12, 13\}, \quad B_{11} = \{3, 8, 9, 14\}, \quad B_{12} = \{4, 5, 10, 15\}.$$

It is easily verified that $\lambda_1 = 3$, $\lambda_{21} = 1$ and $\lambda_{22} = 0$. Since

$$\lambda_1 - d\lambda_{21} = 3 - 2 \cdot 1 = 1 > 0 ,$$

B is a 12×16 2-disjunct matrix.

In a different direction Kautz and Singleton searched among known families of conventional error-correcting codes for those which have desirable superimposition properties. They commented that binary group codes do not lead to interesting super-imposed codes (d-disjunct matrices). First of all, these codes include the zero-vector as a code word, so the corresponding matrix cannot be d-disjunct. The removal of the zero-vector does not solve the problem since the code usually contains a code word of large weight which contains at least one code word of smaller weight. Furthermore, if an error-correcting code of constant weight is extracted from an arbitrary error-correcting code, then Kautz and Singleton showed that the corresponding d-disjunct matrix will have very small values of d. So instead, they looked for codes based on q-nary error-correcting codes.

A q-nary error-correcting code is a code whose alphabets are the set $\{0, 1, \cdots, q - 1\}$. Kautz and Singleton constructed a binary superimposed code by replacing each q-nary alphabet by a unique binary pattern. For example, such binary patterns can be the q-digit binary vectors with unit weight, i.e., the replacement is $0 \to 10 \cdots 0, 1 \to 010 \cdots 0, \cdots, q - 1 \to 0 \cdots 01$. The *distance* l of a code is the minimum number of nonidentical digits between two code words where the minimum is taken over all pairs of code words. Note that the distance l of the binary code is twice the distance l_q of the q-nary code it replaces, and the length t is q times the length t_q. Since the binary code has constant weight $w = t_q$, the corresponding $t \times n$ matrix is d-disjunct with

$$d \geq \left\lfloor \frac{w - 1}{\bar{\lambda}} \right\rfloor = \left\lfloor \frac{t_q - 1}{t_q - l_q} \right\rfloor$$

from Lemma 7.3.2.

To maximize d with given t_q and n_q, one seeks q-nary codes whose distance l_q is as large as possible. Kautz and Singleton suggested the class of *maximal-distance separable* (MDS) q-nary codes where the t_q digits can be separated into k_q information digits and $t_q - k_q$ check digits. Singleton [31] showed that for an MDS code

$$l_q \leq t_q - k_q + 1 .$$

Thus for those MDS codes achieving this upper bound distance,

$$d \geq \left\lfloor \frac{t_q - 1}{k_q - 1} \right\rfloor ,$$

(a deeper analysis proves the equality). Also the k_q information digits imply a total of $n_q = q^{k_q}$ code words.

Kautz and Singleton also commented that the most useful MDS q-nary codes for present purposes has q being an odd prime power satisfying

$$q + 1 \geq t_q \geq k_q + 1 \geq 3 .$$

Therefore for given d

$$q \geq t_q - 1 \simeq (k_q - 1)d ;$$

q is certainly too large for practical use unless k_q is very small, like two or three.

One may replace the q alphabets by binary patterns more general than the aforementioned unit weight type, provided only that the q binary patterns for replacement form a d-disjunct matrix themselves. Clearly, the length of such binary patterns can be much shorter than the unit weight patterns.

Such a replacement can be regarded as a method of composition in which a small $t_0 \times n_0$ d_0-disjunct matrix is converted into a larger $t_1 \times n_1$ d_1-disjunct matrix on the basis of an t_q-digit q-nary code having k_q independent digits where (q is a prime power satisfying $t_q - 1 \leq q \leq n_q$)

$$t_1 = t_0 t_q ,$$

$$n_1 = q^{k_q} ,$$

$$d_1 = \min \left\{ d_0, \left\lfloor \frac{t_q - 1}{k_q - 1} \right\rfloor \right\} .$$

For the unit weight code $t_0 = n_0 = d_0 = q$. Starting with n unit weight code and keeping d fixed, repeated compositions can be carried out to build up arbitrarily large d-disjunct matrices.

By setting $t_1 = qt_q$, Nguyen and Zeisel used a result of Zinoviev [39] and Theorem 7.3.3 to prove

Theorem 7.4.5 *If $d < an^{1/k}$ for some integer $k > 2$ and constant a, then as $d \to \infty$, there exists a constant weight d-disjunct matrix such that*

$$t = (k - 1) \frac{d^2 \log n}{\log d} \quad as \ n \to \infty .$$

Different q-nary codes can be used at each stage of the composition. If the same type of q-nary code is used except that q is replaced by $q = n_1$, then a second composition yields

$$t_2 = t_0[1 + d(k_q - 1)]^2$$

$$n_2 = q^{(k_q)^2}$$

where

$$d(k_q - 1) \le q^{k_q} .$$

Kautz and Singleton also discussed the optimal number of compositions.

Hwang and Sós [17] gave the following construction (with some modification).

Let T be a t-element set and T^k consist of all k-sets of T. Define $r = t/(16d^2)$ (ignoring integrality), $k = 4dr$ and $m = 4r$. Choose C_1 arbitrarily from T^k. Delete from T^k all members which intersect C_1 in at least m rows. Choose C_2 arbitrarily from the updated T^k. Again delete from the updated T^k all members which intersect C_2 in at least m rows. Repeat this procedure until the updated T^k is empty. Suppose $C_1, \cdots, C_n$ have been chosen this way.

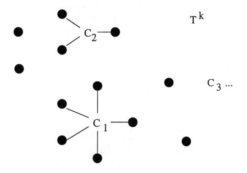

Figure 7.2: Choosing C_i from T^k.

Theorem 7.4.6 $C_1, \cdots, C_n$ constitute a $t \times n$ d-disjunct matrix with $n \ge (2/3)3^{t/16d^2}$.

Proof. By construction, any two columns can intersect in at most $m - 1$ rows. By Lemma 7.3.2, $C_1, \cdots, C_n$ constitute a d-disjunct matrix.

At the jth step the number of members in the updated T^k set which intersect C_j in at least m rows is at most

$$\sum_{i=m}^{k} \binom{k}{i} \binom{t-k}{k-i} .$$

Therefore,

$$n \geq \frac{\binom{t}{k}}{\sum_{i=m}^{k} \binom{k}{i} \binom{t-k}{k-i}} \cdot$$

Set

$$b_i = \binom{k}{i} \binom{t-k}{k-i} \cdot$$

For $3r \leq i < k = 4dr$

$$\frac{b_i}{b_{i-1}} = \frac{(k-i)^2}{(i+1)(t-2k+i+1)} \leq \frac{(4dr-3r)^2}{3r(t-8dr+3r)} \leq \frac{(4d-3)^2}{3(16d^2-8d+3)} < \frac{1}{3} \cdot$$

Hence

$$\sum_{i=m}^{k} b_i < \sum_{i=m}^{k} \left(\frac{1}{3}\right)^{i-3r} b_{3r}$$

$$< b_{3r} \left(\frac{1}{3}\right)^{-3r} \frac{\left(\frac{1}{3}\right)^m}{1-\frac{1}{3}}$$

$$= b_{3r} \frac{\left(\frac{1}{3}\right)^{r-1}}{2} \cdot$$

Since

$$\binom{t}{k} = \sum_{i=0}^{k} b_i > b_{3r} \,,$$

$$n \geq \frac{\binom{t}{k}}{\sum_{i=m}^{k} b_i} > 2 \cdot 3^{r-1}$$

$$\geq 2 \cdot 3^{\frac{t}{16d^2}-1} \cdot$$

$\square$

Corollary 7.4.7 $t(d,n) \leq 16d^2(1 + \log_3 2 + (\log_3 2)\log n)$.

This bound is not as good as the nonconstructive bound given in Theorem 7.2.15.

7.5 The Small d Cases

The definition of a 1-separable matrix is reduced to "no two columns are the same." This was also called a *separating system* by Rényi [25]. For given n then $t \geq \lceil \log n \rceil$ is necessary from Theorem 1.2.1 for a $t \times n$ separating system to exist. A well-known construction which achieves the lower bound is to set column i, $i = 0, 1, \ldots, n-1$, to be the binary representation vector of the number i (a row corresponds to a digit). Since two binary numbers must differ in at least one digit, the matrix, called a *binary representation matrix*, is a separating system. By a similar argument, if column weights are upper bounded by $\bar{w}$, then $n \leq \sum_{i=0}^{\bar{w}} \binom{t}{i}$ for a $t \times n$ separating system to exist.

Rényi asked the question if each row can contain at most k 1s, then what is $t(1, n, k)$, i.e., the minimum t such that a $t \times n$ separating system exists. Katona [19] gave the following answer (Lemma 7.5.1 and Theorem 7.5.2).

Lemma 7.5.1 $t(1, n, k)$ *is the minimum t such that there exist nonnegative integers* $s_0, \cdots, s_t$ *satisfying*

$$tk = \sum_{j=0}^{t} j s_j ,$$

$$n = \sum_{j=0}^{t} s_j ,$$

$$s_j \leq \binom{t}{j} \quad for \ 0 \leq j \leq t .$$

Proof. (sketch). Interpreting s_j as the number of columns with weight j in a separating system, then the above conditions are clearly necessary if each row has exactly k 1s. The proof of sufficiency is involved and omitted here. It can then be proved that the existence of a separating matrix where each row has at most k 1s implies the existence of a separating matrix of the same size where each row has exactly k 1s. □

However, it is still difficult to estimate the minimum t from Lemma 7.5.1. Katona gave lower and upper bounds. His upper bound was slightly improved by Wegener [36] as stated in the following theorem.

Theorem 7.5.2 *Let t^0 denote the minimum t such that a $t \times n$ separating matrix exists. Then*

$$\frac{n \log n}{k \log(en/k)} < t^0 \leq (\lceil \tfrac{n}{k} \rceil - 1) \left\lceil \frac{\log n}{\log \lceil n/k \rceil} \right\rceil .$$

Proof. An information argument proves the first inequality. The total information bits needed to choose one of the n given columns is $\log n$. Each row with k 1s provides

$$\frac{k}{n} \log \frac{n}{k} + \frac{n-k}{n} \log \frac{n}{n-k}$$

bits of information. Thus

$$t^0 \geq \frac{\log n}{\frac{k}{n} \log \frac{n}{k} + \frac{n-k}{n} \log \frac{n}{n-k}}$$

$$> \frac{\log n}{\frac{k}{n} \log \frac{n}{k} + \frac{n-k}{n} \cdot \frac{k}{n-k} \log e} \qquad \text{using } \ln(1+x) < x$$

$$= \frac{n \log n}{k \log \frac{en}{k}} \; .$$

The upper bound is obtained by a construction which is a generalized version of the binary representation matrix given at the beginning of this section. To demonstrate the idea, assume $n/k = g$ and $k = g^x$. At each stage the n elements are partitioned into g groups and a test applies to each group except the last. Thus each stage consumes $g - 1 = n/k - 1$ tests and identifies a contaminated group. The first partition is arbitrary. The second partition is such that each part consists of g^{x-1} elements from each part of the first partition. Thus, the first two partitions divide the n items into g^2 equivalent classes of size g^{x-1} each where the defective is known to lie in one such class. The third partition is then such that each part consists of g^{x-2} elements from each of these classes and so on. After $x + 1 = \log_g n$ stages, each equivalent class is of size 1 and the defective is identified. By considering the possible nonintegrality of n/k, the upper bound is obtained. $\qquad \square$

The definition of a 1-disjunct matrix is reduced to "no column is contained in another column." This was also called a *completely separating system* by Dickson [5] who proved that the minimum t (such that a $t \times n$ completely separating system exists) tends to $\log n$, the same as the separating system. Spencer [32] proved

Theorem 7.5.3 *For a given t the maximum n such that a $t \times n$ completely separating system exists is $\binom{t}{\lfloor t/2 \rfloor}$.*

Proof. M is such a matrix if and only if for all $i \neq j$,

$$C_i \not\subseteq C_j \; .$$

By the Sperner's theorem [33], the largest family of subsets with no subset containing another one consists of the $\binom{t}{\lfloor t/2 \rfloor}$ $\lfloor t/2 \rfloor$-tuples. $\qquad \square$

Schultz, Parnes and Srinivasan [30] generalized Theorem 7.5.3 to

Theorem 7.5.4 *For given t and upper bound $w \leq \binom{t}{\lfloor t/2 \rfloor}$ of the weight, the maximum n such that a $t \times n$ completely separating matrix exists is $\binom{t}{w}$.*

Proof. Implied by Sperner's proof of his theorem. □

When n is large with respect to the maximum number of 1s in a row, Cai [3] gave a more specific result.

Theorem 7.5.5 *If $n > k^2/2$ where $k > 1$ is the maximum number of 1s in a row, then $t = \lceil 2n/k \rceil$ is the minimum t such that a $t \times n$ completely separating system exists.*

Proof. Let M be such a matrix. To avoid trivial discussion assume that M does not contain isolated columns. Then each column has weight at least two since a column with weight one will be contained in another column. Counting the number of 1s by rows and by columns separately, one obtains

$$tk \geq 2n .$$

The reverse inequality is proved by constructing a graph with $\lceil 2n/k \rceil \geq k+1$ vertices and n edges such that the maximum degree is k or less (this can easily be done) and let M be the incidence matrix of the graph. □

For $d = 2$ and $w = 2k - 1$, Lemma 7.2.11 yields

$$r(2k - 1) \leq \frac{\binom{t}{k}}{\binom{2k-2}{k-1}} \quad \text{for } k > 1 .$$

However, Erdös, Frankl and Füredi [9] noted that assuming $t > w$ ($t = w$ is trivial), for any partition of a column into a k-subset and a $(k - 1)$-subset, the 2-disjunctiveness forces either the k-subset or any subset containing the $(k - 1)$-subset to be private. Therefore each column has at least one private k-subset. Hence

$$r(2k - 1) \leq \frac{\binom{t}{k}}{\binom{2k-1}{k}} .$$

They proved that this bound is tight and also solved the even w case in the following theorem. Recall that $S(t, r, n)$ is a t-design on n elements where the block size is r and every t-tuple appears in one block.

Theorem 7.5.6 *Let M be a $t \times n$ constant weight 2-disjunct matrix. Then*

$$n \leq \frac{\binom{t}{k}}{\binom{2k-1}{k}} \quad \text{for } w = 2k - 1$$

and

$$n \le \frac{\binom{t-1}{k}}{\binom{2k-1}{k}} \quad \text{for } w = 2k .$$

Furthermore, equality holds in the former case if and only if there exists an $S(k, 2k - 1, t)$; and equality holds in the latter case if and only if there exists an $S(k, 2k-1, t-1)$.

Proof. In the odd w case, it is clear that a t-design as specified achieves the bound and any constant weight 2-disjunct matrix achieving the bound defines such a t-design. Note that adding a row of 1s to the incidence matrix of this t-design preserves the constant weight 2-disjunct property with $w = 2k$. However, the proof for the bound with even w and the proof that the existence of an $S(k, 2k - 1, t - 1)$ is necessary to achieve the bound are much difficult than the odd w case. The reader is referred to [9] for details.   □

Corollary 7.5.7 $r(1) = t$, $r(2) = t - 1$, $r(3) = t^2/6 + O(t) = r(4)$, $r(5) = t^3/60 + o(t^3) = r(6)$.

Proof. It is well known [18] that $S(2, 3, t)$, which is known as a *Steiner triple system*, exists if and only if $t \ge 7$ and $t = 1$ or $3 \pmod 6$. Hanani [14] proved the existence of $S(3, 5, 4^\alpha + 1)$. Erdös and Hanani [11] proved the existence of matrices with constant weight w where two columns intersect at most twice and $n = \binom{t}{3}/\binom{w}{3} - o(t^3)$.   □

Erdös, Frankl and Füredi also proved

Theorem 7.5.8 *Let M be a $t \times n$ constant weight 2-disjunct matrix. Then*

$$n > \binom{t}{\lceil w/2 \rceil} / \binom{w}{\lceil w/2 \rceil}^2 .$$

Proof. The number of w-sets which can intersect a given w-set at least $\lceil w/2 \rceil$ times is less than

$$\binom{w}{\lceil w/2 \rceil}\binom{t - \lceil w/2 \rceil}{\lfloor w/2 \rfloor} .$$

Using a construction similar to the one discussed in Theorem 7.4.6.

$$n > \frac{\binom{t}{w}}{\binom{w}{\lceil w/2 \rceil}\binom{t-\lceil w/2 \rceil}{\lfloor w/2 \rfloor}} = \frac{\binom{t}{\lceil w/2 \rceil}}{\binom{w}{\lceil w/2 \rceil}^2} .$$

□

Finally, Erdös, Frankl and Füredi proved

Theorem 7.5.9 $\log_{1.25} n < t(2, n) < \log_{1.134} n$.

Proof. The first inequality follows from Theorem 7.5.6, using the Stirling formula and the fact $n \leq \sum_{w=1}^{t} r(w)$. The second inequality is proved by a random construction. Select each of the $\binom{t}{w}$ w-subsets independently with probability $2m/\binom{t}{w}$, the value of m and w to be fixed later. For a given w-set A the number of ordered pairs of w-sets B, C such that $A \subset (B \cup C)$ is

$$R(t, w) = \sum_{i=0}^{w} \binom{w}{i}\binom{t-w}{w-i}\binom{t-w+i}{i} ,$$

where the ith term corresponds to the case that B contains exactly i members of A, and C contains the other $w - i$ members of A. Since

$$R(t, w) = \sum_{i=0}^{w} \binom{w}{i}^2 \binom{t-w+i}{w} \leq \max_{i \leq w} t \binom{w}{i}^2 \binom{t-w+i}{w} \equiv t \max_{i \leq w} g(i) ,$$

the probability that A is covered by two selected w-sets is

$$R(t, w) 4m^2 / \binom{t}{w}^2 < 1/2 \ for \ m < \frac{1}{2\sqrt{2}}\binom{t}{w} / \sqrt{t \max_{i \leq w} g(i)} .$$

After deleting those covered w-sets, the expected number of remaining w-sets is at least $2m - (1/2)2m = m$, and these remaining w-sets form a constant weight 2-disjunct matrix.

To estimate m, note that $g(i)/g(i-1)$ is decreasing in i. Thus the maximum is achieved when this ratio is about one, yielding

$$i_{\max} \sim \frac{1}{2}(3w - 2t + \sqrt{5w^2 - 8wt + 4t^2}) .$$

Setting $w = 0.26t$, one obtains $i_{\max} = 0.1413 \cdots t$ and $m = (1.1348 \cdots)^t$. □

The transpose of the parity check matrix of a conventional binary d-error-correcting code is known (p. 33 [24]) to have the property that the modulo-2 sums of any up to d columns are distinct. This property is exactly what is desired for $\bar{d}$-separable matrices except that the sum is Boolean sum for the latter. Kautz and Singleton suggested the following transformations for small d.

For $d = 2$, transform $0 \rightarrow 01$ and $1 \rightarrow 10$. The modulo-2 addition table before transformation and the Boolean addition table after transformation are given in the following:

$\oplus$	0	1		$\vee$	0	1
0	0	1		0	01	11
1	1	0		1	11	10

Thus if two pairs of columns have different modulo-2 sums, they also have different Boolean sums under this transformation. Namely, the 2-error correcting property is translated to the $\bar{2}$-separable property; while the price paid is that the number of rows is doubled.

The family of Bose-Chaudhuri codes (p. 123 [24]) for $d = 2$ have $2^k - 1$ rows and no more than $2k$ columns for every $k \geq 2$. Hence they yield $\bar{2}$-separable matrices with $4k$ rows and $2^k - 1$ columns; or $n = 2^{t/4} - 1$.

Lindstrom [21] obtained the following result.

Theorem 7.5.10 $n(2, t) = \Theta(2^{t/2})$ *for 2-separability.*

Proof. Theorem 7.5.10 is proved by showing that $n(2, t) \leq 1 + 2^{(t+1)/2}$ and *for t even* $n(2, t) \geq 2^{t/2}$ under the modulo-2 addition and the Boolean sum transformation doubles t.

The upper bound is derived from the fact that there are $\binom{n}{2}$ pairs of columns whose unions must all be distinct t-vectors (there are 2^t of them).

To prove the lower bound, consider the set V of all vectors (x, x^3) with $x \in GF(2^t)$. Then V has cardinality 2^t. If

$$(x, x^3) + (y, y^3) = (u, v)$$

for two elements $x \neq y$ in $GF(2^t)$, then

$$x + y = u \neq 0,$$

and

$$-3xy = v/u - u^2 \ .$$

Since an equation of the second degree cannot have more than two roots in the field, $\{x, y\}$ is uniquely determined by (u, v). Therefore V induces a $2t \times 2^t$ 2-separable matrix. $\qquad\square$

Corollary 7.5.11 $n = \Theta(2^{t/4})$ *for 2-disjunctiveness.*

Proof. Noting $\binom{n}{2} + n \leq 2^t$ and $V \setminus \{0\}$ induces a $2t \times (2^t - 1)$ 2-disjunct matrix. $\square$

Kautz and Singleton also studied the construction of $\bar{2}$-separable matrices with constant weight two. Let M be such a matrix. Construct a simple graph $G(M)$ where vertices are the row indices and edges are the columns. Then $G(M)$ contains no 3-cycle or 4-cycle since such a cycle corresponds to two column-pairs with the same Boolean sum. Regular graphs (each vertex has the same degree r) of this type were studied by Hoffman and Singleton [15] with only four solutions:

$$r = 2 \quad t = 5 \qquad n = 5$$

$$r = 3 \quad t = 10 \qquad n = 15$$

$$r = 7 \quad t = 50 \qquad n = 175$$

$$r = 57 \quad t = 3250 \quad n = 92625$$

which satisfy the conditions $t = 1 + r^2$ and $n = r(1 + r^2)/2$. Thus $n = t\sqrt{t - 1}/2 \rightarrow t^{3/2}/2$ asymptotically. This result was also obtained by Vakil, Parnes and Raghavarao [35].

Relaxing the regularity requirement, one can use a $(v, k, b, r, 1)$ BIBD to construct a $(v + b) \times kb$ 2-separable matrix. Let x_{ij} denote the jth item in block i. Then each column is labeled by an x_{ij}, and each row by an item I or a block B. The column x_{ij} intersects row I if $x_{ij} = I$, and intersects row B if block i is B. (The condition $\lambda = 1$ guarantees the 2-separable property.) For fixed t, n is maximized by using a symmetric BIBD where $v = b$ and $k = r$. From $\binom{v}{2} = v\binom{k}{2}$ or $v - 1 = k(k - 1)$, it can then be shown that

$$n = \frac{t}{4}(1 + \sqrt{2t - 3}) \rightarrow \frac{t^{3/2}}{2\sqrt{2}} .$$

Weideman and Raghavarao [38] proved a relation between $\bar{w}$ and $\bar{\lambda}$ for $\bar{2}$-separable matrix. Huang and Hwang [16] observed that the relation also holds for d-disjuct.

Lemma 7.5.12 *Any $\bar{2}$-separable matrix with $\bar{\lambda} = 1$ can be reduced to one with $\bar{w} = 3$.*

Proof. Replacing all columns of weight greater than three by arbitrary 3-subsets preserves the $\bar{2}$-separability since under the condition $\bar{\lambda} = 1$ no 3-subset can be contained in the union of any two columns. The reduced matrix also preserves $\bar{\lambda}$.

Theorem 7.5.13 *Suppose that $\bar{\lambda} = 1$ in a $\bar{2}$-separable matrix. Then*

$$n \leq t(t + 1)/6 .$$

Proof. From Lemma 7.5.12 assume $\bar{w} = 3$. A column of weight 2 can be represented by the pair of intersecting row indices. The 2-separable property imposes the condition that if columns $\{x, y\}$ and $\{x, z\}$ are in the design, then y, z cannot be collinear. For if C were the collinear column, then

$$\{x, y\} \cup C = \{x, z\} \cup C .$$

Suppose that there are p columns of weight 2. These p pairs generate $2p$ row indices. There are at least $\max\{2p - t, 0\}$ pairs of indices sharing an index ("at least", because $(x, y), (x, z), (x, v)$ generate 3 such pairs). Therefore the p columns of weight 2 generate $p + \max\{2p - t, 0\}$ pairs of indices which cannot be collinear in columns of weight exceeding 2. Thus the number of available pairs to be collinear in columns of weight exceeding 2 is at most

$$\binom{t}{2} - p - \max\{2p - t, 0\} \leq \binom{t}{2} - 3p + t.$$

Since each column of weight exceeding 2 generates at least three collinear pairs,

$$n \le p + \left[\binom{t}{2} - 3p + t \right]/3 = t(t+1)/6.$$

□

Weideman and Raghavarao showed that the upper bound can be achieved for $t \equiv 0$ or $2 \pmod 6$ by taking $t/2$ pairs as groups and the $t(t-2)/6$ blocks of $S(2,3,t)$ as columns. They also showed in a subsequent paper [37] that even for other values of t the upper bound can still often be achieved. Vakil and Parnes [34], by crucially using the constructions of group divisible triple designs of Colbourn, Hoffman and Rees [4], gave the following theorem.

Theorem 7.5.14 *The maximum n in a 2-separable matrix with $\bar{\lambda} = 1$ is*

$$n = \lfloor t(t+1)/6 \rfloor.$$

Since the constructions consist of many subcases, the reader is referred to [34] for details. An example is given here.

Example 7.2. For $t = 8$, the group divisible triple design with the four groups (1,2), (3,4), (5,6), (7,8) consists of the blocks: (1,3,5), (2,4,6), (2,3,7), (1,4,8), (1,6,7), (2,5,8), (3,6,8) and (4,5,7). The $\bar{2}$-separable matrix consists of twelve columns: the four groups and the eight blocks. The eight tests (rows) are: (1,5,8,9), (1,6,7,10), (2,5,7,11), (2,6,8,12), (3,5,10,12), (3,6,9,11), (4,7,9,12), (4,8,10,11).

Note that the n value in Theorem 7.5.14 is slightly bigger than $n(2,t,3)$ from Theorem 7.5.6. A variation of replacing the condition $\bar{\lambda} = 1$ by the weaker one $\bar{w} = 3$ was studied in [30, 34].

Kautz and Singleton tailored the composition method discussed in the last section to the $d = 2$ case. From a $t \times n$ 2-separable matrix M, construct a $(2t + 2p - 1) \times n^2$ 2-separable matrix M'. Column C_i of M' consists of three sections a_i, b_i, c_i, where $a_i \times b_i$ enumerates all column pairs of M, and c_i, depending on a_i and b_i, has length $2p - 1$. The condition on c_i can be more easily seen by constructing a $t \times t$ matrix C whose rows (columns) are code words of M chosen for $a_i(b_i)$ and the entries are $c_i(an(2p-1) \times 1$ vector). Denote the entry in cell (x, y) by C_{xy}. Then the condition, called the *minor diagonal condition*, is

$$C_{xy} \vee C_{uv} \ne C_{xv} \vee C_{uy},$$

since otherwise the column-pair with first two sections $a_x b_y$, $a_u b_v$ and the column-pair with first two sections $a_x b_v$, $a_u b_y$ would have the same Boolean sum.

Starting with a 3×3 weight-one code and using the matrix

$$C_1 = \begin{pmatrix} 1 & 0 & 0 \\ 0 & 1 & 0 \\ 0 & 0 & 1 \end{pmatrix}$$

to construct the third segment ($p = 1$ here), one obtains a 7×9 2-separable matrix. So the next third-section matrix C_2 is of size 9×9. In general at the pth iteration the matrix C_p is of size $3^p \times 3^p$. Kautz and Singleton gave a method to construct C_p from C_{p-1} which preserves the minor diagonal condition where each entry in C_p is a $(2p-1) \times 1$ vector. Thus C_p yields a $t_p \times n_p$ 2-separable matrix with

$$t_p = 2t_{p-1} + 2p - 1 \text{ (or } t_p = 6 \cdot 2^p - 2p - 3)$$

and

$$n_p = 3^{2^p} .$$

It follows that $n \to 3^{t/6}$ asymptotically. Note that this bound is better than the one given in Corollary 7.5.11.

Similar composition can be used to grow a 2-disjunct matrix with parameters

$$t_p = 3 \, t_{p-1} \text{ (or } t_p = 3^{p+1})$$

and

$$n_p = 3^{2^p} .$$

Then $n \to 3^{t^{\log_3 2}/2}$. Note that this construction yields a result inferior to the one given in Theorem 7.5.9.

For $d = 3$ let H denote the parity check matrix of a 3-error-correcting code. Construct M such that every column-pair of H yields four columns of M by the transformation:

$$00 \to 1000, \ 01 \to 0100, \ 10 \to 0010, \ 11 \to 0001 .$$

It can then be verified that M is $\bar{3}$-separable. The Bose-Chaudhuri code for $d = 3$ has $2^k - 1$ rows and no more than $3k$ columns for every $k \geq 3$. Thus M has $t = 4\binom{3k}{2}$ rows and $n = 2^k - 1$ columns; or $n > 2^{\sqrt{t/18}}$ asymptotically.

References

[1] P. Busschbach, Constructive methods to solve the problems of: s-subjectivity, conflict resolution, coding in defective memories, unpublished manuscript, 1984.

[2] K. A. Bush, W. T. Federer, H. Pesotan and D. Raghavarao, New combinatorial designs and their applications to group testing, *J. Statist. Plan. Infer.* 10 (1984) 335-343.

[3] M. C. Cai, On the problem of Katona on minimal completely separating systems with restrictions, *Disc. Math.* 48 (1984) 121-123.

[4] C. Colbourn, D. Hoffman and R. Reed, A new class of group divisible designs with block size three, *J. Combin. Thy.* 59 (1992) 73-89.

[5] T. J. Dickson, On a problem concerning separating systems of a finite set, *J. Combin. Thy.* 7 (1969) 191-196.

[6] A. G. Dyachkov and V. V. Rykov, Bounds of the length of disjunct codes, *Problems Control Inform. Thy.* 11 (1982), 7-13.

[7] A. G. Dyachkov and V. V. Rykov, A survey of superimposed code theory, *Problems. Control Inform. Thy.* 12 (1983) 1-13.

[8] A. G. Dyachkov, V. V. Rykov and A. M. Rashad, Superimposed distance codes, *Problems Control Inform. Thy.* 18 (1989) 237-250.

[9] P. Erdös, P. Frankl and Z. Füredi, Families of finite sets in which no set is covered by the union of two others, *J. Combin. Thy.* A33 (1982) 158-166.

[10] P. Erdös, P. Frankl and D. Füredi, Families of finite sets in which no set is covered by the union of r others, *Israel J. Math.* 51 (1985) 79-89.

[11] P. Erdös and H. Hanani, On a limit theorem in combinatorial analysis, *Publ. Math. Debrecen* 10 (1963) 10-13.

[12] P. Frankl, On Sperner families satisfying an additional condition, *J. Combin. Thy.* A24 (1976) 1-11.

[13] P. Frankl and Z. Füredi, Union-free hypergraphs and probability theory, *Euro. J. Combinatorics* 5 (1984) 127-131.

[14] H. Hanani, On some tactical configurations, *Canad. J. Math.* 15 (1963) 702-722.

[15] A. J. Hoffman and R. R. Singleton, On Moore graphs with diameters 2 and 3, *IBM J. Res. Develop.* 4 (1960) 497-504.

[16] W.T. Huang and F.K. Hwang, private communication.

[17] F. K. Hwang and V. T Sós, Non-adaptive hypergeometric group testing, *Studia Scient. Math. Hungarica* 22 (1987) 257-263.

[18] S. M. Johnson, A new upper bound for error correcting codes, *IEEE Trans. Inform. Thy.* 8 (1962) 203-207.

[19] G. Katona, On separating systems of a finite set, *J. Combin. Thy.* 1 (1966) 174-194.

[20] W. H. Kautz and R. R. Singleton, Nonrandom binary superimposed codes, *IEEE Trans. Inform. Thy.* 10 (1964) 363-377.

[21] B. Lindstrom, Determination of two vectors from the sum, *J. Combin. Thy.* A6 (1969) 402-407.

[22] Q. A. Nguyen and T. Zeisel, Bounds on constant weight binary superimposed codes, *Probl. Control & Inform. Thy.* 17 (1988) 223-230.

[23] W. W. Paterson, *Error Correcting Codes*, (MIT Press, Cambridge, Mass. 1961).

[24] D. Raghavarao, *Constructions and Combinatorial Problems in Designs of Experiments*, (Wiley, New York, 1971).

[25] A. Rényi, On random generating elements of a finite Boolean algebra, *Acta Sci. Math.* (szeged) 22 (1961) 75-81.

[26] M. Ruszinkó, On the upper bound of the size of the r-cover-free families, *J Combin. Thy., series A* 66 (1994) 302-310.

[27] G. M. Saha, H. Pesotan and B. L. Raktoc, Some results on t-complete designs, *Ars Combin.* 13 (1982) 195-201.

[28] G. M. Saha and B. K. Sinha, Some combinatorial aspects of designs useful in group testing experiments, unpublished manuscript.

[29] D. J. Schultz, Topics in Nonadaptive Group Testing, Ph.D. Dissertation, Temple University, 1992.

[30] D. J. Schultz, M. Parnes and R. Srinivasan, Further applications of d-complete designs to group testing, *J. Combin. Inform. & System Sci.* 8 (1993) 31-41.

[31] R. R. Singleton, Maximum distance q-nary codes, *IEEE Trans. Inform. Thy.* 10 (1964) 116-118.

[32] J. Spencer, Minimal completely separating systems, *J. Combin. Thy.* 8 (1970) 446-447.

[33] E. Sperner, Ein Satz Uber Untermengen einer endliche Menge, *Math. Zeit.* 27 (1928) 544-548.

[34] F. Vakil and M. Parnes, On the structure of a class of sets useful in non-adaptive group-testing, *J. Statist. Plan. & Infer.* 39 (1994) 57-69.

[35] F. Vakil, M. Parnes and D. Raghavarao, Group testing with at most two defectives when every item is included in exactly two group tests, *Utilitas Math.* 38 (1990) 161-164.

[36] I. Wegener, On separating systems whose elements are sets of at most k elements, *Disc. Math.* 28 (1979) 219-222.

[37] C. A. Weideman and D. Raghavarao, Some optimum non-adaptive hypergeometric group testing designs for identifying defectives, *J. Statist. Plan. Infer.* 16 (1987) 55-61.

[38] C. A. Weideman and D. Raghavarao, Nonadaptive hypergeometric group testing designs for identifying at most two defectives, *Commun. Statist.* 16A (1987), 2991-3006.

[39] V. Zinoviev, Cascade equal-weight codes and maximal packing, *Probl. Control & Inform. Thy.* 12 (1983) 3-10.

8

Random Designs
and Error Tolerance

In the last chapter we introduced several methods to construct d-disjoinct, d-seperable and $\bar{d}$-separable matrices. A general observation is that these methods may work for a class of n-values, or a class of t-values, but not for most n and t values, since usually they depend on the existences of some combinatorial objects. Furthermore, the constructions are quite complicate. On the other hand, a random construction for given t and n simply assign probability p to each item for being included in test i, $i = 1, \cdots, t$. It is extremely easy to do, and works for all t and n. For given n and d, if t and p are chosen properly, then a random construction yields a desirable matrix with high probability.

Nevertheless, the very concept of a random matrix allows the possibility that the matrix does not have the desired property, and the set of defectives is not completely identified. This type of identification error is called the design error. Another type of error is due to test ambiguity, and can occur to matrices with zero design error. In this chapter we discuss methods to control these errors. It should be noted that although error-control is at a beginning stage without an abundance of results, it is a very important subject which may serve as the bridge between the group testing theory and many applications.

8.1 Random Matrices

Erdos and Renyi [5] first introduced random construction in search problems. Dyachkov [3] proposed a random construction of a d-disjunct matrix for the quantitative model (see Sec. 11.2). Sebo [12] adopted the idea to the group testing model. Note that a random construction cannot guarantee that the resultant matrix is d-disjunct. But with a proper choice of t, the error probability ε can be controlled.

Theorem 8.1.1 *For all $0 < \varepsilon < 1$,*

$$\lim_{n \to \infty} \frac{t(d, n, \varepsilon)}{\log n} \to d.$$

163

Proof. Let $M_{t,n}$ denote the set of all $t \times n$ binary matrices. Construct a random $R \in M_{t,n}$ by selecting t tests where in each test an item is excluded with probability q. Let $P(R)$ denote the probability that there exist two sample points $s \neq s'$ which R cannot distinguish. Suppose that $s \cap s' = s''$ and $|s''| = r$. Note that a test cannot distinguish s from s' only in the following three cases: *(i)* no column from $s \cup s'$ is in the test, *(ii)* some column from s'' is in the test, *(iii)* no column from s'' in the test, but at least one column from each of $s \setminus s''$ and $s' \setminus s''$ is in the test. The probability of test failing to distinguish s from s' is

$$q_r = q^{2d-r} + 1 - q^r + q^r(1 - q^{d-r})^2 = 1 - 2q^d(1 - q^{d-r}).$$

Setting $q = (\frac{1}{2})^{\frac{1}{d}}$,

$$q_r = 1 - 2(\frac{1}{2})^{\frac{d}{d}}[1 - (\frac{1}{2})^{\frac{d-r}{d}}] = (\frac{1}{2})^{\frac{d-r}{d}}.$$

The probability that all t tests failing to distinguish s from s' is simply q_r^t. To compute $P(R)$, we may treat s as fixed. Then there are $\binom{d}{r}\binom{n-d}{d-r}$ ways to select s' such that $|s \cap s'| = r$. Summing over r, we have

$$\sum_{R \in M_{t,n}} P(R) = \sum_{r=0}^{d-1} \binom{d}{r}\binom{n-d}{d-r}(\frac{1}{2})^{\frac{d-r}{d}t}.$$

Setting $t = d\log n + \omega(n)$, where $\omega(n) = o(\log n)$ and $\omega(n) \xrightarrow{n \to \infty} \infty$, and noting $\binom{n-d}{d-r} \leq (n-d)^{d-r}$, we have

$$\sum_{R \in M_{t,n}} P(R) < \sum_{r=0}^{d-1} d^r(n-d)^{d-r}(\frac{1}{2})^{(d-r)\log n}(\frac{1}{2})^{\frac{d-r}{d}\omega(n)}$$

$$= \sum_{r=0}^{d-1} d^r(\frac{n-d}{n})^{d-r}(\frac{1}{2})^{\frac{d-r}{d}\omega(n)} < \varepsilon \text{ for } n > n(\varepsilon).$$

On the other hand, an information-theoretic argument yields

$$2^t \geq \binom{n}{d} \geq (\frac{n}{d})^d$$

or

$$t \geq d\log n - d\log d.$$

$\square$

Dyachkov and Rykov [4] used a random coding method to obtain an upper bound for $t(d,n)$. Busschbach [2] improved this construction to obtain Theorem 8.1.3. It is straightforward to verify

Lemma 8.1.2 *The property of d-disjunct is equivalent to the following statement: For any $d+1$ columns with one of them designated, there always exists a row with 1 in the designated column and 0s in the other d columns.*

Theorem 8.1.3 $t(d,n) \leq 3(d+1)\ln[(d+1)\binom{n}{d+1}]$.

Proof. Let (M_{ij}) be a $t \times n$ random 0–1 matrix where $M_{ij} = 1$ with probability p. For a row i and columns $j_1,\ldots,j_{d+1}$, the probability that $M_{ij_1} = 1$ and $M_{ij_2} = \ldots = M_{ij_{d+1}} = 0$ is $q(1-q)^d$. The probability that there does not exist such a row i (called this event E) is

$$\left[1 - q\,(1-q)^d\right]^t .$$

There are $(d+1)\binom{n}{d+1}$ ways of choosing $d+1$ columns with one designated as j_1. The probability that E occurs to at least one of them is certainly less than the sum of the probability E occurring to each of them. Note that $[1 - q(1-q)^d]^t$ is minimized by choosing $q = 1/(d+1)$. Finally, under the optimal choice of q the probability P that E will happen for every choice of $j_1,\ldots,j_{d+1}$ is less than

$$(d+1)\binom{n}{d+1}\left[1 - \frac{1}{d+1}\left(1 - \frac{1}{d+1}\right)^d\right]^t .$$

From

$$\frac{1}{2} \geq \left(1 - \frac{1}{d+1}\right)^d > \frac{1}{3} \quad \text{for } d \geq 1$$

and

$$-\ln(1-x) \geq x \quad \text{for } 0 \leq x < 1 ,$$

one obtains

$$\ln\left[1 - \frac{1}{d+1}\left(1 - \frac{1}{d+1}\right)^d\right] < \frac{-1}{3(d+1)} .$$

Therefore

$$P < 1 \quad \text{for } t \geq 3(d+1)\ln\left[(d+1)\binom{n}{d+1}\right] ;$$

which implies the existence of an (M_{ij}) which is d-disjunct. □

Corollary 8.1.4 *For $n \gg d$, $t(d,n) \leq 3(d+1)^2 \ln n$.*

Corollary 8.1.5 *The probability that a random $t \times n$ design with $p = 1/(d+1)$ is d-disjunct is at least $(d+1)\binom{n}{d+1}[1 - \frac{1}{d+1}(1 - \frac{1}{d+1})^d]^t$.*

Kautz and Singleton [6] gave a method (see next section) to convert a q-nary code of length t/q to a binary superimposed code of length t with the same number of code words. Nguyen and Zeisel [11] showed that with a proper choice of q, there must exist a random q-nary code whose conversion will yield a d-disjunct matrix with a favorable ratio $t/\log n$.

Theorem 8.1.6 $t(d, n) \leq K(d, n)(d + 1)^2 \log n$, *where*

$$K(d, n) = \min_{d \leq q} \frac{1}{-\frac{d+1}{q} \log \left[1 - \left(1 - \frac{1}{q}\right)^d\right]} + \frac{q}{(d + 1)^2 \log n} \ .$$

Proof. Let M denote the $t \times n$ binary matrix converted from a random q-nary code of length $\lfloor t/q \rfloor$, where q achieves $K(d, n)$. The probability that M is not d-disjunct is less than

$$\binom{n}{d}(n - d)\left[1 - \left(1 - \frac{1}{q}\right)^d\right]^{\lfloor t/q \rfloor}$$

$$< \exp\left\{(d + 1)\ln \ n + \left(\frac{t}{q} - 1\right)\ln\left[1 - \left(1 - \frac{1}{q}\right)^d\right]\right\}$$

$$\leq 1$$

since setting

$$t = (d + 1)^2 \ln\left[\frac{1}{-\frac{d+1}{q}\ln[1 - (1 - \frac{1}{q})^d]} + \frac{q}{(d + 1)^2 \ln n}\right]$$

$$= \frac{q(d + 1)\ln n}{-\ln[1 - (1 - \frac{1}{q})^d]} + q$$

implies

$$\frac{t}{q} = \frac{(d + 1)\ln n}{-\ln[1 - (1 - \frac{1}{q})^d]} + 1,$$

that is

$$(d + 1)\ln n + \left(\frac{t}{q} - 1\right)\ln[1 - (1 - \frac{1}{q})^d] = 0.$$

This implies the existence of a $t \times n$ d-disjunct matrix.   □

Corollary 8.1.7 *As d is fixed and $n \to \infty$,*

$$K(d, n) \leq \frac{\ln 2}{\ln \frac{e}{e-1}} \cong 1.5112 \ .$$

As d also $\to \infty$ but at a much slower rate than n,

$$\lim_{d \to \infty} \ sup \ K(d, n) = \frac{1}{\ln 2} \cong 1.4427 \ .$$

8.2 Macula's Error Tolerance d-Disjunct Matrices

Let $H(x, y)$ denote the Hamming distance between two vertices of the same length, i.e., $H(x, y)$ is the number of bits x differs from y. For a d-disjunct matrix M, define $H(M)$ to be the minimum distance $|p(s) - p(s')|$ between any two sample points s and s'. Macula [9] observed that if $H(M) \geq k$, then M is $(k - 1)$-error detecting and $(\lceil \frac{k}{2} \rceil - 1)$-error correcting. The first part means that if up to $k - 1$ errors occur in test outcomes, we will be alerted to the fact that the algorithm may not yield a correct answer. The second part means that if up to $\lceil \frac{k}{2} \rceil - 1$ errors occur in test outcomes, we could correct them and obtain the correct answer. The first part is accomplished by noting that the observed test outcome vector does not match $p(s)$ for any s; the second part is accomplished by naming s as the correct answer such that $p(s)$ is closest to the observed test outcome vector in Hamming distance.

It is customary to index the rows by the set $T = \{1, \cdots, t\}$ and then label a column by the set of indices from the rows it intersects. For a constant weight w matrix, the columns are labeled by the w-subset of T and the rows by the 1-subset of T. Further, a row intersects a column if and only if the 1-subset is a subset of the w-subset. Macula [8] generalizes this relation between rows and columns by labeling the rows with d-subsets of a set $M = \{1, \cdots, m\}$, the columns with k-subsets, $k > d$, of M, and a row intersects a column if and only if the d-subset is a subset of the k-subset. When the maximum number of rows and columns are taken, the $\binom{m}{d} \times \binom{m}{k}$ matrix is denoted by $\delta(m, d, k)$.

Macula proved:

Theorem 8.2.1 $\delta(m, d, k)$ *is d-disjunct.*

Proof. Let $C_{j_0}, C_{j_1}, ..., C_{j_d}$ be $d + 1$ distinct columns with C_{j_0} being designated. Let $K_0, K_1, ..., K_d$ be the labeling k subsets, respectively. For each $1 \leq i \leq d$, there exists an $x_i \in K_0 \backslash K_i$. Thus the row labeled by $X = \{x_1, ..., x_d\}$ is contained in K_0, but not in any K_i, $1 \leq i \leq d$. Suppose $|X| = d - y, 0 \leq y < d$. Set $X' = X \cup Y$ where Y is a set of y elements from $K_0 \backslash X$. Then X' is a row in $\delta(s, d, k)$ which has a 1 in column C_{j_0}, but 0 in column C_{j_i}, $1 \leq i \leq d$. By Lemma 8.1.2, $\delta(m, d, k)$ is d-disjunct. $\square$

Corollary 8.2.2 $\delta(m, d, k)$ *has column weight $\binom{m}{d}$ and row weight $\binom{m-d}{k-d}$.*

Next we add m new rows to $\delta(m, d, k)$ labeled by $\bar{1}, \bar{2}, ..., \bar{m}$, where row $\bar{i}$ has a zero in any column whose labeling k-subset contains i, and a one otherwise. We call the enhanced matrix $\delta^*(m, d, k)$.

Theorem 8.2.3 *If $k - d \geq 3$, then $H(\delta^*(m, d, k)) \geq 4$.*

Proof. Let $s = (C_{j_1}, ..., C_{j_s})$ and $s' = (C_{h_1}, ..., C_{h_r})$ be two distinct sample points, with $r \leq s \leq d$. Without loss of generality, assume $C_{j_1} \notin s'$. We consider three cases:

Case 1. $r \leq d - 1$. Then for each $1 \leq i \leq r$, there exists an $x_i \in C_{j_1} \backslash C_{h_i}$. So the set $\{x_1, ..., x_r\}$ is in C_{j_1}, but not in C_{h_i}, $1 \leq i \leq r$; or equivalently any row whose label containing $\{x_1, ..., x_r\}$ intersects C_{j_1}, but not C_{h_i}, $1 \leq i \leq r$. Since $r \leq d - 1$ and $k - d \geq 3$, there exist at least four such rows.

Case 2. $r = d$ and $|s \cap s'| = d - 1$. Without loss of generality, assume C_{j_1} is the unique column not in s'. The set $X = \{x_1, x_2, ..., x_r = x_d\}$ still yields a row which intersects C_{j_1} but not C_{h_i}, $1 \leq i \leq d$. If $x_1 \in C_{j_1} \backslash C_{h_i}$ for some $2 \leq i \leq d$, then we can set $x_i = x_1$, and reduce $|X|$ to $d - 1$. The argument of case 1 also works here. We assume that $x_1 \in C_{h_i}$ for all $2 \leq i \leq d$. Since $C_{j_i} = C_{h_i}$ for $2 \leq i \leq d$, $\bar{x}_1$ does not appear in any column of s, but appears in C_{h_1} of s'. Namely, the row labeled by $\bar{x}_1$ intersects s' but not s. Thus we obtain two rows which distinguish s from s'. The other two rows are obtained by symmetry, *i.e.*, using C_{h_1} instead of C_{j_1}.

Case 3. $r = d$ and $|s \cap s'| < d - 1$. There are two columns C_{j_1} and C_{j_2} not in s', which generates two d-sets $X = \{x_1, ..., x_d\}$ and $Y = \{y_1, ..., y_d\}$ which intersect s but not s'. Let $z \in C_{j_1} \backslash C_{j_2}$. If $z \notin C_{h_i}$ for some $1 \leq i \leq d$, we set $x_i = z$, hence $X \neq Y$. If $z \in C_{h_i}$ for all $1 \leq i \leq d$ then z is in every column of s', but not in C_{j_2}. Hence the row labeled by $\bar{z}$ intersects s but not s'. Therefore in either case we obtain two rows which distinguish s from s'. The other two rows are obtained by the symmetry of s and s'.   □

Example 8.1 $\delta(23, 2, 12)$ gives a 2-disjunct matrix with $\binom{23}{2} = 253$ rows and $\binom{23}{12} = 1,352,078$ columns, while $16d^2 \log_2 n \geq 1280$. $\delta^*(23, 2, 12)$ has 276 rows and is 1-error-correcting.

Macula [10] also showed that although $\delta(m, 2, k)$ is 2-disjunct and can only guarantee to solve $(\bar{2}, n)$ problem, it has high probability to solve $(\bar{d}, n)$ problem with $d > 2$.

Let $K = \{K_1, ..., K_d\}$ denote a d-family of k-subsets. Such a subset is called *marked* if for each K_i, there exists a $x_i \in K_i$ which is not in any other K_j in K. x_i is called the *mark* of K_i with respect to K. Note that if the set of defectives is a marked d-family of k-subsets then we can identify K_i by the set of $k - 1$ tests all containing a certain x, which will be identified as the mark of K_i and all having positive outcomes. See the following for an example ($k = 3, d = 3, n = 6$):

	a	a	a	a	a	a	a	a	a	b	b	b	b	b	b	c	c	c	d	p(s)
	b	b	b	b	c	c	c	d	d	e	c	c	c	d	d	e	d	d	e	e
	c	d	e	f	d	e	f	e	f	f	d	e	f	e	f	f	e	f	f	f
ab	1	1	1	1																1
ac	1				1	1	1													1
ad		1			1			1	1											1
ae			1			1		1		1										1
af				1			1		1	1										0
bc	1										1	1	1							1
bd		1									1			1	1					1
be			1									1		1		1				0
bf				1									1		1	1				1
cd					1						1						1	1		0
ce						1						1					1		1	0
cf							1						1					1	1	0
de								1						1			1			1	1
df									1						1			1		1	1
ef										1						1			1	1	0

The set of tests with positive outcomes is $\{ab, ac, ad, ae, bc, bd, bf, de, df\}$. From ac and bc, we obtain the 3-subset abc with mark c. From ae and de, we obtain the 3-subset ade with mark e. From bf and df, we obtain the 3-subset bdf with mark f. Thus if there are truly 3-defectives represented by marked 3-subsets, then they are found.

The probability of obtaining a correct identification is the same as the probability $p(n, d, k)$ that the set of d defectives is a marked set.

Theorem 8.2.4

$$p(n, d, k) \geq \left[\frac{\sum_{i=1}^{k}(-1)^{i+1}\binom{k}{i}\binom{\binom{n-i}{k}}{d-1}}{\binom{\binom{n}{k}-1}{d-1}} \right]^d.$$

Proof. Suppose the d-family $\{K_1, ..., K_d\}$ is randomly chosen. Let E_i denote the event that K_i has a mark. Then

$$p(n, d, k) = P(E_1)P(E_2 \mid E_1)P(E_3 \mid E_1, E_2) \cdots \geq [P(E_1)]^d,$$

since the E_i's are positively correlated.

To compute $P(E_1)$, note that once K_1 is chosen, there are $\binom{\binom{n}{k}-1}{d-1}$ ways to choose the other $d - 1$ K_j's. Such a choice would induce a mark of K_1 if at least one of k alphabets of K_1 does not appear in other K_j's. That number is given in the numerator by using the inclusion-exclusion principle. □

Example 8.2 Suppose $n = 1,000,000, d = 5$. Since $\binom{72}{4} = 1,028,790$ and $\binom{44}{5} = 1,086,008$. We can either use $\delta(72, 2, 4)$ with $\binom{72}{2} = 2556$ tests and $p(72, 5, 4) \geq .9937$ or $\delta(44, 2, 5)$ with $\binom{44}{2} = 946$ tests and $p(44, 5, 5) \geq .97107$.

Macula also proposed a 2-stage modification by testing $\delta(n, 1, k)$ before $\delta(n, 2, k)$. Let i and j be two tests in $\delta(n, 1, k)$ with at least one negative outcomes. Then the test (i, j) can be eliminated from $\delta(n, 2, k)$.

Theorem 8.2.5 *The expected number of tests for the 2-stage algorithm is*

$$n + \binom{n\left[1 - (1 - \frac{k}{n})^d\right]}{2}.$$

Proof. $E(|\cup_{j \in s} C_j|) = n\left[1 - (1 - \frac{k}{n})^d\right].$ □

Example 8.3 Using the 2-stage $\delta(72, 2, 4)$, the expected number of tests is 151.21 and the probability of success is still $\geq .99$.

8.3 *q*-Error-Tolerance *d*-Disjunct Matrices

Let $n(d, t; q)$ denote the maximum number of columns of a matrix with t rows which has the property that $p(s) \neq p(s')$ for any two distinct sample points of $S(\bar{d}, n)$ even when q erroneous test outcomes are allowed. Note that this property is equivalent to q-error detecting (hence $\lfloor (q - 1)/2 \rfloor$-error-correcting). Balding and Torney [1] solved $n(1, t; q)$ and $n(2, t; q)$.

Lemma 8.3.1 *A $t \times n$ matrix M is q-error detecting d-disjunct if and only if $|C_i \backslash p(s)| > q$ for every set s of columns with $|s| \leq d$, and every $i \in \{1, ..., n\} \backslash s$.*

Proof. Necessity. Suppose $|C_i \backslash p(s)| \leq q$. Let $s' = C_i \cup s$. Then $p(s') = p(s)$ if the q tests which intersect C_i but not s are all erroneous.

Sufficiency. Let s and s' be two sets of columns with $|s| \leq d$. If $s' \backslash s \neq \emptyset$, then there exists a column $C' \in s' \backslash s$ such that $|C' \backslash p(s)| > q$. If $s' \backslash s = \emptyset$, then $s \backslash s' \neq \emptyset$ and $|s'| \leq d$. Again, there exists a column $C \in s \backslash s'$ such that $|C \backslash p(s')| > q$. So in either case $p(s)$ and $p(s')$ differ at more than q bits. □

Corollary 8.3.2 *M is q-error detecting d-disjunct if and only if $|C_i \backslash C_j| > q$ for all distinct columns C_i and C_j.*

Corollary 8.3.3 *If M is a $(v, dv + q + 1, t)$-packing (every two columns intersect at most v times), then M is q-error detecting d-disjunct.*

Theorem 8.3.4 *A q-error-detecting 1-disjunct $t \times n$ matrix M satisfies*

$$n \leq \frac{1}{K_q} \binom{t}{\lfloor t/2 \rfloor},$$

where $K_0 = 1$ and for q even,

$$K_q = \sum_{s=0}^{q/2} \binom{\lfloor t/2 \rfloor}{s} \binom{\lceil t/2 \rceil}{s},$$

while for q odd,

$$K_q = K_{q-1} + \frac{1}{T} \binom{\lfloor t/2 \rfloor}{(q+1)/2} \binom{\lceil t/2 \rceil}{(q+1)/2},$$

with $T = \lfloor 2\lfloor \frac{t}{2} \rfloor / (q+1) \rfloor$.

Proof. Lubell's argument for $q = 0$ [7] is extended to general q. Consider the (maximal) chains in the lattice where nodes are subsets of $\{1, ..., t\}$ and the comparison is "containment". Then each chain contains at most one column of M (for otherwise we have one column contained in another). Two k-subsets C, C' are called s-neighbors if $|C \backslash C'| = |C' \backslash C| = s$.

A chain is said to be blocked by a column if it contains an s-neighbor of the column for some $s \leq \frac{q}{2}$. First consider q even. Consider two columns C and C'. Suppose a chain contains both an s-neighbor of C and an s'-neighbor of C'. Without loss of generality, assume $s \leq s'$. Then $|C \backslash C'| \leq s + s'$. It follows from Corollary 8.3.2 that either $s > q/2$ or $s' > q/2$. Therefore a chain cannot be blocked by more than one column of M. So we can associate with C the cost $h(C)$ which is the proportion of chains blocked by C. Consider a node represented by a k-subset. Then it has

$$K_{q,k} = \sum_{s=0}^{q/2} \binom{k}{s} \binom{t-k}{s}$$

s-neighbors for some $s \leq \frac{q}{2}$. Hence

$$h(C) = \frac{K_{q,k}}{\binom{t}{k}}.$$

It is readily verified that $h(C)$ is minimized when $k = \lfloor t/2 \rfloor$ or $\lceil t/2 \rceil$. In either case, the value of $K_{q,k}$ is K_q. Since the total proportion of chains blocked is at most 1, $1/h(C)$ is an upper bound of n.

Next consider q odd. The only difference is that if $|C \backslash C'| = q + 1$ there might exist a chain which contains both a $(q+1)/2$-neighbor of C and a $(q+1)/2$-neighbor of C'; hence such a chain is multiply blocked.

Let C denote the set of columns of M each of which has a $(q+1)/2$-neighbor in the chain $\mathcal{Z} = \{\emptyset, \{1\}, \{1,2\}, ..., \{1,2,...,t\}\}$. Let $C, C' \in \mathcal{C}$ with $|C| = k$, and $|C'| = k' \geq k$. Then

$$|\{1,2,...,k\}\backslash C| = \frac{q+1}{2} = |C \cap \{k+1, k+2, ..., t\}|.$$

Let z denote the number of elements in $\{1,2,...,k\}\backslash C$ not in C'. Then C' can leave out at most $(q+1)/2 - z$ elements in $C \cap \{1,...,k\}$.

Therefore $|C\backslash C' \cap \{1,...,k\}| \leq (q+1)/2 - z$. Since C has only $(q+1)/2$ elements in $\{k+1,...,t\}$, $|C\backslash C' \cap \{k+1,...,t\}| \leq (q+1)/2$. It follows $|C\backslash C'| \leq (q+1)/2 - z + (q+1)/2 \leq q+1$. By Corollary 8.3.2, $|C\backslash C'| \geq q+1$ which can be realized only if $|C\backslash C' \cap \{1,...,k\}| = |C\backslash C' \cap \{k+1,...,t\}| = (q+1)/2$. Namely, C' contains $\{1,...,k\}\backslash C$, is disjoint from $C \cap \{k+1,...,t\}$, and leaves out exactly $(q+1)/2$ elements in $C \cap \{1,...,k\}$.

Since C' is a $(q+1)/2$-neighbor of $\mathcal{Z}$ which differs from the set $\{1,...,k'\}$ in $(q+1)/2$ elements among its first k elements, either $k' = k$, or $k' > k$ but $\{k+1,...,k'\} \subseteq C'$. Note that only one C' of the second type can exist in $\mathcal{C}$. To see this, let C' be a $(q+1)/2$-neighbor of $\{1,...,k\}$ and C'' a $(q+1)/2$-neighbor of $\{1,...,k''\}$, $k'' \geq k' > k$. Then $|C'\backslash C''| = |C'\backslash C'' \cap \{C \cap \{1,...,k\}\}| \leq \frac{q+1}{2} < q+1$.

For $C', C'' \in \mathcal{C}$, let $k'' \geq k'$. Then $k' = k$.

$$\begin{aligned} |C'\backslash C''| &= |C'\backslash C'' \cap \{1,...,k\}| + |C'\backslash C'' \cap \{k+1,...,t\}| \\ &\leq (q+1)/2 + (q+1)/2 = q+1, \end{aligned}$$

where equality assumes only if the left-out parts from $C \cap \{1,...,k\}$ are disjoint, and the parts taken from $\{k+1,...,t\}$ are also disjoint. By treating $C\backslash\{1,...,k\}$ as the left-out part of C from $\{1,...,k\}$, then all columns in $\mathcal{C}$ must have disjoint left-out parts from $\{1,...,k\}$ and disjoint parts from $\{k+1,...,t\}$. Therefore the number of $(q+1)/2$-neighbors of a given chain is at most $\min\{\frac{k}{(q+1)/2}, \frac{t-k}{(q+1)/2}\}$ which is maximized at $k = \lfloor t/2 \rfloor$ with the value T.

Associated with C a cost

$$h'(C) = K'_{q,k}/\binom{t}{k},$$

where

$$K'_{q,k} = K_{q-1,k} + \frac{\text{the number of } (q+1)/2\text{-neighbors of } C}{T}.$$

The cost is minimized at $k = \lfloor t/2 \rfloor$ or $\lceil t/2 \rceil$. In either case $K'_{q,k} = K_q$ and $1/h'(C)$ is an upper bound of n.   □

Corollary 8.3.5 *If $S(\lfloor t/2 \rfloor - 1, \lfloor t/2 \rfloor, t)$ exists, then it yields an optimal 1-error-detecting 1-disjunct matrix.*

Proof. The number of elements in $S(\lfloor t/2 \rfloor - 1, \lfloor t/2 \rfloor, t)$ is

$$
\binom{t}{\lfloor t/2 \rfloor - 1} / \binom{\lfloor t/2 \rfloor}{\lfloor t/2 \rfloor - 1} = \binom{t}{\lfloor t/2 \rfloor} / (t - \lfloor t/2 \rfloor + 1)
$$
$$
= \binom{t}{\lfloor t/2 \rfloor} / (1 + \lceil t/2 \rceil) = \binom{t}{\lfloor t/2 \rfloor} / K_1.
$$

$\square$

Let $\mathcal{F}$ be a family of subsets of $\{1, ..., t\}$. $\mathcal{F}$ is called a $(2, q)$-cover of a k-subset B if

1. $b \in \mathcal{F}$ and $b \subset b' \subseteq B$ implies $b' \in \mathcal{F}$.

2. For every $b \subseteq B$ with $|B \backslash b| \leq q$, at least one part of every 2-partition of b is in $\mathcal{F}$. Note that $b \subseteq B$ and $|b| \geq k - q$ implies $b \in \mathcal{F}$ since b contains both parts of a partition.

Lemma 8.3.6 *M is q-error-detecting 2-disjunct if and only if for each column C the private (with respeat to M) subsets of C form a $(2, q)$-cover of C.*

Proof. Let $b \subset C$ with $|C \backslash b| \leq q$. From Corollary 8.3.2, b is private for if $b \subset C'$, then $|C \backslash C'| \leq q$. If there exists a partition of b into two nonprivate parts, then the union s of the two columns containing them will lead to $|C \backslash p(s)| \leq q$, violating Lemma 8.3.1. This proves necessity.

To prove sufficiency, assume that s is a set of two columns such that $|C \backslash p(s)| \leq q$. Set $b = p(s) \cap C$. Since $b \in \mathcal{F}$ by condition 1, condition 2 of $(2, q)$-cover is violated. $\square$

For $\mathcal{F}$ a $(2, q)$-cover of C, define $h(C, \mathcal{F})$ to be the proportion of all chains which intersect $\mathcal{F}$.

Theorem 8.3.7 *For any k-subset B, $q < k < t - 1$, and $\mathcal{F}$ a $(2, q)$-cover of B,*

$$
h(B, \mathcal{F}) \geq \binom{2x + q - 1}{x} / \binom{t}{x}
$$

where $x = \lfloor (k - q + 1)/2 \rfloor$. Equality is achieved if and only if $k - q$ is odd and $\mathcal{F} = \mathcal{F}^* = \{b \subseteq B : |b| \geq x\}$.

Proof. Suppose that $k - q$ is odd, i.e., $k = 2x + q - 1$. Then every 2-partition of any $(k - q)$-subset of B contains a part b with $|b| \geq x$. Hence $\mathcal{F}^*$ is a $(2, q)$-cover of B. It is easily verified that

$$
h(B, \mathcal{F}^*) = \binom{2x + q - 1}{x} / \binom{t}{x}.
$$

Suppose that $\mathcal{F}$ achieves minimum in $h(B, \mathcal{F})$. Let s denote the largest integer such that there exists some $b \subset B$ with $|b| = x + s$ and $b \notin \mathcal{F}$. If $s \geq x - 1$, $|B \backslash b| \leq q$ and

$b \in \mathcal{F}$ followed from the definition of $(2,q)$-cover. Hence $s < x - 1$. If $s < 0$, then $|b| \leq x - 1$, and $\mathcal{F}^* \subseteq \mathcal{F}$. It follows $h(B, \mathcal{F}^*) \leq h(B, \mathcal{F})$. Therefore we may assume $s \geq 0$. Suppose there exists some $b \in \mathcal{F}$ such that $|b| < x - s - 1$. Let $b \subseteq b' \subseteq B$ such that $|B \backslash b'| \leq q$. Then $|b' \backslash b| > k - q - (x - s - 1) = x + s$. Hence $b' \backslash b \in \mathcal{F}$ and $\mathcal{F} \backslash \{b\}$ is still a $(2,q)$-cover. Therefore we may assume $\mathcal{F}$ contains no such b.

Let f_r and $\bar{f}_r$ denote the number of r-subsets of B in and not in $\mathcal{F}$, respectively. Then each such r-subset appears in $\binom{k-r}{q}(k-q)$-subsets b of B since the q indices of B not in b must not be chosen from the r-subset to keep it intact in b. Clearly, the number of $(x+s)$-subsets of b not in $\mathcal{F}$ cannot exceed the number of $(x-s-1)$-subsets of b in $\mathcal{F}$ due to the $(2,q)$-cover property. Hence

$$\binom{k-x-s}{q} \bar{f}_{x+s} \leq \binom{k-x+s+1}{q} f_{x-s-1},$$

or

$$\frac{\bar{f}_{x+s}(k-x-s)!(x+s)!}{f_{x-s-1}(k-x+s+1)!(x-s-1)!} \leq 1.$$

Construct $\mathcal{F}'$ from $\mathcal{F}$ by removing all $(x-s-1)$-sets and adding any missing $(x+s)$-subsets of B. Then $\mathcal{F}'$ is also a $(2,q)$-cover of B. We compute:

$$\frac{h(B, \mathcal{F}')}{h(B, \mathcal{F})} = \frac{\text{the portion of chains which contain a } (x+s)\text{-subset of } B \text{ but no element of } \mathcal{F}}{\text{the portion of chains which contain a } (x-s-1)\text{-subset of } B \text{ but no other element of } \mathcal{F}}. \qquad (8.1)$$

Let b be a $(x+s)$-subset not in $\mathcal{F}$. Then its lower paths (from this node to node $\emptyset$) does not intersect $\mathcal{F}$. An upper path does not intersect $\mathcal{F}$ if the parent node of b is not contained in B. If it is contained in B, then it intersects $\mathcal{F}$ by our assumption that all subsets of B with size $> x + s$ are in $\mathcal{F}$. A parent node of b is simply $b \cup \{y\}$, for some $y \notin b$. So $b \cup \{y\} \not\subseteq B$ if and only if $y \notin B$, and there are $t - k$ choices of it. So the proportion of chains going through b but not in $\mathcal{F}$ is $(t-k)/(t-x-s)$. Since this is true for every $(x+s)$-subset b not in $\mathcal{F}$, the first term in (8.1) equals

$$\frac{t-k}{t-x-s} \bar{f}_{x+s} / \binom{t}{x+s}.$$

On the other hand, let b now denote a $(x-s-1)$-subset in $\mathcal{F}$. Then an upper path does not intersect $\mathcal{F}$ if and only if the parent node of b is not contained in B, and the proportion is exactly $(t-k)/(t-x+s-1)$. A lower path does not intersect $\mathcal{F}$ since we assume $\mathcal{F}$ contains no subset of size $< x - s - 1$. Therefore the proportion of chains going through b but not containing any other element of $\mathcal{F}$ is $(t-k)/(t-x+s+1)$. Consequently, the second term in (8.1) equals

$$\frac{t-k}{t-x+s+1} f_{x-s-1} / \binom{t}{t-x+s+1}.$$

Thus

$$
\begin{aligned}
\frac{h(B,\mathcal{F}')}{h(B,\mathcal{F})} &= \frac{(t-k)\bar{f}_{x+s}}{(t-x-s)\binom{t}{x+s}} \Big/ \frac{(t-k)f_{x-s-1}}{(t-x+s+1)\binom{t}{t-x+s+1}} \\
&= \frac{\bar{f}_{x+s}(t-x+s-1)!(x+s)!}{f_{x-s-1}(t-x+s)!(x-s-1)!} \\
&< \frac{\bar{f}_{x+s}(k-x-s)!(x+s)!}{f_{x-s-1}(k-x+s+1)!(x-s-1)!} \le 1,
\end{aligned}
$$

contradicting the minimality of $\mathcal{F}$. Therefore $s<0$ and $\mathcal{F}^*$ achieves minimum.

Suppose $k=2x+q$, $q>0$. Then for any $y \in B$, $\{b \in \mathcal{F}: y \notin b\}$ is a $(2,q-1)$-cover for $B\backslash\{y\}$. So the lemma follows from the case $k=2x+q-1$. If $q=0$, then every partition of B has one part in $\mathcal{F}$. Consider the partition of B into two x-sets. Then at least $\binom{2x}{x}/2 = \binom{2x-1}{x}$ x-subsets are in $\mathcal{F}$. Again, we can show that $\mathcal{F}$ contains all $(x+1)$-subsets but no $(x-1)$-subsets. Thus

$$
h(B,\mathcal{F}) \ge \binom{2x-1}{x} \Big/ \binom{t}{x} \quad \text{and } n \le \binom{t}{x} \Big/ \binom{2x-1}{x}
$$

(proved in Lemma 7.2.1, but worse than Theorem 7.5.6).   □

Theorem 8.3.8 *A $t \times n$ q-error-detecting 2-disjunct matrix satisfies*

$$
n \le \binom{t}{x} \Big/ \binom{2x+q-1}{x},
$$

where x is the smallest integer satisfying

$$
t \le 5x+2+q(q-1)/(x+q)(x = \lceil (t-2)/5 \rceil \text{ for } q=0,1). \tag{8.2}
$$

Proof. Define $F(x) = \binom{2x+q-1}{x} / \binom{t}{x}$. Then

$$
\frac{F(x+1)}{F(x)} = \frac{(2x+q+1)(2x+q)}{(t-x)(x+q)},
$$

which exceeds one if and only if (8.2) is not satisfied. Hence $F(x)$ is minimized by (8.2) and n is upper bounded by $\frac{1}{F(x)}$.   □

References

[1] D.J. Balding and D.C. Torney, Optimal pool designs with error detection, *J. Combin. Thy., Series A* 74 (1996) 131-140.

[2] P. Busschbach, Constructive methods to solve the problems of: s-surjectivity conllict resolution, coding in defective memories, unpublished manuscript, 1984.

[3] A.G. Dyachkov, On a problem of false coins, Colloquium in Combinatorics, Keszthely, 1976.

[4] A.G. Dyachkov and V.V. Rykov, A survey of superimposed code theory, *Probl. Control & Inform. Thy.* 11 (1982) 7-13.

[5] P. Erdös and A. Renyi, On two problems of imformation theory, *Publ. Math. Inst. Hung. Acad. Sci.* 8 (1963) 241-254.

[6] W.H. Kautz and R.R. Singleton, Nonrandom binary superimposed code, *IEEE Trans. Inform. Thy.* 10 (1964) 363-377.

[7] D.Lubell, A short proof of Sperner's lemmas, *J. Combin. Theory* 1 (1966) 299.

[8] A.J. Macula, A simple construction of d-disjunct matrices with certain constant weights, *Disc. Math.* 162 (1996) 311-312.

[9] A.J. Macula, Error correcting nonadaptive group testing with d-disjunct matrices, *Disc. Appl. Math.* 80 (1997) 217-222.

[10] A.J. Macula, Probabilistic nonadaptive and two-stage group testing with relatively small pools and DNA library screening, *J. Comb. Optim.* 2 (1999) 385-397.

[11] Q.A. Nguyen and T. Zeisel, Bounds on constant weight binary superimposed codes, *Probl. Control & Inform. Thy.* 17 (1988) 223-230.

[12] A. Sebo, On two random search problems, *J. Statist. Plan. Infer.* 11 (1985) 23-31.

9

DNA Applications

A DNA sequence is a quaternary sequence with four alphabets A, C, G, T, called *nucleotides*. A and T are considered dual, while C and G are considered dual, in the sense that a DNA sequence always appears with its dual while the dual sequence is obtained by interchanging A with T, and C with G. We will talk about a DNA sequence without mentioning its dual.

A DNA sequence is stored by cutting into shorter segments called *clones*. The cut is done by some chemical compound which recognizes a short subsequence like $ACCT$ of the DNA and cuts at T. Usually, the cutting is done several times with different compounds to preserve the information between the two adjacent clones in the first cutting. Note that a cutting provides some information of the content of a clone at its end. In particular, we can use that information to tell the direction of the clone (except in those cases a clone starts with $TCCA$ and ends with $ACCT$, then we need other information to determine the direction). But other than that, the end information is usually ignored since it is not much and since the mixing of clones from several cuttings blurs that information.

The basic question is to determine whether a particular DNA segment, called a *probe*, is contained in a clone. Two technologies are available. *Hybridization* matches the probe with its dual sequence and causes a reaction in the tested clone (if it contains the dual sequence) which can be detected by using radioactivity or fluorescent technology. *Polymerace chain reaction* (PCR) offers a more sensitive and more specific test and the chain reaction product can be observed by human eyes. Both hybridization and PCR can apply to a set of clones simultaneously, the former to up to hundreds of clones and the latter to thousands. By interpreting the probe as the defective ingredient, group testing applies in an obvious way. The reader is referred to [11] for a general background of DNA testing.

9.1 Clone Library Screening

A clone library stores fragments, called *clones*, from a genome of an organism. A clone survives in a host which is usually a bacteria. The action is provided by a *cloning vector* which is constructed from a virus that can infect the host. Commonly used cloning vectors include lambda, plasmid, cosmid and yeast. A vector can insert its chromosome into a bacteria, but the insertion has length limit dependent on the vector. The length unit is 1,000 *base pairs*, abbreviated as kbps. The range of the lambda vector is from 2 kbps to 20 kbps, the range of the cosmid vector is from 20 kbps to 45 kbps, while the range of the yeast vector is from 100 kbps to 1 Mbps = 1000 kbps.

The cloning vector is cut with a restriction enzyme, and a piece of DNA is inserted into the cut. Then the vector is transferred into the host where it can be replicated into an experimentally useful quantity of DNA. Of course if the length of the cut piece is outside of the legitimate range, then it will be discarded. Since a given restriction enzyme cuts at the same places, several different enzymes might be used to get different partitions of the genome. One benefit is that one meaningful subsequence cut by one enzyme could be preserved in a clone cut by another enzyme.

The order of the clones in a genome is not preserved by a cut. The reconstruction of a genome, which is a task currently receiving much attention, depends on the determination of clone overlappings. A sequence-tagged-site (STS) is a subsequence uniquely present in a genome. Two clones having the same STS are overlapped for certain. Therefore *probing* which clones contain a given STS is a crucial part in reconstructing the genome, which is commonly termed as the *physical mapping problem*. To reconstruct the genome, of course we have to use many STSs and even subsequences which are rare, but not necessarily unique, in the genome.

Since a library typically contains between one thousand to a hundred thousands clones, probing the clones one by one is a very costly process. The idea of group testing enters naturally. For a given probe (a given STS), a clone is *positive* if it contains the probe and *negative* if not. Thus a positive clone is like a defective and a negative clone a good item, while a probing is a (group) testing. The subset of clones gathered for testing is often referred to as a *pool*. A *pool design*, which is a collection of pools with the goal to separate positive clones from negative, is like a nonadaptive group testing algorithm. We will also call a pool with positive (negative) outcome a *positive (negative) pool*.

Clones are stored in a library according to some arrangement which is biologically viable and physically convenient. For example, the yeast- artificial-chromosome (YAC) library first reported by Green and Olson [6] has about 23,000 clones stored in 96-well microtiter plates. The clones are grown on nylon filters in a 16×24 grid of 384 colonies following inoculation from four microtiter plates. So the 23,000 clones are spread into 60 such filters. This library was derived from leukocyte DNA of a single male donor, and the average size of a clone is 250 kbps. Note that the physical arrangement of clones does not necessarily have the need of the later probing in mind. Rather, it is the pool design which should accommodate the physical arrangement.

Group testing can also be applied, in a reverse way, to completely identify a DNA fragment. Suppose we take all k-subsequences of $\{A, C, G, T\}$ as probes and find out which k-subsequences are contained in the DNA fragment and with what frequencies.

Then Ho and Hwang [7] showed that the DNA fragment can be determined even when clones are unoriented. By treating the probes as items, and those contained in the given DNA fragment as defectives. We can use a group testing scheme (except it modifies the usually group testing model by specifying the number of defectives in a test, see Sec. 6.3) to minimize the number of probings.

There are other occasions that screening a set of DNA fragments is necessary. For examples, if a rare gene is associated with a decease and we are screening a community for carrier, or a large group of suspects are screened to match DNA left at a crime scene. In either case, group testing is economical.

Up to now we have emphasized the similarities between group testing and DNA screening. But DNA screening presents some unique problem not present in group testing. In group testing, the assembly of groups for testing is usually not a difficult task. In many applications, the population of items is not large and assembly is easy. Even for a large population, if the subjects are people, then the members of a group can respond to the calling of their names or other identification. We cannot expect an automatic response from a set of items. While assembling an arbitrary subset from a large population could be time-consuming, certain algorithms we proposed earlier, like nested algorithms, make the job easier. We showed that if all items are arranged into a line and items are removed from the line upon their identifications, then a nested algorithm always takes the test group from items at the top of the line, thus reducing subset-selection to simple counting.

However, collecting a pool of clones and preparing it for probing is a more involved task. First of all, the population is usually large; so locating the clones from their storage is nontrivial. Then one has to take the right aliquot of each clone and mix them. The pool also has to be purified before subjecting to probing. Since the task is time consuming, and errors introduced by human efforts can be costly, most large libraries intend to automate this process by employing robots, and preprogramming the pools. Note that even though the actual probings are done sequentially, the preprogramming of pools implies that every potential probing present in the algorithm tree must be prepared since before the sequential algorithm is carried out, one doesn't know for sure whether a pool associated with a particular internal node will be probed or not. The consequence is that lots of pools have to be prepared for a sequential algorithm, even though only a few are actually probed. As we commented before that preparing a pool for probing is costly, strong preference is given to nonadaptive algorithms for which only pools actually probed need to be prepared. In practice, s-stage algorithms for very small s are also used. In choosing an algorithm, one has to consider the tradeoff between the number of probings and the number of pools required to be assembled and prepared.

Even assuming that probings are error-free, pool designs which do not guarantee to separate the positive clones from the negative are often used to cut down the cost of probings. Note that a negative clone can be so identified only if it appears in a negative pool. A negative clone so identified is called a *resolved negative*. Also note that a positive clone can be so identified only if it appears in a positive pool whose all other members, if any, must be resolved negative clones. A positive clone so identified is called a *resolved positive*. All other negative clones are called *unresolved negatives*, and all other positive clones are called *unresolved positives*. Since the unresolved negatives and positives must go through costly individual probings to confirm their nature, a good pool design minimizes their numbers. We will let $\bar{N}$ and $\bar{P}$ denote the number of unresolved negatives and unresolved positives, respectively.

Finally, in the clone screening problem, especially before a robot is employed, it is desirable to coordinate the selection of pools with the physical arrangement of clones. For example, if clones are arranged in a grid, then taking the rows or the columns as pools is convenient, time-saving and less likely to pick a wrong clone inadvertently. The physical range of a probing technology, be it hybridization or PCR, should also be a factor in designing an algorithm.

Thus we see that DNA screening has many more goals than group testing; besides the number of tests, we also want to minimize the number of pools, to minimize $\bar{N}$ and $\bar{P}$, and to accommodate the physical arrangement of clones in clone library screening. In practice probings are not error-free and we would like to build in some error-tolerant capability in the pool design. Often we cannot expect to perform all of these. Then we have to select some of the most important factors into the objective function, where "importance" is measured according to the particular application. The reader is referred to Balding *et al.* [1] for an excellent survey on pool designs.

9.2   Deterministic Designs

In this section we consider pool designs in which every pool is deterministic.

Since in some libraries, clones are grown on nylon filters in an $r \times c$ grid, it is convenient to use the rows and columns as pools [2]. Note that a positive clone will yield a positive outcome for the row and the column containing the clone. Hence the clone at the intersection of a positive row and a positive column is a prime suspect for a positive clone. But it does not have to be positive if the grid contains more than one positive clone. For example if the clones a at (i, j) and d at (i', j') are positive, then the clones b and c will also be identified at positive intersections (see Figure 9.1).

One way to resolve the ambiguity is to do individual probings for clones at positive intersections. But as we commented earlier, individual probings are costly and to be minimized. Barillot *et al.* [2] suggested using another grid in which the rows and the columns are again partitions of the rc clones, but two clones are collinear at most once in the two grids, called the *unique collinearity condition*. Since b and c are collinear with a and d in the first grid, they will no longer be collinear with a and d in the second grid. Thus we can distinguish the true positive clones a and d from the false ones by checking whether a clone appears at positive intersections in both grids.

When there are four or more positive clones, then a negative clone can appear at positive intersections in both grids. For example, suppose a, b, c and d are four

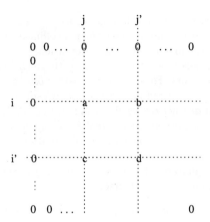

Figure 9.1: Positive clones and positive intersections.

positive clones in grid one. A negative clone e can be in the same row with a and same collumn with b in the first grid, and in the same row with c and same column with d in the second grid. A third grid which together with the first two grids satisfies the unique collinearity condition is needed. In general $2d$ positive clones require $d+1$ grids satisfying the unique collinearity condition. On the other hand, since a clone has $r+c-2$ collinear clones, while the total number of clones other than the given clone itself is $rc-1$, at most $\lfloor (rc-1)/(r+c-2) \rfloor$ grids satisfying the unique collinearity condition exists.

Hwang [9] proved

Theorem 9.2.1 *Necessary and sufficient conditions for the existence of $g \geq 2$ grids satisfying the unique collinearity condition are*
(i) $r = c$,
(ii) there exist $2(g-1)$ orthogonal Latin squares of order r.

Proof. Let $G_1, ..., G_g$ denote the g grids. We first prove necessity.

(i) Suppose to the contrary that $r \neq c$, say, $r > c$. By the pigeonhole principle, a column in G_2 must contain at least two elements from the same row of G_1.

(ii)Label the r^2 clones by the set $\{0, 1, 2, ..., r^2-1\}$. Without loss of generality, assume that G_1 is normalized such that cell (i, j) contains clone (i, j), $0 \leq i \leq r-1$, $0 \leq j \leq r-1$. Then each G_k, $2 \leq k \leq g$, generates two Latin squares L_{k_1} and L_{k_2}. Cell (i, j) of L_{k_1} contains the row index, and cell (i, j) of L_{k_2} contains the column index, of clone (i, j) in G_k. L_{k_1} (or L_{k_2}) is a Latin square since if an index appears twice in a row or a column, then the row (or column) would contain two elements from the same row (or column) of G_1, violating the unique collinearity condition. Furthermore, L_{k_1}

and L_{k_2} are orthogonal since each cell of G_k contains a single element. Finally, L_{k_x} and L_{h_y} must also be orthogonal or two elements collinear in G_k would be collinear again in G_h, violating the unique collinearity condition.

Sufficiency. Let L denote a set of $2(g-1)$ orthogonal Latin squares. Partition L arbitrarily into $g-1$ pairs. For each pair superimpose one square on the other so that each cell contains an ordered pair. Since the two squares are orthogonal, the r^2 ordered pairs represent distinct r-nary numbers in the set $\{0, 1, ..., r^2-1\}$. These $g-1$ squares together with the normalized square (previously designated as G_1) constitute a set of g grids satisfying the unique collinearity condition.   □

It is well known (Raghavarao [10]) that for r an odd prime power, $r-1$ orthogonal Latin squares can be constructed. Therefore

Corollary 9.2.2 *For r an odd prime power, $(r+1)/2$ grids satisfying the unique collinearity condition can be constructed.*

Barrilot *et al.* proposed the use of a $d \times d$ transformation matrix $A = (a_{ij})$ to yield a new d-dimensional grid AG from a given one G. The element in the grid point $(x_1, \cdots, x_d)$ in G will appear in the grid point $(\sum_{j=1}^{d} a_{1j}x_j, \cdots, \sum_{j=1}^{d} a_{dj}x_j)$ in AG. To satisfy the unique collinearity condition, the determinant and all sub-determinants of A must be nonnull and prime to the side length of the grid. To generate three grids, we could either use two different transformation matrices A_1 and A_2, or use the same A twice. In the first case, we have to check the condition on determinants for A_1 and A_1A_2, in the second case A and A^2. For example, the 2-dimensional transformation matrices A and A^2 are shown in Figure 9.2.

$$\begin{pmatrix} 2 & 1 \\ 1 & 1 \end{pmatrix} \quad \begin{pmatrix} 5 & 3 \\ 3 & 2 \end{pmatrix}$$

g_{00}	g_{01}	g_{02}	g_{03}	g_{04}	g_{00}	g_{42}	g_{34}	g_{21}	g_{13}
g_{10}	g_{11}	g_{12}	g_{13}	g_{14}	g_{14}	g_{01}	g_{43}	g_{30}	g_{22}
g_{20}	g_{21}	g_{22}	g_{23}	g_{24}	g_{23}	g_{10}	g_{02}	g_{44}	g_{31}
g_{30}	g_{31}	g_{32}	g_{33}	g_{34}	g_{32}	g_{24}	g_{11}	g_{03}	g_{40}
g_{40}	g_{41}	g_{42}	g_{43}	g_{44}	g_{41}	g_{33}	g_{20}	g_{12}	g_{04}

$A \qquad A^2 \qquad\qquad\qquad G \qquad\qquad\qquad AG$

Figure 9.2:

The determinants and subdeterminants for A and A^2 are 1, 2, 3, 5. Thus it can generate three different $s \times s$ grids if $s \in \{1, 2, 3, 5\}$, but only two if s is a prime to $\{1, 2, 3, 5\}$.

Suppose the total number n of clones is much greater than the size rc of a grid. Assuming n divides rc, then the n clones can be stored in n/rc grids. We can either treat a grid as a unit to duplicate partitions of its rc clones (as discussed above), or we can duplicate partitions of the whole n clones (each partition consists of a set of n/rc grids). The latter problem has not been dealt with in the design literature.

Barillot et al. also extended the 2-dimensional grid to higher dimensions. They proposed taking the set of hyperplanes as pools. Note that the pool size of a d-dimensional hypercube is about $n^{\frac{d-1}{d}}$, which Barillot et al. warned would be too large if $d > 4$. An option would be to take lower-dimensional hyperplanes as pools to reduce the pool size. Of course, the price paid is a larger number of probings. The pros and cons of this trade-off have not been studied.

The unique collinearity condition is tied down with a hypercube structure with orthogonal hyperplanes. By generalizing the "unique collinearity" to "multiple intersections", we might as well discard the associated geometrical structure. Instead of hyperplanes, we now have a set of subsets of the set $\{1, ..., n\}$ and the condition is that no two subsets can intersect in more than λ elements. This condition of course leads us to the packing designs which were studied in Chapter 7.

9.3 Random Designs

Random designs refer to the fact that the pools are generated by a probabilistic scheme. In Sec. 8.1, we study the random design in which there are t pools where a pool contains each item with probability p. Note that p is a design parameter which can be chosen to maximize certain design objective. In Theorem 9.1.2 we gave an asymptotic analysis how large t must be for the design to be a d-disjunct matrix. Here, our focus is on $\bar{N}$ and $\bar{P}$ for given t and n. Hwang [8] extended a formula of Balding, Bruno, Knill and Torney [1] for $P(\bar{N} = 0)$ to $P(\bar{N} = j)$.

Lemma 9.3.1

$$P_p(\bar{N} = j) =$$
$$\sum_{i=0}^{t} \binom{t}{i} (1-p)^{id} [1 - (1-p)^d]^{t-i} \binom{n-d}{j} (1-p)^{ij} [1 - (1-p)^i]^{n-d-j}.$$

Proof. The probability that a given pool doesn't contain a positive clone is $(1-p)^d$. Hence the probability that none of i given pools contains a positive clone is $(1-p)^{id}$. The probability that the other $t-i$ pools each containing a positive clone is $[1 - (1-p)^d]^{t-i}$. Finally, the probability that a negative clone is contained in (one of) the i pools is $1 - (1-p)^i$. Hence the probability that exactly j negative clones is contained in the $t-i$ pools is the $\sum_l$ term at the end of Lemma 9.3.1 obtained by the inclusion-exclusion formula. $\qquad\square$

Corollary 9.3.2

$$P_p(\bar{N} = 0) =$$
$$\sum_{i=1}^{t} \binom{t}{i} (1-p)^{id} [1 - (1-p)^d]^{t-i} [1 - (1-p)^i]^{n-d} \quad .$$

Balding *et al.* gave the following three results concerning $E(\bar{N})$.

Theorem 9.3.3 $E_p(\bar{N}) = (n - d)[1 - p(1 - p)^d]^t$.

Proof. In the proof of Theorem 4.3.9 we showed that in a random $t \times n$ design the probability that there does not exist a row which contains a given column but none of other d given columns is $[1 - p(1-p)^d]^t$. This can be interpreted as the probability that a given negative clone does not appear in a pool absent of a positive clone. Since this argument applies to any of the $n - d$ negative clones and expectation is a linear function, Lemma 9.3.3 follows.   □

Of course, Theorem 9.3.3 can also be obtained by Lemma 9.3.1 through the definition $E_p(\bar{N}) = \sum_{j=0}^{n-d} jP(\bar{N} = j)$.

Define $E(\bar{N}) = \min_p E_p(\bar{N})$.

Theorem 9.3.4 $E(\bar{N}) = (n - d)[1 - d^d/(d + 1)^{d+1}]^t$.

Proof. Set $\frac{\partial E_p(\bar{N})}{\partial p} = (n - d)t[1 - p(1 - p)^d]^{t-1}[-(1 - p)^d + pd(1 - d)^{d-1}] = 0$. We obtain $(1 - p) = dp$, or $p = 1/(d + 1)$.   □

Corollary 9.3.5 *If $E(\bar{N}) \leq a$ is required, then*

$$t \geq \frac{\log a - \log n}{\log[1 - d^d/(d + 1)^{d+1}]} \xrightarrow{d \text{ large}} (d + 1)e(\log n - \log a).$$

Proof.

$$\log[1 - d^d/(d + 1)^d] \cong$$
$$-d^d/(d + 1)^{d+1} = -(1 - \frac{1}{d + 1})^d/(d + 1) \cong -e^{-1}/(d + 1).$$

□

It should be noted that all the above results do not take into consideration that a pool cannot be empty and should not be identical to another pool. Therefore the actual case should be slightly better than the results showed.

A design which misses a clone completely has no way to identify the nature of that clone. On the other hand, a design which contains a clone in every pool is also bad since if the clone is positive, then every pool would yield a positive response, thus withholding information on other clones. Stretching the reasoning a little bit, a clone (column) with either too small or too big a weight is not good. Setting conditions on the weight of a clone will increase the efficiency of the design, but will also harden the analysis since such conditions would almost certainly destroy the independence among pools. If the conditions are complicated, then the analysis could become impossible. Bruno *et al.* [4] introduced such a condition in its simplest type by fixing the weight of each clone at w, where w is an integer to be optimized later (note that independence among clones is preserved). They called it a *random k-set design* (they use the parameter k instead of w), which we will rename as a random weight-w design to differentiate from the random size-k design (each pool is a k-set) to be introduced later.

Bruno *et al.* and Balding *et al.* gave the following results concerning $P_w(\bar{N})$ and $E_w(\bar{N})$. They assume that the pools are independent to facilitate the analysis.

Lemma 9.3.6 *Let I be a given set of i pools. The probability that I is exactly the set of pools not containing any positive clone is*

$$W(i) = \sum_{h=i}^{t} (-1)^{h-i} \binom{t-i}{h-i} \left[\binom{t-h}{w} / \binom{t}{w} \right]^d.$$

Proof. The probability that h pools including I not containing any positive clone is $\binom{t-i}{h-i} [\binom{t-h}{w} / \binom{t}{w}]^d$, where $\binom{t-i}{h-i}$ is the number of ways of choosing the other $h - i$ pools, and $\binom{t-h}{w} / \binom{t}{w}$ is the probability that the h pools do not contain a specific positive clone. Lemma 9.3.6 follows from the inclusion-exclusion principle. $\square$

Again, we extend their result of $P_w(\bar{N} = 0)$ to $P_w(\bar{N} = j)$, using an argument similar to the proof of Lemma 9.3.1.

Lemma 9.3.7

$$P_w(\bar{N} = j) =$$

$$\sum_{i=0}^{t} \binom{t}{i} W(i) \binom{n-d}{j} \left[1 - \binom{t-i}{w} / \binom{t}{w} \right]^{n-d-j} \left[\binom{t-i}{w} / \binom{t}{w} \right]^j.$$

Corollary 9.3.8 $P_w(\bar{N} = 0) = \sum_{i=0}^{t} \binom{t}{i} W(i) \left[1 - \binom{t-i}{w} / \binom{t}{w} \right]^{n-d}.$

Lemma 9.3.9 $E_w(\bar{N}) = (n-d) \sum_{i=0}^{w} \binom{w}{i} \left[\binom{t-i}{w} / \binom{t}{w} \right]^d.$

Proof. Consider a negative clone which is represented by the w-subset W. The probability that a given positive clone does not appear in i given pools of W is $\binom{t-i}{w} / \binom{t}{w}$. Hence the probability that all d positive clones do not appear in i given pools of W is $[\binom{t-i}{w} / \binom{t}{w}]^d$. Using the inclusion-exclusion formula, the probability that there exists a pool containing C but not any positive clone is given by the sum term in Lemma 9.3.9. Since the above argument is true for any negative clone and expectation is a linear function, Lemma 9.3.9 follows.   □

An explicit expression for the optimal w which minimizes $E_w(\bar{N})$ is not known. Bruno *et al.* also compared the random weight-w design with the random design and found that the former is usually better.

Just like in the random design, identical w-sets randomly chosen should not be allowed, since the design would not be able to differentiate the clones they represent. This fact was ignored in the analysis for it is difficult to be dealt with. Recently, Hwang [8] studied this case and computed $P(\bar{N} = j)$, $E(\bar{N})$. With a similar reasoning, it would be desirable to forbid w-sets with heavy intersection. If the limit of intersections is set at v, then it becomes a random (v, w, t)-packing.

In a similar vein, a pool containing too few or too many clones also yields little information and hence is not efficient. Although an empty pool, which yields no information at all, is not counted as a pool, one would like to rule out more of the extreme cases to bring up efficiency. On the other hand, ruling out the extreme cases destroys the independence of the clones and makes the analysis more difficult. A compromise is to consider the simplest kind of dependence by fixing the weight of a pool at k, which is an integer to be determined later to maximize efficiency. Such a pool design will be called the *random size-k design*.

Lemma 9.3.10

$$P(\bar{N} = n - d) = [1 - \binom{n-d}{k}/\binom{n}{k}]^t.$$

$$P(\bar{N} = j) = \sum_{i=1}^{t} \binom{t}{i} \left[\binom{n-d}{k}/\binom{n}{k}\right]^i \left[1 - \binom{n-d}{k}/\binom{n}{k}\right]^{t-i}$$
$$\cdot \sum_{l=j}^{n-d} (-1)^{l-j} \binom{n-d}{l} \left[\binom{n-d-l}{k}/\binom{n-d}{k}\right]^i$$
$$for\ 0 \leq j < n - d.$$

Proof. Suppose the set of negative pools has cardinality i. If $i = 0$, then every pool contains a positive clone and no negative clone is identified. Thus $\bar{N} = n - d$. This implies that $j < n - d$ implies $i \geq 1$. In $P(\bar{N} = j)$, the term between the two sums is the probability that there exist exactly i negative pools, while the term after the second sum is the probability that exactly j negative clones are not contained in any of the negative pools, computed by the inclusion-exclusion principle.   □

Note that if $i \geq 1$, then at least the k clones in a negative pool are identified; thus $j \leq n - d - k$. This fact is reflected in Lemma 9.3.10 since $\binom{n-d-l}{k} = 0$ for $l > n - d - k$.

Theorem 9.3.11

$$E_k(\bar{N}) = (n-d)[1 - \binom{n-d-1}{k-1}/\binom{n}{k}]^t.$$

Proof. Given a negative clone C, the number of ways of choosing a pool T containing C but not any of the d positive clones is $\binom{n-d-1}{k-1}$, namely, besides C, the other $k-1$ members of T must be chosen from the $n-d-1$ other negative clones. Therefore the probability that there does not exist a pool containing C but no positive clones is given by the second factor of $E_k(\bar{N})$ in Theorem 9.3.11.

The k which minimizes $E_k(\bar{N})$ does not have an exact expression. If we choose k to be $n/(d+1)$ (assuming divisibility), then k equals the expected size of a random pool with optimal choice of p.

Again, the reader should be reminded of two facts true in practice but not reflected in the analysis.

1. An empty pool is not allowed.

2. Identical pools are not allowed since they are redundant.

The problem of generating random k-sets and random (v,k,t)-packing efficiently seems to need more attention.

Finally, we discuss the problem of computing $E_x(\bar{P})$ for $x \in \{p, w, k\}$. The reason that we didn't do it separately for p, w, k is that there is a uniform treatment. Namely, there is a relation between $E_x(\bar{N})$ and $E_x(\bar{P})$ for all x. To show such a relation, we need to denote $E_x(P)$ by $E_x^d(P)$.

Theorem 9.3.12

$$\frac{E_x^d(\bar{P})}{d} = \sum_{j=0}^{n-d} P(\bar{N}=j)E_x^{d-1+j}(\bar{N})/(n-d+1-j) \quad \text{for all } x \in \{p, w, k\}.$$

Proof. Given that $\bar{N}=j$, then a positive clone C is unresolved if and only if there does not exist a pool which contains C but no other positive clones or unresolved negatives. This is the same condition for a negative clone to be unresolved except that only the nonexistence of positive clones is required. Therefore the former probability can be obtained from the latter by replacing d, the number of positives, with $d-1+j$, the number of other positives and unresolved negatives. Since the selection is on a per clone basis, we have to divide $E_x^{d-1+j}(\bar{N})$ by $d-1+j$ and to multiply by d to obtain $E_x(\bar{P})$. $\square$

One may also seek to compute $E_x(\bar{N}+\bar{P})$, the expected number of unresolved clones. This is easily done since

$$E_x(\bar{N}+\bar{P}) = E_x(\bar{N}) + E_x(\bar{P}).$$

Furthermore, since both $E_x^d(\bar{P})$ and $E_x^d(\bar{N}+\bar{P})$ can be expressed as linear functions of $E_x^j(\bar{N})$, $j=d-1,...,n-1$, finding the minimum of $E_x^d(\bar{P})$ and $E_x^d(\bar{N}+\bar{P})$ are reduced to finding the minimums of those linear functions.

9.4   Some Additional Problems

In this section we will let p denote the number of pools. Let $N_d(p, h)$ denote the maximum number of clones which can be screened given at most d pools and h confirmatory tests, and let $\bar{N}_d(p, h)$ denote the same except h is the expected number of confirmatory tests. Define

$$f(d, t) = \limsup_{p \to \infty} \frac{\log N_d(p, h)}{p}, \, \bar{f}(d, t) = \limsup_{p \to \infty} \frac{\log \bar{N}_d(p, h)}{p}.$$

Farach *et al.* [5] proved the surprising result.

Theorem 9.4.1 $\bar{f}(d, h)$ *is independent of h.*

They also give lower and upper bounds for $\bar{f}(d, h)$, and stated that the bounds of $\bar{f}(d, 1)$ differ only by constants.

Theorem 9.4.2 $\frac{\ln 2}{d}(1 + o(1)) \leq \bar{f}(d, 1) \leq \frac{1}{d}(1 + o(1))$.

Suppose that the n clones are arranged into a line and the positive set is an interval. Farach *et al.* [5] gave

Theorem 9.4.3 $t(n) \sim 2 \log n$ *for sequential algorithms.*

Proof. There are $\binom{n}{2}$ intervals. Hence $2 \log n$ is about the information lower bound of $t(n)$. On the other hand, a halving procedure can be implemented as a line algorithm, which identifies the first positive in $\log n$ probings. By working on the line and then its reverse line, we can identify the two endpoints of the interval (thus identifying the interval) in $2 \log n$ probings.   □

Theorem 9.4.4 $t(n) = n$ *for nonadaptive algorithms.*

Proof. Clearly, n pools suffices since individual testing takes n pools. To prove necessity, assume that the interval starts at i. To identify that i, not $i - 1$, is the starting point, it is necessary to have a pool in which i is the smallest index. Since i can assume any value from 1 to n, n pools are needed.   □

Farach *et al.* also consider an algorithm between sequential and nonadaptive.

Theorem 9.4.5 *Consider an s-stage algorithm. Then*

$$p \leq 2^s - 1 + n, \quad t \leq 4s - 5 + 2\lceil n/2^{s-1} \rceil.$$

Proof. Let T be an algorithm tree of depth $s - 1$. Let the root be at level 0. Then each subsequent level corresponds to a stage. Each node v is associated with an interval $I(v)$, while $I(root) = (1, \cdots, n)$. Note that if u and w are the two children of node v, then $I(u) + I(w) = I(v)$. Let $v_1, \cdots, v_{2^l}$ denote the 2^l nodes in level l. Then $I(v_i), I(v_{i+1}), \cdots, I(v_j)$ for any $1 \le i \le j \le 2^l$ is an interval.

At each level l, there exist two indices i and j (equality is allowed) such that $I(v_1), \cdots, I(v_{i-1}), I(v_{i+1}), \cdots, I(v_{2^l})$ are negative, and $I(v_i), I(v_{i+1}), \cdots, I(v_j)$ are positive. Namely, the two endpoints of the interval reside in $I(v_i)$ and $I(v_j)$, respectively. Since it suffices to identify the two endpoints of the interval, only the children of v_i and v_j need to be probed at the next level. Therefore at most four probings are required at each level except only one is needed at level 0 and two at level 1. Thus T contains at most $3 + 4(s - 2)$ probings. At stage s, individual probings are conducted for the two nodes containing the two endpoints. Hence

$$t \le 3 + 4(s - 2) + 2\lceil \frac{n}{2^{s-1}} \rceil.$$

Since T has $2^s - 1$ nodes and the s-stage has n probes since each clone can be an endpoint, we have

$$p \le 2^s - 1 + n.$$

□

The knowledge of d does not seem to be helpful for the arguments given in Theorems 9.4.3 and 9.4.5. But it should improve the nonadaptive case.

Farach *et al.* also considered a model with three kinds of clones, positives, negatives and inhibitors, where the presence of an inhibitor in a pool would dictate the outcome to be negative, regardless of whether the pool contains positive clones. There are two different problems. In the *positive classification problem*, only the positives need to be identified; in the *classification problem*, every clone needs to be identified.

Lemma 9.4.6 *Let A be an algorithm for the positive classification problem in which a positive clone exists. Then there exists a sequential algorithm A' for the classification problem which requires at most twice as many probings as A.*

Proof. At the end of A, the set U of unidentified clones consists of negatives or inhibitors. Delete all pools with positive outcomes, and delete all identified clones from pools with negative outcomes. Consider $u \in U$. Suppose u appears in pool j with clone v_j. Then changing u to a positive and v_j to an inhibitor would preserve the outcomes of all probings, contradicting the fact that A has identified all positives. Therefore there exists a pool in which u is the only clone. Let c be a positive clone (identified). Probe $c \cup u$ to identify u. Thus the number of additional probings does not exceed $|U|$, while the number of probings in A is at least $|U|$ since we have shown each $u \in U$ must have been probed without the presence of any other clone in U. □

The condition "a positive clone exists" was not in the original statement of the lemma but is necessary for otherwise A could be the individual testing algorithm, but there is no way to differentiate negatives from inhibitors in A'.

Let $n = p + r + m$, where p, r, n are the numbers of positives, inhibitors and negatives.

Theorem 9.4.7 *The positive classification problem requires* $\Omega[\log \binom{n}{p}\binom{n-p}{r}]$ *probings.*

Proof. $\log \binom{n}{p}\binom{n-p}{r}$ is the information lower bound for the classification problem. Theorem 9.4.7 now follows from Lemma 9.4.6. $\qquad\square$

Corollary 9.4.8 *For $p + r << n$, the positive classification problem requires $\Omega((p + r)\log n)$ probings.*

Boris and Vaccaro [3] improved the lower bound of Theorem 9.4.7 by extending the concept of an r-cover-free family (which is equivalent to an r-disjunct matrix) to a (p, r)-*cover-free family*, which is a binary matrix with no union of p columns being a subset of the union of any other r columns. Clearly, a $(1, r)$-cover is an r-cover. Let $t(n, p, r)$ denote the smallest t such that a $t \times n$ (p, r)-cover exists. Boris and Vaccaro gave a lower bound of $t(n, p, r)$ based on a known lower bound of $t(n, 1, r)$ obtained in Chapter 8.

Lemma 9.4.9 *Suppose $n - p\lfloor n/p \rfloor = q$ and $n \geq p+q$. Define $Q = \lfloor (r-q)/p \rfloor$. Then*

$$t(n, p, r) \geq \frac{Q^2}{\alpha_Q \log Q} \cdot \log\lfloor n/p \rfloor.$$

Proof. Let M be a (p, r)-cover-free family. Partition the n columns of M into $\lfloor n/p \rfloor$ groups such that each group, except possibly one, has p columns. Let g_i denote the union of the columns in group i. The $(g_1, \cdots, g_{\lfloor n/p \rfloor})$ must be a Q-cover-free family, or a Q-disjunct matrix. By Theorem 8.3.5,

$$t(Q, \lfloor n/p \rfloor) = \frac{Q^2}{\alpha_Q \log Q} \cdot \log\lfloor n/p \rfloor.$$

Lemma 9.4.9 follows immediately. $\qquad\square$

In the original text of [3], $\lfloor (r - q)/p \rfloor$ was simply written as $\lfloor r/p \rfloor$. Then the argument does not follow. Let M be a $(2,4)$-cover-free family with seven columns. Then the partition is into (2 columns, 2 columns, 3 columns). Note that $\lfloor r/p \rfloor = 2$. But it is possible that (g_1, g_2, g_3) is not 2-disjunct since g_1 is contained in $g_2 \cup g_3$, a union of five columns.

Corollary 9.4.10 *An $(n, \bar{p}, \bar{r})$ positive classification problem, $r \geq p + q$, requires*

$$\Omega \left(\frac{Q^2}{\alpha_Q \log Q} \cdot \log \lfloor n/p \rfloor \right)$$

probings.

Proof. For $t < \frac{Q^2}{\alpha_Q \log Q} \cdot \log \lfloor n/p \rfloor$, there exists a set of p columns whose union is covered by a set of r other columns. Let this set of p columns be the set of inhibitors. Then the probing outcomes are all negative. Thus we cannot tell whether there exists any positive clones. $\qquad \square$

Even when p and r are constants, not bounds, Boris and Vaccaro showed that there exist two sets of p columns covered by some r-unions. Hence

Theorem 9.4.11 *An (n, p, r) positive classification problem requires $\Omega \left(\frac{Q^2}{\alpha_Q \log Q} \cdot \log \lfloor n/p \rfloor \right)$ probings.*

Note that the bound of Theorem 9.4.11 is better than the bound of Corollary 9.4.8 whenever

$$\frac{Q^2}{\log Q} > p + r,$$

or $r = \Omega(p^2 \log p)$.

Knil *et al.* gave a probabilistic algorithm for the positive classification problem.

Theorem 9.4.12 *The (n, p, r) positive classification problem can be solved in $O((p + r) \log n)$ probings, assuming $p + r << n$ and $1 \leq p$.*

Proof. The problem hinges at finding a set S containing some positives but no inhibitor. By making T a constant part of each probing, all inhibitors can be identified by using regular group testing (in which the inhibitors play the role of "defectives" and both positives and negatives play the role of "good items". Remove the inhibitors and use regular group testing to separate the positives from the negatives.

Let P and R denote the sets of positives and inhibitors, respectively. For $j \in P$, define $D = \prod_{i \in R} (j - i)$ which is nonzero. Let q be a prime such that $D \not\equiv 0 \pmod{q}$. Consider the pools $T_i = \{ x \in \{ 1, \cdots, n \} \mid x \equiv i \pmod{q} \}$, $i = 0, 1, \cdots, q - 1$. Then the pool containing j contains no inhibitor and hence its outcome is positive. j can then be identified using binary splitting in another $\log(r/q)$ probings, with a total of $q + \log(r/q)$ probings. The problem is then reduced to finding q. A well-known fact from number theory states that for $n \geq 17$, the product of all primes less than or equal to k is greater than 2^k. Let Q, $|Q| = \pi(\log D)$, be the set of all primes q less than or equal to $\log D$. Then $\prod_{q \in Q} q > D$, implying that the product of any $\pi(\log D)$ primes is greater than D, or $D \equiv 0 \pmod{q}$ can hold for fewer than $\pi(\log D)$ primes.

Another fact from number theory states that there are at least $2\pi(\log D)$ primes less than or equal to $4\log D$. Hence a random prime q from this set of $2\pi(\log D)$ primes satisfies $D \not\equiv 0 \pmod{q}$ with probability at least $1/2$. Thus such a q is expected to be found in two trials. Since $D \le n^r$, $\log D \le r\log n$. So each trial takes $O(r\log n)$ time.

By our results in Chapter 2, identifying the inhibitors takes $O(r\log n)$ time and separating the positives from the negatives takes $O(p\log n)$ time. Therefore $O((r + p)\log n)$ time suffices. □

Boris and Vaccaro gave a deterministic algorithm.

Theorem 9.4.13 *The positive classification problem can be solved in $O(r^2\log n + p\log(n/p))$ probings.*

Proof. By Theorem 8.4.6 we can construct a $t \times n$ $(1,r)$-cover-free family, where $t = O(r^2\log n)$, to identify one positive clone. Using this positive clone we can find all inhibitors in $r\log(n/r)$ probings. Deleting all inhibitors, we can find all positive clones in $p\log(n/p)$ probings. □

References

[1] D.J. Balding, W.J. Bruno, E. Knill and D.C. Torney, A comparative survey of nonadaptive probing designs, in *Genetic Mapping and DNA Sequencing, IMA Vol. in Mathematics and Its Applications*, Springer-Verlag, 133-154, 1996.

[2] E. Barillot, B. Lacroix and D. Cohen, Theoretical analysis of library screening using an n-dimensional pooling strategy, *Nucl. Acids Res.* 19 (1991) 6241-6247.

[3] A.D. Boris and U. Vaccaro, Improved algorithms for group testing with inhibitors, *Inform. Proc. Lett.* 67 (1998) 57-64.

[4] W.J. Bruno, E. Knill, D.J. Balding, W.J. Bruno, N.A. Doggett, W.W. Sawhill, R.L. Staltings, C.C. Whittaker and D.C. Torney, Efficient probing designs for library screening, *Genomics* 26 (1995) 21-30.

[5] M. Farach, S. Kannen, E. Knill and S. Muthukrishnan, Group testing problems in experimental molecular biology, in B. Carpentieri, A. DeSantis, J. Storer, U. Vaccaro (Eds.), *Proc. Compression and Complexity of Sequences*, IEEE Computer Soc., 357-367, 1997.

[6] E.D. Green and M.V. Olson, Systematic screening of yeast artificial-chnomosome libraries by use of the polymerase chain reaction, *Proc. Nat. Acad. Sci. USA* 87 (1990) 1213-1217.

[7] C.C. Ho and F.K. Hwang, A class of DNA graphs, preprint, 1999.

[8] F.K. Hwang, Random k-set pool designs with distinct columns, preprint, 1999.

[9] F.K. Hwang, An isomorphic factorization of the complete graph, *J. Graph Theory* 19 (1995) 333-337.

[10] D. Raghavarao, *Constructive and Combinatorial Problems in Designs of Experiments*, Wiley, New York, 1971.

[11] M.S. Waterman, *Introduction to Computational Biology*, Chapman and Hall, 1995.

Part III
Extended Group Testing Models

10
Multiaccess Channels and Extensions

Consider a communication network where many users share a single multiaccess channel. A user with a message to be transmitted is called an *active user*. For convenience, assume that each message is of unit length and can be transmitted in one time slot. The transmission is done by broadcasting over the channel which every user, active or not, can receive. However, if at any given time slot more than one active user broadcasts, then the messages conflict with each other and are reduced to noise. The problem is to devise an algorithm which schedules the transmissions of active users into different time slots so that the transmissions can be *successful*.

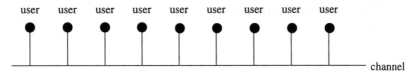

Figure 10.1: A multiaccess channel.

The algorithms to be considered in this chapter do the scheduling in epochs. At the start of an epoch, the users are classified either as active or inactive according as whether they have messages at that particular moment. An inactive user remains labeled as inactive even though a message is generated during the epoch. An epoch ends when all active users have transmitted successfully in different time slots, and then the next epoch starts.

When the set of active users is known, they can then be scheduled to transmit in successive time slots in some order and no conflict can occur. But active users are usually unknown at the beginning of an epoch. One simple protocol, called TDM (*time-division-multiplexing*), is to assign each user a time slot in which the user can transmit if active. When there are n users, n time slots will be needed. This is very inefficient since the number of active users is typically small (or the sharing of a multiaccess channel would not be practical). Hayes [9] proposed a bit reservation algorithm which first identifies all active users using a group query; and then schedules the known active users to transmit in order. In a bit reservation algorithm a set of

197

users is queried and the active users among them are requested to transmit a bit. When the channel is quiet after the query, the queried set cannot contain an active user. If the channel is not quiet, then the queried set is known to contain active users, but not how many or whom. The feedback is identical to the feedback of group testing. Usually the number of active users in an epoch, or an upper bound of it can be estimated from the length of the previous epoch (since the active users were generated during that epoch). Then a (d, n) or $(\bar{d}, n)$ algorithm can serve as a bit reservation protocol.

Capetanakis [4], also Tsybakov and Mikhailov [13], proposed a direct transmission algorithm which also queries sets of users, but requests active users among the queried set to transmit. If the channel is quiet in the next time slot, the queried set will contain no active user. If the channel broadcasts a message, the queried set will contain exactly one active user who has transmitted successfully. If the channel is noisy, then the queried set contains at least two active users who have transmitted, but their messages collide, thus fail to get through. Further queries are needed to separate the transmissions of these active users. Note that the type of feedback of a query is ternary: $0, 1, 2^+$, where 2^+ means at least 2. The reader should be warned that the bulk of literature on multiaccess channels employs probabilistic models and will not be covered in this volume.

10.1   Multiaccess Channels

Capetanakis [4, 5] (also see Tsybakov and Mikhailov [13]), gave the following tree algorithm C for $n = 2^k$ users:

Let T_n denote a balanced binary tree with n leaves. Label each leaf by a distinct user, and label each internal node u by the set of users which label the descendants of u. Thus the root of T_n is labeled by the whole set of n users. Starting from the root, using either a breadth-first or a depth-first approach to visit the nodes and query the set of users labeling them, except that if the feedback of a query is 0 or 1, then all descendants of the node will not be visited.

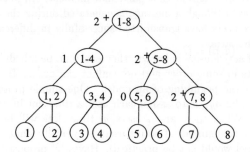

Figure 10.2: T_8 with three active users: 2, 7, 8.

Clearly, after all the nodes are visited, all active users have successfully transmitted. The number of queries is just the number of nodes visited. Let $C(d \mid n)$ denote the number of queries required by algorithm C when d of the n users are active (d is unknown). Then

$$C(1 \mid 2^k) = 1,$$
$$C(d \mid 2^k) = 1 + \max_{0 \le i \le \lfloor \frac{d}{2} \rfloor} \{C(i \mid 2^{k-1}) + C(d-i \mid 2^{k-1})\} \quad \text{for } d \ge 2 .$$

It is easily solved that

Theorem 10.1.1 $C(d \mid 2^k) = 2\lfloor \frac{d}{2} \rfloor k - 2\lfloor \frac{d}{2} \rfloor (D-1) + 2^D - 1$, *where* $D = \lceil \log d \rceil$ *for* $d \ge 2$.

Namely, the worst case occurs when active users label the leaves in pairs, but are otherwise scattered evenly over the tree.

Corollary 10.1.2 $C(d \mid n) \xrightarrow[n \to \infty]{} d \log n$ *for every fixed d.*

Capetanakis also proposed a variant tree algorithm in which the visit starts at nodes at level l (the root is at level 1). Let $C_l(d \mid n)$ denote the corresponding number of queries. Since the worst-case distribution of active users is the same as before

$$C_l(d \mid n) = C(d \mid n) - (2^{l-1} - 1) + \sum_{i=\lceil \log d \rceil + 1}^{l} (2^{i-1} - 2\lfloor \frac{d}{2} \rfloor)$$
$$= C(d \mid n) - 2^{\lceil \log d \rceil} - 2\lfloor \frac{d}{2} \rfloor (l - \lceil \log d \rceil) + 2^{l-1} + 1 ,$$

where $2^{l-1} - 1$ is the number of nodes skipped in C_l, and $2^{i-1} - 2\lfloor \frac{d}{2} \rfloor$ is the number of nodes at level i skipped in C.

If d is known, then l can be optimally chosen to be approximately $1 + \log(d/\ln 2)$ with

Corollary 10.1.3 $C(d,n) \cong C(d \mid n) - d(2 - \log \ln 2 - 1/\ln 2) + 1.$

Several improvements over the tree algorithm have been suggested. Massey [11] pointed out that if node u has two child-nodes x and y such that the feedback of querying u and x are 2^+ and 0 respectively, then one can skip the visit to y and go directly to the child-nodes of y, since the feedback of querying y can be predicted to be 2^+.

There is also no reason to restrict the size of queried sets to powers of two. Suppose that the n users are divided into g groups of n/g users each. Apply the tree algorithm on each group. Assume that group i contains d_i active users. The total number of queries is at most

$$g + \sum_{i=1}^{g} d_i \log(n/g) = g + d \log(n/g) .$$

If g is selected to be approximately $\log n$, then the number of queries is about $(d + 1) \log n - d \log \log n$. If d is known, g can be optimally selected to be approximately $d/\ln 2$. Then the number of queries is about $d \log n - d \log \frac{d \log e}{e}$.

When d is known, it should be better to let the query size vary as a function of the updated values of d and n. Define a nested algorithm as one for which whenever a set of users is known to contain active users, then subsequent queries must be directed to this set until the implied number of active users have successfully transmitted from this set. Let $H(d, n)$ denote the maximum number of queries required under a minimax nested algorithm given the (d, n) sample space. Let $G(m; d, n)$ $(F(m; d, n))$ denote the number of queries required under a minimax nested algorithm given the (d, n) sample space and a subset of m users known to contain at least two (one) active users. Then the recurrence equations are:

$$H(d, n) = 1 + \min_{1 \le k < n} \{\max\{H(d, n - k), \ H(d - 1, n - k), G(k : d, n)\}\} ,$$

$$G(m; d, n) = 1 + \min_{1 \le k < m} \{\max\{G(m - k; d, n - k), F(m - k; d - 1, n - k), G(k; d, n)\}\} ,$$

$$F(m; d, n) = 1 + \min_{1 \le k < m} \{\max\{F(m - k; d, n - k), H(d - 1, n - k), G(k; d, n)\}\} ,$$

where $H(0, n) = 0$, $H(1, n) = 1$, $G(2; d, n) = 2 + H(d - 2, n - 2)$ and $F(1; d, n) = 1 + H(d - 1, n - 1)$.

Let $Q(d, n)$ denote the number of queries required given a (d, n) sample space. Greenberg and Winograd [8] proved a lower bound of $Q(d, n)$ which is asymptotically close to the upper bounds discussed earlier. They first proved two looser lower bounds whose combination yields the tighter lower bound desired.

Lemma 10.1.4 $Q(d, n) \ge d + \log(n/d)$ *for* $d \ge 2$.

Proof. An oracle argument is used. Let A_0 denote the original set of active users and let A_t denote the updated set of active users after the tth query Q_t.

Given any sequence of queries $Q_1, \cdots, Q_t$, define $S_1 = \{1, \cdots, n\}$ and

$$S_{t+1} = \begin{cases} S_t \cap Q_t & \text{if } |S_t \cap Q_t| \ge |S_t|/2 \\ \\ S_t - Q_t & \text{otherwise .} \end{cases}$$

Then $|S_{t+1}| \ge |S_t|/2 \ge n/2^t$. It follows that $|S_{t+1}| \ge d$ as long as $t \le \log(n/d)$. The oracle selects A_0 as a subset of S_{t+1}; thus $A_{t+1} = A_0$. Since $|A_0| = d$, at least d queries are needed to allow the active users in A_0 to transmit. Hence $Q(d, n) \ge d + \log(n/d)$. $\qquad \square$

Lemma 10.1.5 $Q(d, n) \geq (L/\log L)(\log \lfloor n/L \rfloor) - L$ for $8 \leq d \leq \sqrt{2n}$, where $L = \lfloor d/2 \rfloor$ (hence $4 \leq L \leq n/L$).

Proof. Consider a new problem of having L sets $N_0(1), \cdots, N_0(L)$, of $\lfloor n/L \rfloor$ users each, where each set contains exactly two active users. Let $Q(L)$ denote the number of queries required for this new problem. Then

$$Q(L) \leq Q(d, n) .$$

Define the cost of $N_t(i)$ by $\log |N_t(i)|$. Let $N_t(i)$ denote the updated set of $N_0(i)$ still containing exactly two active users after t queries. Then the cost at step t is

$$\sum_{i=1}^{L} \log |N_t(i)|.$$

The following oracle scheme is used such that the cost reduced at each query is upper bounded.

(i) Suppose that for some j, $| N_t(j) | > L$ and $| N_t(j) \cap Q_t | \geq | N_t(j) | /L$. Then select one such j and set

$$\begin{aligned} N_{t+1}(j) &= N_t(j) \cap Q_t , \\ N_{t+1}(i) &= N_t(i) \quad \text{for all } i \neq j . \end{aligned}$$

(ii) Otherwise, for every i with $| N_t(i) | > L$, set

$$N_{t+1}(i) = N_t(i) - Q_t .$$

For every i with $| N_t(i) | \leq L$, set

$$N_{t+1}(i) = \text{any two users of } N_t(i) .$$

Let L_t denote the number of $N_t(i)$ such that $| N_t(i) | \leq L$. The cost reduced at query t is

$$\begin{aligned} E(t) &= \sum_{i=1}^{L} \log |N_t(i)| - \sum_{i=1}^{L} \log |N_{t+1}(i)| \\ &\leq \begin{cases} \log L + L_t \log L & \text{in case (i)} \\ (L - L_t) \log \frac{L}{L-1} + L_t \log L & \text{in case (ii)} . \end{cases} \end{aligned}$$

Since for each i, $|N_t(i)|$ is reduced to 2 for only one t, the total cost reduced in q queries is chosen as the smallest integer satisfying the inequalities.

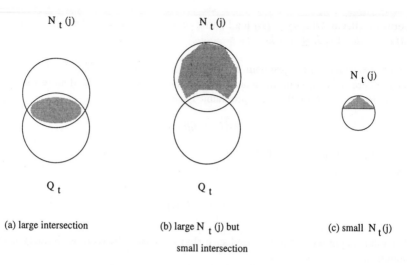

Figure 10.3: $N_{t+1}(j)$ (shaded area).

The total cost reduced in q queries is

$$
\sum_{t=0}^{q-1} E(t) \;<\; q \max\left\{\log L,\; L\log\frac{L}{L-1}\right\} + L\log L
$$
$$
= \; q\log L + L\log L \quad \text{for } L \geq 4 \,.
$$

The problem is unsolved whenever this number does not exceed the initial cost, i.e.,

$$
\sum_{i=1}^{L} \log |N_0(i)| = L\log\lfloor n/L\rfloor \,.
$$

Hence

$$
Q(d,n) \geq \frac{L\{\log\lfloor n/L\rfloor - L\log L\}}{\log L} \,.
$$

$\square$

Theorem 10.1.6 $Q(d,n) = \Omega(d\log n/\log d)$.

Proof. For $d < 8$ or $d > \sqrt{2n}$, use Lemma 10.1.4. For $8 \leq d \leq \sqrt{2n}$, use Lemma 10.1.5. $\square$

10.2 Nonadaptive Algorithms

A nonadaptive algorithm for the multiaccess channel problem can also be represented by a $0-1$ matrix M with columns as users, rows as queries and $M_{ij} = 1$ implying that query i contains user j. Since an active user can transmit successfully in a query if and only if no other active user is also transmitting, M must have the property that for any sample from the given sample space and a given column in that sample, there exists a row with 1 in the given column and 0 in all other columns in that sample. When the sample space is $S(d, n)$ or $S(\bar{d}, n)$, by Lemma 4.3.8, this property is satisfied if and only if M is $(d - 1)$-disjunct. Therefore all results on d-disjunct matrices apply here.

However, there is a weaker sense of nonadaptive algorithms for the multiaccess channel problem with less stringent requirements. This occurs when all queries are specified simultaneously but carried out one by one in the order of the row index. Any active user who has already transmitted successfully will not transmit in any subsequent query even though its column entry is 1. Translating this property to the matrix M, then for every sample s there exists a permutation of the columns in s such that there exists $\mid s \mid$ rows which form an $\mid s \mid \times \mid s \mid$ lower triangular submatrix with the columns in s, i.e., the submatrix has 1's in the diagonal but only 0's above the diagonal. Busschbach [3] gave an upper bound using a random code construction similar to the one given in Theorem 4.3.9 except the coefficient 3 is replaced by $\log 3$.

Komlos and Greenberg [10] used a probability argument to derive a better upper bound for nonadaptive algorithms. For convenience, assume d divides n. Let S_k denote the set of all k-subsets of the set of n users. Let $Q_1, \cdots, Q_q$ denote a list of queries which are distinct but random members of $S_{n/d}$. Let A_j denote an arbitrary member of S_d. A query Q_i is said to *isolate* a user in A_j if $\mid Q_i \cap A_j \mid = 1$.

Lemma 10.2.1 *For every i, $1 \leq i \leq d$, with probability at least $(4e)^{-1}$, there is a user x in A_j isolated by Q_i, but not by any Q_k for $1 \leq k < i$.*

Proof.

$$\text{Prob} \ (Q_i \text{ isolates } x \text{ and } Q_k \text{ not isolates } x \text{ for } 1 \leq k < i)$$

$$= \ \text{Prob} \ (Q_i \text{ isolates } x) \ \text{Prob} \ (Q_k \text{ not isolates } x \text{ for } 1 \leq k < i).$$

Since the expected value of $\mid Q_i \cap A_j \mid$ is one,

$$\text{Prob} \ (\mid Q_i \cap A_j \mid \geq z) \leq 1/z \ .$$

Furthermore, it is easily verified that

$$\text{Prob} \ (\mid Q_i \cap A_j \mid = 1) \geq \text{Prob} \ (\mid Q_i \cap A_j \mid = 0).$$

Hence

$$\begin{aligned} \text{Prob} \ (\mid Q_i \cap A_j \mid = 1) &\geq \ [1 - \text{Prob} \ (\mid Q_i \cap A_j \mid \geq 2)]/2 \\ &\geq \ (1 - 1/2)/2 \ = \ 1/4 \ . \end{aligned}$$

Prob $(Q_j$ not isolates x for $1 \leq j < i)$

$$\geq \text{Prob}\left(x \notin \bigcup_{k=1}^{i-1} Q_k\right)$$

$$= \left(\binom{n-1}{n/d} \Big/ \binom{n}{n/d}\right)^{i-1} = \left(\frac{n-n/d}{n}\right)^{i-1} = \left(1-\frac{1}{d}\right)^{i-1}$$

$$\geq \left(1-\frac{1}{d}\right)^{d-1} > e^{-1} .$$

□

Lemma 10.2.2 *A random query list $Q_1, \cdots, Q_d$ isolates at least $d/(4e)^2$ users in A_j with probability at least $1 - e^{-bd}$ for any $A_j \in S_d$, where $b = (4e)^{-2}\left[1-(4e)^{-1}\right]/2$.*

Proof. Let $B(m, M, p)$ denote the probability of m or more successes in M independent trials, each of which succeeds with probability p. Angluin and Valiant [1] proved that

$$B((1+\beta)Mp, M, p) \leq e^{-\beta^2 Mp/2} .$$

Call Q_i a failure if it isolates a user in A_j not isolated by any Q_k, $k < i$; call Q_i a success otherwise. Then the probability of a success is less than $1 - (4e)^{-1}$ for every Q_i. Thus the probability of getting $[1-(4e)^{-2}]d$ successes or more in the random list of queries $Q_1, \ldots, Q_d$ is less than

$$B([1+(4e)^{-1}]d[1-(4e)^{-1}], d, 1-(4e)^{-1}) \leq e^{-bd} .$$

□

Lemma 10.2.3 *For $d \geq 2$ there exists a list of queries of length $O(d\log(n/d))$ such that it isolates at least $d/(4e)^2$ users in A_j for any $A_j \in S_d$.*

Proof. Consider a random list Q of t queries $Q_1, \cdots, Q_t$ where $t = md$. From Lemma 10.2.2 each disjoint sublist of d queries fails to isolate $1/(4e)^2$ users in a given A_j with probability at most e^{-bd}. Hence the probability for the t queries to fail is at most e^{-mbd}. Setting

$$m = \left\lceil \frac{ln\binom{n}{d}}{bd} \right\rceil + 1,$$

then $e^{-mbd} < 1/\binom{n}{d}$.

For a given $A_j \in S_d$, define random variables

$$X_j(Q) = \begin{cases} 0 & \text{if } Q_1, \cdots, Q_t \text{ isolates at least } d/(4e)^2 \text{ users in } A_j \\ 1 & \text{otherwise} . \end{cases}$$

Let

$$X(Q) = \sum_{A_j \in S_d} X_j(Q) \ .$$

Treating $Q_1, \cdots, Q_t$ as a random list of t queries,

$$E(X) = \sum_{A_j \in S_d} E(X_j) < \sum_{A_j \in S_d} \frac{1}{\binom{n}{d}} = 1 \ .$$

Therefore, there must exist a list Q' such that $X(Q') = 0$, or equivalently, Q' isolates at least $d/(4e)^2$ users in every $A_j \in S_d$. It is easily verified that $t = md = O(d \log(n/d))$. □

Theorem 10.2.4 For $d \geq 2$, there exists a list of queries of length $O(d \log(n/d))$ which isolates all users in A_j for every $A_j \in S_d$.

Proof. Define $c = 1/(4e)^2$. Lemma 10.2.3 guarantees the existence of lists L_i, $i = 0, 1, \ldots, p-1$, each of length $O(d_i \log(n/d_i))$ which isolates at least $cd_i \equiv c(1-c)^i d$ users in every $A_j \in S_{d_i}$. Note that the length of the concatenation $L_0, L_1, \cdots, L_{i-1}$ is

$$\sum_{j=0}^{i-1} d(1-c)^j \log \left(\frac{n}{d(1-c)^j} \right) \geq d \cdot \frac{1-(1-c)^i}{c} \log \frac{n}{d[1-(1-c)^i]/c},$$

since

$$\sum_{j=0}^{i-1} (1-c)^j = \frac{1-(1-c)^i}{c}.$$

By Lemma 10.2.3, $L_0, \ldots, L_{i-1}$ fail to isolate at most

$$d - d[1 - (1-c)^i] = (1-c)^i d$$

users. Set p to be

$$\left\lceil \frac{\log d}{-\log(1-c)} \right\rceil + 1 \ ,$$

such that $(1-c)^p d < 1$, then all users are identified. The length of the concatenated list is easily verified to be $O(d \log(n/d))$. □

10.3   Two Variations

Berger, Mehravari, Towsley and Wolf [2] introduced two variations to the multiaccess channel problem by considering two ways to combine the ternary feedbacks of the latter to binary feedbacks (a third way leads to the group testing model). Although their discussion was in the context of PGT, the essence of their results can be easily transplanted to CGT.

Since an active user needs more than identification, i.e., the message must be transmitted successfully, the term *satisfied* is introduced to denote the latter state. For an inactive user, satisfaction simply means identification. In the *conflict/no conflict* model, the feedbacks of 0 and 1 are combined into a "no conflict" feedback. Note that all users in a queried set with a no-conflict feedback are satisfied; so they are not affected by the suppression of information. There are two possible consequences for unsatisfied users:

1. If a subset G' of a conflict set G is queried with a no-conflict feedback, then it is not known whether $G\backslash G'$ contains at least 1 or 2 active user.

2. The number of satisfied active users is no longer known. So one cannot deduce that all unsatisfied users are inactive from the knowledge that d active users have been satisfied.

Berger *et al.* suggested ways to test $G\backslash G'$ in the situation described in the first case. Then one can simulate an algorithm for the multiaccess channel for the current model. The second case can be taken care of by testing the set of unidentified items whenever the situation is unclear.

In the *success/failure* model, the feedbacks 0 and 2^+ are combined into a "failure" feedback. This may occur when the channel has another source of noise indistinguishable from the conflict noise. Berger *et al.* proposed an algorithm B for PGT which, whenever a failure set is identified, queries all users in that set individually. Adapting it to $S(d,n)$ and let $Q_B(d,n)$ denote the maximum number of queries required by B. Then

$$Q_B(0,n) = 0, \ Q_B(1,n) = 1, \ Q_B(n,n) = n$$

and for $n > d \geq 2$

$$Q_B(d,n) = 1 + \min_{1\leq k\leq n-d+1} \max\{Q_B(d-1,n-k),$$
$$k-1+Q_B(d,n-k), \ k+\max_{2\leq i\leq k} Q_B(d-i,n-k)\}.$$

Note that if the failure set contains no active user, then one can deduce this fact after querying the first $k-1$ users individually. This explains the term $k-1$ added to $Q_B(d,n-k)$. Since it is easily verified by induction that

$$Q_B(d,n) \geq Q_B(d-1,n) ,$$

the above recursive equation can be reduced to

$$Q_B(d,n) = 1 + \min_{1\leq k\leq n-d+1} \max\{k-1+Q_B(d,n-k), k+Q_B(d-2,n-k)\} .$$

For $d=2$ it follows

$$Q_B(2,n) = \min_{1\leq k\leq n-1}\{k+Q_B(2,n-k)\} .$$

Using the initial condition $Q_B(2,2) = 2$, it is easily verified by induction that

$$Q_B(2,n) = n .$$

Since $Q_B(d,n)$ is clearly nondecreasing in d,

$$Q_B(d,n) = n \text{ for } d \geq 2 ,$$

i.e., Algorithm B is simply the individual testing algorithm.

Are there better algorithms than individual testing for $d \geq 2$? The answer is yes, and surprisingly we already have it. Namely, all the nonadaptive algorithms reported in Sec. 5.2, be they regular or weak-sense, apply to the success/failure model. This is because the matrices in these algorithms have the property that for any sample of d columns including a designated one, there exists a row with 1 in the designated column and 0s in the other columns of the sample. So each active user in the sample has a query to its own to transmit. Therefore all the $(d-1)$-disjunct matrices can be used in the current model for the sample space $S(\bar{d}, n)$. In particular, Theorem 4.5.3 says that the $(\bar{2}, n)$ problem can be done in t queries where t is the smallest integer satisfying

$$\binom{t}{\lfloor t/2 \rfloor} \geq n .$$

Since the feedbacks for the success/failure model is a subset of the multiaccess channel model, the above t is also the minimax number of queries for nonadaptive algorithms for the former model as it is for the latter.

One can do better for sequential algorithms. For example, for $d = 2$, one can use the binary representation matrix given in Sec. 4.5 (sequentially). Since 1-separable implies that for every pair of columns there exists a row with 1 in one column and 0 in the other, one active user will transmit through that row and the other through a complementary subset (not in the matrix). Thus it requires $1 + \lceil \log n \rceil$ queries. This algorithm can be modified into a weak-sense nonadaptive algorithm by attaching an all-1 row at the end of the binary representation matrix. For $d = 3$, a modified scheme works. Query the users labeled by all 0s and all 1s (if they exist) individually and delete these two columns from the binary representation matrix. Query the set of 1s in each row and their complementary sets. It is easily verified that every active user has a query to its own to transmit. The total number of queries is $1 + \lceil \log n \rceil + \lceil \log(n+1) \rceil$.

An example for $n = 8$ and $d = 2$ is given in the following table:

query\user	0	1	2	3	4	5	6	7
1	0	0	0	0	1	1	1	1
2	0	0	1	1	0	0	1	1
3	0	1	0	1	0	1	0	1

If 6 and 7 are the two active users, then 7 transmits in query 3, and 6 in query 4 which consists of the complementary set of query 3.

10.4   The k-Channel

The k-channel is a generalization of the multiaccess channel such that any fewer than k users can transmit successfully in the same time slot ($k = 2$ is the multiaccess case). The simultaneous transmission is possible in several scenarios. The channel may be able to transmit the Boolean sum of messages received. If the messages are coded into a superimposed code (see Chap. 4) where each supercode word consists of up to $k - 1$ code words, then the superimposed message, which is a concatenation of supercode words, can also be uniquely deciphered. A typical application is to use a superimposed code on users' identifications. A reservation algorithm requests active users to transmit their identifications. If the number of active users is less than k, then all active users are identified in one time slot. Another scenario is when a time slot has capacity $k - 1$ ($k - 1$ subslots), or the channel is a pool of $k - 1$ subchannels.

The k-channel was first studied by Tsybakov, Mikhailov and Likhanov [14] for probabilistic models. Let $Q_k(\bar{d}, n)$ denote the number of queries required for a minimax algorithm for the k-channel with a $(\bar{d}, n)$ set of users. Chen and Hwang [7] used an argument similar to the proof of Theorem 10.1.6 to prove

Theorem 10.4.1 $Q_k(\bar{d}, n) = \Omega((d/k) \ \log n / \log d)$.

They also proposed an algorithm which is an extension of the generalized binary splitting algorithm (see Sec. 2.2):

Partition the set of unsatisfied users into two different groups L and U, called *loaded* and *unloaded*. Namely, a loaded group is known to contain some active users and this knowledge comes from querying, not from the nature of the sample space. Originally, all users are in the unloaded group. Let $\alpha(u)$ be a parameter to be determined later when u is the size of the updated U.

Step 1. Query any set S of $(k - 1)2^{\alpha(u)}$ users in U (set $S := U$ if $k\alpha(m) > m$).

Step 2. If the feedback on S is at most $k - 1$, set $U := U \setminus S$ and go back to Step 1.

Step 3. If the feedback on S is k^+, set $L := S$ and $c := k$.

Step 4. Let ℓ be the size of L. If $\ell \leq k - 1$, query L and go back to Step 1. If $\ell \geq k$, query any set S' of $\lfloor \ell/2 \rfloor$ users from L.

Step 5. Suppose the feedback on S' is k'. If $k' < c$, set $L := L \setminus S'$, $c := c - k'$ and go back to Step 4. Otherwise, move $L \setminus S'$ to U. If $c \leq k' < k$, go back to Step 1. If $k' = k^+$, set $L := S'$ and go back to Step 4.

Let $Q_k(d, n : \alpha)$ denote the maximum number of queries required by the above algorithm. Note that every time Step 3 is taken, at least k active users will be satisfied before going back to Step 1. Therefore Step 3 can be entered at most $\lfloor d/k \rfloor$ times. Once Step 3 is entered, the size of L is reduced by half by every new query until the size is at most $k - 1$. Hence a total of $\alpha(u) + 1$ queries (counting the queries entering Step 3) is needed. Making the conservative assumption that no inactive user is identified in the process of satisfying active users, then the $n - d$ inactive users are identified in Step 1 in a total of at most $\lceil (n - d)/((k-)2^\alpha(u)) \rceil$ queries. So

$$Q_k(d, n : \alpha) \leq \left\lfloor \frac{d}{k} \right\rfloor (\alpha(u) + 2) + \left\lceil \frac{n - d}{(k - 1)2^{\alpha(u)}} \right\rceil .$$

Ideally, $\alpha(u)$ should be a function of u. For easier analysis, set $\alpha(u) = \log(n/d)$.

Theorem 10.4.2 $Q_k(d, n) = O((d/k) \log(n/d))$.

For d small or large, more accurate information on $Q_k(d, n)$ can be derived. A TDM algorithm for the k-channel will query $k - 1$ users at a time. Thus it requires $\lceil n/(k - 1) \rceil$ queries. Clearly, a TDM algorithm will be minimax if d is sufficiently large. Chang and Hwang [6] gave a lower bound on such d.

Theorem 10.4.3 If $\left\lceil \frac{n}{k-1} \right\rceil \leq \left\lceil \frac{d+1}{k} \right\rceil + \left\lceil \frac{d}{k-1} \right\rceil - 1$, then

$$Q_k(d, n) = \left\lceil \frac{n}{k - 1} \right\rceil .$$

Proof. It suffices to prove that

$$Q_k(d, n) \geq \left\lceil \frac{n}{k - 1} \right\rceil .$$

An oracle argument is used. If a query is of size at most $k - 1$, then the oracle always orders the feedback 0 (if 0 is impossible, then an integer as small as possible). Otherwise, the feedback is k^+, whenever possible. Under this oracle, an algorithm will not query a set larger than k, unless it is known that the number of active users contained therein is less than k.

An active user can be satisfied only in the following two situations:

(i) The user is in a queried set of size at most $k - 1$.

(ii) The user is in a queried set of size at least k, but this set can contain at most $k - 1$ active users since at least $d - k + 1$ active users are known to be elsewhere.

Let S be the first queried set to arise in situation (ii). Since S contains inactive users, all sets of size at most $k - 1$ queried before S must contain no active user (since otherwise the feedback to such a set could be reduced by switching active users with the inactive users in S). So the $x \geq d - k + 1$ active users known to lie elsewhere must lie in sets of size at least k. By the definition of the oracle, the feedback of these sets are k^+. Since only k active users can be counted from each such set, to count up to $d - k + 1$ active users, there must be at least $\lceil (d - k + 1)/k \rceil$ such sets. Furthermore

---

the x active users have to be satisfied in at least another $\lceil (d-k+1)/(k-1) \rceil$ queries. Counting the query on S, the minimum total number of queries is

$$\left\lceil \frac{d+1}{k} \right\rceil + \left\lceil \frac{d}{k-1} \right\rceil - 1 \ .$$

If situation (ii) never arises, then the total number of queries is at least $\lceil n/(k-1) \rceil$. $\Box$

Let $n_q(k,d)$ denote the largest n such that q queries suffice given d and k. Since $Q_k(d,n)$ is clearly increasing in n, a complete specification of $n_q(k,d)$ is equivalent to one of $Q_k(d,n)$. If $d < k$, then $Q_k(d,n) = 1$. For $d \geq k$ but d small, Chang and Hwang [6] proved

Theorem 10.4.4 *For $2 \leq k \leq d < 2k$ and $q \geq 2$,*

$$n_q(k,d) = 2^{q-2}(3k-2-d) + d - k \ .$$

Proof. A construction is first given to show

$$n_q(k,d) \geq 2^{q-2}(3k-2-d) + d - k \ .$$

For $q = 2$ the RHS of the above inequality is $2k - 2$ which can certainly be handled by two queries of $k - 1$ users each. The general $q \geq 3$ case is proved by induction on q. Let S be the first query set with $2^{q-3}(3k-2-d)$ users. If the feedback on S is less than k, then by induction, $q - 1$ more queries suffice for the remaining users. So assume the feedback is k^+ and S is a loaded set. For the next $q - 3$ queries, use the halving technique as described in the Chen-Hwang algorithm until a loaded set of size $3k - 2 - d$ is left, or all $2^{q-3}(3k-2-d)$ users are satisfied. In the former case, this set can either be a set which has been queried with feedback k^+ or the only unqueried subset of such a set. Next query a subset of $k - 1$ users from this loaded set. Then the remaining $2k - 1 - d$ users are the only unsatisfied users from a set with feedback k^+. The number of satisfied active users during this process is at least

$$k - (2k-1-d) = d+1-k \ .$$

Hence there are at most $k - 1$ active users among all unsatisfied users. One more query takes care of them. In the latter case, in the remaining $d - k$ users at most $d - k \leq k - 1$ are active. Again, one more query suffices.

Next the reverse inequality on $n_q(k,d)$ is proved. For $q = 2$, $2k - 1$ users require three queries by Theorem 10.4.3. The general $q \geq 3$ case is again proved by induction on q. Let

$$n = 2^{q-2}(3k-2-d) + d - k + 1 \ .$$

Suppose that the first query is on x users. If $x \leq 2^{q-3}(3k-2-d)$, consider the feedback 0. Then the remaining $n - x$ users cannot be satisfied by $q - 1$ more queries by induction. If $x \geq 2^{q-3}(3k - 2 - d) + 1$, consider the feedback k^+. Clearly, if $x \geq 2^{q-3}(3k - 2 - d) + d - k + 1$, then the x users cannot be satisfied by $q - 1$ more queries by induction. So assume

$$1 \leq x - 2^{q-3}(3k - 2 - d) \leq d - k .$$

Now an oracle reveals $2^{q-3}(3k - 2 - d)$ inactive users among the unqueried users; then these users are satisfied. So the number of unqueried, unsatisfied users is

$$n - x - 2^{q-3}(3k - 2 - d) = d - k + 1 - [x - 2^{q-3}(3k - 2 - d)] \leq d - k .$$

These up to $d - k$ users can still all be active since the queried x users guarantee to contain only k active users. Therefore the set of $n' = 2^{q-3}(3k - 2 - d) + d - k + 1$ unsatisfied users form an $S(d, n')$. By induction they cannot be satisfied in $q - 1$ queries. $\square$

10.5 Quantitative Channels

In a bit reservation channel each active user transmits a bit. Although bits transmitted by active users collide, the channel may have the capability to sense the "loudness" of this collision and hence deduces the number of active users, though still not knowing who they are. Such a channel will be called a *quantitative channel* since it provides quantitative information about the number of active users. It will be shown that this quantitative information leads to more efficient algorithms than ordinary group testing which provides only qualitative information.

Long before Tsybakov [12] introduced the quantitative channel to multiaccess communication (for probabilistic models), the combinatorial version had been studied as a problem of detecting counterfeit coins by using a spring scale. Therefore the mathematical results will be discussed in the next chapter, Sec. 6.2.

References

[1] D. Angluin and L. Valiant, Fast probabilistic algorithms for Hamiltonian paths and matchings, *J. Comput. Syst. Sci.* 18 (1979) 155-193.

[2] T. Berger, N. Mehravari, D. Towsley and J. Wolf, Random multiple-access communications and group testing, *IEEE Trans. Commun.* 32 (1984) 769-778.

[3] P. Busschbach, Constructive methods, to solve the problem of: *s*-subjectivity, conflict resolution, coding in defective memories, unpublished manuscript, 1984.

[4] J. I. Capetanakis, Tree algorithms for packet broadcast channels, *IEEE Trans. Inform. Theory* 25 (1979) 505-515.

[5] J. I. Capetanakis, Generalized TDMA: The multi-accessing tree protocol, *IEEE Trans. Commun.* 27 (1979) 1479-1485.

[6] X. M. Chang and F. K. Hwang, The minimax number of calls for finite population multi-access channels, in *Computer Networking and Performance Evaluation*, Ed: T. Hasegawa, H. Takagi and Y. Takahashi, (Elsevier, Amsterdam, 1986) 381-388.

[7] R. W. Chen and F. K. Hwang, K-definite group testing and its application to polling in computer networks, *Congress Numerantium* 47 (1985) 145-159.

[8] A. G. Greenberg and S. Winograd, A lower bound on the time needed in the worst case to resolve conflicts deterministically in multiple access channels, *J. Assoc. Comput. Math.* 32 (1985) 589-596.

[9] J. F. Hayes, An adaptive technique for local distribution, *IEEE Trans. Commun.* 26 (1978) 1178-1186.

[10] J. Komlos and A. G. Greenberg, An asymptotically fast nonadaptive algorithm for conflict resolution in multiple access channels, *IEEE Trans. Inform. Theory* 31 (1985) 302-306.

[11] J. L. Massey, Collision-resolution algorithms and random-access communications, Tech. Rep. UCLA-ENG-8016, School of Engineering and Applied Science, Univ. Calif. Los Angeles, 1980.

[12] B. S. Tsybakov, Resolution of a conflict with known multiplicity, *Probl. Inform. Transm.* 16 (1980) 65-79.

[13] B. S. Tsybakov and V. A. Mikhailov, Free synchronous packet access in a broadcast channel with feedback, *Probl. Inform. Transm.* 14 (1978) 259-280.

[14] B. S. Tsybakov, V. A. Mikhailov and N. B. Likhanov, Bounds for packet transmissions rate in a random-multiple-access system, *Prob. Inform. Transm.* 19 (1983) 61-81.

11
Additive Model and Others

We introduce other group testing models with different types of outcomes. Some of these models can be classified as parametric group testing since there is a parameter to represent the degree of defectiveness and a test outcome is a function of the parameters of items in that test group. In particular, all possible patterns of outcomes for two (possibly different) defectives are examined.

11.1 Symmetric Group Testing

Sobel, Kumar and Blumenthal [23] studied a symmetrized version of group testing for PGT which is asymmetric with respect to defectives and good items. In the symmetric model, there are ternary outcomes; all good, all defective, and mixed (which means containing at least one defective and one good item each). Hwang [13] studied the symmetric model for CGT. He proved

Theorem 11.1.1 $M(\overline{n-1}, n) = n$.

Proof. That
$$M(\overline{n-1}, n) \leq n$$
is obvious since individual testing needs only n tests. The reverse inequality is proved by an oracle argument. Let G denote the graph whose vertices are the unidentified items and an edge exists between two vertices if they have been identified as a "mixed pair," one good and one defective. At the beginning the graph has n vertices and no edges. After each test, the graph is updated by either adding one edge or removing a component (a connected subgraph). Note that if the state of a vertex is known, then the states of all vertices in the same component can be deduced. Therefore one can assume without loss of generality that a test group does not contain two vertices from the same component. The oracle will dictate the "mixed" outcome to each test of size two or more and add an edge between two arbitrary vertices in the test group. It will also dictate the "all good" outcome to each test of size one and remove the component containing that vertex from G. In either case the number of components is reduced

by one for each test. Since G starts with n components, n tests are required.   □

Next we prove a complementary result.

Theorem 11.1.2 $M(\overline{n-2}, n) < n.$

Proof. Test the group (1,2), (1,3), $\cdots$, until a group $(1, i)$, $2 \le i \le n$, yields a non-mixed outcome. Then the states of items 1, 2, $\cdots$, i are all known in $i - 1$ tests and the states of the remaining $n - i$ items can be learned through individual testing in $n - i$ tests. If all outcomes of $(1, 2)$, ..., $(1, n)$ are mixed, then items 1 must be the only defective.   □

For small d, the ordinary group testing model is not too different from the symmetric model since the "all defective" outcome is unlikely to occur except for small test groups. Therefore good group testing algorithms can be simulated here without giving up too much. The same goes for small $n - d$ by reversing the definition of good items and defectives. For general d, Hwang proposed the following two algorithms.

The chain algorithm

Step 1. Test items 1 and 2 as a group.

Step 2. Suppose the current test group is $\{i, i + 1\}$. If the outcome is mixed, test the group $\{i + 1, i + 2\}$; if not, test the group $\{i + 2, i + 3\}$.

The star algorithm

Step 1. Test items 1 and 2 as a group.

Step 2. Suppose the current test group is $\{i, j\}$, $i < j$. If the outcome is mixed, test the group $\{i, j + 1\}$ next; if not, test the group $\{j + 2, \ j + 3\}$.

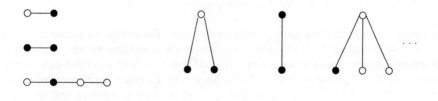

Figure 11.1: The chain algorithm and the star algorithm.

It should be understood that for both procedures, any specified item having a label beyond n should be excluded. Furthermore, an empty group should not be tested.

Note that for both algorithms, the number of tests equals n subtracting the number of nonmixed outcomes. The maximum size of a chain or a star is $1 + 2\min\{d, n - d\}$ or $1 + \max\{d, n - d\}$. Thus, the star algorithm is better if d and $n - d$ are close and worse if otherwise.

11.2 Some Additive Models

Consider the (d, n) sample space and assume that the ith defective x_i has a defectiveness measurable by θ_i. For an additive model, the outcome of a test on group G is $\sum_{x_i \in G} \theta_i$.

In the *power-set* model it is assumed that $\sum_{x_i \in s'} \theta_i$ are distinct over all $s' \subseteq s$. Therefore there exists a one-to-one mapping from the outcomes to the power set of s, i.e., there are 2^d possible outcomes. Since there are $\binom{n}{d}$ samples in the (d, n) sample space, the information lower bound yields

$$M(d, n) \geq \lceil \log_{2^d} n(n - 1) \cdots (n - d + 1) \rceil .$$

Here we give a stronger lower bound and a construction to achieve it (the special case $d = 2$ was given in [14]).

Theorem 11.2.1 $M(d, n) = \lceil \log n \rceil$.

Proof. To identify the d defectives, one certainly has to identify a particular defective, say, x. For the purpose of identifying x, the only relevant information in an outcome is whether it contains x. Therefore

$$M(d, n) \geq \lceil \log n \rceil$$

since the right hand side is the lower bound of identifying a single defective with the binary outcome "contained" or "not contained."

On the other hand the binary representation matrix given in the first paragraph of Sec. 4.5 to identify a single defective also identifies all d defectives. Namely, defective x_i is I_k where k is the number corresponding to the binary vector with 1s in all rows whose outcomes contain x_i and 0s elsewhere. $\square$

Example 11.1. In the following table, $x_1 = I_k$ where $k = (0, 0, 1, 1) = 3$ and $x_2 = I_j$ where $j = (1, 0, 1, 0) = 10$.

I_0	I_1	I_2	I_3	I_4	I_5	I_6	I_7	I_8	I_9	I_{10}	I_{11}	outcome
0	0	0	0	0	0	0	0	1	1	1	1	x_2
0	0	0	0	1	1	1	1	0	0	0	0	ϕ
0	0	1	1	0	0	1	1	0	0	1	1	$x_1 x_2$
0	1	0	1	0	1	0	1	0	1	0	1	x_1

In the *residual* model it is assumed that nothing is known about θ_i. So the only inference one can draw from the outcomes is the "containment" relation. For example, if group G induces an outcome θ and a subgroup G' induces an outcome $\theta' < \theta$, then without testing, one can infer that the outcome on the group $G\backslash G'$ is $\theta - \theta'$, hence $G\backslash G'$ is a contaminated group. The residual model was first studied by Pfeifer and Enis [21] for PGT.

For $d = 1$ the residual model is reduced to the ordinary group testing model; thus $M(1, n) = \lceil \log n \rceil$. For $d = 2$, the residual model is identical to the quantitative model (see below). Not much is known for $d \geq 3$.

In the *quantitative* model it is assumed that $\theta_i = \theta$, a constant. Thus the set of outcomes is mapped to the number of defectives in the test group. The quantitative model has a long history in combinatorial search literature. Shapiro [22] and Fine [9] raised the question that if counterfeit coins weigh nine grams and genuine coins weigh ten grams, given a scale which weights precisely, what is the minimum number of weightings required to extract all counterfeit coins from a set of n coins? A $t \times n$ 0-1 matrix M is called a *detecting matrix* if the vectors MX_i, $i = 1, \ldots, 2^n$ are all distinct, where X_i ranges over all binary n-tuples. An immediate extension of Theorem 1.2.1 to the case of $n + 1$ outcomes yields

$$(n + 1)^t \geq 2^n .$$

Let $g(n)$ denote the minimum t such that a $t \times n$ detecting matrix exists. Cantor [3] proved that $g(n) = O(n/\log\log n)$, while Söderberg and Shapiro [24] proved $g(n) = O(n/\log n)$. Erdös and Rényi [8], and many others independently, proved

Theorem 11.2.2 $\lim\limits_{n\to\infty} \inf \dfrac{g(n)\log n}{n} \geq 2$.

Proof. Let M denote a $t \times n$ detecting matrix. Partition the rows $r_1, \ldots, r_t$ of M into two classes according as whether the weight of a row is less than $h = \lfloor \sqrt{n\log n} \rfloor$. Let s denote a sample (a subset of columns) and let M_s denote the submatrix of M consisting of s whose rows are denoted by $r'_1, \ldots, r'_t$. Let v_s denote the $1 \times t$ vector whose component $v_s(j)$ is the weight of r'_j.

If r_j belongs to class 1, then $v_s(j)$ can take on at most h different values. If r_j belongs to class 2 and has weight $w \geq h$, then the number of samples s such that $v_s(j)$ does not lie between $w/2 \pm \lambda\sqrt{w\log w}$ (λ is a positive constant to be chosen later) is

$$2^{n-w} \sum_{|k-\frac{w}{2}|>\lambda\sqrt{w\log w}} \binom{w}{k} .$$

A sample is called "bad" if it contains such a $v_s(j)$ and "good" otherwise. According to the Moivre-Laplace theorem,

$$\sum_{|k-\frac{w}{2}|>\lambda\sqrt{w\log w}} \binom{w}{k} = O\left(\frac{2^w}{w^{2\lambda^2}}\right) .$$

Let b denote the number of bad samples. Then

$$b = O\left(\frac{n2^n}{h^2\lambda^2}\right)$$
$$= O\left(\frac{2^n}{n^{\lambda^2-1}(\log n)^{\lambda^2}}\right)$$
$$= O\left(\frac{2^n}{\log n}\right) \qquad \text{for } \lambda^2 \geq 1 .$$

On the other hand, let v denote the number of different vectors v_s ranging over the good samples. Then

$$v \leq \left(2\lambda\sqrt{n\log n}\right)^t .$$

Since M is a detecting matrix, necessarily

$$v \geq 2^n - b$$

which implies

$$t \geq \frac{2n}{\log n + O(\log\log n)} .$$

Theorem 11.2.2 follows immediately. □

Lindstrom [19, 20] (see also Cantor and Mills [4]) gave a construction of $(2^k - 1) \times k2^{k-1}$ detecting matrices M_k to show that the asymptotic lower bound of Theorem 11.2.2 can be achieved. The rows of M_k are labeled by all nonempty subsets Y of $K = \{1,\ldots,k\}$. The columns of M_k are divided into groups which are also labeled by nonempty subsets of K. The group labeled by $X \subseteq K$ contains $|X| = x$ columns $v_1,\ldots,v_x$. Let $c(Y,X,v_i)$ denote the entry at the intersection of row Y and column (X,v_i). Furthermore, let $R(X)$ be the set of 2^{x-1} rows contained in X and whose numbers of intersections with X have odd cardinalities and let $R_i(X)$ be an arbitrary 2^{x-i}-subset of $R(X)$.

$$c(Y,X,v_i) = \begin{cases} 1 & \text{if } Y \cap X \in R_i(X) \\ 0 & \text{otherwise .} \end{cases}$$

M_3 is given in the following table:

	{1}	{2}	{3}	{1,2}		{1,3}		{2,3}		{1,2,3}		
{1}	1	0	0	1	1	1	1	0	0	1	1	1
{2}	0	1	0	1	0	0	0	1	1	1	1	0
{3}	0	0	1	0	0	1	0	1	0	1	0	0
{1,2}	1	1	0	0	0	1	1	1	1	0	0	0
{1,3}	1	0	1	1	1	0	0	1	0	0	0	0
{2,3}	0	1	1	1	0	1	0	0	0	0	0	0
{1,2,3}	1	1	1	0	0	0	0	0	0	1	0	0

To prove that M_k is a detecting matrix, the following lemma is crucial.

Lemma 11.2.3 *Let X and Z be two column-groups such that $Z \nsubseteq X$. Then*

$$\sum_{Y \in R(Z)} c(Y, X, v_i) = \sum_{Y \notin R(Z)} c(Y, X, v_i) \ .$$

Proof. Since $Z \nsubseteq X$, there exists an element $j \in Z - X$. Clearly,

$$(Y \cup \{j\}) \cap X = Y \cap X \ .$$

By construction

$$c(Y \cup \{j\}, X, v_i) = c(Y, X, v_i)$$

for every row Y not containing j. Since $Y \cap Z$ and $(Y \cup \{j\}) \cap Z$ have different parities, one of them is in $R(Z)$ and the other not. Furthermore, $c(\{j\}, x, v_i) = 0$. Hence the terms in the two sums of Lemma 11.2.3 are pairwise equal.

Theorem 11.2.4 $\displaystyle \lim_{n \to \infty} \frac{g(n) \log n}{n} = 2.$

Proof. It is shown first that M_k is a detecting matrix. Let s be a sample and let $I_i(s)$ be the indicator function such that

$$I_i(s) = \begin{cases} 1 & \text{if column } C_i \in s \\ 0 & \text{otherwise .} \end{cases}$$

Let $I(s)$ be the column vector consisting of $I_i(s)$, $i = 1, \ldots, k2^{k-1}$. Then M_k is a detecting matrix if $I_i(s)$ can be solved from the equation

$$M_k I(s) = m(s) \ ,$$

where $m(s) = (m_1, \ldots, m_{2^k-1})$ is a column vector and m_j is the outcome yielded by row j. The $I_i(s)$ are solved in the partial order of the subsets labeling the column groups. $I_i(s)$ in the same subset are solved simultaneously. Columns which have been solved are deleted from the partial order and columns in a group which is a maximal element in the current partial order are next to be solved. Suppose that Z is such a group with columns $v_1, \ldots, v_z$. Add up the rows in $R(Z)$ and subtract from it rows not in $R(Z)$. Due to Lemma 11.2.3, the coefficients of $I_i(s)$ for all unsolved columns C_i not in Z are zero. Thus we are left with one equation with z variables. Since the coefficients of the z variables form a representation system, these columns can be uniquely solved.

Note that

$$n = \sum_{i=0}^{k} i \binom{k}{i} = k2^{k-1} = \frac{(t+1)\log(t+1)}{2} < \frac{(t+1)\log n}{2} .$$

Thus

$$\lim_{n \to \infty} \sup \frac{g(n)\log n}{n} \leq 2 .$$

Theorem 11.2.4 now follows from Theorem 11.2.2. □

One might also consider the quantitative model for the (d, n) sample space or when the row weight is restricted to be k. Koubek and Rajlich [18] showed that $\lim g(n)$ exists for the latter case. Aigner and Schughart [2] gave a minimax (sequential) line algorithm for the former case. Their model actually allows testing the items from both ends. But since a set which contains x defectives implies its complementary set contains $d - x$ defectives, it can be assumed that all tests are from the top order. Furthermore, it doesn't matter whether identified items are removed from the line or not since if a test set contains identified items, then the number of unidentified defectives contained in the subset can be deduced.

Consider a line algorithm whose first test is on the first y items and the second on the first z items. The first test partitions the n items into two disjoint sets G of the first y items, and G' of the remaining $n - y$ items. If $z \leq y$, then the second test yields no information on G'; while if $z \geq y$, then no information on G. Let $A(d, n)$ denote the minimum number of tests required by a minimax line algorithm. The above argument yields the recursive equation

$$A(d, n) = 1 + \min_{\lceil n/2 \rceil \leq i < n} \max_{0 \leq j \leq d} \{A(d - j, i) + A(j, n - i)\} .$$

Aigner and Schughart showed that this recursive equation has the following solution.

Theorem 11.2.5 Define $k = \lceil \log \frac{n}{2d-1} \rceil + 1$ and $h = \lceil \frac{n}{2^{k-1}} \rceil - d$. Then $A(d, n) = kd + h - 1$.

Sequential algorithms for the $(2, n)$ sample space have been extensively studied. Let $g(2, n)$ denote the number of tests required by a minimax algorithm. Christen [6] (see also Aigner [1]) showed that $g(2, n) \leq \log_\phi n \cong 2.28 \log_3 n$, where $\phi = (1 + \sqrt{5})/2$ is the golden ratio. Hao [12] considered the problem of identifying two defectives from two disjoint sets of size m and n each containing exactly one defective. Let $H(m, n)$ denote the number of tests required by a minimax algorithm.

Lemma 11.2.6 $H(ab, cd) \leq H(a, c) + H(b, d)$.

Proof. Partition the ab(or cd) items into a(or c) classes of b(or d) items each. Use $H(a, c)$ tests to identify the two classes containing defectives. Then use $H(b, d)$ tests to identify the two defectives from the two contaminated classes. □

Lemma 11.2.7 *There exist infinitely many n such that $H(n, n) > g(2, n)$.*

Proof. If not, then there exists an N such that for all $n > N$, $H(n, n) \leq g(2, n)$. Now consider a set of $n = 2^r N$ items and the algorithm which first tests a set of $2^{r-1}N$ items and then uses the minimax subalgorithm. Then

$$g(2, 2^r N) \leq 1 + \max\{H(2^{r-1}N, 2^{r-1}N), g(2, 2^{r-1}N)\} = 1 + g(2, 2^{r-1}N) .$$

Repeat this to obtain

$$g(2, 2^r N) \leq r + g(2, N) ,$$

which implies

$$\lim_{n \to \infty} \sup \frac{g(2, n)}{\log_3 n} \leq \log 3 .$$

But an application of Theorem 1.2.1 yields

$$\frac{g(2, n)}{\log_3 n} \geq \frac{\log_3 \binom{n}{2}}{\log_3 n} ,$$

which implies

$$\lim_{n \to \infty} \inf \frac{g(2, n)}{\log n} \geq 2 > \log 3,$$

a contradiction. □

Using the above two lemmas Hao proved that $H(n, n)/\log_3 n$, hence $g(2, n)/\log_3 n$, converges to a constant $\leq 12/\log_3 330 \cong 2.27$.

Recently, Gargano, Montuori, Setaro and Vaccaro [11] obtained a better upper bound of $g(2, n)$ by strengthening Lemma 11.2.7.

Lemma 11.2.8 *For any positive integers m and n, $m < n$,*

$$g(2,n) \leq \max_{0 \leq k \leq \lceil \log n \rceil} \left\{ k + H\left(m^{K(m)}, m^{K(m)} \right) \right\},$$

where

$$K(m) = \lceil \log_m n - k \log_m 2 \rceil .$$

Proof. Consider the algorithm which tests half of the current set containing two defectives until this set is split into two subsets each containing one defective. Then invoke $H(x,x)$. Suppose that k halving tests are used. Then

$$x \leq \lceil \frac{n}{2^k} \rceil \leq m^{K(m)} .$$

$\square$

By displaying the binary tree demonstrating $H(32,32) = 7$, and using Lemma 11.2.8, the following is proved.

Theorem 11.2.9 $g(2,n) \leq 2.18 \ldots \log_3 n + O(1)$.

Proof.

$$\begin{aligned} g(2,n) &= \max_k \left\{ k + H(32^{K(32)}, 32^{K(32)}) \right\} \\ &\leq \max_k \left\{ k + 7K(32) \right\} = 2.18 \ldots \log_3 n + O(1) . \end{aligned}$$

$\square$

11.3   A Maximum Model

Let θ_i denote the defectiveness measure as in the last section. In the model M, the outcome of testing a group G is $\max_{x_i \in G} \theta_i$ (0 if G contains no defective). This model applies where there exist different degrees of defectiveness and what is observed in a test is the consequence caused by the most severe defectiveness. Clearly,

$$\log_{d+1} n(n-1) \cdots (n-d+1) \sim d \log_{d+1} n$$

is an information lower bound. On the other hand the d defectives can be identified one by one, in the order of severeness, by treating the currently most severe one as the only defective (and removing it after identification). The ith severest defective then requires at most $\lceil \log(n-i+1) \rceil$ tests, yielding the upper bound

$$\sum_{i=0}^{d-1} \lceil \log(n-i) \rceil \sim d \log n .$$

Obviously, this upper bound has not made full use of the information about those defectives which are not most severe. For example, if θ_i is the currently largest θ and the outcome of a test of group G is θ_j, $j \neq i$, then the information that x_j, is the most severe defective in G is ignored.

For $d = 2$ Hwang and Xu [16] gave a significantly better algorithm than the above naive one. Let x denote the less severe defective and y the more severe one. They considered two configurations $[a \times b]$ and $[n, b]$. The former denotes the case that x is known to lie in a set A of a items and y a set B of b items where A and B are disjoint. The latter denotes the case that x is known to lie in a set N of n items of which a subset B of b items contains y. Note that $[n, n]$ denotes the original sample space. Let $M[a \times b]$ and $M[n, b]$ denote the minimax numbers for these two configurations. Let $b_m(a)$ denote the largest b such that $M[a \times b] \leq m$.

Lemma 11.3.1 *Suppose $2^\alpha \geq a > 2^{\alpha-1}$. Then $b_m(a)$ is undefined for $m < \alpha$ and*

$$b_m(a) = \sum_{i=\alpha}^{m} \binom{m}{i} \quad \text{for} \quad m \geq \alpha.$$

Proof. Clearly, $M[a \times b]$ is decreasing in both a and b. Suppose $\alpha > m$. Then

$$M[a \times b] \geq M[a \times 1] = \lceil \log a \rceil = \alpha > m,$$

hence $b_m(a)$ is undefined. It is also clear that

$$b_m(a) = 1 = \sum_{i=m}^{m} \binom{m}{i} \quad \text{for} \quad m = \alpha.$$

The general m case is proved by induction on both m and a.

Let $0, x, y$ denote the three outcomes in a natural way. Assume that the first test group G consists of i items from A and j items from B. Then the new configuration after the testing is

$$\begin{array}{ll} [(a-i) \times (b-j)] & \text{if the outcome is } 0, \\ [i \times (b-j)] & \text{if the outcome is } x, \\ [a \times j] & \text{if the outcome is } y. \end{array}$$

Since $M[a \times j] \leq m - 1$ is required, $j \leq b_{m-1}(a)$. Similarly,

$$b - j \leq \min\{B_{m-1}(a-i), B_{m-1}(i)\}.$$

By the induction hypothesis, $i = \lfloor a/2 \rfloor$ maximizes the above minimum. Therefore

$$\begin{aligned} b_m(a) &= b_{m-1}(a) + b_{m-1}(\lfloor a/2 \rfloor) \\ &= \sum_{i=\alpha}^{m-1} \binom{m-1}{i} + \sum_{i=\alpha-1}^{m-1} \binom{m-1}{i} \\ &= \sum_{i=\alpha}^{m} \binom{m}{i}. \end{aligned}$$

$\square$

Define

$$
\begin{aligned}
f(0,0) &= f(0,1) = 1 \\
f(4t,0) &= 2^{3t-1} + 1 \quad for \ t \geq 1 \\
f(4t,k) &= f(4t-1, k-1) \quad for \ t \geq 1, k = 1, \ldots, t+1,
\end{aligned}
$$

$$
f(4t+i,k) = \min \left\{ \sum_{j=k}^{t+i} f(4t+i-1, j), 2^{3t+i-1} + \epsilon(k) \right\} \quad for \ t \geq 0, i = 1,2,3,
$$

$$
k = 0, 1, \ldots, t+1,
$$

where $\epsilon(k) = 1$ if $k = 0$ and $\epsilon(k) = 0$ otherwise. $f(4t+i,k)$ will later be used as the b value in $[n, b]$. Hwang and Xu proved

Lemma 11.3.2
 (i) $1 \leq f(4t+i,k) \leq \sum_{j=3t-1+i}^{4t+i-k} \binom{4t+i-k}{j}$.
 (ii) $\sum_{k=2}^{t+1} f(4t+3,k) > 2^{3t}/5 \ for \ t \geq 4$.
 (iii) $f(4t+2,1) > 2^{3t-1} \ for \ t \geq 0$.
 (iv) $f(4t+3,0) > 2^{3t+1} \ for \ t \geq 0$.

The proofs are skipped as they are quite involved.

Theorem 11.3.3 $M[2^{3t-1+i} + 1, f(4t+i,k)] \leq 4t+i-k \ for \ 4t+i \geq 1$.

Proof. The proof is by induction on $(4t+i, k)$ in the lexicographical order. By Lemma 11.3.2(i), $f(4t+i, t+1) = 1$ for all t and i, and

$$
M[2^{3t-1+i} + 1, f(4t+i, t+1)] = M[2^{3t-1+i} + 1, 1] = 3t - 1 + i = 4t + i - (t+1) .
$$

For the pair $(4t + i, k)$, $k \neq t + 1$, $i \neq 0$, first test a group of 2^{3t-2+i} items with $f(4t+i, k+1)$ items from the set of $f(4t+i,k)$ items. The new configuration after the testing is

$$
\begin{aligned}
&[2^{3t-2+i} + 1, f(4t+i-1,k)] \quad &\text{if the outcome is } 0, \\
&[2^{3t-2+i} \times f(4t+i-1,k)] \quad &\text{if the outcome is } x, \\
&[2^{3t-1+i} + 1, f(4t+i,k+1)] \quad &\text{if the outcome is } y.
\end{aligned}
$$

By induction, Lemmas 11.3.1 and 11.3.2(i), $4t + i - 1 - k$ more tests suffice.
   For the pair $(4t, k)$, $t \geq k \geq 1$,

$$
\begin{aligned}
M[2^{3t-1} + 1, f(4t,k)] &= M[2^{3(t-1)-1+3} + 1, f(4(t-1)+3, k-1)] \\
&\leq 4(t-1) + 3 - k + 1 = 4t - k .
\end{aligned}
$$

Finally, for the pair $(4t, 0)$ first test a group of $f(4t - 1, 0)$ items. The new configuration after the testing is

$$
\begin{array}{ll}
[2^{3t-1} + 1 - f(4t - 1, 0), 2^{3t-1} + 1 - f(4t - 1, 0)] & \text{if the outcome is } 0, \\
[f(4t - 1, 0) \times (2^{3t-1} + 1 - f(4t - 1, 0))] & \text{if the outcome is } x, \\
[2^{3t-1} + 1, f(4t - 1, 0)] & \text{if the outcome is } y.
\end{array}
$$

By Lemma 11.3.2(iv),

$$
2^{3t-1} + 1 - f(4t - 1, 0) < f(4t - 1, 0),
$$

hence

$$
M[2^{3t-1} + 1 - f(4t - 1, 0), 2^{3t-1} + 1 - f(4t - 1, 0)] \le M[2^{3t-1} + 1, f(4t - 1, 0)] = 4t - 1
$$

by induction. Furthermore

$$
M[f(4t - 1, 0) \times (2^{3t-1} + 1 - f(4t - 1, 0))] \le M[2^{3t-1} \times f(4t - 1, 0)] \le 4t - 1
$$

by Lemmas 11.3.1 and 11.3.2(i). $\square$

Corollary 11.3.4 $M(2, f(4t + i, k)) \le 4t + i - k$ for $4t + i \ge 1$.

Since $f(4t + i, k)$ is roughly 2^{3t}, $M(2, n)$ is approximately $\frac{4}{3} \log n$, which is an improvement over the naive upper bound $2 \log n$. How to extend this improvement for general d is still an open problem.

11.4   Some Models for $d = 2$

Let x and y be the two defectives. In the *candy factory* model there are three possible outcomes: x, y and $0/xy$, meaning the test group contains x only, y only, none or both. Christen [6] gave a picturesque setting for the model. Workers of a candy factory pack boxes containing a fixed number of equally heavy candy pieces but one mischievous worker shifts a piece of candy from one box to another (Figure 11.2). So one box becomes too heavy and the other too light, but their total weight remains constant. If a test group contains both the heavy and light box, a weighing cannot differentiate the group from a group containing neither.

Christen noted that the division of the sample space induced by the three outcomes is not balanced (in favor of the $0/xy$ outcome). Therefore the usual information lower bound, which depends only on counting but not on the structure of the problem, is an underestimate. For example, a set of eight items consists of $8 \times 7 = 56$ possible pairs of (x, y). If a group of four items is tested, then the distribution of these 56 pairs into the three subspaces induced by the three outcomes $x, y, 0/xy$ is $16 : 16 : 24$. In general after j tests all with the $0/xy$ outcome, the n items are partitioned into up to 2^j subsets where both x and y lie in one of these subsets. Christen proved

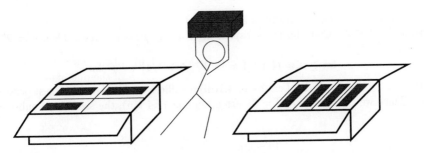

Figure 11.2: One mischievous worker shifts a piece of candy from one box to another.

Lemma 11.4.1
　(i) The minimum of $2\sum_{i=1}^{m}\binom{r_i}{2}$ under the constraint $\sum_{i=1}^{m} r_i = n$ occurs exactly when $m - n + \lfloor n/m \rfloor m$ of the r_k are equal to $\lfloor n/m \rfloor$ and the others to $\lceil n/m \rceil$.
　(ii) The above minimum is equal to $(\lceil n/m \rceil - 1)(2n - \lceil n/m \rceil m)$.
　(iii) For fixed $n \geq m$ the minimum is decreasing in m.

　The proof is straightforward and omitted.
　The oversize of the subspace induced by a sequence of $0/xy$ outcomes forces a better lower bound which, amazingly, was shown by Christen to be achievable. In using Lemma 11.4.1, m represents the number of disjoint $0/xy$ subsets.

Theorem 11.4.2 *The maximum number $f(t)$ of items such that the two defectives in the candy factory can be identified in t tests is*

$$
f(t) = \begin{cases}
7 & \text{if } t = 4, \\
(3^{t-h} - 1 + 2^{1+h})/2 & \text{if } 1 + 2^h < 3^{t-h}, \\
\lfloor 3(3^{t-h} + 2^h)/4 \rfloor & \text{otherwise,}
\end{cases}
$$

where $h = t - \lfloor (1+t)/\log 6 \rfloor$.

Proof. First it is shown that $n = f(t) + 1$ items need at least $t + 1$ tests. The case $t = 4$ can be directly verified. For $t \geq 5$, it is easily shown that

$$
\frac{3^{t-h} + 1}{2} \leq 2^h \leq 3^{t-h+1} - 1 .
$$

Set $n = f(t) + 1$ in Lemma 11.4.1. Two cases have to be distinguished. (i) $2^h < 3^{t-h} - 1$. Consider the subspace after h $0/xy$ outcomes. Then $m = 2^h$ and

$$
2m > n = f(t) + 1 = (3^{t-h} + 1 + 2^{h+1})/2 > m .
$$

Hence $\lceil n/m \rceil = 2$. From Lemma 11.4.1(ii), the size of the subspace is

$$
2(n - m) = 3^{t-h} + 1 .
$$

Thus at least $t - h + 1$ more tests are required.

(ii) $3^{t-h} + 1 \le 2^h$. Consider the subspace after $h - 1$ $0/xy$ outcomes. Then $m = 2^{h-1}$ and

$$4m \ge n = f(t) + 1 = \lfloor 3(3^{t-h} + 2^h)/4 \rfloor + 1 > 2m .$$

Hence $4 \ge \lceil n/m \rceil \ge 3$. By Lemma 11.4.1(iii) it suffices to consider the largest possible m. Hence we consider $\lceil n/m \rceil = 3$. From Lemma 11.4.1(ii), the size of the subspace is

$$4n - 6m \ge 3^{t-h+1} + 1 .$$

Thus at least $t - h + 2$ more tests are required. That $f(t)$ items can always be done in t tests is proved by construction.

Let $[\sum_{i=1}^m r_i]$ denote the configuration that there are m disjoint sets of size $r_1, \cdots, r_m$, and the two defectives lie in one of the m sets. Let $[\sum_{i=1}^m (p_i \times q_i)]$ denote the configuration that there are m disjoint sets each of which is further partitioned into two subsets of p_i and q_i items each. The two defectives always lie in the same set i, with x among the p_i items and y among the q_i items. It can be easily seen that once an x or y outcome is obtained, then the n items are partitioned in this manner. In this configuration the prescribed algorithm takes $\lceil p_i/2 \rceil$ and $\lfloor q_i/2 \rfloor$ items from each set i, as long as $p_i \ge 4$ and $q_i \ge 4$ for each i, for a group test. In the $[\sum_{i=1}^m r_i]$ configuration, the algorithm takes $\lfloor r_i/2 \rfloor$ items from each set, as long as $r_i \ge 4$ for each i, for a group test. Whenever the $p_i \ge 4$, $q_i \ge 4$, $r_i \ge 4$ condition is violated, Christen gave some *ad hoc* procedures to take care of the situations. Then he showed that this algorithm does $f(t)$ items in t tests. The detailed verification is omitted here. $\square$

Suppose that in the candy factory example, a weighing can only identify an underweight box. Then the possible outcomes are x and $0/y/xy$, the former indicating that the group contains x but not y. This model was called the *underweight* model by Hwang [14] who gave an algorithm requiring $3 \log n - 1$ tests.

Ko [17] gave a recursive algorithm with better asymptotic results. Let $[m(p \times q)]$ denote the configuration $[\sum_{i=1}^m (p_i \times q_i)]$ if $p_i = p$ and $q_k = q$ for all i, and let $m(r)$ denote the configuration $[\sum_{i=1}^m r_i]$ if $r_i = r$ for all i.

Lemma 11.4.3 *Let* $0 < k < l$ *and* $p = \binom{l}{k}$. *Given the configuration* $[m(pq)]$ *there exist* l *tests such that*

(i) if one test outcome is x, then the new configuration is $\left[m \left(\frac{kpq}{l} \times \frac{(l-k)pq}{l} \right) \right]$,

(ii) if none of the test outcomes is x, then the new configuration is $[mp(q)]$.

Proof. First assume $m = q = 1$. Construct an $l \times p$ matrix M by having the k-subsets of the set $\{1, \ldots, l\}$ as columns. Then each row has kp/l 1s. Associate each column with an item and treat rows as tests. Suppose row j yields the outcome x. Then x must be one of the columns having a 1-entry in row j, and y must not be. So the new configuration is $\left[\left(\frac{kp}{l} \times \frac{(l-k)p}{l}\right)\right]$. (i) is verified. Clearly, for any two columns C, C' of M, there must exist a row with 1 in C and 0 in C'. So (ii) holds trivially.

In the general case partition the $m(pq)$ items into p sets of mq items each, with q items coming from each of the m groups. Associate the columns of M with the p sets. Then (i) and (ii) are easily verified. $\qquad \square$

Ko's algorithm $K(l)$: For given l, set $k = \lfloor l/2 \rfloor$ and $p = \binom{l}{k}$. Suppose $p^{\alpha-1} < n \le p^{\alpha}$. Add dummy items to make the initial configuration $[(p^{\alpha})]$. There are 2α steps, starting with Step 0.

Step m $(0 \le m < \alpha)$. Assume that the current configuration is $[p^m(p^{\alpha-m})]$. Apply Lemma 11.4.3 to find l tests satisfying (i) and (ii) of Lemma 11.4.3. If one of the tests has outcome x, go to Step m'. If not, go to Step $m+1$.

Step m' $(0 \le m < \alpha)$. Assume that the current configuration is $[p^m(kp^{\alpha-m}/l \times (l - k)p^{\alpha-m}/l)]$. Using binary splitting to identify x among the kp^{α}/l items. Then by inserting x into every test, y can be identified from the $(l-k)p^{\alpha-m}/l$ items again by binary testing.

Lemma 11.4.3 assures that $K(l)$ is a correct algorithm.

Theorem 11.4.4 *The number of tests required by $K(l)$ is*
$$M_{K(l)}(n) \le (2 + \epsilon_l) \log n + 3l,$$

where
$$\epsilon_l = 2\left(\frac{l}{\log p} - 1\right) \sim \frac{\log l}{\log p}.$$

Proof. Suppose $K(l)$ completes Step m before switching to Step m'. Then
$$M_{K(l)}(n) = (m+1)l + \log(kp^{\alpha}/l) + \log[(l-k)p^{\alpha-m}/l] < \alpha l + \alpha \log p + \log p < (2\alpha+1)l,$$
since $l > \log p$ and the function achieves maximum at $m = \alpha - 1$.

$$
\begin{aligned}
(2\alpha + 1)l &\le \left[2\left(\frac{\log n}{\log p} + 1\right) + 1\right]l \\
&= 2l\frac{\log n}{\log p} + 3l \\
&= 2\log n + 2\left(\frac{l}{\log p} - 1\right)\log n + 3l \\
&\sim 2\log n + \epsilon_l \log n + 3l.
\end{aligned}
$$
$\qquad \square$

By setting $l = \lceil \sqrt{\log n} \rceil$, one obtains

Corollary 11.4.5

$$M_{K(l)}(n) = 2 \log n + O(\sqrt{\log n} \log \log n).$$

Gargano, Korner and Vaccaro [10] considered the subproblem of identifying only x in the underweight model. Let $M(\{x\}, n)$ denote the minimax number of tests for this subproblem.

Theorem 11.4.6 *If* $n = \binom{k}{\lceil k/2 \rceil}$ *for some integer* k, *then*

$$M(\{x\}, n) = k - 1 + \left\lceil \log \left(\frac{k-1}{\lceil (k-1)/2 \rceil - 1} \right) \right\rceil.$$

Proof. For any algorithm A represent its first $k - 1$ tests by a binary matrix. By the Sperner's theorem, there exist at most $\binom{k-1}{\lceil (k-1)/2 \rceil}$ columns not containing each other. Since n is greater than this number, there exist columns a, b such that b contains a. Let a and b also denote the corresponding items. Then for each such pair (a, b), $x = a$(with $y = b$) is a solution consistent with the test outcomes.

Let X denote the set of such items a. Then the set of columns labeled by items not in X constitute a Sperner family with $k - 1$ elements. Thus

$$|X| \geq n - \binom{k-1}{\lceil (k-1)/2 \rceil} = \binom{k-1}{\lceil (k-1)/2 \rceil - 1},$$

which means that A needs at least $\lceil \log X \rceil$ tests.

On the other hand, let the n items be represented by the $\lfloor k/2 \rfloor$-subsets of the set $\{1, \cdots, k\}$. Since no column is contained in another column, one of the tests must yield the x outcome. But the last test can be skipped since its x outcome can be deduced if the first $k - 1$ tests yield no x outcome. Since each row has $n \lfloor k/2 \rfloor / k = \binom{k-1}{\lceil (k-1)/2 \rceil - 1}$ 1s once a row with the x outcomes is found, it takes at most $\left\lceil \log \binom{k-1}{\lceil k/2 \rceil - 1} \right\rceil$ more tests. □

Corollary 11.4.7 $M(\{x\}, n) \geq 2 \log n + \frac{1}{2} \log \log n - 4.$

Proof. Assume that

$$\binom{k-1}{\lceil (k-1)/2 \rceil} \leq n < \binom{k}{\lceil k/2 \rceil}.$$

Using Sterlings formula, it is easily verified that

$$k > \log n + \frac{\log \log n}{2}.$$

Since $M(\{x\}, n)$ is nondecreasing in n

$$M(\{x\}, n) \geq M\left(\{x\}, \binom{k-1}{\lceil (k-1)/2 \rceil}\right) \geq k - 2 + \left\lceil \log \binom{k-2}{\lceil k/2 \rceil - 2} \right\rceil$$

$$\geq 2 \log n + \frac{\log \log n}{2} - 4 .$$

$\square$

Clearly, a lower bound of $M(\{x\}, n)$ is also a lower bound of $M(n)$ for the underweight model. From Corollaries 11.4.5 and 11.4.7, $M(n) - 2 \log n$ lies between $\log \log n$ and $\log \log n \sqrt{\log n}$.

Hwang also studied the parity model whose outcomes are odd and even, the parity of the number of defectives in the test group. He observed that by using the 1-separable property of the binary representation matrix, there always exists a row containing one defective but not the other. Suppose that row j is the first such row. Since each row has at most $n/2$ 1s, by binary splitting, one defective can be identified in $\lceil \log n \rceil - 1$ more tests. The other defective must lie in the set of 0s in row j, but in the same set as the identified defective in row i for $i = 1, \ldots, j-1$. There are at most $n/2^j$ items satisfying this requirement. Hence the other defective can be identified in $\lceil \log n \rceil - j$ more tests. The total number of tests is

$$j + \lceil \log n \rceil - 1 + \lceil \log n \rceil - j = 2 \lceil \log n \rceil - 1 ,$$

which is at most one more than the information bound $\lceil \log \binom{n}{2} \rceil$.

Chang, Hwang and Weng [5] proposed a better algorithm H which achieves the information lower bound except on a set of n with measure zero. Their algorithm encounters only the two configurations $[\sum_{i=1}^{m} r_i]$ and $[\sum_{i=1}^{m} (p_i \times q_i)]$ defined as before. In the former configuration, the next test group consists of $\lfloor r_i/2 \rfloor$ items from each r_i. In the latter configuration, the next test group will take items from each $p_i \times q_i$ group in such a way that the sizes of the two configurations split $\sum_{i=1}^{m} (p_i \times q_i)$ evenly (it is easily verified that this can always be done). Represent the algorithm H by a binary tree with the left branch always denoting the "odd" outcome. Then it can be shown that the sizes of the configurations corresponding to the nodes at a given level are ordered from left to right. Therefore, only the leftmost node at each level needs to be concerned. Furthermore, since the split of the leftmost node is always even, the number of tests is simply

$$1 + \left\lceil \log \left(\lfloor \tfrac{n}{2} \rfloor \lceil \tfrac{n}{2} \rceil \right) \right\rceil ,$$

where $\left\lfloor \lfloor \tfrac{n}{2} \rfloor \times \lceil \tfrac{n}{2} \rceil \right\rfloor$ is the configuration after the first test yielding an "odd" outcome. Thus H achieves the information lower bound except when

$$\lceil \log \lfloor \tfrac{n}{2} \rfloor \times \lfloor \tfrac{n}{2} \rfloor \rceil > \lceil \log \binom{n}{2} \rceil - 1 .$$

Define integer i_k by

$$\lceil \log \binom{i_k}{2} \rceil = k \ .$$

Chang, Hwang and Weng showed that the above inequality holds if and only if $n \in N$ where $N = \{n : n = I(2l) = 2I(2l - 2) = \cdots = 2^j I(2l - 2j) > 2^{j+1} I(2l - 2j - 2)$ for some $j \geq 0\}$. They also showed that although N is an infinite set, its density is $(\log n)/2n$.

Hwang [13, 14] surveyed all nonequivalent models for two possibly different defectives.

References

[1] M. Aigner, Search problems on graphs, *Disc. Appl. Math.* 14 (1986) 215-230.

[2] M. Aigner and M. Schughart, Determining defectives in a linear order, *J. Statist. Plan. Inform.* 12 (1985) 359-368.

[3] D. G. Cantor, Determining a set from the cardinalities of its intersections with other sets, *Canad. J. Math.* 16 (1964) 94-97.

[4] D. G. Cantor and W. H. Mills, Determination of a subset from certain combinatorial properties, *Canad. J. Math.* 18 (1966) 42-48.

[5] X. M. Chang, F. K. Hwang and J. F. Weng, Optimal detection of two defectives with a parity check device, *SIAM J. Disc. Math.* 1 (1988) 38-44.

[6] C. Christen, A Fibonaccian algorithm for the detection of two elements, Publ. 341, Dépt. d'IRO, Univ. Montreal, 1980.

[7] C. Christen, Optimal detection of two complementary defectives, *SIAM J. Alg. Disc. Methods* 4 (1983) 101-110.

[8] P. Erdös and A. Rényi, On two problems of information theory, *Publ. Math. Inst. Hung. Acad. Sci.* 8 (1963) 241-254.

[9] N. J. Fine, Solution E1399, *Amer. Math. Monthly* 67 (1960) 697-698.

[10] L. Gargano, J. Korner and U. Vaccaro, Search problems for two irregular coins with incomplete feedback, *Disc. Appl. Math.* 36 (1992) 191-197.

[11] L. Gargano, V. Montuori, G. Setaro and U. Vaccaro, An improved algorithm for quantitative group testing, *Disc. Appl. Math.* 36 (1992) 299-306.

[12] F. H. Hao, The optimal procedures for quantitative group testing, *Disc. Appl. Math.* 26 (1990) 79-86.

[13] F. K. Hwang, Three versions of a group testing game, *SIAM J. Alg. Disc. Method* 5(1984) 145-153.

[14] F. K. Hwang, A tale of two coins, *Amer. Math. Monthly* 94 (1987) 121-129.

[15] F. K. Hwang, Updating a tale of two coins, *Graph Theory and Its Applications: East and West*, ed. M. F. Capobianco, M. Guan, D. F. Hsu and F. Tian, (New York Acad. Sci., New York) 1989, 259-265.

[16] F. K. Hwang and Y. H. Xu, Group testing to identify one defective and one mediocre item, *J. Statist. Plan. Infer.* 17 (1987) 367-373.

[17] K. I. Ko, Searching for two objects by underweight feedback, *SIAM J. Disc. Math.* 1 (1988) 65-70.

[18] V. Koubek and J. Rajlich, Combinatorics of separation by binary matrices, *Disc. Math.* 57 (1985) 203-208.

[19] B. Lindstrom, On a combinatory detection problem I, *Publ. Math. Inst. Hung. Acad. Sci.* 9 (1964) 195-207.

[20] B. Lindstrom, Determining subsets by unramified experiments, *A Survey of Statistical Designs and Linear Models*, ed. J. N. Srivastava, (North Holland, Amsterdam, 1975) 407-418.

[21] C. G. Pfeifer and P. Enis, Dorfman type group testing for a modified binomial model, *J. Amer. Statist. Assoc.* 73 (1978) 588-592.

[22] H. S. Shapiro, Problem E1399, *Amer. Math. Monthly* 67 (1960) 82.

[23] M. Sobel, S. Kumar and S. Blumenthal, Symmetric binomial group-testing with three outcomes, *Statist. Decision Theory and Related Topics*, ed. S. S. Gupta and J. Yackel, (Academic Press, 1971) 119-160.

[24] S. Söderberg and H. S. Shapiro, A combinatory detection problem, *Amer. Math. Monthly* 70 (1963) 1066-1070.

12
Group Testing on Graphs

Consider the group testing problem studied in Sec. 3.1, i.e., there exist two disjoint sets each containing exactly one defective. By associating each item with a vertex, the sample space can be represented by a bipartite graph where each edge represents a sample point of the space $S(2, n)$. This observation was first made by Spencer as reported in [9]. Chang and Hwang [9] conjectured that a bipartite graph with 2^k $(k > 0)$ edges always has a subgraph, induced by a subset of vertices, with 2^{k-1} edges. While the conjecture remains open, it has stimulated forthcoming research casting group testing on graphs.

12.1   2-Optimal Graphs

A graph is an ordered pair of disjoint sets (V, E) such that E is a set of pairs of elements in V and $V \neq \emptyset$. The set V is called the *vertex set* and the set E is called the *edge set*. When a graph is denoted by G, its vertex set and edge set are denoted by $V(G)$ and $E(G)$, respectively. Two vertices are *adjacent* if there is an edge between them. Two graphs are *isomorphic* if there exists a one-to-one correspondence between their vertex sets, which preserves adjacency. A graph H is a subgraph of G if $V(H) \subseteq V(G)$ and $E(H) \subseteq E(G)$. Furthermore, the subgraph H is said to be *induced* by W if $W = V(H)$ and $E(H) = E(G) \cap \{(x, y) \mid x, y \in W\}$. In this case, denote $H = G[W]$. A graph is *bipartite* if its vertices can be partitioned into two disjoint sets such that every edge is between these two sets. A bipartite graph is denoted by (A, B, E) where A and B are the two vertex sets and E is the edge set.

Aigner [1] proposed the following problem: Given a graph G, determine the minimum number $M[1, G]$ such that $M[1, G]$ tests are sufficient in the worst case to identify an unknown edge e where each test specifies a subset $W \subseteq V$ and tests whether the unknown edge e is in $G[W]$ or not.

An equivalent form of the Chang-Hwang conjecture is that for any bipartite graph G,

$$M[1, G] = \lceil \log |E(G)| \rceil$$

where $|E(G)|$ is the number of edges in G. In fact, a bipartite graph G with m edges, $2^{k-1} < m \leq 2^k$, can always be embedded into a larger bipartite graph with 2^k edges.

If the conjecture of Chang and Hwang is true, then every test can identify exactly half of the edges. Thus, k tests are enough. Clearly, k is a lower bound for $M[1, G]$. Thus, $M[1, G] = k = \lceil \log m \rceil$. Conversely, if $m = 2^k$ and $M[1, G] = k$, then the first test has to identify 2^{k-1} edges. Thus, the conjecture of Chang and Hwang is true.

It is worth mentioning that it is not true that any bipartite graph can be evenly split. A counterexample was given by Foregger (as reported in [9]) as follows: Let $K_{x,y}$ be the complete bipartite graph with two vertex sets containing x and y vertices, respectively. Then in any induced subgraph of $K_{x,y}$, the number of edges is in the form $x'y'$ where $0 \le x' \le x$ and $0 \le y' \le y$. For $x = 5$, $y = 9$, neither the number $\lceil \frac{xy}{2} \rceil = 23$ nor the number $\lfloor \frac{xy}{2} \rfloor = 22$ is in this form. This means that the conjecture of Chang and Hwang is quite special.

A graph is *2-optimal* if $M[1, G] = \lceil \log |E(G)| \rceil$. Aigner [1] proved

Theorem 12.1.1 *For any forest F, $M[1, F] = \lceil \log |E(F)| \rceil$, i.e., any forest is 2-optimal.*

Proof. It suffices to prove that a forest F with q edges can always be split evenly (into two integers differing by at most 1). This can be done in the following way: Initially, set $A := V(F)$. For each step $i = 1, 2, \cdots, \lfloor q/2 \rfloor$, choose a leaf u of $F[A]$ and set $A := A - \{u\}$. Note that at each step, $F[A]$ has exactly one edge removed. Therefore, after $\lfloor q/2 \rfloor$ steps, $F[A]$ contains exactly $\lceil q/2 \rceil$ edges. □

Andreae [7] proved two other classes of 2-optimal graphs. A graph is called *k-orderable* if its vertices can be ordered into a sequence such that a vertex has at most k neighbors in its predecessors.

Lemma 12.1.2 *A 2-orderable graph $G(V, E)$ with $|E| = 2^t$ can be evenly split.*

Proof. Lemma 12.1.2 can be easily verified for $t = 1, 2$. So assume $t \ge 3$. Let $v_1, \cdots, v_n$ be a 2-orderable sequence. Let G_i denote the subgraph induced by $v_1, \cdots, v_i$. Then there exists an i such that $|E(G_i)| = 2^{t-1}$ or $2^{t-1} - 1$. If it is the former, we are done. So assume $|E(G)| = 2^{t-1} - 1$.

Call a vertex in $V(G) \setminus V(G_i)$ a *r-vertex* if it has exactly r neighbors in G_i. Since G is 2-orderable, $0 \le r \le 2$. If there exists a 1-vertex u, then $G_i \cup \{u\}$ induces an even split. If there exist two 0-vertices u and w with an edge (u, w), then $G_i \cup \{u, w\}$ induces an even split. If there exist two 2-vertices u, w with an edge (u, w), or there exist a 0-vertex having three 2-vertices as neighbors, then one of the induced vertex would have three neighbors in its predecessors, contradicting the assumption of 2-orderable sequence. To summarize, the vertices in $V(G) \setminus V(G_i)$ are 0-vertices or 2-vertices, and the only possible edges among them are between the 0-vertices and the 2-vertices, with at most two edges from a 0-vertex. Since $|E(G \setminus G_i)| = 2^{t-1} + 1$ is odd, there exists a 0-vertex u having a unique 2-vertex w as a neighbor.

Let v be an arbitrary vertex in G_i. We may assume $d_{G_i}(v) > 0$ for otherwise v can be deleted from G_i, where $d_{G_i}(v)$ is the degree of v in G_i. Suppose $d_{G_i}(v) = 1$. If $(w, v) \notin E(G)$, then $(G_i \cup \{w\}) \setminus \{v\}$ induces an even split. If $(w, v) \in E(G)$, then $(G_i \cup \{u, w\}) \setminus \{v\}$ induces an even split. So assume $d_{G_i}(v) = 2$. If $(w, v) \notin E(G)$, then again, $(G_i \cup \{u, w\}) \setminus \{v\}$ induces an even split. Consider the case $(w, v) \in E(G)$. There must exist another vertex in $G \setminus G_i$ for otherwise

$$|E(G)| = |E(G_i)| + 3 = 2^{t-1} + 2 < 2^t \text{ for } t \geq 3.$$

Suppose that there exists a 2-vertex $x \neq u, w$ in $G \setminus G_i$. If $(x, v) \notin E(G)$, then $(G_i \cup \{w, x\}) \setminus \{v\}$ induces an even split. If $(x, v) \in E(G)$, then $(G_i \cup \{u, w, x\}) \setminus \{v\}$ induces an even split. So assume that no 2-vertex other than w exists. Let x be a 0-vertex. Since $d_G(x) \geq 1$, $(x,, v) \in E(G)$. Now $(G_i \cup \{u, w, x\}) \setminus \{v\}$ induces an even split. $\qquad \square$

Theorem 12.1.3 *All 2-orderable graph are 2-optimal.*

Proof. Let $G(V, E)$ be a 2-orderable graphs. Suppose

$$2^{t-1} < |E| \leq 2^t.$$

Add $2^t - |E|$ independent edges (on new vertices) to obtain G', which is clearly still 2-orderable. By Lemma 12.1.2, $E(G')$ can be evenly split, and such a split induces a split on $E(G)$ into two parts with sizes at most 2^{t-1}. Theorem 12.1.3 can now be proved by induction. $\qquad \square$

Since all series-parallel graphs are 2-orderable, we have

Corollary 12.1.4 *All series-parallel graphs are 2-optimal.*

Note that a planar graph has a vertex of degree at most five and is therefore 5-orderable (recursively placing a vertex of minimum degree at the end). It is still unknown whether all planar graphs are 2-optimal.

Andeae gave another class of 2-optimal graphs.

Theorem 12.1.5 *A graph G with maximum degree at most three is 2-optimal.*

Proof. Analogous to the proof of Theorem 12.1.3, it suffices to prove Theorem 12.1.5 under the restriction that $|E(G)| = 2^t$. The case $t \leq 3$ can be easily verified. So, we assume $t \geq 4$. Note that G cannot be 3-regular since this would imply

$$3n = 2|E(G)| = 2^{t-1}.$$

We consider two cases.

Case 1. G has a vertex u of degree one. Let w be the unique neighbor of u. Consider a sequence $u, w, v_3, \cdots, v_n$. Then there exists an $i \geq 4$ such that $|E(G_i)| = 2^{t-1}, 2^{t-1} + 1$ or $2^{t-1} + 2$, In the first two subcases, either G_i or $G_i \setminus \{u\}$ induces an even split. So assume $|E(G_i)| = 2^{t-1} + 2$.

If G_i contains two vertices of G_i-degree one, or a vertex of G_i-degree two, then an even split cannot be easily obtained. Thus assume that all vertices in G_i except u have G_i-degree 3. Namely, no edge exists between G_i and $G \setminus G_i$. Since $E(G) \neq E(G_i)$, $G \setminus G_i$ contains an edge (x, y). Then $G_i \cup \{x, y\} \setminus \{w\}$ induces an even split.

Case 2. G has a vertex u of degree two. Let w_1 and w_2 be the two neighbors of u. Consider a sequence $u, w_1, w_2, v_4, \cdots, v_n$. Again, there exists an $i \geq 4$ such that $|E(G_i)| = 2^{t-1}, 2^{t-1} + 1$ or $2^{t-1} + 2$. It suffices to consider the case $|E(G_i)| = 2^{t-1} + 1$ and G_i contains no vertex of G_i-degree at most one. Define an r-vertex as before (in the proof of Lemma 12.1.2). We may assume the nonexistence of a 1-vertex or two adjacent 0-vertices to rid of the easy cases. If $G \setminus G_i$ contains a 0-vertex, then it must be adjacent to a 2-vertex. Therefore $G \setminus G_i$ contains a 2-vertex x adjacent to (y, z) in G_i. From previous arguments, $2 \leq d_{G_i}(y) \leq 3$. Hence $d_{G_i}(y) = 2$. Then $G_i \cup \{x\} \setminus \{y\}$ induces an even split.

Consequently, we only need to settle the case that all vertices in $G \setminus G_i$ are 3-vertices. Since $t \geq 4$, there exist two vertices x and x' in $G \setminus G_i$. Note that x and x' have disjoint sets of neighbors (or one vertex would be of degree at least four). Furthermore, x must have a neighbor y which is not a neighbor of v. Therefore $d_{G_i}(y) = 2$ and $y \neq v$. $G_i \cup \{x\} \setminus \{v, y\}$ induces an even split. $\square$

12.2 Solution of the Du-Hwang Conjecture

By Theorem 2.1.1,

$$M[1, G] \geq \lceil \log |E(G)| \rceil$$

for any graph G. Aigner [2] conjectured that for all graphs G,

$$M[1, G] \leq \log |E(G)| + c$$

where c is a constant. Althöfer and Triesch [6] settled this conjecture by proving that for all graphs G,

$$M[1, G] \leq \lceil \log |E(G)| \rceil + 3.$$

Du and Hwang [11] pointed out that there are infinitely many complete graphs K_n such that

$$M[1, K_n] \geq \lceil \log |E(K_n)| \rceil + 1.$$

They believed that for all graphs G,

$$M[1, G] \leq \lceil \log |E(G)| \rceil + 1.$$

Damaschke [10] proved truth of this upper bound. We withhold the proof now in anticipation of a more general result (Theorem 12.2.1).

Aigner's problem can be extended to hypergraphs.

A hypergraph H is an ordered pair of disjoint sets (V, E) such that E is a collection of subsets of V and $V \neq \emptyset$. The set V is the vertex set of H and the set E is the hyperedge set. They are also denoted by $V(H)$ and $E(H)$, respectively. The *rank* of H is defined by

$$rank(H) = \max_{e \in E} |e|.$$

For any $u \in V$, the degree of u in H is defined by

$$deg_H(u) = |\{e \in E \,|\, u \in e\}|.$$

A hypergraph H' is a subhypergraph of H if $V(H') \subseteq V(H)$ and $E(H') \subseteq E(H)$. Furthermore, the subhypergraph H' is said to be *induced* by W if $W = V(H')$ and $E(H') = \{e \in E(H) \,|\, e \subseteq W\}$. In this case, write $H' = H[W]$.

Generalized Aigner's problem on hypergraphs is as follows: Given a hypergraph H, what is the minimum number $M[1, H]$ such that $M[1, H]$ tests are sufficient in the worst case to identify an unknown edge e. Here, a test, as before, is on a subset W of vertices, and the outcome informs whether e is in $H[W]$ or not.

If all hyperedges of H are considered as items, then this problem is the CGT with constraint $\mathcal{I}$ on the testable groups where

$$\mathcal{I} = \{E(H[W]) \,|\, W \subseteq V(H)\}.$$

(If viewing the vertices as items, then constraints are on the sample space.) From the lower bound of the CGT, it is easily seen that for any graph G,

$$M[1, H] \geq \lceil \log |E(H)| \rceil.$$

Althöfer and Triesch [6] also proved that all hypergraphs H of rank r,

$$M[1, H] \leq \log |E(H)| + c_r$$

where c_r is a constant depending on r.

Based on the above results and relation between Aigner's problem and the prototype group testing problem, Du and Hwang [11] conjectured that

$$M[1, H] \leq \log |E| + cr$$

for any hypergraph $H = (V, E)$ of rank r and a constant c. This conjecture was proved by Triesch [19] with a surprisingly strong result.

Theorem 12.2.1 *For any hypergraph $H = (V, E)$ of rank r,*

$$M[1, H] \leq \log |E| + r - 1.$$

This section contributes to the proof of this theorem. Before doing so, let us introduce a relation between the prototype group testing problem and Aigner's problem in hypergraphs.

The prototype group testing problem with more than one defective can also be transformed into a special case of the problem of Aigner's problem in hypergraphs. In fact, for the prototype group testing problem with n items and d defectives, consider a hypergraph $H = (V, E)$ where V is the set of n items and E is the family of all subsets of d items. One can obtain the following correspondence between the two problems:

the prototype CGT	CGT on hypergraph H
test T	test $V \setminus T$
T pure (contaminated)	$V \setminus T$ contaminated (pure)
$i_1, i_2, \cdots, i_d$ are defectives	$\{i_1, i_2, \cdots, i_d\}$ is the defective hyperedge

According to this correspondence, it is easy to transform algorithms from one problem to the other. So, the two problems are equivalent and the following holds.

Theorem 12.2.2 *Let $H = (V, E)$ where $|V| = n$ and E is the family of all subsets of d elements in V. Then*

$$M[1, H] = M(d, n).$$

The correspondence described in the above table also tells us that Aigner's problem in hypergraphs has an equivalent version as follows: Given a hypergraph $H(V, E)$ with a defective edge, find the minimum number of tests for identifying the defective edge where each test on a subset of vertices has two outcomes, whether the subset contains a defective vertex or not (a vertex is defective if it is in the defective edge).

In the following we will work on this version. The advantage of this version is that it is easy to see what is a legitimate test.

First, we choose a vertex-cover $C = \{v_1, \cdots, v_s\}$ by the following greedy algorithm.

begin
  Initially, $C := \emptyset$;
      $V := V(H)$;
      $i := 1$;
  while $E(H[V - C]) \neq \emptyset$
    do choose a vertex $v_i \in V - C$ with maximun degree in $H[V - C]$,
        set $C := C \cup \{v_i\}$ and $i := i + 1$;
  $s := i - 1$;
end.

Denote $H_i = H[V - \{v_1, \cdots, v_{i-1}\}]$. From the choice of C, it is easy to see that for any $1 \le i \le s$,

$$d_{H_1}(v_1) \ge d_{H_2}(v_2) \ge \cdots \ge d_{H_s}(v_s) \qquad (12.1)$$

and

$$\sum_{i=1}^{s} d_{H_i}(v_i) = |E|.$$

Thus,

$$\sum_{i=1}^{s} 2^{-\lceil \log \frac{|E|}{d_{H_i}(v_i)} \rceil} \le 1. \qquad (12.2)$$

Next, we give a lemma.

Lemma 12.2.3 *Suppose s positive integers $l_1 \le l_2 \le \cdots \le l_s$ satisfying $\sum_{i=1}^{s} 2^{-l_i} \le 1$. Then there exists a binary tree T with leaves $1, 2, \cdots, s$ ordering from left to right such that the length of the path from the root to leaf i is at most l_i.*

Proof. It is proved by induction on l_s. For $l_s = 1$, since $\sum_{i=1}^{s} 2^{-l_i} \le 1$, $s \le 2$. Thus, the existence of the binary tree T is trivial. For $l_s \ge 2$, let j be the index such that $l_j < l_{j+1} = \cdots = l_s$. Denote $q = \lceil (s-j)/2 \rceil$ and $l'_{j+1} = \cdots = l'_{j+q} = l_s - 1$. We claim that

$$\sum_{i=1}^{j} 2^{-l_i} + \sum_{i=j+1}^{j+q} 2^{-l'_i} \le 1.$$

In fact, if $s - j$ is even, then it is trivial that

$$\sum_{i=1}^{j} 2^{-l_i} + \sum_{i=j+1}^{j+q} 2^{-l'_i} = \sum_{i=1}^{s} 2^{-l_i} \le 1.$$

If $s - j$ is odd, then

$$\sum_{i=1}^{j} 2^{-l_i} + \sum_{i=j+1}^{j+q} 2^{-l'_i} = \sum_{i=1}^{s} 2^{-l_i} + 2^{-l_s} \le 1 + 2^{-l_s}.$$

Multiplying $2^{l_s - 1}$ on both sides, it becomes

$$2^{l_s - 1} \left(\sum_{i=1}^{j} 2^{-l_i} + \sum_{i=j+1}^{j+q} 2^{-l'_i} \right) \le 1 + 2^{-1}.$$

Since the left hand side is an integer, we have

$$2^{l_s - 1} \left(\sum_{i=1}^{j} 2^{-l_i} + \sum_{i=j+1}^{j+q} 2^{-l'_i} \right) \le 1.$$

Therefore,

$$\sum_{i=1}^{j} 2^{-l_i} + \sum_{i=j+1}^{j+q} 2^{-l'_i} \le 1.$$

By the induction hypothesis, there exists a binary tree T with leaves $1, 2, \cdots, j, (j + 1)', \cdots, (j + q)'$ such that the length of path from the root to i for $1 \le i \le j$ is at most l_i and the length of path from the root to leaf i' for $j + 1 \le i \le j + q$ is at most $l'_i = l_s - 1$. Now, if $s - j$ is even, we put two sons to every leaf i' for $j + 1 \le i \le j + q$ and name those $s - j$ new leaves by $j + 1, \cdots, s$, and if $s - j$ is odd, we put two sons to every leaf i' for $j + 2 \le i \le j + q$ and name leaf $(j + 1)'$ together with $s - j - 1$ new leaves by $j + 1, \cdots, s$. The resulting binary tree meets the requirement. □

Now, we give the proof of Theorem 12.2.1.

Proof of Theorem 12.2.1. It is proved by induction on the rank r. For $r = 1$, the problem is simply the prototype group testing problem with one defective item and hence $M[1, H] = M(1, |E(H)|) = \lceil \log |E(H)| \rceil$. For $r \ge 2$, consider the vertex cover $C = \{v_1, \cdots, v_s\}$ obtained by the greedy algorithm. Set $l_i = \lceil \log \frac{|E|}{d_{H_i}(v_i)} \rceil$. By Lemma 12.2.3, there is a binary tree T with leaves $1, 2, \cdots, s$ ordering from left to right such that the length of the path from the root to leaf i is at most l_i. Since C is a vertex cover, there must exist a defective vertex v_i in C. Denote by T_a the subtree of T rooted at vertex a. One searches this v_i with the binary tree T as follows.

> **begin**
>   Ininitially, set $i := 0$;
> $a :=$ the root of T
>   **while** a is not a leaf
>   **do begin** $b :=$ the left son of a;
>   test on $\{v_j \mid j$ is a leaf of $T_b\}$;
>   **if** the outcome is negative
>   **then** $a :=$ the right son of a
>   **else** $a := b$;
>   **end-while**;
> $i := a$;
> **end.**

Note that this algorithm can find a defective vertex v_i through at most l_i tests. Moreover, when v_i is found, all $v_1, \cdots, v_{i-1}$ have been found to be good. Therefore, the remaining suspected edges are those incident to v_i in H_i. The total number of them is $d_{H_i}(v_i)$. Removing v_i from them results in a hypergraph of rank at most

$r - 1$. By the induction hypothesis, $\lceil \log d_{H_i}(v_i) \rceil + r - 2$ tests are enough to identify remaining defective vertices. Therefore, the total number of tests is at most

$$l_i + \lceil \log d_{H_i}(v_i) \rceil + r - 2 \le \lceil \log |E| \rceil + r - 1.$$

$\square$

For the prototype group testing problem, Theorem 12.2.1 implies

Corollary 12.2.4 $M(d,n) \le \lceil \log \binom{n}{d} \rceil + d - 1$.

Every graph is a hypergraph of rank 2.

Corollary 12.2.5 *For any graph G,*

$$M[1, G] \le \lceil \log |E(G)| \rceil + 1.$$

This bound is tight. In fact, for a complete graph K_n of n vertices, $M[1, K_n] = M(2, n)$. In Sec. 3.3, it is proved that if i_t satisfies

$$\binom{i_t}{2} < 2^t < \binom{i_t + 1}{2},$$

then $n_t(2) \le i_t - 1$ for $t \ge 4$ (see Lemma 3.3.3). It follows that for $t \ge 4$,

$$M(2, i_t) \ge t + 1.$$

Moreover, for $t \ge 4$, $i_t \ge 3$. Thus,

$$\binom{i_t + 1}{2} \Big/ \binom{i_t}{2} = \frac{i_t + 1}{i_t - 1} \le 2.$$

Thus,

$$t = \lceil \log_2 \binom{i_t}{2} \rceil.$$

Hence,

$$M(2, i_t) \ge \lceil \log_2 \binom{i_t}{2} \rceil + 1.$$

Thus, the following can be concluded.

Theorem 12.2.6 *There are infinitely many n such that*

$$M[1, K_n] \ge \lceil \log_2 \binom{n}{2} \rceil + 1.$$

Motivated by this result, we conjecture that there exists hypergraph H of rank r such that $M[1, H] = \lceil \log |E(H)| \rceil + r - 1$.

Here, we raise another problem on searching more unknown edges. Let $M[d, H]$ be the minimum number k such that k tests are enough in the worst case to identify d defective (or unknown) edges in hypergraph H. Then by the lower bound of $M(d, n)$, it is easily seen that for all hypergraphs H and $d \geq 1$,

$$M[d, H] \geq d \log \frac{|E(H)|}{d}.$$

We conjecture that there exists a constant c such that for every hypergraph G and $d \geq 1$,

$$M[d, H] \leq d(\log \frac{|E(H)|}{d} + c).$$

12.3   Defective Vertices

Given a graph G with two defective vertices at two ends of an edge, what is the minimum number $M(G)$ of tests to identify the two defectives where each test on a subset W of vertices has two outcomes, W contains a defective vertex or not?

It was observed in section 12.2 that for any graph G, $M(G) = M[1, G]$, that is, the above problem is an equivalent version of Aigner's problem. For this version, Aigner and Triesch[3] considered the constraint that each test must be on a single vertex (the test outcome shows the state of the vertex, it is defective or not). Let $M^*(G)$ denote the minimax number of test for the graph $G(V, E)$ under this constraint, and let $\#G$ denote the number of connected components of G. They proved

Theorem 12.3.1 *Suppose G has no multiple edge. Then*
(i) $|E| \leq \binom{M^*(G)+1}{2} + 1$, and
(ii) $|V| \leq \binom{M^*(G)+1}{2} + 1 + \#G \leq \binom{M^*(G)+2}{2} + 1$.

Proof. (i) Trivially true for $M^*(G) = 0$. The general $M^*(G)$ case is proved by induction. Suppose a minimax algorithm tests vertex v first. Clearly, the degree of v is at most $M^*(G)$, for otherwise a positive outcome can induce $M^*(G)$ or more tests. Suppose the outcome is negative. The problem is reduced to $M^*(G) - 1$ tests on the graph $G \setminus \{v\}$. By the induction hypothesis,

$$|E(G)| \leq |E(G \setminus \{v\})| + M^*(G) \leq \binom{M^*(G)}{2} + 1 + M^*(G) = \binom{M^*(G) + 1}{2} + 1.$$

(ii) The first inequality follows immediately from (i). The second holds since each component needs at least one test.   □

By solving the inequalities in Theorem 12.3.1, we obtain

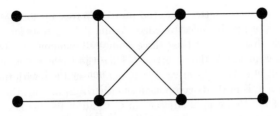

Figure 12.1: $M^*(G) = 4$, $|E| = 11$.

Corollary 12.3.2 *(i)* $M^*(G) \geq \sqrt{2|E| - 7/4} - 1/2$,
   (ii) $M^*(G) \geq \sqrt{2|V| - 7/4} - 3/2$.

Theorem 12.3.3 *For nonadaptive algorithms a graph $G(V, E)$ achieves the bound of Theorem 12.3.1(i) if and only if there exists an $M^*(G)$-subset $W \subseteq V$ such that $G(W)$ is complete, each vertex of W has degree $M^*(G)$, and there is exactly one edge not intersecting W.*

Proof. Clearly, the defective edge in G can be identified by testing the $M^*(G)$ vertices in W. Next we prove the "only if" part. Theorem 12.3.3 is easily verified for $M^*(G) \leq 3$. The general case is proved by induction. Let G be a graph achieving the bound. From the proof of Theorem 12.3.1(i), the test must be on a vertex v of degree $M^*(G)$. Consider the case that the test outcome is negative. By the induction hypothesis, $G \setminus \{v\}$ contains a complete graph on a vertex subset W' where $|W'| = M^*(G) - 1$, and other vertices of degree at most 2. Since the bound is achieved under a nonadaptive algorithm, any of the $M^*(G)$ tests can be chosen first. Therefore there must exist $M^*(G)$ vertices of degree $M^*(G)$. Inspecting the subgraph $G \setminus \{v\}$, the other $M^*(G) - 1$ vertices of degree $M^*(G)$ must be the vertices in W', therefore, $\{v\} \cup W$ constitutes a complete graph. $\square$

An example is shown in Figure 12.1.
Since the state of the last vertex can be deduced, at most $|V| - 1$ tests are required. The extreme case is completely characterized in the next theorem.

Theorem 12.3.4 $M^*(G) = |V| - 1$ *if and only if the dual graph $\bar{G}$ has at least three components.*

Proof. Suppose that $\bar{G}$ has at most two connected components. Order the vertices in each component into $v_1, \cdots, v_r$ and $w_1, \cdots, w_s$ such that in $\bar{G}$ each v_i, $i \geq 2$, and each w_j, $j \geq 2$, is adjacent to at least one of its predecessors. Test the vertices in the order of $v_r, v_{r-1}, \cdots, v_2, w_s, w_{s-1}, \cdots, w_2, w_1, v_1$ until a positive outcome or w_1 is reached. In the former case, test all neighbors of the positive vertex. Since no vertex in this sequence except possibly w_1, is adjacent to all of its successors, only $|V| - 2$

tests are required. In the latter case, (no positive vertex up to w_2), we are able to conclude that (w_1, v_1) is the defective edge. Again, $|V| - 2$ tests are consumed.

Next suppose that $\bar{G}$ has at least three connected components. Let $v_1, v_2, \cdots, v_n$ denote any test sequence of the n vertices. Then there exists a v_i not belonging to the $\bar{G}$-component of either v_{n-1} or v_n. Let v_j denote such a v_i with the largest index. Since each v_i, $i > j$, is in the $\bar{G}$-component of either v_{n-1} and v_n, they are not in the $\bar{G}$-component of v_j. Hence v_j is adjacent in G to all of its successors. Let the test outcome be negative up to v_j, and positive on v_j. Then $|V| - 1$ tests are required. □

Aigner [1] considered the additive model for graphs. Namely, when a result of vertices is tested, the test outcome reveals the number of defective vertices contained in the subset. He identified some classes of 3-optimal graphs; a graph G is said to be 3-optimal if the number of tests on this graph in the worst case equals $\lceil \log_3 |E(G)| \rceil$. First, a lemma.

Lemma 12.3.5 *Let $G(V, E)$ be a path $v_0, v_1, \cdots, v_n$. Then there are subsets $B, B' \subseteq V$ with $v_0 \in B \cup B'$ such that $G[B]$ and $G[B']$ have $\lfloor n/2 \rfloor$ and $\lceil n/2 \rceil$ edges, respectively, and $G \setminus G[B]$ and $G \setminus G[B']$ contains no edge at all.*

Proof. Choose $C = \{v_j \mid j \not\equiv 0 \pmod 4\}$. $G(C)$ has $n/2$ edges for n even, $\lfloor n/2 \rfloor$ edges for $n \equiv 1 \pmod 4$ and $\lceil n/2 \rceil$ edges for $n \equiv 3 \pmod 4$. In the first case, set $B = B' = C$; in the second case, set $B = C$ and $B' = C \cup \{v_{n-1}\}$; in the third case, set $B = C \setminus \{n\}$ and $B' = C$.   □

Theorem 12.3.6 *(i) A forest G consisting of a set of paths is optimal.*
(ii) A cycle C_n is optimal if and only if $n > 3$ and n is not a power of 3.

Proof. (i) Let l_i be the length of path i, $i = 1, \cdots, p$. Suppose

$$3^{k-1} < \sum_{i=1}^{p} l_i \leq 3^k.$$

Add $3^k - \sum_{i=1}^{p} l_i$ arbitrary edges to G to obtain G'. It suffices to prove that G' is optimal.

Since by collecting the vertices of a path in order, we can absorb the edges one by one into an induced subgraph, it is easy to find a vertex set A such that $|E(G[A])| = 3^{k-1}$ and the edges taken from a path are consecutive and starting from the beginning. Delete $E(G[A])$ to obtain a graph G^*. Apply Lemma 12.3.5 to each updated path to obtain a set B such that $|E(G[B])| = 3^{k-1}$ and $G^* \setminus B$ contains no edge. Test $A \cup V(G^*) \setminus B$.

(ii) Suppose $3^{k-1} < n < 3^k$. Let $A = \{v_1, v_2, \cdots, v_{3^{k-1}+1}\}$. Let C be an independent set of $(3^{k-1} - 3)/2$ points not intersecting the set $A \cup \{v_{3^{k-1}+2}, v_n\}$. Test $A \cup C$. If the outcome is 2, then the edge is in A, there are 3^{k-1} choices. If the outcome is 1, then the edge is between $A \cup C$ and $V \setminus (A \cup C)$ and there are $3^{k-1} - 1$ choices.

If $n = 3^k$, let A be the test set. Then the number of edges between A and $V \setminus A$ is even which is also the number of sample points for outcome 1. Thus, a 3-way even split is impossible. □

Aigner commented that the condition that the degree of any vertex in G is at most two is necessary in (i) since $K_{1,3}$ is not 3-optimal. Andreae [7] showed that a forest of maximum degree three is 3-optimal except for five cases, and conjectured that for every maximum degree, only a finite number of exception exists.

12.4   On Trees

While a tree is certainly a bipartite graph, this section is different from Sec. 12.1 in that the number of defective is one here, not two, and the tree structure represents restriction on the sample space, not the test space.

The following is a classic problem:

Consider a rooted tree T. Suppose that each leaf is associated with an item. There exists exactly one defective. Identify it by a sequence of tests $\{T_i\}$. Each T_i is on the set of all leaves which are descendants of the node i. (Namely, each test is on a subtree T_i rooted at i.) The test-outcome of T_i indicates whether T_i has the defective leaf or not.

This problem has a large number of applications. When a hierarchical organization of concepts form the framework of an identification process, usually tests exist to determine whether the unknown concept can be identified with a given category in the hierarchy. For instance, the problems of identifying an unknown disease that a patient has, identifying an unknown chemical compound, and finding a faulty gate in a logic circuit fit the above description.

Let $|T|$ denote the number of leaves in a tree T. Pratt [15] and Spira [18] proved the following.

Lemma 12.4.1 *Every nonempty finite binary tree T contains a subtree T' such that*

$$\frac{1}{3} \le \frac{|T'|}{|T|} \le \frac{2}{3}.$$

Proof. Let r be the root of T. For each node v, denote by T_v the subtree rooted at v. For each internal node v denote by v_0 and v_1, respectively, its left and right sons. Without loss of generality, assume that $|T_{v_0}| \le |T_{v_1}|$ for every v. First, one looks at the two sons r_0 and r_1 of the root r. If $|T_{r_1}| < \frac{2}{3}|T|$, then the subtree T_{r_1} meets the requirement. If $|T_{r_1}| \ge \frac{2}{3}|T|$, then one considers the son r_{11} of r_1. If $|T_{r_{11}}| < \frac{2}{3}|T|$, then the subtree $T_{r_{11}}$ meets the requirement since

$$|T_{r_{11}}| \ge \frac{1}{2}|T_{r_1}| \ge \frac{1}{3}|T|.$$

If $|T_{r_{11}}| \geq \frac{2}{3}|T|$, then consider the son r_{111} of r_{11}. This process cannot go forever because one must have $|T_{r_{1...1}}| < \frac{2}{3}|T|$ when $r_{1...1}$ is a leaf. Thus, the subtree with the required property exists.   □

From this lemma, it is easy to see that the minimax number of tests required to determine a defective leaf in the binary tree T is at most $\lceil \log_{3/2} |T| \rceil$. However, this upper bound is not tight. In fact, if a test reduces only one third of the number of leaves, then the next test would be able to reduce a larger fraction. From this observation, Rivest [16] showed that k tests are sufficient to reduce the number of possibilities by a factor of $2/F_{k+3}$, where F_i is the ith Fibonacci number. Rivest's bound is tight. To see this, consider the Fibonacci trees $\{\mathcal{F}_i\}$ constructed as follows (see Figure 12.2):

$\mathcal{F}_1 = \mathcal{F}_2 =$ the empty tree (i.e., the tree has only one node and no edge),
$\mathcal{F}_i =$ the binary tree whose root has two sons $\mathcal{F}_{i-2}$ and $\mathcal{F}_{i-1}$.

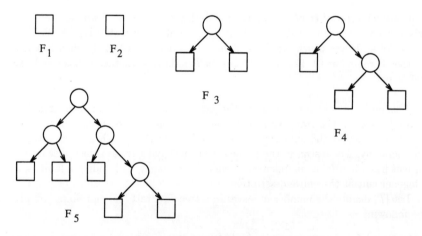

Figure 12.2: Fibonacci trees

Let $R_k(T)$ denote the minimax number of leaves after k tests.

Theorem 12.4.2 $R_k(\mathcal{F}_{k+3}) \geq 2$.

Proof. One proves this by induction on k. For $k = 0$, $R_0(\mathcal{F}_3)$ is the number of leaves in $\mathcal{F}_3$ which equals 2. For the inductive step, one first notices that if a tree T contains two disjoint subtrees $\mathcal{F}_{k+1}$ and $\mathcal{F}_k$, then $R_{k-1}(T) \geq R_{k-1}(\mathcal{F}_{k+2})$. Now, suppose that the first test is on a subtree T of $\mathcal{F}_{k+3}$. Then

$$R_k(\mathcal{F}_{k+3}) \geq \max\{R_{k-1}(T), R_{k-1}(\mathcal{F}_{k+3} \setminus T)\}.$$

Note that $\mathcal{F}_{k+3}$ has two disjoint subtrees $\mathcal{F}_{k+1}$ and $\mathcal{F}_{k+2}$ rooted at the second level. If $T = \mathcal{F}_{k+2}$, then $R_{k-1}(T) \geq 2$. If $T \neq \mathcal{F}_{k+2}$, then T must be contained in one of three disjoint subtrees isomorphic to $\mathcal{F}_{k+1}$, $\mathcal{F}_k$, and $\mathcal{F}_{k+1}$, respectively. Thus, the complement of T must contain disjoint subtrees isomorphic to $\mathcal{F}_k$ and $\mathcal{F}_{k+1}$, respectively. Hence, $R_{k-1}(\mathcal{F}_{k+3} \setminus T) \geq R_{k-1}(\mathcal{F}_{k+2}) \geq 2$.   □

Rivest [16] proposed the following greedy algorithm.

Greedy Algorithm. Given a tree T with a defective leaf, if T has at least two nodes, then carry out the following stages in each iteration.

Stage 1. Find the lowest node a such that $|T_a|/|T| > 1/2$.

Stage 2. If a is a leaf, then test a. Otherwise, let b be a son of a such that T_b has more or the same number of leaves in $T_a \setminus T_b$. If $|T| - |T_a| > |T_b|$, then test T_a. Otherwise, test T_b.

Stage 3. Suppose that the test on T' is performed in Stage 2. If T' is contaminated, then set $T := T'$; else, set $T := T \setminus T'$. If T is the empty tree, then stop; else, go back to Stage 1.

Lemma 12.4.3 *Suppose that a test on subtree T' is chosen in Stage 2. Then*

$$\max\{|T'|, |T| - |T'|\} = \min_{v \in V(T)} \max\{|T_v|, |T| - |T_v|\}.$$

Proof. Clearly, if v is an ancestor of a, then

$$\max\{|T_a|, |T| - |T_a|\} = |T_a| \leq |T_v| = \max\{|T_v|, |T| - |T_v|\}.$$

If v is not comparable with a, then $|T_v| < \frac{1}{2}|T|$. Let u be the lowest ancestor for both v and a. Then

$$|T_a| \leq |T_u| \leq |T| - |T_v| = \max\{|T_v|, |T| - |T_v|\}.$$

If v is a descendant of a other than b, then

$$\max\{|T_b|, |T| - |T_b|\} = |T| - |T_b| \leq |T| - |T_v| = \max\{|T_v|, |T| - |T_v|\}.$$

Finally, the proof is completed by noting that

$$\max\{|T'|, |T| - |T'|\} \leq \min\{|T_a|, |T| - |T_b|\}.$$

□

Let $G_k(T)$ be the maximum number of leaves in the tree after k tests chosen by the greedy algorithm.

Theorem 12.4.4 *For any binary tree T with $|T| \geq F_{k+3}$, $k \geq 1$,*

$$\frac{G_k(T)}{|T|} \leq \begin{cases} \frac{2}{F_{k+2}} \cdot \frac{G_1(T)}{|T|} & for \quad \frac{1}{2} \leq \frac{G_1(T)}{|T|} \leq \frac{F_{k+2}}{F_{k+3}} \\ \frac{2}{F_{k+1}} \cdot (1 - \frac{G_1(T)}{|T|}) & for \quad \frac{F_{k+2}}{F_{k+3}} \leq \frac{G_1(T)}{|T|} \leq \frac{2}{3}. \end{cases}$$

First, note that if $1/2 \leq G_1(T)/|T| \leq F_{k+2}/F_{k+3}$, then

$$\frac{2}{F_{k+2}} \cdot \frac{G_1(T)}{|T|} \leq \frac{2}{F_{k+3}};$$

if $F_{k+2}/F_{k+3} \leq G_1(T)/|T| \leq 2/3$, then

$$\frac{2}{F_{k+1}} \cdot (1 - \frac{G_1(T)}{|T|}) \leq \frac{2}{F_{k+1}} \cdot (1 - \frac{F_{k+2}}{F_{k+3}}) \leq \frac{2}{F_{k+3}}.$$

Thus, this theorem implies the following.

Corollary 12.4.5 *For any binary tree T with $|T| \geq F_{k+3}$,*

$$G_k(T) \leq \frac{2}{F_{k+3}}|T|.$$

Now, go back to the proof of Theorem 12.4.4.

Proof of Theorem 12.4.4. One proves it by induction on k. For $k = 1$, it follows from Lemma 12.4.1. For $k \geq 2$, let U denote the subtree of T (either the first tested subtree or its complement) such that $|U| = G_1(T)$ and V is the complement of U with respect to T. Clearly, $|V| \leq \frac{1}{2}|T|$.

Case 1. V contains the defective leaf. In this case, after the first test, the tree V is left. Thus,

$$\frac{G_k(T)}{|T|} \leq \frac{G_{k-1}(V)}{|V|} \cdot \frac{|V|}{|T|} \leq \frac{2}{F_{k+2}} \cdot \frac{1}{2} = \frac{1}{F_{k+2}}.$$

Note that $\frac{1}{2} \leq \frac{G_1(T)}{|T|} \leq \frac{2}{3}$. Thus,

$$\frac{1}{F_{k+2}} \leq \frac{2}{F_{k+2}} \cdot \frac{G_1(T)}{|T|}$$

and

$$\frac{1}{F_{k+2}} = \frac{1}{F_{k+1} + F_k} < \frac{1}{F_{k+1} + 0.5F_{k+1}} = \frac{2}{3F_{k+1}} \leq \frac{2}{F_{k+1}} \cdot (1 - \frac{G_1(T)}{|T|}).$$

Case 2. U contains the defective leaf. In this case, one claims that $G_1(U) \leq |V|$. In fact, if $U = T_a$, then

$$G_1(U) \leq |T_b| \leq |T| - |T_a| = |V|.$$

If $U = T \setminus T_b$, then $|T_a| \geq |T| - |T_b|$, so

$$G_1(U) \leq \max\{|T_a| - |T_b|, |T| - |T_a|\} \leq \max\{|T_b|, |T| - |T_a|\} = |T_b| = |V|.$$

Thus, it is always true that $G_1(U) \leq |V|$. For $1/2 \leq G_1(T)/|T| \leq F_{k+2}/F_{k+3}$, one has

$$\frac{G_k(T)}{|T|} \leq \frac{|U|}{|T|} \cdot \frac{G_{k-1}(U)}{|U|} \leq \frac{G_1(T)}{|T|} \cdot \frac{2}{F_{k+2}}.$$

For $F_{k+2}/F_{k+3} \leq G_1(T)/|T| \leq 2/3$, one has

$$\frac{1}{2} \leq \frac{G_1(U)}{|U|} \leq \frac{|V|}{|U|} = \frac{|T| - G_1(T)}{G_1(T)} \leq (\frac{F_{k+3}}{F_{k+2}} - 1) \leq \frac{F_{k+1}}{F_{k+2}}.$$

Therefore,

$$\begin{aligned}
\frac{G_k(T)}{|T|} &\leq \frac{|U|}{|T|} \cdot \frac{G_{k-1}(U)}{|U|} \\
&\leq \frac{|U|}{|T|} \cdot \frac{G_1(U)}{|U|} \cdot \frac{2}{F_{k+1}} \\
&\leq \frac{|U|}{|T|} \cdot \frac{|V|}{|U|} \cdot \frac{2}{F_{k+1}} \\
&= (1 - \frac{|U|}{|T|}) \cdot \frac{2}{F_{k+1}} \\
&= (1 - \frac{G_1(T)}{|T|}) \cdot \frac{2}{F_{k+1}}.
\end{aligned}$$

$\square$

Let $M(T)$ be the minimax number of tests for identifying a defective leaf from T. Then by Corollary 12.4.5, the following holds.

Corollary 12.4.6 $M(T) \leq \min\{k + 1 \mid |T| \leq F_{k+3}\}$.

Pelc [14] studied the same problem allowing a lie. Let $M^r(T)$ denote the minimax number of tests for identifying a defective leaf from T with at most r lies.

Theorem 12.4.7 *Let $T(n)$ be the complete balanced binary tree of n levels. Then*

$$M^1(T(n)) = 2n + 1 - \max\{k \mid M^1(T(k)) \leq n\}.$$

The problem of determining $M^r(T(n))$ for $r \geq 2$ is still open.

The tree search problem studied in this section is also investigated by Garey and Graham [13] and Garey [12]. But they did the analysis on the average-case complexity.

12.5   Other Constraints

Other constraints have been studied in the literature. We give a brief survey in this section.

Aigner [2] considered an additional constraint that each test set has at most k items. For searching an edge in a graph with this additional constraint, he argued that the problem is not so simple even for $k = 1$. For $k \geq 2$, no nontrivial result has been derived.

Aigner and Triesch [3] studied the problem of searching for subgraphs as follows: Let $\mathcal{G}$ be a collection of graphs with the same vertex set V. Determine the minimum number $L(\mathcal{G})$ such that $L(\mathcal{G})$ tests are sufficient in the worst case to identify G if each test is on an edge e and tells whether e is in G or not. This problem is also a constrained group testing problem if graphs in $\mathcal{G}$ are items with the constraint that only items in I can be tested, where

$$\mathcal{I} = \{\{G \in \mathcal{G} \mid e \in E(G)\} \mid e \subset V\}.$$

Two interesting results obtained in [4] are as follows.

Theorem 12.5.1 *Let $\mathcal{M}$ be the collection of matchings on n vertices, $n \geq 2$ even. Then $L(\mathcal{M}) = \frac{n(n-2)}{2}$.*

Theorem 12.5.2 *Let $\mathcal{T}$ be the collection of trees on n vertices. Then $L(\mathcal{T}) = \binom{n}{2} - 1$.*

A potential area of research about constrained testing is software testing. Software testing is an important and largely unexplored area. It can be formulated as a testing problem on graphs with possible failure edges and failure vertices. (See [17].) It is a complicated problem and worth studying.

References

[1] M. Aigner, Search problems on graphs, *Disc. Appl. Math.* 14 (1986) 215-230.

[2] M. Aigner, *Combinatorial Search*, (Wiley-Teubner, 1988).

[3] M. Aigner and E. Triesch, Searching for an edge in a graph, *J. Graph Theory* 12 (1988) 45-57.

[4] M. Aigner and E. Triesch, Searching for subgraphs, *Contemporary methods in graph theory*, (Bibliographisches Inst., Mannheim, 1990) 31-45.

[5] M. Aigner, E. Triesh, and Z. Tuza, Searching for acyclic orientations of graphs, *Disc. Math.* 144 (1995) 3-10.

[6] I. Althöfer and E. Triesch, Edge search in graphs and hypergraphs of bounded rank, *Discrete Mathematics* 115 (1993) 1-9.

[7] T. Andreae, A ternary search problem on graphs, *Disc. Appl. Math.* 23 (1987) 1-10.

[8] T. Andreae, A search problem on graphs which generalizes some group testing problems with two defectives, *Disc. Math.*, 88 (1991) 121-127.

[9] G.J. Chang and F.K. Hwang, A group testing problem, *SIAM J. Alg. Disc. Meth.*, 1 (1980) 21-24.

[10] P. Damaschke, A tight upper bound for group testing in graphs, *Disc. Appl. Math.* 48 (1994) 101-109.

[11] D.-Z. Du and F.K. Hwang, *Combinatorial Group Testing and its Applications* (1st ed.), (World Scientific, Singapore, 1993) pp. 203-211.

[12] M. R. Garey, Optimal binary identification procedures, *SIAM J. Appl. Math.* 23 (1972) 173-186.

[13] M. R. Garey and R. L. Graham, Performance bounds on the splitting algorithm for binary testing, *Acta Informatica* 3 (1974) 347-355.

[14] A. Pelc, Prefix search with a lie, *Journal of Combinatorial Theory* 48 (1988) 165-173.

[15] V. R. Pratt, The effect of basis on size of boolean expressions, *Proc. 16th FOCS* (1975) 119-121.

[16] R. L. Rivest, The game of "N questions" on a tree, *Disc. Math.* 17 (1977) 181-186.

[17] S. Sahni, *Software Development in Pascal*, (The Camelot Publishing Co., Fridley, Minnesota, 1985) pp. 325-368.

[18] P. M. Spira, On time hardware complexity tradeoffs for boolean functions, *Proc. 4th Hawaiian Inter. Symp. System Science* (1971) 525-527.

[19] E. Triesch, A group testing problem for hypergraphs of bounded rank, *Disc. Appl. Math.* 66 (1996) 185-188.

Part IV
Other Related Searching Problems

13

Optimal Search in One Variable

Many optimal search problems in one variable have the same flavor as CGT. We study them in this chapter.

13.1 Midpoint Strategy

When gas pipe line has a hole, one may find it by testing the pressure at some points on the line. If the pressures at two points are different, then a hole must be between them.

(a) Suppose there exists exactly one hole between points A and B. How does one choose the test points on segment AB to optimize the accuracy in the worst case?

(b) Suppose there exists at most one hole between A and B. How does one solve the same question in (a)?

Problems of this type provide continuous versions of combinatorial group testing. If the pressures at A and B are already known, then the best choice for one test is the midpoint in both problems (a) and (b). In fact, from each test, one can break the segment into two parts; one of them may contain a hole. In the worst case, the hole always falls in the longer part. So, the midpoint would minimize the longer part.

If the pressures at A and B are unknown, then the optimal strategy for (a) is that initially, test one of A and B, say A and then for each of the rest tests, choose the midpoint of the segment containing a hole. In fact, suppose that the initial two tests are at points C and D in $[A, B]$. Then the test outcome is either $[C, D]$ contains a hole or $[A, B] \setminus [C, D]$ contains a hole. That is, the tests break the segment into two parts; one contains the hole, the other one does not. Moreover, adding any new test will reduce at most half of the part with a hole. So, the worst-case optimal strategy is to let the two parts have equal length. The above midpoint strategy meets this requirement.

For (b), if the pressures at A and B are unknown, the midpoint strategy is also a good one in some sense, but not necessary the optimal. To see this, let us compare the midpoint strategy with another strategy. Suppose one uses three tests. Initially, test A.

255

By the midpoint strategy, the second test is performed at the midpoint C. In the worst case, the two pressures at A and C are the same. So, in order to know whether segment CB contains a hole or not, the third point has to be chosen at B. If C and B have different pressures, then one finds a segment of length $\frac{1}{2}|AB|$ containing a hole.

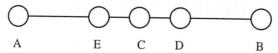

Figure 13.1: Test points

However, if the second test is performed at point D such that $|AD| = \frac{2}{3}|AB|$ (see Figure 13.1), then one gets a better result. In fact, if A and D have the same pressure, then test B; if A and D have different pressures, then test the midpoint E of AD. In this way, one can determine either the nonexistence of a hole or the position of a hole with accuracy $\frac{1}{3}$.

In general, the following holds.

Theorem 13.1.1 *Suppose there exists at most one hole between A and B and the pressures at A and B are unknown. For a natural number k, let $\epsilon(k)$ denote the smallest ϵ such that k tests are sufficient in the worst case to determine either a hole with accuracy $\epsilon|AB|$ or nonexistence of a hole in $[A,B]$. Then $\epsilon(k) = \frac{1}{2^{k-1}-1}$.*

Proof. First consider a similar problem under a slightly different assumption that the pressure at A is known and the pressure at B is unknown. Let $\epsilon^*(k)$ denote the smallest ϵ such that k tests are sufficient in the worst case to determine either a hole with accuracy ϵ or the nonexistence of a hole in $[A,B]$ $\epsilon^*(k) = \frac{1}{2^{k-1}}$ is proved by induction on k. For $k = 1$, the unique test must be made at point B (otherwise, it cannot be known whether a hole exists at B or not). In the induction step, suppose the first test is made at point C with $|AC| = x|AB|$. There are two cases.

Case 1. A and C have the same pressure. So, $[A, C]$ has no hole. The rest $k - 1$ tests are sufficient in the worst case to determine either a hole with accuracy $\epsilon^*(k - 1)|CB|$ or $[C, B]$ having no hole.

Case 2. A and C have different pressures. So, $[A, C]$ contains a hole and $[C, B]$ does not. The rest $k - 1$ tests would be performed in $[A, C]$. Since both pressures at A and C are known, the optimal strategy is to choose the midpoint. In this way, one can determine a hole with accuracy $2^{1-k}|AC|$.

Summarizing the two cases, one sees that

$$\epsilon^*(k) = \min_{0 \le x \le 1} \max\left(\frac{x}{2^{k-1}}, \epsilon^*(k-1)\cdot(1-x)\right).$$

Since $\frac{x}{2^{k-1}}$ is increasing and $\epsilon^*(k-1)(1-x)$ is decreasing as x increases, $\max(\frac{x}{2^{k-1}}, \epsilon^*(k-1)\cdot(1-x))$ achieves its minimum when $\frac{x}{2^{k-1}} = \epsilon^*(k-1)(1-x)$, i.e., $x = \frac{2^{k-1}}{2^{k}-1}$. Therefore, $\epsilon^*(k) = \frac{1}{2^{k}-1}$.

To prove $\epsilon(k) = \frac{1}{2^{k-1}-1}$, it suffices to prove that in the situation that both pressures at A and B are unknown, an optimal strategy must first test one of A and B. Suppose to the contrary that the first test is taken place at C other than A and B. Without loss of generality, assume $|AC| > \frac{2^{k-2}-1}{2^{k-1}-1}|AB|$. Since $\epsilon^*(k-2)|AC| > \epsilon^*(k-1)|AB|$, the rest $k-1$ tests must apply to $[A, C]$. This leaves $[C, B]$ uncertain. So, the first test must be made at either A or B. $\square$

Note that if both pressures at A and B are unknown then the first test in an optimal strategy must be made at either A or B. So, The problem can be reduced to the situation that either the pressure at A or the pressure at B is known and the other is unknown. The following corollary establishes an advantage of the midpoint strategy.

Corollary 13.1.2 *Suppose that there exists at most one hole between points A and B and the pressure at A is known and the pressure at B is unknown. Assume that the first test is made at C. Let $d(C, k)$ denote the smallest d such that k tests are sufficient to determine either a hole with accuracy d or the nonexistence of a hole in $[A, B]$. Let C^* denote the midpoint of $[A, B]$. If $C \neq C^*$, then there exists k_0 such that for $k \geq k_0$, $d(C, k) > d(C^*, k)$.*

Proof. Denote $x = \frac{|AC|}{|AB|}$. From the proof of Theorem 13.1.1, it is easy to see that

$$d(C, k) = \max(\frac{x}{2^{k-1}}, \epsilon^*(k-1)(1-x))|AB|.$$

So, $d(C, k)$ is increasing for $0 \leq x \leq \frac{2^{k-1}}{2^k-1}$ and decreasing for $\frac{2^{k-1}}{2^k-1} \leq x \leq 1$. Thus, if $|AC| > |CB|$, then for all $k \geq 2$, $d(C, k) > d(C^*, k)$. If $|AC| < |CB|$, then there exists k_0 such that for $k \geq k_0$, $|AC| > \frac{2^{k-1}}{2^k-1}|AB|$. For those k, $d(C, k) > d(C^*, k)$. $\square$

13.2   Fibonacci Search

Consider a unimodal function $f : [a, b] \to R$ (see Figure 13.2). Choose two points x_0 and x_1 from $[a, b]$ with $x_0 < x_1$. Compare $f(x_0)$ with $f(x_1)$. If $f(x_0) \geq f(x_1)$, then the maximum point of f falls into $[a, x_1]$; otherwise, the maximum point falls into $[x_0, b]$. This fact provides an iterative method to search the maximum point in $[a, b]$. Initially, choose a point x_0 as above. At the kth step, choose one new point x_k which together with a point x_i ($i < k$) forms a new pair in the interval of uncertainty. in which the maximum must lie. Then delete a piece from the uncertain interval by the above fact. What is the best choice for points x_k's? The situation is similar to the problem (b) in the last section. Let $F_0 = F_1 = 1$ and $F_k = F_{k-1} + F_{k-2}$ for $k \geq 2$. Then the characteristic equation for this recursive formula is

$$x^2 - x - 1 = 0$$

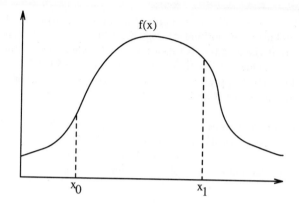

Figure 13.2: Unimodal function

which has two roots $\frac{1 \pm \sqrt{5}}{2}$. So, in general,

$$F_k = \frac{1}{\sqrt{5}} \left(\left(\frac{1 + \sqrt{5}}{2} \right)^k + \left(\frac{1 - \sqrt{5}}{2} \right)^k \right).$$

The sequence $\{F_k\}$ is the well-known Fibonacci sequence.

Theorem 13.2.1 *For a natural number k, let ϵ be a number such that k tests are sufficient in the worst case to determine the maximum point with accuracy $\epsilon|b - a|$. Then $\epsilon \geq \frac{1}{F_k}$.*

Proof. The theorem is proved by induction on k. For $k = 1$ and $k = 2$, it is trivial. In the induction step, suppose x_0 and x_1 are chosen in the initial step and the first step. Consider two cases.

   Case 1. $|a - x_1| \geq \frac{F_{k-1}}{F_k}|a - b|$. In the worst case, it may happen that $f(x_0) > f(x_1)$. So, $[a, x_1]$ is left for the interval of uncertainty. By the induction hypothesis, $\epsilon \frac{|b-a|}{|x_1-a|} \geq \frac{1}{F_{k-1}}$. So,

$$\epsilon \geq \frac{|x_1 - a|}{|b - a|} \cdot \frac{F_{k-2}}{F_{k-1}} \geq \frac{F_{k-1}}{F_k} \frac{1}{F_{k-1}} = \frac{1}{F_k}.$$

   Case 2. $|a - x_1| < \frac{F_{k-1}}{F_k}|b - a|$. Then $|x_1 - b| > \frac{F_{k-2}}{F_k}|a - b|$. In the worst case, the interval $[x_0, b]$ may be left in uncertainty at the first step and the interval $[x_1, b]$ is then left in uncertainty at the second step. Applying the induction hypothesis to $[x_1, b]$, one obtains

$$\epsilon \frac{|a - b|}{|x_1 - b|} \geq \frac{1}{F_{k-2}}.$$

So,

$$\epsilon \geq \frac{|x_1 - b|}{|a - b|} \frac{1}{F_{k-2}} \geq \frac{1}{F_k}.$$

$\square$

To reach the lower bound $1/F_k$, it is easy to see from the above proof that x_0 and x_1 must be chosen such that

$$\frac{|x_0 - b|}{|a - b|} = \frac{|x_1 - a|}{|a - b|} = \frac{F_{k-1}}{F_k}.$$

As k goes to infinity, this ratio goes to $\frac{\sqrt{5}-1}{2}$, the well-known golden ratio.

Using the golden ratio to determine points x_k is a well-known line search procedure in nonlinear programming [19]. The method drew a special attention from Lou-Geng Hua [10] [11]. He promoted the golden section search[1] as the most important method in optimum seeking. By using the continued fraction, he established the optimality of the golden section search, which is similar to that of the middle point strategy. In the following, his theorem is given with a proof provided by Tao [26].

For any algorithm α and any unimodal function f on interval $[0, 1]$ of length one, let $L_f(\alpha, n)$ denote the total length of the intervals of uncertainty after n tests on the function f. Let

$$L(\alpha, n) = \sup_{\text{unimodal } f} L_f(\alpha, n).$$

Theorem 13.2.2 *For any algorithm α, there exists $n(\alpha) > 0$ such that for $n \geq n(\alpha)$, $L(\alpha, n) \leq q^n$ where $q = \frac{\sqrt{5}-1}{2}$. Moreover, the equality sign holds if and only if α is the golden section method.*

To prove this theorem, Tao first established two lemmas.

Lemma 13.2.3 *For any algorithm α, one of the following holds:*

$$L(\alpha, 1) > q, \tag{13.1}$$
$$L(\alpha, 2) \geq q^2. \tag{13.2}$$

Proof. Suppose that the first and the second test points are x_1 and x_2. Without loss of generality, assume $x_1 < x_2$. If $x_1 < 1 - q$, then

$$L(\alpha, 1) = \max(1 - x_1, x_2) \geq 1 - x_1 > q.$$

If $x_1 \geq 1 - q$, then

$$L(\alpha, 2) \geq L(\alpha, 1) - (x_2 - x_1) \geq x_2 - (x_2 - x_1) = x_1 \geq 1 - q = q^2.$$

$\square$

---

[1]The golden section search is as follows: At each step with an interval $[a, b]$ of uncertainty, choose x_0 and x_1 such that $|x_0 - a|/|x_1 - a| = |x_1 - a|/|b - a| = \frac{\sqrt{5}-1}{2}$ and then compare $f(x_0)$ and $f(x_1)$.

Lemma 13.2.4 *For any algorithm α, there exists a sequence of natural numbers $\{n_k\}$ such that*
(a) For $n \in \{n_k\}$,

$$L(\alpha, n) = \prod_{i=1}^{m}(q + \epsilon_i^*) \prod_{j=1}^{r}(q^2 + \epsilon_j)$$

where $m + 2r = n$, $\epsilon^* > 0$, $\epsilon_j \geq 0$, $i = 1, 2, \cdots, m$, $j = 1, \cdots, r$.
(b) $1 \leq n_{k+1} - n_k \leq 2$.

Proof. By Lemma 13.2.3, either $L(\alpha, 1) = q + \epsilon_1^*$ or $L(\alpha, 2) = q^2 + \epsilon_2$ for some $\epsilon_1^* > 0$ and $\epsilon_j \geq 0$. If the former case occurs, then set $n_1 = 2$; if the latter case occurs, then set $n_1 = 2$. Similarly, consider the remainder interval and in general, define

$$n_{k+1} = \begin{cases} n_k + 1 & \text{if} \quad L(\alpha, n_k + 1) > qL(\alpha, n_k) \\ n_k + 2 & \text{if} \quad L(\alpha, n_k + 2) \geq q^2 L(\alpha, n_k). \end{cases}$$

This sequence meets the requirement. $\square$

Now, Theorem 13.2.2 can be readily proved.
Proof of Theorem 13.2.2. By Lemma 13.2.4, for any natural number n, either $n \in \{n_k\}$ or $n = n_k + 1$ for some k. In the latter case,

$$L(\alpha, n) = \prod_{i=1}^{m}(q + \epsilon_i^*) \prod_{j=1}^{r}(q^2 + \epsilon_j)(q - \epsilon_{r+1}')$$

where $m + 2r = n_k = n - 1$, $\epsilon_i^* > 0$, $0.5 > \epsilon_j \geq \epsilon_j' \geq 0$ for $i = 1, 2, \cdots, m$ and $j = 1, 2, \cdots, r + 1$. Thus,

$$\frac{L(\alpha, n)}{q^n} = \prod_{i=1}^{m}\left(1 + \frac{\epsilon_i^*}{q}\right) \prod_{j=1}^{r}\left(1 + \frac{\epsilon_j}{q^2}\right)\left(1 - \frac{\epsilon_{r+1}'}{q}\right).$$

Next, it is shown that for sufficiently large n, $\frac{L(\alpha,n)}{q^n} > 1$.
Case 1. $\{\epsilon_j\}$ is a finite sequence, i.e., for sufficiently large n, $n \in \{n_k\}$. In this case, it is clear that for sufficiently large n, $\frac{L(\alpha,n)}{q^n} > 1$.
Case 2. $\{\epsilon_j\}$ is an infinite sequence, but it does not converge to 0. In this case, there exists $\epsilon_0 > 0$ such that for infinitely many j, $\epsilon_j \geq \epsilon_0$. Thus,

$$\frac{L(\alpha, n)}{q^n} \geq \left(1 + \frac{\epsilon_0}{q}\right)^v \left(1 - \frac{1}{2q}\right) \to \infty \text{ as } n \to \infty.$$

Case 3. $\lim_{j\to\infty} \epsilon_j = 0$. Since $\epsilon_j \geq \epsilon_j'$, $\lim_{j\to\infty} \epsilon_j' = 0$. Note that α is different from the golden section search. Therefore, either $m \geq 1$ or ($m = 0$ and $\epsilon_j > 0$ for some j, say $\epsilon_1 > 0$, without loss of generality). Thus, either

$$\frac{L(\alpha, n)}{q^n} \geq \left(1 + \frac{\epsilon_1^*}{q}\right)\left(1 - \frac{\epsilon_{r+1}'}{q}\right) \to \left(1 + \frac{\epsilon_1^*}{q}\right) > 1$$

or

$$\frac{L(\alpha, n)}{q^n} \geq (1 + \frac{\epsilon_1^*}{q})(1 - \frac{\epsilon_{r+1}'}{q}) \rightarrow (1 + \frac{\epsilon_1}{q^2}) > 1.$$

$\square$

Theorem 13.2.1 was proved by Kiefer [13]. Karp and Miranker [12], Avriel and Wilder [2], and Beamer and Wilder [3] parallelized the testing process. They considered a sequence of stages. In the ith stage, exactly k_i tests are performed parallelly. When the total number of tests is predetermined, they generalized Kiefer's result to determine the test points. Hong [9] considered the case that the number of tests are not predetermined. He established a generalization of Theorem 13.2.2.

Let $\{k_i\}$ be an infinite sequence of natural numbers. For any algorithm α and any unimodal function f on interval $[0, 1]$ of length one, let $L_f(\alpha, k_1, \cdots, k_n)$ denote the total length of the intervals of uncertainty after n stages on the function f. Let

$$L(\alpha, k_1, \cdots, k_n) = \sup_{\text{unimodal} f} L_f(\alpha, k_1, \cdots, k_n).$$

Theorem 13.2.5 (a) If $\{k_i\}$ contains an infinite subsequence of odd numbers or k_1 is odd, then there exists a strategy α^* such that for any strategy α,

$$L(\alpha^*, k_1, \cdots, k_n) \leq L(\alpha, k_1, \cdots, k_n)$$

for sufficiently large n.

(b) In general, for any $0 < \beta < 1$, there exists a strategy α_β such that for any strategy α,

$$\beta \cdot L(\alpha_\beta, k_1, \cdots, k_n) \leq L(\alpha, k_1, \cdots, k_n)$$

for sufficiently large n.

Beamer and Wilder [3] raised the following problem: Given N, determine $\{k_i\}_{1 \leq i \leq n}$ such that $k_1 + \cdots + k_n = N$ and $\inf_\alpha L(\alpha, k_1, \cdots, k_n)$ achieves the minimum. Through efforts made by Wu [27], Qi, Yuan, and Wu [23, 24], Li [15, 16, 17], Luo [20], and Li and Weng [18], the problem was finally solved.

Due to Hua's popularization efforts, many results on optimal searchs in one variable were obtained. The reader may refer to [11] for more information.

A unimodal function has only one maximal point. In general, a function may have more than one maximal points. To find the global maximum point, one may need to identify all maximal points. Could some ideas in previous chapters be helpful to do this job? It might. But, not enough attention has been given to the question.

13.3   Minimum Root Identification

A lot of problems in the optimal search can be reduced to the following form.

Minimum Root Identification: Given m continuous functions h_i's on $[0,1]$ with property that

(*) $h_i(0) \leq 0$ for all $i = 1, \cdots, m$ and each h_i has at most one root in $[0,1]$,

identify
$$\min\{z \in [0,1] \mid h_i(z) = 0 \text{ for some } i\}.$$

For example, consider the following optimization problem:

$$\begin{aligned} \text{maximize} \quad & f(x) \\ \text{subject to} \quad & g_1(x) \leq 0, \cdots, g_m(x) \leq 0 \\ & x \in R^n \end{aligned}$$

where f is continuously differentiable in the *feasible region* Ω, the set of all points satisfying the constraints, and all g_i are continuously differentiable convex functions in the n-dimensional Euclidean space R^n. There are a family of classical iterative methods solving it, called *feasible direction methods*, which work as follows: Initially, find a feasible point x_1 (i.e., a point in Ω). At the kth iteration with a feasible point x_k, first find a direction d_k satisfying that (1) $\nabla f(x_k)^T d_k > 0$, and (2) there exists $\alpha_0 > 0$ such that for $\alpha \in [0, \alpha_0]$, $x_k + \alpha d_k$ is a feasible point. Such a direction is called a *feasible ascent direction*. Once a feasible ascent direction d_k is found, one then obtains a new feasible point x_{k+1} with $f(x_k + 1) > f(x_k)$ by a line search procedure, e.g., the golden section search described in the last section.

Since all g_i are convex, the feasible region Ω is a convex set. Define $\alpha^* = \max\{\alpha \mid x_k + \alpha d_k \text{ is a feasible point}\}$. Then for all $\alpha \in [0, \alpha^*]$, $x_k + \alpha d_k$ is feasible and for any $\alpha > \alpha^*$, $x_k + \alpha d_k$ is not feasible. In general, finding α^* involves unbounded search which will be studied in the next chapter. However, when the feasible region Ω is bounded or when α_0 is defined by

$$\alpha_0 = \min\{1, \alpha^*\},$$

the problem of finding α^* or α_0 can be reduced to the minimum root identification problem. To do so, define $h_i(\alpha) = g_i(x_k + \alpha d_k)$. Then h_i will have the property (*) described in the problem and

$$\alpha_0 = \min\{z \in [0,1] \mid h_i(z) = 0 \text{ for some } i\}.$$

A naive bisecting method can compute α_0 with uncertainty at most 2^{-n} in nm evaluations of h_i's. (At each step, one tests the feasibility of the midpoint of the interval of uncertainty and each test for the feasibility of a point requires values of all h_i at the point.) However, there are several obvious ways which can save the number of evaluations significantly. These methods can be found in [7, 4, 6, 8, 14, 21, 25]. In particular, Rivest *et al.* [25] discovered an equivalent relation between the minimum root identification and a problem with unreliable tests as follows.

Half-Lie Problem: Suppose there is an unknown $x \in (0, 1]$. Given a natural number r, the problem is to identify x by using only questions of the form "Is $x < c$?" with $c \in (0, 1]$, where up to r of the "No"-answers but none of the "Yes"-answers may be erroneous.

The equivalence of the two problems is in the sense that an optimal strategy for one problem can be trivially transformed to an optimal strategy for the other one, vice versa.

This equivalence is now shown.

Consider each evaluation of function h_i at α as an answer for the question "Is $h_i(\alpha) > 0$?". Associated with a questioning history (together with answers), the state S is given through a sequence of $m + 1$ numbers

$$0 \le L_1 \le \cdots \le L_m \le 1, 0 \le R \le 1$$

and a permutation π of $\{1, \cdots, m\}$ chosen such that L_i is the largest α for which the question "Is $h_{\pi(i)}(\alpha) > 0$?" has received a "No"-answer ($L_i = 0$ if no such answer has been received yet) and R is the smallest α for which there exists a question "Is $h_i(\alpha) > 0$?" which has received a "Yes"-answer. ($R = 1$ if no "Yes"-answer has been received yet.) Clearly, the interval of uncertainty at this state is $(L_1, R]$.

Lemma 13.3.1 *The optimality of any strategy is unchanged if a question "Is $h_{\pi(i)}(c) > 0$?" is replaced by a question "Is $h_{\pi(0)}(c) > 0$?".*

Proof. Let α be an optimal strategy in which the question "Is $h_{\pi(i)}(c) > 0$?" is asked at the state $(L_1, \cdots, L_m, R)$. Clearly, $L_i < c \le R$. Let $\Delta_k(L_1, \cdots, L_m, R)$ denote the minimum length of interval of uncertainty after k more questions starting from the state $(L_1, \cdots, L_m, R)$. Clearly, $L_i < c \le R$. If the answer is "Yes", then the next state is $(L_1, \cdots, L_m, c)$. If the answer is "No", then the next state is $(L_1, \cdots, L_{i-1}, L_{i+1}, \cdots, L_k, c, L_{k+1}, \cdots, L_m, R)$ for some k with $L_k \le c \le L_{k+1}$. Thus,

$$\Delta_m(L_1, \cdots, L_m, R) = \max(\Delta_{m-1}(L_1, \cdots, L_m, c),$$
$$\Delta_{m-1}(L_1, \cdots, L_{i-1}, L_{i+1}, \cdots, L_k, c, L_{k+1}, \cdots, L_m, R).$$

Note that $\delta_m(L_1, \cdots, L_m, R)$ is a nonincreasing function with respect to $L_1, \cdots, L_m$. Thus,

$$\Delta_{m-1}^\alpha(L_2, \cdots, L_k, c, L_{k+1}, \cdots, L_m, R)$$
$$\le \Delta_{m-1}^\alpha(L_1, \cdots, L_{i-1}, L_{i+1}, \cdots, L_k, c, L_{k+1}, \cdots, L_m, R).$$

It follows that

$$\Delta_m(L_1, \cdots, L_m, R) \ge \max(\Delta_{m-1}(L_1, \cdots, L_m, c),$$
$$\Delta_{m-1}(L_2, \cdots, L_k, c, L_{k+1}, \cdots, L_m, R)).$$

This means that if the question "Is $h_{\pi(i)}(c) > 0$?" is replaced by the question "Is $h_{\pi(0)}(c) > 0$?", then the optimality of the strategy is unchanged.   □

Now, consider the half-lie problem. The state of this problem can be summarized by a sequence of number

$$L_1 \leq \cdots \leq L_r, \quad 0 < R \leq 1$$

where L_i's are the r largest numbers c such that the question "Is $x < c$?" has received a "No"-answer ($L_1 = \cdots = L_k = 0$ if only $r - k$ "No"-answers have been received) and R is the smallest c such that the question "Is $x < c$?" has received a "Yes"-answer ($R = 1$ if no "Yes"-answer has been received).

Now, let $m = r$ and map the question "Is $x < c$?" to the question "Is $h_{\pi(0)}(c) > 0$?". Then in both problems, from the state $(L_1, \cdots, L_m, R)$ the answer "Yes" yields the state $(L_1, \cdots, L_m, c)$ and the answer "No" yields the state $(L_2, \cdots, L_k, c, L_{k+1}, \cdots, L_m, R)$. Thus, this mapping gives a one-to-one correspondence between strategies for the half-lie problem and strategies, which use only questions of the form "Is $h_{\pi(0)}(c) > 0$?", for the minimum root identification problem.

Moreover, by Lemma 13.3.1, the optimality of any strategy is unchanged if a question "Is $h_{\pi(i)}(c) > 0$?" is replaced by a question "Is $h_{\pi(0)}(c) > 0$?". Thus, the images of optimal strategies for the half-lie problem under the above mapping are actually optimal strategies for the minimum root identification problem.

Conversely, an optimal strategy for the minimum root identification problem can first be transformed to an optimal strategy using only questions in the form "Is $h_{\pi(0)}(c) > 0$?" and then transformed to an optimal strategy for the half-lie problem. Thus, Rivest *et al.* [25] concluded.

Theorem 13.3.2 *The minimum root identification problem and the half-lie problem are equivalent.*

Clearly, the optimal strategy in Sec. 8.2 for the problem of identifying an unknown $x \in (0, 1]$ with up to m lies is also a strategy for the half-lie problem. However, it may not be an optimal strategy. Let us restate the strategy here directly for the minimum root identification problem for convenience of the reader.

Associated with a natural number j (the number of remaining tests) and a state $S = (L_1, \cdots, L_m, R)$, a weight is given as follows:

$$w(j, S) = \sum_{i=1}^{t-1} \left(\binom{j}{i} \right) (L_{i+1} - L_i) + \left(\binom{j}{t} \right) (R - L_t)$$

where $L_t \leq R \leq L_{t+1}$ (denote $L_{m+1} = 1$).

Suppose that a new question "Is $h_{\pi(0)}(\alpha)$?" is asked at the state S where $L_r \leq \alpha \leq L_{r+1} \leq R$. Let $S_y(\alpha)$ and $S_n(\alpha)$ denote two states obtained respectively from answers "Yes" and "No". Then the strategy can result in the following algorithm.

Algorithm: For a given accuracy ϵ, find k such that $\left(\binom{k}{m}\right) 2^{-k} \leq \epsilon$. ($k$ is the total number of tests needed for the given accuracy.) Then carry out the following:

for $j = k, k-1, \cdots, 1$ **do begin**
    compute $w(j-1, S_y(R))$;
    find $\alpha \in (L_1, R]$ such that
        $w(j-1, S_y(\alpha)) \leq 0.5 \cdot w(j, S)$ and
        $w(j-1, S_n(\alpha)) \leq 0.5 \cdot w(j, S)$;
    answer question "Is $h_{\pi(0)}(\alpha) > 0?$";
end-for

Note that at the initial state, the weight is $\left(\binom{k}{m}\right)$. After answering a question "Is $h_{\pi(0)}(\alpha) > 0?$", the weight is reduced to a half. Thus, k questions would reduce the weight to a number less than $\left(\binom{k}{m}\right) 2^{-k}$. Moreover, $w(0, S) = |R - L_1|$. That is, after k questions, the weight is exactly the length of the interval of uncertainty which contains α_0. So, the following can be concluded.

Theorem 13.3.3 *Using k questions "Is $h_i(\alpha) > 0?$", one can determine the minimum root with accuracy* $\left(\binom{k}{m}\right) 2^{-k}$.

The minimum root identification problem can also be solved by using the chip game. To use the chip game, the domain has to be transformed from the continuous one to a discrete one. To do so, given an accuracy ϵ, choose $n = \lceil 1/\epsilon \rceil$ and consider the domain $\{\frac{i}{n} \mid j = 1, 2, \cdots, n\}$. Now, the chip game can be performed on this domain by Aslam-Dhagat's method. Namely, a j^* can be obtained to satisfy

$$j^* = \max\{j \mid h_i(\frac{j}{n}) \leq 0 \text{ for every } i = 1, \cdots, m\}.$$

Clearly, $\frac{i^*}{n}$ is within distance ϵ from the minimum root.

By Theorem 13.3.3, to identify the minimum root with accuracy 2^{-n}, k questions are enough if $\left(\binom{k}{m}\right) 2^{-k} \leq 2^{-n}$. By Lemma 5.3.2, it is sufficient if k satisfies

$$2^{kH(m/k)-k} \leq 2^{-n},$$

that is,

$$k(1 - H(m/k)) \geq n.$$

Note that $k(1 - H(m/k))$ is an increasing function of k. Thus, $\lceil k_0 \rceil$ questions are enough if k_0 satisfies

$$k_0(1 - H(m/k_0)) = n.$$

Note that

$$k_0 - (n + m\log n - m\log m)$$
$$= k_0 - k_0(1 - H(m/k_0)) - m\log\{k_0(1 - H(m/k_0))\} + m\log m$$
$$= k_0 H(m/k_0) + m\log(m/k_0) - m\log(1 - H(m/k_0))$$
$$= -k_0(1 - m/k_0)\log(1 - m/k_0) - m\log(1 - H(m/k_0)).$$

Since

$$\lim_{k_0\to\infty} -k_0(1 - m/k_0)\log(1 - m/k_0) - m\log(1 - H(m/k_0)) = m\log e$$

and $-k_0(1 - m/k_0)\log(1 - m/k_0) - m\log(1 - H(m/k_0))$ is increasing as k_0 increases, one has that

$$k_0 = n + m\log n - m\log m + O(m).$$

Rivest *et al.* [25] also established a matching lower bound as follows.

Theorem 13.3.4 *Suppose k questions "Is $x < c$?" are enough to determine an unknown $x \in (0,1]$ with accuracy 2^{-n} when up to r of the "No"-answers, but none of the "Yes"-answers, may be erroneous. Then $k \geq n + r\log n - r\log r + O(r)$.*

Since the set of uncertainty is always an interval, Theorem 13.3.4 is equivalent to the following.

Theorem 13.3.5 *Suppose k questions "Is $x < c$?" are enough to determine an unknown $x \in \{1,\cdots,2^n\}$ when up to r of the "No"-answers, but none of the "Yes"-answers, may be erroneous. Then $k \geq n + r\log n - r\log r + O(r)$.*

Proof. Consider an optimal strategy S which is represented by a binary "decision tree" T_S. Each internal node of T_S is a question "Is $x \leq c$?"; the two edges from the internal node to its right and left sons correspond to the "Yes"-answer and "No"-answer, respectively. Each leaf ℓ is associated with a value $value(\ell)$ which is the determined value of the unknown x. Since the optimality is considered in the worst case, without loss of generality, T_S can be assumed to be completely balanced, that is, the strategy S always asks exactly k questions. (If x is identified in less than k questions, then asks some dumb questions like "Is $x \leq 2^n$?" for the rest times.)

Let $lies(\ell)$ and $yes(\ell)$ be two subsets of $\{1,\cdots,k\}$ which indicate on the path from the root to the leaf ℓ which questions were answered incorrectly and which questions were answered "Yes". That is, if $i \in lies(\ell)$, then the ith question along the path from the root to ℓ must be answered "No" which is also a lie; if $i \in yes(\ell)$, then the i question on the path must be answered "Yes" which cannot be a lie. Suppose $value(\ell) = x$. If $|lies(\ell)| < r$, then for each $i \in yes(\ell)$, the "No"-answer will give one more lie without providing any information. Therefore, the "No" branch of the ith question must have a leaf ℓ' such that $value(\ell) = x$ and $|lies(\ell')| = |lies(\ell)| + 1$.

Now, one considers a x which satisfies the following property:

On every path from the root to a leave ℓ with $value(\ell) = x$ and every $i \in \{1, \cdots, r\}$, at least one fourth of k/r answers between $1 + i \cdot (k/r)$th and $(i+1)(k/r)$th answers are "Yes"-answers.

Such an x is called a *regular value*.

Claim. For every regular x, there are at least $(k/(4r))^r$ leaves with value x.

Proof. Define

$$N_x(i) = \{t \mid t \text{ is a node in } T_S \text{ on level } i \cdot (k/r) + 1 \text{ and}$$
$$\text{has a leaf } \ell \text{ with } value(\ell) = x \text{ and } |lies(\ell)| = i$$
$$\text{but no leaf } \ell' \text{ with } value(\ell) = x \text{ and } lies(\ell') < i\}.$$

Clearly, $N_x(0)$ consists of the root, so $|N_x(0)| = 1$. For $i < r$, note that each "Yes"-answer on the path from a node $t \in N_x(i)$ to a leaf ℓ with $value(\ell) = x$ and $|lies(\ell)| = i$, between level $1 + i \cdot (k/r)$ and level $(i+1)(k/r)$, provides a node in $N_x(i+1)$. Since x is regular, there exist at least $k/(4r)$ such "Yes"-answers for each node t in $N_x(i)$. Therefore,

$$N_x(i+1) \geq \frac{k}{4r} N(i).$$

It follows that

$$N_x(r) \geq \left(\frac{k}{4r} \right)^r.$$

$\square$

To prove the theorem, it suffices to prove that for sufficiently large n, there exist at least 2^{n-1} regular values among $\{1, \cdots, 2^n\}$. In fact, if this is done, then for sufficiently large n, by the Claim, the total number of leaves in T_S is at least

$$2^{n-1} \left(\frac{k}{4r} \right)^r.$$

Thus, the depth of T_S is

$$k \geq \log(2^{n-1} \left(\frac{k}{4r} \right)^r) = n - 1 + r \log k - r \log r - 2r.$$

By the information lower bound, $k \geq n$. Thus, for sufficiently large n,

$$k \geq n + r \log n - r \log r - 2r - 1,$$

that is,

$$k \geq n + r \log n - r \log r + O(r).$$

Now, it will be proved that there are at least 2^{n-1} regular values among $\{1, \cdots, 2^n\}$. First, note that the number of "Yes"-"No" sequences of length k/r with less than $k/(4r)$ "Yes"-answers is

$$\left(\binom{k/r}{k/(4r)}\right) \le 2^{(k/r)H(1/4)}.$$

Thus,

the number of irregular values among $\{1, \cdots, 2^n\}$

$\le$ the number of paths each of which does not satisfy the condition in the definition of the regular value

$\le$ $r2^{(k/r)H(1/4)} \cdot 2^{k-k/r}$

$\le$ $2^{kd+\log r}$

where

$$d = 1 - \frac{1}{r} + \frac{1}{r} \cdot H(\frac{1}{4}) = 1 - \frac{0.18...}{r} < 1.$$

Since $k \le n + r \log n - r \log r + O(r)$, one has that for sufficiently large n,

$$kd + \log r \le (n + r \log n - r \log r + O(r))d + \log r < n - 1.$$

This completes the proof of the theorem. $\square$

References

[1] M. Aigner, *Combinatorial Search*, (John Wiley & Sons, New York, 1988).

[2] M. Avriel and D.J. Wilder, Optimal search for a maximum with sequences of simultaneous function evaluations, *Management Science* 12 (1966) 722-731.

[3] J.H. Beamer and D.J. Wilder, Minimax optimization of unimodal functions by variable block search, *Management Science* 16 (1970) 529-541.

[4] J.H. Beamer and D.J. Wilder, A minimax search plan for constrained optimization problems, *J. Optimization Theory Appl.* 12 (1973) 439-446.

[5] E.R. Berlekamp, Block for the binary symmetric channel with noiseless delayless feedback in *Error-Correcting Codes*, (Wiley, New York, 1968) 61-85.

[6] S. Gal, Multidimensional minimax search for a maximum, *SIAM J. Appl. Math.* 23 (1972) 513-526.

[7] S. Gal, B. Bacherlis, and A. Ben-Tal, On finding the maximum range of validity of a constrained System, *SIAM J. Control and Optimization* 16 (1978) 473-503.

[8] S. Gal and W.L. Miranker, Sequential and parallel search for finding a root, *Tech. Rep.* 30, IBM Israel Scientific Center, Haifa, Israel, 1975.

[9] J.-W. Hong, Optimal strategy for optimum seeking when the number of tests is uncertain, *Scientia Sinica* No.2 (1974) 131-147 (in Chinese).

[10] L.-G. Hua and Y. Wang, *Popularizing Mathematical Methods in the People's Republic of China*, (Boston, Birkhäuser, 1989).

[11] L.-G. Hua, *Optimum Seeking Methods*, (Science Press, Beijing, 1981)(in Chinese).

[12] R.M. Karp and W.L. Miranker, Parallel minimax search for a maximum, *J. Combinatorial Theory* 4 (1968) 19-35.

[13] J. Kiefer, Sequential minimax search for a maximum, *Proceedings of Amer. Math. Soc.* 4 (1953) 502-506.

[14] J. Kiefer, Optimum sequential search and approximation methods under minimum regularity assumptions, *SIAM J. Appl. Math.* 5 (1957) 105-136.

[15] W. Li, The solution of optimal block search problem for $N \geq 3n$, *Acta Mathematicae Sinica* No.4 (1974) 259-269 (in Chinese).

[16] W. Li, Solution of optimal block search problem for $N \geq 3n$ (continuation), *Acta Mathematicae Sinica* No.1 (1975) 54-64 (in Chinese).

[17] W. Li, *Optimal Sequential Block Search*, (Heldermann, Berlin, 1984).

[18] W. Li and Z. Weng, All solutions of the optimal block search problem, *Acta Mathematicae Sinica* No.1 (1979) 45-53 (in Chinese).

[19] D.G. Luenberger, *Linear and Nonlinear Programming*, (Addison-Wesley, Reading, 1984).

[20] S. Luo, All solutions of the optimal block search problem for $N < 3n$, *Acta Mathematicae Sinica* No.3 (1977) 225-228 (in Chinese).

[21] Y. Milman, Search problems in optimization theory, Ph.D. thesis, Technion-Israel Institute of Technology, Haifa, 1972.

[22] A. Pelc, Searching with known error probability, *Theoretical Computer Science* 63 (1989) 185-202.

[23] J. Qi, Y. Yuan, and F. Wu, An optimization problem (II), *Acta Mathematicae Sinica* No.2 (1974) 110-130 (in Chinese).

[24] J. Qi, Y. Yuan, and F. Wu, An optimization problem (III), *Acta Mathematicae Sinica* No.1 (1975) 65-74 (in Chinese).

[25] R.L. Rivest, A.R. Meyer, D.J. Kleitman, K. Winklmann, and J. Spencer, Coping with errors in binary search procedures, *J. Computer and System Sciences* 20 (1980) 396-404.

[26] X. Taó, Proving the optimality of optimum seeking method, *Acta Mathematicae Sinica* 24:5 (1981) 729-732 (in Chinese).

[27] F. Wu, An optimization problem (I), *Scientia Sinica* No.1 (1974) 1-14 (in Chinese).

14

Unbounded Search

In this chapter, we deal with unbounded domains, that is, tested objects from an unbounded area, e.g., a half line, the set of natural numbers, etc..

14.1 Introduction

Many problems involve searching in an unbounded domain. The following are some examples.

(1) In Sec. 14.3, we will discuss the minimum root identification problem which searches a boundary point α_0 satisfying

$$\alpha_0 = \begin{cases} 1, & \text{if } h_i(1) \leq 0 \text{ for } i = 1, \cdots, m, \\ \max\{\alpha \mid h_i(\alpha) \leq 0 \text{ for } i = 1, \cdots, m\}, & \text{otherwise} \end{cases}$$

where every $h_i(\alpha)$ $(= g_i(x + \alpha d))$ is a convex function in α. The problem arose from solving the following optimization problem:

$$\begin{aligned} \text{maximize} \quad & f(x) \\ \text{subject to} \quad & g_1(x) \leq 0, \cdots, g_m(x) \leq 0 \\ & x \in R^n \end{aligned}$$

where f is continuously differentiable in the constrained area and all g_i are continuously differentiable convex functions in R^n. A more natural version of the minimum root identification problem is to find α^* in $[0, \infty]$ such that

$$\alpha^* = \max\{\alpha \mid h_i(\alpha) \leq 0 \text{ for } i = 1, \cdots, m\}.$$

This version is a search problem with an unbounded domain.

(2) In unconstrained optimization, one considers the problem

$$\max f(x)$$

and uses a line search procedure to solve the following subproblem

$$\max\{f(x + \alpha d) \mid 0 \leq \alpha\}.$$

271

This subproblem gives another example in unbounded search.

(3) In the recursive function theory, there is an important operation, called the μ-*operation*, as follows.

$$h(x) = \begin{cases} \min\{y \mid g(x, y) = 0\}, & \text{if } \exists y, g(x, y) = 0, \\ \text{undefined}, & \text{otherwise} \end{cases}$$

where $g(x, y)$ is a total recursive function. Suppose that one uses the question " Is there $y \le a$ such that $g(x, y) = 0$?" as a primitive operation. Then this problem can be formulated as follows: Identify the unknown $h(x)$ from the natural numbers by questions of the type "Is $h(x) \le a$?". (Actually, in the recursive function theory, it is well-known that in general there is no way, unless the domain of $h(x)$ is a recursive set, to tell whether $h(x)$ is defined at x or not. Thus, one studies only the algorithm for computing $h(x)$ in case that $h(x)$ is defined. When $h(x)$ is undefined, the algorithm runs forever and outputs nothing.)

The most straightforward algorithm for unbounded search is the unary search. For example (3), it will ask questions "Is $h(x) \le 0$?", "Is $h(x) \le 1$?", $\cdots$, until a "Yes"-answer is obtained. But, the unary search is clearly not a good one.

Let n denote the value of $h(x)$. (n is considered to be the input size.) The cost of the unary search is $n+1$. The following binary search gives a significant improvement.

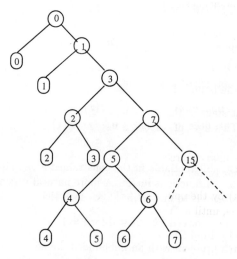

Figure 14.1: The decision tree of the unbounded binary search

The binary search has two stages. The first stage of the binary search is to find a bounded area containing the unknown by successively asking "Is $n \le 2^i - 1$?" for $i = 0, 1, \cdots$, until a "Yes"-answer is obtained. Then the unknown n is identified in the second stage by a standard bounded binary search. Suppose that the first stage stops at a "Yes"-answer for the question "Is $n \leq 2^m - 1$?". Then $2^{m-1} - 1 < n \leq 2^m - 1$. n has 2^{m-1} possibilities. Thus, the second stage takes $m - 1$ and the first stage takes $m + 1$ tests. The total number of tests is $2m = 2\lfloor \log n \rfloor + 2$. The decision tree of the unbounded binary search is shown in Figure 14.1. Each internal node of the tree is labeled by a number i corresponding to a test "Is $n \leq i$?". Each leaf is labeled by the identified value of the unknown.

14.2   Bentley-Yao Algorithms

Based on the binary search, Bentley and Yao [2] discovered a family of interesting algorithms. The basic idea is as follows: Note that the binary search is an improvement of the unary search. However, the first stage of the binary search is still a unary search along sequence $\{2^i - 1 \mid i = 0, 1, \cdots\}$. Thus, this stage can also be improved by the binary search again. Let $\ell(n) = \lfloor \log n \rfloor + 1$ and $\ell^{(i)}(n) = \overbrace{\ell(\cdots \ell(n) \cdots)}^{i}$. Then the second improved algorithm runs as follows:

Stage 1. Find $\ell^{(2)}(n)$ by the unary search, i.e., ask questions "Is $\ell^{(2)}(n) \leq 0$?", "Is $\ell^{(2)}(n) \leq 1$?", $\cdots$, until a "Yes"-answer is obtained. (Note that $\ell(x) \leq i$ if and only if $x \leq 2^i - 1$. Thus, the question "Is $\ell^{(k)}(n) \leq i$?" is equivalent to the question "Is $n \leq f^{(k)}(i)$?" where $f(y) = 2^y - 1$.)

Stage 2. Find $\ell(n)$ by the bounded binary search with question of type "Is $\ell(n) \leq i$?". (Note that $2^{\ell^{(2)}(n)-1} + 1 \leq \ell(n) \leq 2^{\ell^{(2)}(n)}$. Thus, this stage takes at most $\ell^{(2)}(n) - 1$ tests.)

Stage 3. Find n by the bounded binary search.

Note that the first stage of this algorithm still uses the unary search. So, it can be improved again. This kind of improvement can be done forever. So, a family of algorithms is obtained.

Let B_0 denote the unary search and B_1 denote the binary search. In general, the algorithm B_k is obtained from improving the algorithm B_{k-1} and runs as follows.

Stage 1. Find $\ell^{(k)}(n)$ by the unary search, i.e., ask questions "Is $\ell^{(k)}(n) \leq 0$?", "Is $\ell^{(k)}(n) \leq 1$?", $\cdots$, until a "Yes"-answer is obtained.

Stage i ($2 \leq i \leq k+1$). Find $\ell^{(k-i+1)}(n)$ by the bounded binary search with question of type "Is $\ell^{(k-i+1)}(n) \leq i$?" (note: $2^{\ell^{(k-i+2)}(n)-1} + 1 \leq \ell^{(k-i+1)}(n) \leq 2^{\ell^{(k-i+2)}(n)}$).

Here $\ell^{(0)}(n) = n$. To analyze the cost of the algorithm B_k, notice that the first stage needs $\ell^{(k)}(n) + 1$ tests and the ith stage needs at most $\ell^{(k-i+2)}(n) - 1$ tests. Thus, the total number of tests is at most

$$\ell(n) + \ell^{(2)}(n) + \cdots + 2\ell^{(k)}(n) - k + 1.$$

From the theoretical point of view, the algorithm B_k is better than the algorithm B_{k-1} for any k. However, for a particular instance, it may not be the case. In fact, $\ell^{(k-1)}(n) - 2\ell^{(k)}(n) - 1$ decreases monotonely as k increases and it becomes a negative number when k gets sufficiently large. Clearly, the best choice for k is the largest j such that

$$\ell^{(j-1)}(n) > 2\ell^{(j)}(n) - 1,$$

which is also the smallest j such that

$$\ell^{(j)}(n) \leq 2\ell^{(j+1)}(n) - 1.$$

Since the largest positive integer x satisfying

$$x \leq 2\ell(x) - 1 = 2(\lfloor \log x \rfloor + 1) - 1$$

is 5, the best choice for k is the smallest integer j satisfying

$$\ell^{(j)}(n) \leq 5.$$

This j is denoted by $\ell^*(n)$. The following algorithm, denoted by B^*, was also suggested by Bentley and Yao [2].

Step 1. Find $\ell^*(n)$ by the unary search, i.e., ask questions "Is $\ell^{(i)}(n) \leq 5$?" for $i = 0$, $1, \cdots$, until a "Yes"-answer is obtained.

Step 2. Find n by the algorithm $B_{\ell^*(n)}$.

The reader may immediately find that the algorithm B^* is still improvable because the first step is still the unary search. Actually, the technique of Bentley and Yao can be used in this situation forever and a family of uncountably many algorithms will be obtained.

Note that in the algorithm B^*, the first step takes $1 + \ell^*(n)$ tests. The number of tests in the second step is at most

$$\sum_{i=1}^{\ell^*(n)} \ell^{(i)}(n) + \ell^{(\ell^*(n))}(n) - \ell^*(n) + 1$$

$$\leq \sum_{i=1}^{\ell^*(n)} \ell^{(i)}(n) + 6 - \ell^*(n).$$

So, the total cost of the algorithm B^* is

$$\sum_{i=1}^{\ell^*(n)} \ell^{(i)}(n) + 7.$$

Bentley-Yao algorithms are nearly optimal. To show this, a lower bound result was also presented in [2].

Theorem 14.2.1 *Let $f(n)$ be the cost function of an unbounded searching algorithm. Then for infinitely many n,*

$$f(n) > \log n + \log^{(2)} n + \cdots + \log^{(\log^* n)} n - 2 \log^* n$$

where $\log^* n$ is the least number j such that $\log^{(j)} n \le 1$.

The following lemma is an infinite version of Lemma 1.2.2.

Lemma 14.2.2 (Kraft's Inequality) *Let $f(n)$ be the cost function of a correct unbounded searching algorithm. Then*

$$\sum_{i=0}^{\infty} 2^{-f(i)} \le 1.$$

Proof. The decision tree T of each correct unbounded searching algorithm is an infinite binary tree. A node is said at the jth level if the path from the root to the node has length j. For each node v at the jth level, define $g(v) = 2^{-j}$. Then $g(v) = g(v') + g(v'')$ when v' and v'' are two children of v. From this relation, it is easy to see that for any finite subtree T' obtained from T by cutting off at a certain level, the sum of $g(v)$ over all leaves v of T' is one. Now, for any natural number n, let $j = \max\{f(i) \mid i = 0, \cdots, n\}$. Then all leaves corresponding to sample points $0, \cdots, n$ are in levels not lower than level j. Cut off all nodes at level lower than j from T. Denote the remainder by T'. Clearly,

$$\sum_{i=1}^{n} 2^{-f(i)} < \sum_{v \text{ over leaves of } T'} g(v) = 1$$

for every n. Thus,

$$\sum_{i=1}^{\infty} 2^{-f(i)} \le 1.$$

$\square$

Proof of Theorem 14.2.1. Suppose to the contrary that Theorem 14.2.1 does not hold. Then there exists an algorithm such that the inequality holds for only finitely many n. It means that for sufficiently large n,

$$2^{-f(n)} > \frac{4^{\log^* n}}{n(\log n)(\log^{(2)} n) \cdots (\log^{(\log^* n - 1)} n)}.$$

By Kraft's inequality, to obtain a contradiction, it is sufficient to prove that the series

$$\sum_{n=1}^{\infty} \frac{4^{\log^* n}}{n(\log n)(\log^{(2)} n) \cdots (\log^{(\log^* n - 1)} n)}$$

is divergent. Define $k(n) = \log^* n - \log^*(\log^* n) - 2$ and, for positive integers i and n,

$$k_i = -i - 2 + \left.2^{2^{\cdot^{\cdot^{2}}}}\right\}^i$$

$$n_i = 1 + \left.2^{2^{\cdot^{\cdot^{2}}}}\right\}^{k_i+i+1}$$

$$n_i' = \left.2^{2^{\cdot^{\cdot^{2}}}}\right\}^{k_i+i+2}.$$

Then for $n_i \le n \le n_i'$, $k(n) = k_i$ and $\log^{(k(n)+2)} n \le \log^* n$. Hence, for $n_i \le n \le n_i'$,

$$\begin{aligned}
&\log^{(k(n)+2)} n + \cdots + \log^{(\log^* n)} n \\
\le\ & log^* n + \log(\log^* n) + \cdots + \log^{(\log^*(\log^* n))}(\log^* n) \\
<\ & 2\log^* n.
\end{aligned}$$

Thus,

$$\begin{aligned}
&\sum_{n=1}^{\infty} \frac{4^{\log^* n}}{n(\log n)(\log^{(2)} n)\cdots(\log^{(\log^* n-1)} n)} \\
\ge\ & \sum_{n=n_i}^{n_i'} \frac{4^{\log^* n}}{n(\log n)(\log^{(2)} n)\cdots(\log^{(\log^* n-1)} n)} \\
\ge\ & \sum_{n=n_i}^{n_i'} \frac{2^{\log^{(k(n)+2)} n+\cdots+\log^{(\log^* n)} n}}{n(\log n)(\log^{(2)} n)\cdots(\log^{(\log^* n-1)} n)} \\
=\ & \sum_{n=n_i}^{n_i'} \frac{1}{n(\log n)(\log^{(2)} n)\cdots(\log^{(k(n))} n)} \\
\ge\ & \int_{n_i}^{n_i'} \frac{dx}{x(\log x)(\log^{(2)} x)\cdots(\log^{(k_i)} x)} \\
=\ & (\ln 2)^{k_i+1} \log^{(k_i+1)} x \ |_{x=n_i}^{x=n_i'} \\
>\ & (\ln 2)^{k_i+1}(2^{k_i} - k_i - i - 3) \\
=\ & (2\ln 2)^{k_i+1}(0.5 + o(1))
\end{aligned}$$

where the following facts have been used:

$$\begin{aligned}
\log^{(k_i+1)} n_i' &> 2^{k_i} \\
\log^{(k_i+1)} n_i &< k_i + i + 3.
\end{aligned}$$

Note that $2\ln 2 > 1$. Therefore, as k_i goes to infinity, $(2\ln 2)^{k_i}(0.5 + o(1))$ also goes to infinity. This completes the proof. $\square$

Remark. It is worth mentioning that the above lower bound cannot be improved by the same technique. In fact, the series

$$\sum_{n=1}^{\infty} \frac{1}{n(\log n)(\log^{(2)} n) \cdots (\log^{(\log^* n-1)} n)}$$

is convergent. To see this, let $I_k = \{x \mid \log^* x = k\}$. Then $I_k = (a, b]$ where $\log^k a = 0$ and $\log^k b = 1$. Thus,

$$\int_{I_k} \frac{dx}{x(\log x)(\log^{(2)} x) \cdots (\log^{(k-1)} x)}$$
$$= (\ln 2)^k \log^k x \mid_{x=a}^{b}$$
$$= (\ln 2)^k.$$

Therefore,

$$\int_{1}^{\infty} \frac{dx}{x(\log x)(\log^{(2)} x) \cdots (\log^{(\log^* x-1)} x)} = \sum_{k=1}^{\infty} (\ln 2)^k,$$

which is convergent. It follows that

$$\sum_{n=1}^{\infty} \frac{1}{n(\log n)(\log^{(2)} n) \cdots (\log^{(\log^* n-1)} n)}$$

is convergent. Thus, there exists a positive integer n_0 such that

$$\sum_{n=n_0}^{\infty} \frac{1}{n(\log n)(\log^{(2)} n) \cdots (\log^{(\log^* n-1)} n)} < 1.$$

From this fact, one can prove that there exists an algorithm whose cost function f satisfies that for $n \geq n_0$,

$$f(n) \leq \log n + \log^{(2)} n + \cdots + \log^{(\log^* n)} n$$

and

$$\sum_{n=0}^{n_0-1} 2^{-f(n)} + \sum_{n=n_0}^{\infty} \frac{1}{n(\log n)(\log^{(2)} n) \cdots (\log^{(\log^* n-1)} n)} \leq 1.$$

In fact, the inverse of Lemma 14.2.2 holds. Its proof can be obtained by reversing the proof of Lemma 14.2.2. The reader may work out the detail as an exercise.

14.3 Search with Lies

Similar to the bounded minimum root identification problem, the unbounded minimum root identification problem can also be transformed to an unbounded search problem with lies. In fact, the unbounded minimum root identification is equivalent to the unbounded half-lie problem.

In Sec. 9.3, the bounded half-lie problem was dealt with. In this section, the results are extended from the bounded erroneous searching to the unbounded erroneous searching (i.e., search for a unknown natural number n by "Yes"-"No" tests with errors with certain restriction).

For the unbounded erroneous searching, the search usually occurs in two stages. In the first stage, a bound of the unknown number n is determined. In the second stage, apply the algorithm for the bounded erroneous searching.

The first stage can be performed by a brute force search in the following way: Ask questions "Is $n < 2^{2^i}$?" for $i = 0, 1, \cdots$, until a "Yes"-answer is confirmed. If the number of lies is bounded by a constant r, then each question needs to repeat at most $2r + 1$ times in order to obtain a confirmed answer. Thus, totally, this stage takes at most $(2r + 1)\lceil \log \log n \rceil$ tests. If the number of lies is linearly bounded with a ratio q, then the total number of tests in this stage is bounded by

$$O\left(\left(\frac{1}{1-q}\right)^{\lceil \log \log n \rceil}\right) = o(\log n).$$

For the second stage, if the number of lies is bounded by a constant, then the bounded searching algorithm can be used to find n from $[1, 2^{2^{\lceil \log \log n \rceil}}]$. Note that

$$2^{2^{\lceil \log \log n \rceil}} \le 2^{2^{\log \log n + 1}} = n^2.$$

From Sec. 8.3, there exists an algorithm executing this stage with at most $O(\log n^2) = O(\log n)$ tests.

If the number of lies is linearly bounded, then in the second stage, when the chip game is employed, the boundary line has to be set to start at level $q \cdot o(\log n)$ instead of level 0. But, this does not affect very much the quantity of the number of tests. Aslam and Dhagat [1] indicated that it still takes $O(\log n)$ tests for $0 \le q < 1/2$.

Summarizing the above discussion, the following has been obtained.

Theorem 14.3.1 *Any unknown natural number n can be identified with $O(\log n)$ "Yes"-"No" tests with a constant number of lies. For $0 < q < 1/2$, any unknown natural number n can be identified with $O(\log n)$ "Yes"-"No" tests linearly bounded with ratio q.*

For the known error probability model, Pelc [3] proved the following.

Theorem 14.3.2 *If $q < 1/2$, then for any positive $p < 1$, the unknown natural number n can be identified with reliability p in $O(\log^2 n)$ queries. If $q < 1/3$, then for any positive $p < 1$, the unknown natural number n can be identified with reliability p in $O(\log n)$ queries.*

14.4 Unbounded Fibonacci Search

Bentley and Yao [2] proposed the following question: "Is the corresponding unbounded Fibonacci search interesting?" In Sec. 14.1, it was made clear that in
the nonlinear optimization theory, unbounded searching for maximum is certainly
important.

Suppose that one wants to find the maximum of the unimodal function $f(x)$ on
$[0, \infty)$. Given an accuracy $\epsilon > 0$, define $x_{-1} = 0$, $x_0 = F_0^- \epsilon$, $x_i = F_i \epsilon$ for $i \geq 1$ where
$F_0 = F_1 = 1$, $F_{i-1} + F_i = F_{i+1}$, which are Fibonacci numbers. (F_0^- is a number very
close to F_0 but smaller than F_0.) The unbounded Fibonacci search can be performed
in the following way.

Stage 1. Compute the function values $f(x_0)$, $f(x_1)$, $\cdots$, until $f(x_i) \geq f(x_{i+1})$ is
found.

Stage 2. Apply the bounded Fibonacci search to the interval $[x_{i-1}, x_{i+1}]$.

Suppose that the maximum point is x. Then the first stage needs to compute
$1 + \min\{i \mid x \leq F_i \epsilon\}$ function values. The second stage needs to compute at most
$\min\{i \mid x \leq F_i \epsilon\}$ function values. Thus, the total number of function values computed
is $1 + 2\min\{i \mid x \leq F_i \epsilon\}$.

Similarly, the unbounded golden section search can be described as follows.

Stage 1. Compute the function values $f(\epsilon)$, $f(\rho\epsilon)$, $\cdots$, until $f(\rho^i \epsilon) \geq f(\rho^{i+1}\epsilon)$ is
found where $\rho = \frac{3-\sqrt{5}}{2}$.

Stage 2. Apply the bounded Fibonacci search to the interval $[\rho^{i-1}\epsilon, \rho^{i+1}\epsilon]$.

Both the unbounded Fibonacci search and the unbounded golden section search
can be improved infinitely many times by refining the first stage. The improvements
are similar to those in Sec. 14.2. The detail is left to the reader as exercises.

There also exist problems on unbounded searching in high dimensional spaces.
For example, consider an unconstrained maximization problem

$$\max f(x) \text{ for } x \in R^n.$$

The simplex method for this problem can be described as follows: Initially, compute
$n+1$ function values $f(x_1)$, $\cdots$, $f(x_{n+1})$. At each step, there are $n+1$ function values,
for simplicity, still denoted by $f(x_1)$, $\cdots$, $f(x_{n+1})$, storaged in the algorithm. The
algorithm first finds the minimal function value, say $f(x^{n+1})$, from the $n+1$ function
values, then compute $f(\bar{x}_{n+1})$ where $\bar{x}_{n+1}$ is the symmetric point of x_{n+1} with respect
to the hyperplane determined by x_1, $\cdots$, x_n (see Figure 14.2).

Note that in the above algorithm, two simplices $x_1 x_2 \cdots x_{n+1}$ and
$x_1 x_2 \cdots x_n \bar{x}_{n+1}$ are symmetric. So, they have the same size. The algorithm can be
improved to enlarge or reduce the size of the second simplex by using the technique
for unbounded searching.

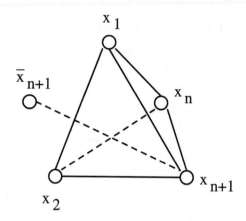

Figure 14.2: The simplex method

References

[1] J.A. Aslam and A. Dhagat, Searching in presence of linearly bounded errors, *Proceedings of 23rd STOC*, 1991, pp. 486-493.

[2] J.L. Bentley and A.C. Yao, An almost optimal algorithm for unbounded searching, *Information Processing Letters*, 5 (1976) 82-87.

[3] A. Pelc, Searching with known error probability, *Theoretical Computer Science*, 63 (1989) 185-202.

[4] M. Avriel, *Nonlinear Programming: Analysis and Methods*, (Prentice-Hall, Englewood Cliff, New Jersey, 1976).

15

Membership Problems

Consider a set of n items having d defective ones. Given a family of subsets of items, what is the minimum number t such that there exists an algorithm, using at most t tests on subsets in the family, for identifying whether a given item is defective or not? This problem is called the *membership* problem which is a variation of group testing.

15.1 Examples

Clearly, for the membership problem, if individual testing is allowed, then the solution is trivial, i.e., individual testing is optimal. So, usually, the given family of subsets does not contain singletons.

Suppose the given family consists of all subsets of two items. Clearly, if $d + 1 = n$, then there exists no solution for the membership problem because all tests receive the same answer. If $d + 2 \leq n$, then $d + 1$ tests are sufficient. In fact, for any item x, choose the other $d + 1$ items to form $d + 1$ pairs with x. Tests these $d + 1$ pairs. If one of these pairs is pure, then x is good; otherwise, x is defective. Actually, $d + 1$ is the minimum number of tests in the worst case to identify whether an arbitrarily given item is good or not. The proof is as follows.

Given a family of subsets of two items, a subset of items is called a *vertex-cover* of the family if it intersects each subset in the family with at least one item. To do the worst-case analysis, consider a test history in which every test obtains the positive outcome. (If for some test, the positive outcome is impossible, then the test group must consist of all already-known good items and this test should be removed.) Suppose that the history contains t tests and x is identified to be defective in the history. Then any vertex-cover of the t contaminated sets not containing x must contain at least $d + 1$ elements. (Otherwise, one cannot know that x must be defective.) Thus, $t \geq d + 1$.

Suppose that the given family consists of all subsets of three items. Similarly, consider a test history consisting of t tests; every test produces the positive outcome. Suppose that x is identified to be defective in this history. Then, every subset of items not containing x, which has nonempty intersection with every test group in the

281

history, must have size at least $d + 1$. Delete x and take away an item from each test set not containing x. Then the resulting graph has at most $n - 1$ vertices and a vertex-cover of size at least $d + 1$. Thus, t is not smaller than the minimum number of edges for a graph with at most $n - 1$ vertices which has the minimum vertex-cover of size at least $d + 1$. Conversely, suppose G is a graph with at most $n - 1$ vertices which has the minimum vertex-cover of size at least $d + 1$. Associate every vertex with an item other than x. For each edge give a test set consisting of x and the two items associated with the two endpoints of the edge. Then x can be identified by these tests. In fact, if one test has the negative outcome, then x is good; if all tests have the positive outcome, then x is defective. Thus, the minimum number of tests for identifying an item with 3-size test sets is exactly the minimum number of edges in a graph with at most $n - 1$ vertices which has the minimum vertex-cover of size at least $d + 1$. Since a complete graph of $n - 1$ vertices has the minimum vertex-cover of size $n - 2$. The membership problem has solutions if and only if $n \geq d + 3$.

In general, if the given family consists of all subsets of k (≥ 2) items, then the problem has solutions if and only if $n \geq d + k$. However, computing the optimal solution seems not so easy for $k > 3$.

The membership problem can also be represented as a game of two players. The first player keeps an item x in his mind; the second one asks questions in the form "Is $x \in S$?" for some S in the given family. Then the first one answers the question according to what x he has. The game ends when the second player identifies the membership of x based on the questions and answers. The problem is to find the optimal strategy for the second player. The game-theoretic formulation is used to study the following examples.

A *polyhedron* is a convex set with a linear boundary. A *polyhedral set* is a union of finitely many disjoint open polyhedrons. Given a polyhedral set P and a point x, decide whether x is in P or not by using the minimum number of linear comparisons, i.e., asking question "Is $\ell(x) < 0$, $\ell(x) = 0$, or $\ell(x) > 0$?" for a linear function $\ell(\cdot)$. This problem is called the *polyhedral membership problem*. Several natural problems can be transformed to this problem. The following is one of them, which was initially studied by Dobkin and Lipton [5]: Given n real numbers $x_1, x_2, ..., x_n$, decide whether they are distinct by using pairwise comparisons with answers: "bigger", "equal", or "less". Represent the n real numbers by an n-dimensional vector $x = (x_1, \cdots, x_n)$. Let $P = \{(y_1, \cdots, y_n) \mid y_i \neq y_j, 1 \leq i < j \leq n\}$. Then the problem is to determine whether x is in P or not, a polyhedral membership problem. It is worth mentioning that P does not have to be a polyhedron.

A binary string is a finite sequence of symbols 0 and 1. Consider 2^n items encoded by binary strings. Suppose each test corresponds to a question on a symbol of a given string whether the symbol is 0 or 1. Let the set of defectives consist of all strings having an odd number of 1's. Then for any item x chosen by the first player, the second player has to ask at least n questions to identify whether the item is defective or not. In fact, from each question the second player can learn one symbol of x. But, to identify whether x is defective or not, the second player has to know all symbols of x. This is due to the fact that x can change from defective to good or from good to defective as a symbol of x changes between 0 and 1. Since n questions are clearly sufficient, the minimum number of questions that the second player needs to ask is n.

A large class of membership problems is about graphs. Consider the set of all graphs with a fixed vertex set V of n vertices. Suppose a graph is defective if and only if it is connected. In the game the first player chooses a graph on V and the second player determines whether the graph is connected by asking whether selected edges exist in the chosen graph. Then in the worst case, the second player has to ask $n(n-1)/2$ questions. To see this, note that the worst-case scenario means that the first player may change his choice as long as it does not contradict his previous answers during the game. Now, assume that the first player always wants to keep the game going as long as possible. Note that from each question the second player knows only whether an edge exists or not. Consider the following strategy of the first player: Choose the "Yes"-answer only in the case that if he gives the "No"-answer, then the second player can find immediately that the graph is disconnected. In this way, the second player has to know whether each possible edge exists or not. This fact is proved by contradiction. Note that according to the strategy of the first player, the final graph he chooses is connected. Suppose on the contrary that this strategy does not work, i.e., there is an edge (s,t) which has not been asked by the second player but the second player finds that all edges (i,j) received the "Yes"-answer already form a connected graph G. Adding the edge (s,t) to G results in a cycle containing (s,t). From this cycle, choose an edge (k,h) other than (s,t). Then $(G \cup (s,t)) \setminus (k,h)$ is still a connected graph, contradicting the strategy for giving the "Yes"-answer for the question about edge (k,h).

15.2 Polyhedral Membership

In the last section, we mentioned the polyhedral membership problem. Suppose that a polyhedral set P and a point x are given. If the boundary of P can be described by m linear functions, g_i for $1 \le i \le m$, a naive way to determine whether a point x is in P or not is to compute all $g_i(x)$. Thus, m tests are required. However, some preliminary work may reduce the number of tests. For example, consider a polygon P in the plane (see Figure 15.1). P has m vertices and m edges determined by g_i's. Choose a point o in the interior of P. Let vertices $v_1, \cdots, v_m$ of P be arranged counterclockwise. Through each pair of o and vertex v_i, a line is determined.

With such preparation, the *wedge* ov_iv_{i+1} containing the point x can be determined with at most $\lceil \log(m+1) \rceil$ tests. In fact, the first test uses a line through some ov_i such that the line cuts the plane into two parts each of which contains at most $\lceil (m+1)/2 \rceil$ wedges. (Note: One of the m wedges may be cut into two pieces.) Such a line exists because rotating the line around o, the number of wedges on each side of the line

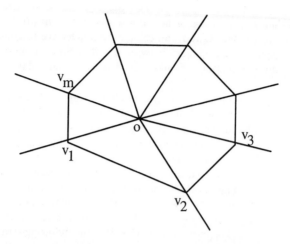

Figure 15.1: A polygon in the plane.

is changed by at most one; and when the line is rotated $180°$, the two sides of the line are interchanged. So there exists a step at which the number of wedges at the two sides differ by at most one. Clearly, the rest of tests can also remove half of the remaining wedges. Thus, with at most $\lceil \log(m + 1) \rceil$ tests, only one wedge is left. Now, one more test with the line $v_i v_{i+1}$ is enough to determine whether the point x is in P or not. So, the total number of tests is $\lceil \log(m + 1) \rceil + 1$. Yao and Rivest [8] proved an elegant lower bound as follows.

Theorem 15.2.1 *Let P be a polyhedral set in R^n. Let $C(P)$ be the minimum number of tests sufficient in the worst case to determine whether a given point is in P or not. Then*

$$C(P) \geq \lceil \tfrac{1}{2} \log f_d(P) \rceil \text{ for any } d$$

where $f_d(P)$ is the number of d-dimensional facets of P. (A facet of $P = \{x \in R^n \mid h_i(x) = a_i^T x - b_i \leq 0, i = 1, \cdots, m\}$ is a subset in the form $\{x \in R^n \mid h_i(x) < 0 \text{ for } i \in I, h_i(x) = 0 \text{ for } i \notin I\}$ where $I \subseteq \{1, \cdots, m\}$.)

Proof. Let $h(x) = a^T x - b$ be a linear function specifying a test. For any polyhedral set P, denote $P^- = \{x \in P \mid h(x) \leq 0\}$ and $P^+ = \{x \in P \mid h(x) \geq 0\}$. Then for each d-dimensional facet F, at least one of F^- and F^+ is a d-dimensional facet of P^- or P^+. So,

$$f_d(P^-) + f_d(P^+) \geq f_d(P). \tag{15.1}$$

Suppose t tests are sufficient in the worst case to determine the membership of a point x^* in P. x^* may be asked always to lie in the part with more d-dimensional facets. When the testing ends, the t linear inequalities given by the t tests must form a polyhedron falling inside of P (otherwise, x^* cannot be identified to be in P). So, each facet can be represented through these t linear functions. Clearly, a polyhedron represented by t linear inequalities can have at most $\binom{t}{n-d}$ d-dimensional facets. Moreover, by (15.1), this polyhedron has at least $f_d(P)2^{-t}$ d-dimensional facets. Thus,

$$\binom{t}{n-d} \geq f_d(P)2^{-t}.$$

So,

$$\binom{C(P)}{n-d}2^{C(P)} \geq f_d(P).$$

It follows that $C(P) \geq \lceil \frac{1}{2}\log f_d(P) \rceil$.   □

This theorem was also discovered by Kalinová [7], Morávek [10] (for $d = 0$), and Morávek and Pudlák [11]. Dobkin and Lipton [5] showed

$$C(P) \geq \Omega(\log_2(\beta_0(P)))$$

where $\beta_0(P)$ is the number of connected components of P. Steele and Yao [16] and Ben-Or [1] did further investigation on this lower bound. Recently, Björner, Lovász, and Yao [3] proved a new bound

$$C(P) \geq \log_3 |\chi(P)|$$

where $\chi(P)$ is the Euler characteristic of P, that is,

$$\chi(P) = f_0(P) - f_1(P) + f_2(P) - \cdots + (-1)^n f_n(P).$$

Yao [22] generalized this bound from polyhedral sets to semi-algebraic sets.

15.3   Boolean Formulas and Decision Trees

A Boolean function is a function whose variables' values and function value are all in $\{true, false\}$. Usually, one denotes "true" by 1 and "false" by 0. In the following table, there are three Boolean functions, conjunction $\wedge$, disjunction $\vee$, and negation $\neg$. The first two have two variables and the last one has only one variable.

x	y	$x \wedge y$	$x \vee y$	$\neg x$
0	0	0	0	1
0	1	0	1	1
1	0	0	1	0
1	1	1	1	0

Exclusive-or $\oplus$ is also a Boolean function of two variables, which is given by $x \oplus y = ((\neg x) \wedge y) \vee (x \wedge (\neg y))$. For simplicity, one also writes $x \wedge y = xy$, $x \vee y = x + y$ and $\neg x = \bar{x}$. The conjunction, disjunction and exclusive-or all follow the commutative law and the associative law. The distributive law holds for conjunction to disjunction, disjunction to conjunction, and conjunction to exclusive-or, i.e. $(x + y)z = xz + yz$, $xy + z = (x + z)(y + z)$, and $(x \oplus y)z = xz \oplus yz$. An interesting and important law about negation is De Morgan's law, i.e., $\overline{xy} = \bar{x} + \bar{y}$ and $\overline{x + y} = \bar{x}\bar{y}$.

An assignment for a Boolean function of n variables is a binary string of n symbols; each symbol gives a value to a variable. A partial assignment is an assignment to a subset of variables. A *truth-assignment* for a function is an assignment x with $f(x) = 1$. Suppose that $x_1 = e_1, \cdots, x_k = e_k$ form a partial assignment for function f. Then $f|_{x_1=e_1,\cdots,x_k=e_k}$ denote the function obtained by substituting $x_1 = e_1, \cdots, x_k = e_k$ into f, which is a function of variables other than $x_1, \cdots, x_k$.

The membership problem with binary strings as items and $\mathcal{F}$ as the given family can be interpreted as the problem of evaluating a Boolean function. Suppose that a binary string is defective if and only if it is a truth-assignment. Note that each question "Is the string in $\{x_1 \cdots x_n \mid x_i = 1\}$?" is equivalent to the question " Is $x_i = 1$?". So, one can also describe the game-theoretic formulation in the following way: The second player picks a variable and then the first player gives a value to the variable. A tool for studying this game is the decision tree defined as follows.

A *decision tree* of a Boolean function f is a binary tree whose internal nodes are labeled by variables, leaves are labeled by 0 and 1. Each variable goes to its two children along two edges labeled by 0 and 1, corresponding to the two values that the variable may take. Given an assignment to a Boolean function represented by a decision tree T, T computes the function value in the following way: Find a path from the root to a leaf such that all variables on the path take values in the assignment. Then the value of the leaf on the path is the value of the Boolean function at the assignment.

For example, a decision tree is given in Figure 15.2 which computes the function

$$f(x_1, x_2, x_3) = (x_1 + x_2)(\bar{x}_2 + x_3).$$

A decision tree for the function involved in the game is a strategy of the second player. As the first player always plays adversary to the second player, the second player has to go along the longest path on the tree. So, the optimal strategy for the second player is to choose a decision tree with the minimum longest path. (The length of paths is the number of edges on the path.) For a Boolean function f, the minimum length of the longest path of a decision tree computing f is denoted by $D(f)$. $D(f)$ is the minimum number of questions that the second player has to ask in order to identify the membership of an item in the worst case. Clearly, $D(f) \leq n$ when f has n variables. For convenience, assume that for constant function $f \equiv 0$ or $f \equiv 1$, $D(f) = 0$. Note that for every nonconstant function f, $D(f) \geq 1$. So,

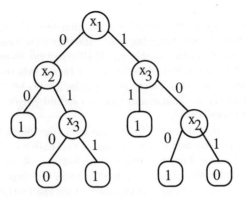

Figure 15.2: A decision tree.

$D(f) = 0$ if and only if f is a constant.

A Boolean function f of n variables is *elusive* if $D(f) = n$. The following are some examples on the elusiveness of Boolean functions.

Example 1. In a tournament, there are n players $1, \cdots, n$. Let x_{ij} be the result of the match between players i and j, i.e.

$$x_{ij} = \begin{cases} 1 & \text{if } i \text{ beats } j, \\ 0 & \text{if } j \text{ beats } i. \end{cases}$$

(Note that this is not necessarily a transitive relation.) Consider the following function:

$$t(x_{12}, \cdots, x_{n-1,n}) = \begin{cases} 1 & \text{if there is a player who beats all other players,} \\ 0 & \text{otherwise.} \end{cases}$$

Then $D(t) \leq 2(n-1) - \lfloor \log_2 n \rfloor$. To show this, one needs to design a tournament such that within $2(n - 1) - \lfloor \log_2 n \rfloor$ matches, the value of function t can be determined. This tournament has two stages. The first stage consists of a balanced knockout tournament. Let i be the winner of the knockout tournament. In the second stage, the player i plays against every one whom he did not meet in the knockout tournament. If i wins all his matches, then t equals 1; otherwise, t equals 0. A knockout tournament for n players contains $n - 1$ matches, in which the winner i plays at least $\lfloor \log_2 n \rfloor$ times. So, the total number of matches is at most $2(n - 1) - \lfloor \log_2 n \rfloor$. t is not elusive.

Example 2. Consider the following function

$$m(x_{11}, \cdots, x_{1n}, \cdots, x_{n1}, \cdots, x_{nn}) = \prod_{i=1}^{n} \sum_{j=1}^{n} x_{ij}.$$

Then m is elusive. To see this, consider a decision tree computing m. The first player looks for a path in the following way. Starting from the root, suppose that currently he faces a question on variable x_{ij}. If all other variables in row i have been assigned the value 0, then the first player assigns 1 to x_{ij}; otherwise, assigns 0 to x_{ij}. In this way, it is easy to see that before all variables are assigned, the second player cannot know the value of m. This means that the second player has to encounter all variables. Thus, m is elusive.

A Boolean function is *monotone* if it contains only operations $\wedge$ and $\vee$. A Boolean function is called a *tree function* if it is monotone and each variable appears exactly once in its expression. The above function m is an example of the tree function. By a similar argument, one can show that every tree function is elusive. To find the longest path, consider the following strategy: If variable x_i that the first player meets appears in a sum in the expression, then set $x_i = 0$; otherwise, x_i must appear in a product in the expression, set $x_i = 1$. After assigning x_i a value, simplify the expression. This strategy will only make assigned variables disappear from the expression. Therefore, the second player has to encounter all variables by this strategy.

The following are some general results on elusiveness.

Theorem 15.3.1 *A Boolean function with an odd number of truth-assignment is elusive.*

Proof. The constant functions $f \equiv 0$ and $f \equiv 1$ have 0 and 2^n truth-assignments, respectively. Hence, a Boolean function with an odd number of truth-assignments must be a nonconstant function. If f has at least two variables and x_i is one of them, then the number of truth-assignments of f is the sum of those of $f|_{x_i=0}$ and $f|_{x_i=1}$. Therefore, either $f|_{x_i=0}$ or $f|_{x_i=1}$ has an odd number of truth-assignments. Thus, tracing the odd number of truth-assignments, one will encounter all variables in a path of any decision tree computing f. $\square$

Define $p_f(t) = \sum_{x \in \{0,1\}^n} f(x)t^{\|x\|}$ where $\|x\|$ is the number of 1s in string x. It is easy to see that $p_f(1)$ is the number of truth-assignments for f. The following theorem is an extension of the above.

Theorem 15.3.2 *For a Boolean function of n variables, $(t+1)^{n-D(f)} \mid p_f(t)$.*

Proof. First, note that if $f \equiv 0$ then $p_f(t) = 0$ and if $f \equiv 1$ then $p_f(t) = (t+1)^n$. This means that the theorem holds for $D(f) = 0$. Now, consider f with $D(f) > 0$ and a decision tree of depth $D(f)$ computing f. Without loss of generality, assume that the root is labeled by x_1. Denote $f_0 = f|_{x_1=0}$ and $f_1 = f|_{x_1=1}$. Then

$$
\begin{aligned}
p_f(t) &= \sum_{x \in \{0,1\}^n} f(x)t^{\|x\|} \\
&= \sum_{x \in \{0,1\}^{n-1}} f(0x)t^{\|x\|} + \sum_{x \in \{0,1\}^{n-1}} f(1x)t^{1+\|x\|} \\
&= p_{f_0}(t) + t p_{f_1}(t).
\end{aligned}
$$

Note that $D(f_0) \leq D(f) - 1$ and $D(f_1) \leq D(f) - 1$. Moreover, by the induction hypothesis, $(t+1)^{n-1-D(f_0)} \mid p_{f_0}(t)$ and $(t+1)^{n-1-D(f_1)} \mid p_{f_1}(t)$. Thus, $(t+1)^{n-D(f)} \mid p_{f_0}(t)$ and $(t+1)^{n-D(f)} \mid p_{f_1}(t)$. Hence, $(t+1)^{n-D(f)} \mid p_f(t)$. $\square$

An important corollary is as follows. Denote $\mu(f) = p_f(-1)$.

Corollary 15.3.3 *If $\mu(f) \neq 0$, then f is elusive.*

Next, we present an application of the above criterion.

Let H be a subgroup of permutation group S_n on $\{1, \cdots, n\}$. H is *transitive* if for any $i, j \in \{1, \cdots, n\}$, there exists $\sigma \in H$ such that $\sigma(i) = j$.

Let f be a Boolean function of n variables. f is *weakly symmetric* if there exists a transitive subgroup H of S_n such that for any $\sigma \in H$, $f(x_1, \cdots, x_n) = f(x_{\sigma(1)}, \cdots, x_{\sigma(n)})$. Denote $\mathbf{0} = (0, \cdots, 0)$ and $\mathbf{1} = (1, \cdots, 1)$.

Theorem 15.3.4 *Let n be a prime power, i.e. $n = p^m$ where p is a prime and m is a positive integer. If f is weakly symmetric and $f(\mathbf{0}) \neq f(\mathbf{1})$, then f is elusive.*

Proof. Let n_k be the number of truth-assignments with exactly k 1s. Since f is weakly symmetric, each variable takes 1 in the same number of truth-assignments with exactly k 1s, say a_k such truth-assignments. Then $p^m a_k = n a_k = n_k k$. If $0 < k < n$, then $p \mid n_k$. Thus, $\mu(f) = \sum_{k=0}^{n} n_k(-1)^k \equiv f(\mathbf{0}) + f(\mathbf{1})(-1)^n \pmod{p}$. Since $f(\mathbf{0}) \neq f(\mathbf{1})$, $\mu(f) \equiv 1$ or $(-1)^n \pmod{p}$. Thus, $\mu(f) \neq 0$. By Corollary 15.2.3, f is elusive. $\square$

15.4 Recognition of Graph Properties

Let $\{1, \cdots, n\}$ be the vertex set of a graph $G = (V, E)$. Its adjacency matrix is (x_{ij}) defined by

$$x_{ij} = \begin{cases} 1 & \text{if } \{i, j\} \in E, \\ 0 & \text{otherwise.} \end{cases}$$

Note that $x_{ij} = x_{ji}$ and $x_{ii} = 0$. So, there are only $n(n-1)/2$ independent variables, e.g., x_{ij}, $1 \leq i < j \leq n$. If one uses the string $x_{12}x_{13} \cdots x_{1n}x_{21} \cdots x_{n-1,n}$ to represent the graph G, then all graphs, with n vertices, having a certain property form a set of strings which are truth-assignments of a Boolean function. This Boolean function characterizes the property. For example, the connectivity corresponds to a Boolean function f_{con} such that $f_{con}(x_{12}, \cdots, x_{n-1,n}) = 1$ if and only if the graph G with adjacency matrix (x_{ij}) is connected. For simplicity of notation, a graph itself will be viewed as a string or a Boolean assignment to $n(n-1)/2$ variables.

Not every Boolean function of $n(n-1)/2$ variables is a graph property. Because a graph property should be invariant under graph isomorphism, a Boolean function

f of $n(n-1)/2$ variables is a graph property if and only if for every permutation σ on $\{1, \cdots, n\}$,

$$f(x_{12}, \cdots, x_{n-1,n}) = f(x_{\sigma(1)\sigma(2)}, \cdots, x_{\sigma(n-1)\sigma(n)}).$$

There is a lot of research that has been done on decision trees of graph properties [4]. In 1973, Aanderaa and Rosenberg (as reported in [13]) conjectured that there exists a positive constant ϵ such that for any nontrivial monotone graph property P, $D(P) \geq \epsilon n^2$. Rivest and Vuillemin [12] proved the conjecture in 1975. In this section, their result is presented.

First, monotone nontrivial bipartite graph properties are studied. A bipartite graph property is a Boolean function $f(x_{11}, x_{12}, \cdots, x_{1n}, x_{21}, \cdots, x_{mn})$ such that for any permutation σ of $1, 2, \cdots, m$ and permutation τ of $1, 2, \cdots, n$,

$$f(x_{\sigma(1)\tau(1)}, \cdots, x_{\sigma(m)\tau(n)}) = f(x_{11}, \cdots, x_{mn}).$$

Lemma 15.4.1 *Let P be a monotone nontrivial property of bipartite graphs between vertex sets A and B with $|A| \cdot |B|$ a prime power. Then P is elusive.*

Proof. This is a corollary of Theorem 15.3.4. In fact, in order to transform an edge (i, j) to another edge (i', j') where $i, i' \in A$ and $j, j' \in B$, one needs only to choose a permutation σ on A and a permutation τ on B such that $\sigma(i) = i'$ and $\tau(j) = j'$. Thus, the bipartite graph property is weakly symmetric. Since the number of edges for a complete bipartite graph between A and B is a prime power $|A| \cdot |B|$, all conditions of Theorem 15.3.4 hold. $\square$

Lemma 15.4.2 *Let P be a nontrivial monotone property of graphs of order n. If $2^m < n < 2^{m+1}$, then*

$$D(P) \geq \min\{D(P'), 2^{2m-2}\}$$

for some nontrivial monotone property P' of graphs of order $n-1$.

Proof. The idea is to reduce the computation of P on n vertices to the computation of a nontrivial monotone graph property on $n-1$ vertices (in cases 1 and 2) or a nontrivial monotone bipartite graph property (in case 3). Let K_{n-1} be the complete graph on $n-1$ vertices $2, \cdots, n$ and $K_{1,n-1}$ the complete bipartite graph between 1 and $\{2, \cdots, n\}$.

Case 1. $\{1\} \cup K_{n-1}$ has property P. In this case, let P' be the property that a graph G on vertices $2, \cdots, n$ has property P' if and only if $\{1\} \cup G$ has property P. Then the empty graph does not have property P' and K_{n-1} has. So, P' is nontrivial. Clearly, P' is monotone since P is. Now, in a decision tree computing P, 0 is assigned to all edges in $K_{1,n-1}$. Then a decision tree computing P' is obtained. Thus, $D(P) \geq D(P')$.

Case 2. $K_{1,n-1}$ does not have property P. In this case, let P' be the property that a graph G on vertices $2, \cdots, n$ has property P' if and only if $K_{1,n-1} \cup G$ has property P. Then P' is a nontrivial monotone property of graphs of order $n-1$ and $D(P) \geq D(P')$.

Case 3. $K_{1,n-1}$ has property P and $\{1\} \cup K_{n-1}$ does not have property P. Let $A = \{1, \cdots, 2^{m-1}\}$, $B = \{n - 2^{m-1}+1, \cdots, n\}$ and $C = \{2^{m-1}+1, \cdots, n-2^{m-1}\}$. Let $K_{B \cup C}$ denote the complete graph on vertex set $B \cup C$. Then $A \cup K_{B \cup C}$ is a subgraph of $\{1\} \cup K_{n-1}$. Since $\{1\} \cup K_{n-1}$ does not have property P and P is monotone, $A \cup K_{B \cup C}$ does not have property P. Let $K_{A,B}$ be the complete bipartite graph between A and B. Then $K_{1,n-1}$ is a subgraph of $K_{A,B} \cup K_{A \cup C}$ which is isomorphic to $K_{A,B} \cup K_{B \cup C}$. Since $K_{1,n-1}$ has property P, so has $K_{A,B} \cup K_{B \cup C}$. Now, let P' be the property such that a bipartite graph G between A and B has property P' if and only if $G \cup K_{B \cup C}$ has property P. Then P' is a nontrivial monotone property of bipartite graphs between A and B with $|A| = |B| = 2^{m-1}$ and $D(P) \geq D(P')$. By Lemma 15.4.1, $D(P') \geq 2^{2m-2}$. This completes the proof of Lemma 15.4.2. $\qquad\square$

Lemma 15.4.3 *If P is a nontrivial monotone property of graphs of order $n = 2^m$ then $D(P) \geq n^2/4$.*

Proof. Let H_i be the disjoint union of 2^{m-i} copies of the complete graph of order 2^i. Then $H_0 \subset H_1 \subset \cdots \subset H_m = K_n$. Since P is nontrivial, H_m has property P and H_0 does not have property P. Thus, there exists an index j such that H_{j+1} has property P and H_j does not have property P. Partition H_j into two parts with vertex sets A and B, respectively; each contains exactly 2^{m-j-1} disjoint copies of the complete graph of order 2^j. Let $K_{A,B}$ be the complete bipartite graph between A and B. Then H_{j+1} is a subgraph of $H_j \cup K_{A,B}$. So, $H_j \cup K_{A,B}$ has property P. Now, let P' be a property of bipartite graphs between A and B such that a bipartite graph between A and B has property P' if and only if $H_j \cup G$ has property P. Then P' is a nontrivial monotone property of bipartite graphs between A and B with $|A| \cdot |B| = 2^{2m-2}$. By Lemma 15.4.1, $D(P) \geq D(P') = 2^{2m-2} = n^2/4$. $\qquad\square$

Theorem 15.4.4 *If P is a nontrivial monotone property of graphs of order n, then $D(P) \geq n^2/16$.*

Proof. It follows immediately from Lemmas 15.4.2 and 15.4.3. $\qquad\square$

The lower bound in Theorem 15.4.4 has been improved subsequently to $n^2/9 + o(n^2)$ by Kleitman and Kwiatkowski [9] and to $n^2/4 + o(n^2)$ by Kahn, Saks, and Sturtevant [6]. Kahn, Sake, and Sturtevant discovered a new criterion using some concept from algebraic topology. With such a criterion and some results on fixed point theory, they established the elusiveness of nontrivial monotone properties of graphs of order a prime power. In general, Karp conjectured that every nontrivial monotone graph property is elusive. This conjecture is still open.

With the approach of Kahn, *et al.* [6], Yao [20] proved that every monotone nontrivial bipartite graph property is elusive. With Yao's result, the recursive formula in Lemma 15.4.2 has been improved to

$$D(P) \geq \min\{D(P'), \frac{n^2 - 1}{2}\}$$

(see [8] for details). There are also many results on probabilistic decision trees in the literature. The interested reader may refer to [4, 14, 18, 19].

References

[1] M. Ben-Or, Lower bounds for algebraic computation trees, *Proceedings of 15th STOC* (1983) 80-86.

[2] M.R. Best, P. van Emde Boas, and H.W. Lenstra, Jr. A sharpened version of the Aanderaa-Rosenberg Conjecture, *Report ZW 30/74*, Mathematisch Centrum Amsterdam (1974).

[3] A. Björner, L. Lovász, and A. Yao, Linear decision trees: volume estimates and topological bounds, *Proceedings of 24th STOC* (1992) 170-177.

[4] B. Bollobas, *Extremal Graph Theory*, Academic Press (1978).

[5] D. Dobkin and R.J. Lipton, On the complexity of computations under varying sets of primitives, *J. of Computer Systems Sci.* 18 (1979) 86-91.

[6] J. Kahn, M. Saks, and D. Sturtevant, A topological approach to evasiveness, *Combinatorica* 4 (1984) 297-306.

[7] E. Kalinová, The localization problem in geometry and Rabin-Spira linear proof (czech), M. Sci. thesis, Universsitas Carolina, Prague, 1978.

[8] V. King, My thesis, Ph.D. Thesis at Computer Science Division, University of California at Berkeley, 1989.

[9] D.J. Kleitman and D.J. Kwiatkowski, Futher results on the Aanderaa-Rosenberg Conjecture, *J. Combinatorial Theory (Ser B)*, 28 (1980) 85-95.

[10] J. Morávek, A localization problem in geometry and complexity of discrete programming, *Kybernetika* (Prague) 8 (1972) 498-516.

[11] J. Morávek and P. Pudlák, New lower bound for polyhedral membership problem with an application to linear programming, in *Mathematical Foundation of Computer Science*, edited by M. P. Chytil and V. Koubek, (Springer-Verlag, 1984) 416-424.

[12] R. Rivest and S. Vuillemin, On recognizing graph properties from adjacency matrices, *Theor. Comp. Sci.* 3 (1976) 371-384.

[13] A.L. Rosenberg, On the time required to recognize properties of graphs: A problem, SIGACT News, 5:4 (1973) 15-16.

[14] M. Snir, Lower bounds for probabilistic linear decision trees, *Theor. Comp. Sci.* 38 (1985) 69-82.

[15] P.M. Spira, Complete linear proof of systems of linear inequalities, *J. Computer Systems Sci.* 6 (1972) 205-216.

[16] M. Steele and A. Yao, Lower bounds for algebraic decision trees, *J. Algorithms* 3 (1982) 1-8.

[17] A.C. Yao, On the complexity of comparison problems using linear functions, *Proc. 16th IEEE Symposium on Switching and Automata Theory* (1975) 85-99.

[18] A.C. Yao, Probabilistic computations: towards a unified measure of complexity, *Proc. 18th FOCS* (1977) 222-227.

[19] A.C. Yao, Lower bounds to randomized algorithms for graph properties, *28th FOCS* (1987) 393-400.

[20] A.C. Yao, Monotone bipartite graph properties are evasive, manuscript, 1986.

[21] A.C. Yao and R.L. Rivest, On the polyhedral decision problem, *SIAM J. Computing* 9 (1980) 343-347.

[22] A. Yao, Algebraic decision trees and Euler characteristics, *Proceedings of 33rd FOCS* (1992) 268-277.

16
Counterfeit Coins

This chapter is dedicated to the counterfeit coin problem, the most famous search problem historically [20, 19, 11], which recently draws on an unexpected connection to some deep mathematical theory to yield new results [4, 2, 3, 15].

16.1 One Counterfeit Coin

A man has twelve coins including possibly a counterfeit one. The counterfeit coin has a weight different from genuine coins. *Assume all genuine coins have the same weight.* (We will assume it throughout this chapter.) How can one tell in no more than three weighings with a balance (a) whether a counterfeit coin exists, (b) if so which one is and (c) whether the counterfeit coin is heavier or lighter than a genuine coin.

Here, the balance has two dishes, the right side and the left side. By *weighing*, one means that two equal sized subsets of coins are placed in the two dishes respectively and the outcome is one of the following: (1) *left side light*, i.e., the total weight of the coins on the left dish is smaller than that on the right dish; (2) *right side light*, i.e., the total weight of the coins on the right dish is smaller than that on the left dish; (3) *balanced*, i.e., two sides have the same total coin-weight.

This is a well-known problem with a long history in the literature [12]. A general solution will be presented in this section. Before doing so, let us first show some simple results.

Theorem 16.1.1 *Suppose there are n coins with possibly a light counterfeit coin. Then, $2 \leq n \leq 3^k - 1$ if and only if one can always tell in no more than k weighings (a) whether a counterfeit coin exists, and (b) if so which one is.*

Proof. For $n = 1$, the balance is useless and hence one has no way to tell (a). For $n \geq 2$, note that there are $n + 1$ sample points. By the information lower bound, $k \geq \log_3(n + 1)$, that is, $n \leq 3^k - 1$.

Next, assume $2 \leq n \leq 3^k - 1$. One proves by induction on k that k weighings are enough to tell (a) and (b). For $k = 1$, n must equal 2. Put them on two sides;

one in each. If balanced, then no counterfeit coin exists. If unbalanced, then the lighter one is counterfeit. Therefore, one weighing is enough. Now, consider $k \geq 2$. If $2 \leq n \leq 3^{k-1} - 1$, then by the induction hypothesis, $k - 1$ weighings are enough to tell (a) and (b). Thus, assume $3^{k-1} \leq n \leq 3^k - 1$. Let $h = \lceil (n - 3^{k-1} + 1)/2 \rceil$. Clearly,

$$1 \leq h \leq 3^{k-1} \text{ and } n - 2h \leq 3^{k-1} - 1.$$

Put h coins to each side of the balance.

If balanced, then $2h$ coins on the balance are genuine. By the induction hypothesis, additional $k - 1$ weighing are enough to tell (a) and (b) for the remaining $n - 2h$ coins. (Remark: since there are $2h$ genuine coins in hand, one can still tell (a) and (b) when $n - 2h = 1$.)

If unbalanced, then the h coins in the lighter side contains a counterfeit coin. ((a) is answered.) Moreover, if $h \leq 3^{k-1} - 1$, then by the induction hypothesis, additional $k - 1$ weighing are enough. If $h = 3^{k-1}$, then one can still use $k - 1$ weighing to tell (b) by equally dividing unknown coins into three groups in each weighing.   □

From the proof of Theorem 16.1.1, it is easy to see the following.

Corollary 16.1.2 *Suppose there are n coins with exactly one counterfeit coin which is light. Then $2 \leq n \leq 3^k$ if and only if one can always tell in no more than k weighings (b) which one is counterfeit.*

This corollary can be generalized as follows.

Lemma 16.1.3 *Suppose there are two groups of coins. The first group S_0 has n_0 coins with possibly a light counterfeit coin. The second group S_1 has n_1 coins with possibly a heavy counterfeit coin. Assume that $S_0 \cup S_1$ contains exactly one counterfeit coin and there exists additional $\min(1, n_0, n_1)$ genuine coin which can be used for helping. Then $n_0 + n_1 \leq 3^k$ if and only if one can always tell in no more than k weighings (b) which one is counterfeit and (c) whether the counterfeit coin is heavier or lighter than a genuine coin.*

Proof. One proves it by induction on k. First, note that if $\min(n_0, n_1) = 0$, then this lemma reduces to Corolllary 16.1.2. Therefore, one may assume $\min(1, n_0, n_1) = 1$. For $k = 1$, there are two cases as follows.

Case 1. $n_0 = n_1 = 1$. Put the one in S_0 on the left side and the genuine coin on the right side of the balance. If balanced, then the one in S_1 is a heavy counterfeit coin. If unbalanced, then the one in S_0 is a light counterfeit coin.

Case 2. $n_0 = 1$ and $n_1 = 2$ (or $n_0 = 2$ and $n_1 = 1$). Put the two unknown coins in S_1 on the balance, one on each side. If balanced, then the one in S_0 is a light counterfeit coin. If unbalanced, then the one on the heavy side of the balance is a heavy counterfeit coin.

Next, consider $k \geq 2$. One may assume $3^{k-1} < n_0 + n_1 \leq 3^k$. Let $h = \lceil (n_0 + n_1 - 3^{k-1})/2 \rceil$. Then

$$1 \leq h \leq 3^{k-1} \quad \text{and} \quad 3^{k-1} - 1 \leq n_0 + n_1 - 2h \leq 3^{k-1}.$$

Since $k \geq 2$, $3^{k-1} - 1 \geq 2$. This enables one to take $2h$ coins from $S_0 \cup S_1$ with even numbers of coins from S_0 and S_1, respectively. Now, put the $2h$ chosen coins on the balance such that the two sides contain the same number of coins from S_0 and the same number of coins from S_1. If balanced, then the counterfeit coin is among the $n_0 + n_1 - 2h$ coins not on the balance. By the induction hypothesis, $k - 1$ more weighings are enough to tell (b) and (c). If unbalanced, then the counterfeit coin is among coins from S_0 on the lighter side and coins from S_1 in the heavier side. Thus, the total number of unknown coins is h. By the induction hypothesis, $k - 1$ more weighings are enough to solve the problem. □

Theorem 16.1.4 *Suppose there are n coins with possibly a counterfeit coin and there exists one additional genuine coin. Then $n \leq (3^k - 1)/2$ if and only if one can always tell in no more than k weighings (a) whether a counterfeit coin exists, (b) if so which one is and (c) whether the counterfeit coin is heavier or lighter than a genuine coin.*

Proof. There are $2n + 1$ sample points. By the information lower bound, $k \geq \lceil \log_3(2n + 1) \rceil$. Thus, $n \leq (3^k - 1)/2$.

Next, assume $n \leq (3^k - 1)/2$. One shows by induction on k that k weighings are enough to tell (a), (b), and (c). For $k = 1$, one must have $n = 1$. Thus, one weighing is enough with helping of the additional genuine coin. Consider $k \geq 2$. Let $h' = (n - \frac{3^{k-1}-1}{2})/2$ and $h = \lfloor h'/2 \rfloor$. Then

$$h' \leq 3^{k-1} \quad \text{and} \quad n - h' = (3^{k-1} - 1)/2.$$

Put h unknown coins on the left side and $h' - h$ unknown coins on the right side of the balance. When $h' - h > h$, put one genuine coin on the left side, too. If unbalanced, then the h' unknown coins on the balance contains exactly one counterfeit coin which is light when it is in the light side and is heavy when it is in the heavy side. By Lemma 16.1.3 $k - 1$ more weighings are enough to solve the problem. If balanced, then all coins on the balance are genuine and one needs to deal with only $n - h'$ coins not on the balance. By the induction hypothesis, $k - 1$ more weighing are enough to solve the problem. □

It is interesting to point out that in the literature, the problem dealt in Theorem 16.1.4 is usually given condition "there are enough additional genuine coins". Actually, one additional genuine coin is enough.

Theorem 16.1.5 *Suppose there are n coins with possibly a counterfeit coin. Then $3 \leq n \leq (3^k - 3)/2$ if and only if one can always tell in no more than k weighings (a) whether a counterfeit coin exists, (b) if so which one is and (c) whether the counterfeit coin is heavier or lighter than a genuine coin.*

Proof. Suppose that k weighings are enough and that in the first weighing, each side of the balance has x coins. If the outcome of the first weighing is balanced, then there are $2(n - 2x) + 1$ possible sample points. By the information lower bound, $\log_3(2(n - 2x) + 1) \le k - 1$, i.e., $n - 2x \le (3^{k-1} - 1)/2$. If the outcome of the first weighing is unbalanced, then there are $2x$ possible sample points. By the information lower bound, $\log_3(2x) \le k - 1$, i.e., $2x \le 3^{k-1}$. Note that $2x$ is an even number. Thus, $2x \le 3^{k-1} - 1$. Therefore,

$$n \le \frac{3^{k-1} - 1}{2} + 3^{k-1} - 1 = \frac{3^k - 3}{2}.$$

Moreover, if $n = 1$, then one has no way to do any weighing; if $n = 2$, then one has only one way to do weighing which can tell (a) but not (b) and (c).

Next, assume $3 \le n \le (3^k - 3)/2$. One proves by induction on k that k weighings are enough to tell (a), (b), and (c). For $k = 2$, one must have $n = 3$. Put two coins on the balance, one on each side. If balanced, then the two coins on the balance are genuine and only one coin is still unknown. Hence, one more weighing can solve the problem. If unbalanced, then the one not on the balance is genuine. By Theorem 16.1.4, one more weighing is enough to solve the problem. Now, consider $k \ge 3$. If $n \le (3^{k-1} - 3)/2$, then by the induction hypothesis, $k - 1$ weighings are enough. Thus, one may assume $(3^{k-1} - 1)/2 \le n \le (3^k - 3)/2$. Let $h = \max(1, \lceil (n - \frac{3^{k-1}-1}{2})/2 \rceil)$. Then

$$1 \le h \le (3^{k-1} - 1)/2 \quad \text{and} \quad 1 \le n - 2h \le (3^{k-1} - 1)/2.$$

Put $2h$ coins on the balance, h coins on each side. If balanced, then there remain $n - 2h$ coins unknown; they are not on the balance. By Theorem 16.1.4, $k - 1$ more weighing are enough to solve the problem. If unbalanced, then there remain $2h$ coins unknown; they are on the balance. By Lemma 16.1.3, $k - 1$ more weighings are enough. □

Theorem 16.1.5 can be made stronger.

Theorem 16.1.6 *Suppose there are n coins with possibly a counterfeit coin. Then $3 \le n \le (3^k - 3)/2$ if and only if one can always tell in no more than k nonadaptive weighings (a) whether a counterfeit coin exists, (b) if so which one is and (c) whether the counterfeit coin is heavier or lighter than a genuine coin.*

The proof can be done by implementing k weighings, in the proof of Theorem 16.1.6, nonadaptive. To explain this, consider an example that there are twelve coins with possibly one counterfeit coin. A sequential algorithm for it is shown in Figure 16.1, where $1, 2, 3, 4 : 5, 6, 7, 8$ represents a weighing with coins 1, 2, 3, 4 on the left side and coins 5, 6, 7, 8 on the right side. The edge-labels e, l, and r denote three weighing outcomes, balanced, left side light, and right side light, respectively. $12L$ and $12L$ denote respectively the outcomes that coin 12 is a light counterfeit coin and that

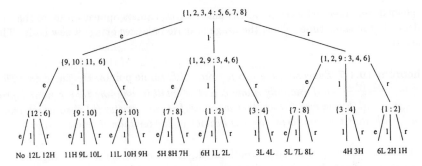

Figure 16.1: A sequential algorithm for 12 coins.

coin 12 is a heavy counterfeit coin. This sequential algorithm can be implemented by the following three nonadaptive weighings:

$$W_1 = \{1,2,3,4 : 5,6,7,8\},$$
$$W_2 = \{9,10,1,2 : 11,6,3,4\},$$
$$W_3 = \{12,9,7,1,3 : 6,10,8,2,4\}.$$

The following table contains the outcome of these three weighings.

W_1	e	e	e	e	e	e	e	e	e
W_2	e	e	e	l	l	l	r	r	r
W_3	e	l	r	e	l	r	e	l	r
	No	$12L$	$12H$	$11H$	$9L$	$10L$	$11L$	$10H$	$9H$
W_1	l	l	l	l	l	l		l	l
W_2	e	e	e	l	l	l		r	r
W_3	e	l	r	e	l	r		l	r
	$5H$	$8H$	$7H$	$6H$	$1L$	$2L$		$3L$	$4L$
W_1	r	r	r		r	r	r	r	r
W_2	e	e	e		l	l	r	r	r
W_3	e	l	r		l	r	e	l	r
	$5L$	$7L$	$8L$		$4H$	$3H$	$6L$	$2H$	$1H$

Not every sequential algorithm for a problem on one counterfeit coin can be implemented nonadaptively. However, for optimal algorithm in the proof of Theorem 16.1.5, it is not hard to do with minor modification. A general argument can be found in Halbeisen and Hungerbühler[12].

Halbeisen and Hungerbühler also studied weighing with more than one balance. Note that although three weighings W_1, W_2, and W_3 are nonadaptive, they cannot implement on three balances parallelly since a coin cannot appear on more than one balance in the same time. Thus, the usage of more balances brings a new issue. They showed

Theorem 16.1.7 *Suppose there are n coins with possibly a counterfeit coin. Then $3 \leq n \leq \frac{(2b+1)^k - 1}{2} - b$ if and only if one can always tell in no more than k nonadaptive weighings with b balances (a) whether a counterfeit coin exists, (b) if so which one is and (c) whether the counterfeit coin is heavier or lighter than a genuine coin.*

Linial and Tarsi [18] found the optimal algorithm in the sense of average number of weighings. They showed the following.

Theorem 16.1.8 *Suppose there are n coins with exactly one counterfeit coin. Let $2n = 3^t + 2k + 1, (3^t > k \geq 0)$. Then the smallest average number of weighings for any algorithm to find (b) which one is the counterfeit coin and (c) whether the counterfeit coin is heavier or lighter than a genuine coin is $F(n)/(2n)$ where*

$$F(n) = 2nt + 3k + \begin{cases} 4, & k \text{ even,} \\ 3, & k \text{ odd.} \end{cases}$$

Theorem 16.1.9 *Suppose there are n coins with exactly one counterfeit coin and there is an additional genuine coin. Let $2n = 3^t + 2k + 1, (3^t > k \geq 0)$. Then the smallest average number of weighings for any algorithm to find (b) which one is the counterfeit coin and (c) whether the counterfeit coin is heavier or lighter than a genuine coin is $S(n)/(2n)$ where*

$$S(n) = 2nt + 3k + \begin{cases} 2, & k \text{ even,} \\ 3, & k \text{ odd.} \end{cases}$$

Linial and Tarsi also indicated that Theorems 16.1.8 and 16.1.9 still hold if one replace "any algorithm" by "any nonadaptive algorithm".

This may encourage the reader to think that that every result about one counterfeit coin for sequential algorithm would hold for nonadaptive algorithm. However, it is not the case. The following is a counterexample.

Aigner [1] proposed a generalized balance. A *multi-arms balance* has $r(\geq 2)$ arms each with a dish. For each weighing, r equally sized subsets of coins are placed on r dishes. When there is at most one counterfeit coin and $r \geq 3$, the multi-arms balance can always tell which dish contains a counterfeit coin and, if it contains, whether the counterfeit coin is lighter or heavier.

De Bonis, Gargano, and Vaccaro [7] studied optimal algorithms for the average number of weighings with a multi-arms balance. They obtained the following result for sequential algorithms.

Theorem 16.1.10 *Suppose there are n coins with exactly one counterfeit coin which is lighter. Let $n = (r+1)^L + kr + j \geq r$ where $0 \leq k < (r+1)^L$ and $0 \leq j \leq r-1$. Then the smallest average number of weighings with an r-arms balance for any algorithm to find which one is the counterfeit coin is*

$$\frac{H(n)}{n} + \begin{cases} j & \text{if } 2(r+1) \leq n \leq 3r, \\ (r-k)/n & \text{if } 3r+1 \leq n \leq r(r+1) \\ 0 & \text{otherwise,} \end{cases}$$

where

$$H(n) = nL + \left\lceil (kr+j)\frac{r+1}{r} \right\rceil.$$

However, the smallest average number of weighings with an r-arms balance for all nonadaptive algorithms in the same situation is much harder to determine. De Bonis [6] determined this number for almost all k, which is different from that in Theorem 16.1.10 in many cases.

16.2 Two, Three, and More Counterfeit Coins

A general counterfeit coin problem is described as follows: Given a set of n coins with at most two different weights. Lighter coins are counterfeit ones. Identify all counterfeit coins with the minimum number of weighings of a regular balance.

Let $g(d,n)$ denote the minimax number of weighings under condition that the number d of counterfeit coins is known. Clearly, $g(0,n) = 0$. By Theorem 16.1.1, $g(1,n) = \lceil \log_3 n \rceil$. A surprising result on $g(2,n)$ was obtained by Li [16].

Theorem 16.2.1 $g(2,n) = \lceil \log_3 \binom{n}{2} \rceil$.

The proof of Theorem 16.2.1 is based on a result of Tošić [23]. It is a very complicated case-by-case argument.

Li [16] also showed the following.

Theorem 16.2.2 $\lceil \log_3 \binom{n}{3} \rceil \leq g(3,n) \leq \lceil \log_3 \binom{n}{3} \rceil + 2$.

Bošnjak [5] obtained a similar result for three counterfeit coins. In general, Pyber [21] obtained the following.

Theorem 16.2.3 $\lceil \log_3 \binom{n}{d} \rceil \leq g(d,n) \leq \lceil \log_3 \binom{n}{d} \rceil + 15d$.

Following the idea of Du and Hwang [8], Hu and Hwang [14] initiated a study on competitive algorithms for the counterfeit coin problem. They encountered a complication in dealing with case $d = 0$. To see this, let $g_\alpha(d \mid n)$ denote the maximum number of weighings by the algorithm α on samples with d counterfeit coins where d is unknown. Then for any algorithm α, there do not exist constants c and a such that $g_\alpha(0 \mid n) \leq cg(0,n) + a$. In fact, $g(0,n) = 0$ and no algorithm could tell in a constant number of weighings whether $d = 0$.

To solve this problem, Hu and Hwang proposed a new definition of competitive algorithms for counterfeit coin problem. Define

$$g(d \mid n) = \min_\alpha g_\alpha(d \mid n).$$

An algorithm α is called a *c-competitive* algorithm if there exists a constant a such that for $0 \leq d \leq n-1$, $g_\alpha(d \mid n) \leq cg(d \mid n) + a$.

Unfortunately, they were still unable to establish a nontrivial lower bound for $g(0 \mid n)$. Therefore, they had to restrict their *c*-competitive algorithm to satisfy $g_\alpha(d \mid n) \leq cg(d \mid n) + a$ for $1 \leq d \leq n-1$ and a constant a. The competitive ratio c in this sense has been improved several times [13, 25, 24]. The best known c is $\log_2 3 + \frac{1}{2}$, obtained by Wan and Du [24].

16.3   The All-Equal Problem

To establish a nontrivial lower bound for $g(0 \mid n)$, Hu and Hwang [14] proposed the following problem:

The All-Equal Problem: Given a set of n coins of at most two different weights, decide whether all coins have the same weight or not.

They also gave an algorithm as follows: In the first step, compare two coins; if the weighing is not balanced, then stop, else go to the next step. In general, in the $(k+1)$th step, compare the set of coins used in the kth step and a set of the same number of new coins; if the weighing is balanced, then stop, else go to the next step until no unweighed coin is left. Clearly, if every weighing was balanced, then all coins have the same weight. This algorithm solves the all-equal problem in $\lceil \log_2 n \rceil$ weighings. Hu and Hwang conjectured that this is an optimal algorithm. In other words, $g(0 \mid n) = \lceil \log_2 n \rceil$. However, their conjecture was disproved by Kozlov and Vu [15].

Kozlov and Vu discovered a surprising connection between the all-equal problem and lattice geometry. To explain it, let S denote the set of n given coins. Consider m weighings and let A_i and B_i be the sets of coins on the left dish and on the right dish, respectively, in the ith weighing. For each coin $c \in S$, define an m-dimensional vector v_x by the rule that the ith coordinate of v_x equals 1 if $c \in A_i$, -1 if $c \in B_i$, and 0 if $c \notin A_i \cup B_i$. Since $|A_i| = |B_i|$ for all i, one has

$$\sum_{c \in S} v_c = 0. \tag{16.1}$$

Let W be the set of all m-dimensional vectors with coordinates in $\{1, -1, 0\}$. Then $|W| = 3^m$ and $v_c \in W$ for all $c \in S$. For each $w \in W$, let $\lambda_w = |\{c \mid v_c = w, c \in S\}|$. Then

$$\sum_{w \in W} \lambda_w = n \qquad (16.2)$$

and (16.1) can be rewritten as

$$\sum_{w \in W} \lambda_w w = 0. \qquad (16.3)$$

Thus, $(\lambda_w, w \in W)$ is a 3^m-dimensional vector in the following cone

$$K = \{(\mu_w, w \in W) \mid \sum_{w \in W} \mu_w w = 0, \mu_w \geq 0 \text{ for } w \in W\}.$$

Note that all coordinates of $(\lambda_w, w \in W)$ are non-negative integers. Thus, $(\lambda_w, w \in W)$ is actually a nonzero lattice point in cone K. (A *lattice point* is an integral vector.)

What does it mean that every weighing is balanced? Let C_1 (C_2) denote the set of all lighter (heavier) coins in S. The ith weighing balanced means that $|A_i \cap C_1| = |B_i \cap C_1|$ and $|A_i \cap C_2| = |B_i \cap C_2|$. For each $c \in C_j$, define $v_c^{(j)} \in W$ by the rule that the ith coordinate is 1 if $c \in A_i$, -1 if $c \in B_i$, and 0 otherwise. For each $w \in W$, denote

$$\lambda_w^{(j)} = |\{c \in C_j \mid v_c^{(j)} = w\}|. \qquad (16.4)$$

It is easy to see that if all weighings are balanced, then for $j = 1, 2$,

$$(\lambda_w^{(j)}, w \in W) \in K, \sum_{w \in W} \lambda_w^{(j)} = |C_j|,$$

and

$$\lambda_w = \lambda_w^{(1)} + \lambda_w^{(2)} \text{ for all } w \in W. \qquad (16.5)$$

Suppose the m weighings, represented by (A_i, B_i) for $1 \leq i \leq m$, being balanced cannot guarantee all coins having the same weight. Then (16.5) holds for some sample (C_1, C_2) with $|C_1| > 0$ and $|C_2| > 0$. Thus, $(\lambda_w, w \in W)$ can be represented by the sum of two nonzero lattice points in K.

Conversely, if $(\lambda_w, w \in W)$ can be represented by the sum of two nonzero lattice points in K as shown in (16.5), then it is easy to choose nonempty coin sets C_1 and C_2 to satisfy (16.4). This means that the m weighings, represented by (A_i, B_i) for $1 \leq i \leq m$, being balanced cannot guarantee all coins having the same weight.

Therefore, the m weighings represented by (A_i, B_i) for $1 \leq i \leq m$ form a correct algorithm for the all-equal problem if and only if $(\lambda_w, w \in W)$ cannot be represented by the sum of two nonzero lattice points in K.

A finite set of vectors $\{a_1, a_2, \cdots, a_t\}$ in K is called an *integral Hilbert basis* if each lattice point in K is a non-negative integral linear combination of $a_1, a_2, \cdots, a_t$. An integral Hilbert basis is *minimal* if no proper subset of it is also an integral Hilbert basis. It is known that K has a unique minimal Hilbert basis (see Theorem 16.4 in [22]). From the above discussion, the following is obtained.

Theorem 16.3.1 *The m weighings represented by (A_i, B_i) for $1 \leq i \leq m$ form a correct algorithm for the all-equal problem if and only if $(\lambda_w, w \in W)$ is in the minimal Hilbert basis of K.*

Proof. Let H denote the minimal Hilbert basis of K. First, assume that m weighings represented by (A_i, B_i) for $1 \leq i \leq m$ form a correct algorithm for the all-equal problem. Then $(\lambda_w, w \in W)$ cannot be written as the sum of two lattice points in K. By contradiction, suppose $(\lambda_w, w \in W)$ is not in H. Then

$$(\lambda_w, w \in W) = \sum_{y \in H} \alpha_y y$$

where α_y's are non-negative integers and $\sum_{y \in H} \alpha \geq 2$. So, there exists $z \in H$ such that $\alpha_z \geq 1$. z and $\sum_{y \in H} \alpha_y - z$ would be lattice points in K such that $(\lambda_w, w \in W) = z + (\sum_{y \in H} \alpha_y - z)$, a contradiction.

Next, consider $x \in H$. We will show that x cannot be written as the sum of two lattice points in K. By contradiction, suppose

$$x = y + z \tag{16.6}$$

for two lattice points y and z in K. Write y and z as non-negative integral combinations of vectors in H and substitute them into (16.6). Then x is represented by a non-negative integral combination of vectors in H such that the sum of all coefficients is at least two, i.e.,

$$x = \sum_{a \in H} \alpha_a a \tag{16.7}$$

where α_a's are non-negative integers such that $\sum_{a \in H} \alpha_a \geq 2$.

We claim that $\alpha_x = 0$. In fact, by contradiction, suppose $\alpha_x > 0$. Then $\sum_{a \in H \setminus \{x\}} \alpha_a a + (\alpha_x - 1)x = 0$. This implies that H contains zero vector, contradicting the minimality of H.

Now, $\alpha_x = 0$. It follows from (16.7) that x can be removed from H, contradicting the minimality of H. $\square$

By Theorem 16.3.1 and (16.2), for each vector x in the minimal Hilbert basis of K, there exists a correct algorithm of m weighings for the all-equal problem with the number of given coins equal to the sum of coordinates of x. Let $n(m, 2)$ denote the maximum possible number of coins with at most two different weights for which the all-equal problem can be solved in m weighings. Then $n(m, 2)$ is equal to the maximum of the sum of coordinates of lattice points in the minimal Hilbert basis of K.

If the conjecture of Hu and Hwang holds, then $n(m, 2) = 2^m$. However, Kozlov and Vu disproved the conjecture of Hu and Hwang by showing that $n(3, 2) \geq 10 > 2^3 = 8$. They also showed that $n(m, 2) \leq (3^m - 1)(m + 1)^{(m+1)/2}/2$, which yields $g(0 \mid n) = \Omega(\log n / \log \log n)$.

To show $n(3,2) \geq 10$, one needs to find a lattice point in the minimal Hilbert basis of K such that the sum of coordinates of the lattice point is 10. To do it, one first gives a sufficient condition for a lattice point to be in the minimal Hilbert basis of K.

A nonzero vector x in K is called an *extremal direction* of K if x cannot be written as $x = y + z$ for linearly independent vectors $u, v \in K$. From the theory of polyhedral, it is well-known that for any cone, there exist finitely many extremal directions such that every vector in the cone is a non-negative combination of those extremal directions.

Lemma 16.3.2 *If a lattice point x is an extremal direction of K and its coordinates are relatively prime, i.e. their greatest common divisor is 1, then it is in the minimal Hilbert basis of K.*

Proof. By contradiction, suppose $x = y + z$ for nonzero lattice points y and z in K. Since x is an extremal direction of K, y and z cannot be linearly independent. Thus, $y = \alpha x$ and $z = \beta x$ for some positive scalars α and β. Since the coordinates of x are relatively prime, α and β must be positive integers. Thus, $\alpha + \beta \geq 2$. However, since $x = y + z = (\alpha + \beta)x$, one has $\alpha + \beta = 1$, a contradiction. $\qquad\square$

A vector in the minimal Hilbert basis of K is called a *minimum generator* if it is an extremal direction of K.

The next lemma indicates how to find all minimum generators.

Lemma 16.3.3 *Let $L = (w_1, w_2, \cdots, w_{m+1})$ for $w_1, w_2, \cdots, w_{m+1} \in W$ such that $rank(L) = m$. Define $x \in K$ by*

$$
x_w = \begin{cases} \dfrac{(-1)^{i-1} \det L_i}{gcd(|\det L_1|, |\det L_2|, \cdots, |\det L_{m+1}|)} & \text{if } w = w_i \text{ for } 1 \leq i \leq m+1, \\ 0 & \text{otherwise}, \end{cases}
$$

where L_i is obtained from L by deleting the ith column, i.e.,

$$
L_i = (w_1, \cdots, w_{i-1}, w_{i+1}, \cdots, w_{m+1}).
$$

If $x \geq 0$, then x is a minimum generator of K. Moreover, every minimum generator x of K can be obtained in the above way.

Proof. Clearly, $\sum_{w \in W} x_w = 0$. If $x \geq 0$, then $x \in K$. Since x is a lattice point and its coordinates are relatively prime, it suffices to show that x is an extremal direction. By contradiction, suppose $x = y + z$ for linearly independent $y, z \in K$. Since $y \geq 0$ and $z \geq 0$, $x_w = 0$ implies $y_w = z_w = 0$. Thus, $\sum_{i=1}^{m+1} y_{w_i} w_i = \sum_{i=1}^{n+1} z_{w_i} w_i = 0$. That is, both $(y_{w_1}, y_{w_2}, \cdots, y_{w_{m+1}})^T$ and $(z_{w_1}, z_{w_2}, \cdots, z_{w_{m+1}})^T$ are in subspace $\{x' \mid Lx' = 0\}$ (the kernel of L). However, $rank(L) = m$. Thus the kernel of L is a line. This means that $(y_{w_1}, y_{w_2}, \cdots, y_{w_{m+1}})$ and $(z_{w_1}, z_{w_2}, \cdots, z_{w_{m+1}})$ are linearly dependent, so are y and z, a contradiction.

Conversely, suppose x is a minimum generator of K. Let s denote the sum of coordinates of x. Then $s > 0$. Consider polyhedron $K' = \{y \in K \mid \sum_{w \in W} y_w = s\}$. Clearly, $x \in K'$. Since x is an extremal direction of K, it is easy to show that x is an extremal point of K'. (A point in a polyhedron is an *extremal point* x if it cannot be written as a convex combination of other points in the polyhedron.) Note that K' is in the standard form of feasible region of linear programming. From the theory of linear programming, it is known that each extremal point of the feasible region is a basic feasible solution whose nonzero coordinates are included in the solution of a system of linear equations as follows:

$$\begin{pmatrix} 1 & 1 & \cdots & 1 \\ w_1 & w_2 & \cdots & w_{m+1} \end{pmatrix} x' = \begin{pmatrix} s \\ 0 \end{pmatrix} \tag{16.8}$$

where

$$rank \begin{pmatrix} 1 & 1 & \cdots & 1 \\ w_1 & w_2 & \cdots & w_{m+1} \end{pmatrix} = m + 1.$$

The solution of this system of equations is unique, which equals

$$\alpha(\det L_1, -\det L_2, \cdots, (-1)^m \det L_{m+1})$$

for some scaler α. It follows that

$$x_{w_i} = \frac{(-1)^{i-1} \det L_i}{gcd(|\det L_1|, |\det L_2|, \cdots, |\det L_{m+1}|)}$$

for $1 \le i \le m + 1$.   □

Now, for $m = 3$, consider

$$L = \begin{pmatrix} -1 & 1 & 1 & -1 \\ 0 & -1 & 1 & -1 \\ 1 & 0 & -1 & -1 \end{pmatrix}.$$

It is easy to verify that $rank(L) = 3$ and

$$\frac{(\det L_1, -\det L_2, \det L_3, -\det L_4)}{gcd(|\det L_1|, |\det L_2|, |\det L_3|, |\det L_4|)} = (4, 2, 3, 1).$$

Thus, one can obtain a minimum generator in which the sum of coordinates is equal to 10. Properly choosing A_i and B_i, one may obtain the following algorithm:

$$S = \{1, 2, 3, 4, 5, 6, 7, 8, 9, 10\}$$

$$A_1 = \{1, 2, 3, 4, 10\} \quad B_1 = \{5, 6, 7, 8, 9\},$$
$$A_2 = \{1, 2, 3, 4\} \quad B_2 = \{7, 8, 9, 10\},$$
$$A_3 = \{7, 8, 9\} \quad B_3 = \{5, 6, 10\}.$$

To establish a lower bound for $n(m, 2)$, one first notes that every extremal direction x can be obtained from solving an equation system (16.8). The following lemma follows from this fact and the proof of Lemma 16.3.3.

Corollary 16.3.4 *For every extremal direction x, there exists a minimum generator y such that $x = \alpha y$ for a positive scalar α.*

As a consequence of this corollary, one has that every point in K is a non-negative combination of minimum generators. More importantly, one has

Lemma 16.3.5 *Every vector in the minimal Hilbert basis of K is a non-negative combination of at most $(3^m - 1)/2 - m$ minimum generators.*

Proof. Note that if $w \in W$, then $-w \in W$. For any vector x in the minimal Hilbert basis of K, either $x_w = 0$ or $x_{-w} = 0$. In fact, by contradiction, suppose $x_w > 0$ and $x_{-w} > 0$. Define a lattice point $y \in K$ by

$$y_u = \begin{cases} 1 & \text{if } u = w \text{ or } -w, \\ 0 & \text{otherwise.} \end{cases}$$

Then $x = y + (x - y)$ and $x - y$ is also a lattice point in K, a contradiction. Similarly, the coordinate of x corresponding to zero vector in W is also zero. Therefore, each vector x in the minimal Hilbert basis of K has at most $(3^m - 1)/2$ nonzero coordinates.

By Corollary 16.3.4, every vector x in the minimal Hilbert basis of K is a non-negative combination of minimum generators. Since x is nonzero, it is actually a positive combination of minimum generators. For every $x_w = 0$, the corresponding coordinate of every minimum generator in the positive combination is also equal to 0. This means that all minimum generators in the positive combination belong to cone $K' = \{y \in K \mid y_w = 0 \text{ for } x_w = 0\}$. The dimension of K' is $(3^m - 1)/2 - m$. By Caratheodory Theorem[1] in polyhedral cones, x is a positive combination of at most $(3^m - 1)/2 - m$ minimum generators. $\square$

Let $\gamma(m)$ denote the maximum of the sum of coordinates of minimum generators of K.

Theorem 16.3.6 $\gamma(m) \leq n(m, 2) \leq (\frac{3^m - 1}{2} - m)\gamma(m).$

---

[1]Caratheodory Theorem states that if a convex cone generated by p vectors is in a k-dimensional space, then every vector in the cone is a positive combination of at most k vectors from the p vectors.

Proof. The first inequality follows immediately from the fact that every minimum generator is in the minimal Hilbert basis of K. To prove the second inequality, by Lemma 16.3.5, write each vector x in the minimal Hilbert basis of K as a non-negative combination of $(3^m - 1)/2 - m$ minimum generators

$$x = \sum_{i=1}^{\frac{3^m-1}{2}-m} \alpha_i x^{(i)}$$

where $x^{(i)}$'s are minimum generators of K. Note that $x - x^{(i)} \notin K$. Hence, $\alpha_i < 1$. Let $s(x)$ denote the sum of coordinates of X. Then

$$s(x) = \sum_{i=1}^{\frac{3^m-1}{2}-m} \alpha_i s(x^{(i)}) < \sum_{i=1}^{\frac{3^m-1}{2}-m} s(x^{(i)}) \le (\frac{3^m - 1}{2} - m)\gamma(m).$$

Therefore, $n(m, 2) \le (\frac{3^m-1}{2} - m)\gamma(m)$. $\square$

An upper bound of $\gamma(m)$ is established by Hadamard inequality as follows.

Lemma 16.3.7 *If A is an $n \times n$ matrix with entry a_{ij} in the ith row and the jth column, then*

$$|\det A| \le \prod_{i=1}^{n}(\sum_{j=1}^{n} a_{ij}^2)^{1/2}.$$

By Lemma 16.3.3, for each minimum generator x, there is an $m \times (m+1)$ matrix L with entries in $\{1, -1, 0\}$ such that

$$\begin{aligned}
s(x) &= \frac{\det L_1 - \det L_2 + \cdots + (-1)^m L_{m+1}}{gcd(|\det L_1|, |\det L_2|, \cdots, |\det L_{m+1}|)} \\
&\le \det \begin{pmatrix} e \\ L \end{pmatrix} \\
&\le (m+1)^{(m+1)/2},
\end{aligned}$$

where e is an $(m+1)$-dimensional row vector with all coordinates 1. Thus, one has

Theorem 16.3.8 $n(m, 2) \le (\frac{3^m-1}{2} - m)(m+1)^{(m+1)/2}$.

16.4   Anti-Hadamard Matrices

To establish a good lower bound for $\gamma(m)$, Alon and Vu [3] studied anti-Hadamard matrices. What are the anti-Hadamard matrices?

For a real matrix A, the *condition number* $c(A) = \|A\| \cdot \|A^{-1}\|$ where $\|A\| = \sup_{x \ne 0} \|Ax\|/\|x\|$ is very important in numerical linear algebra. A is called *ill-conditioned* if $c(A)$ is large. *Anti-Hadamard matrices* are ill-conditioned matrices with entries in the set $\{0,1\}$ or in the set $\{1,-1\}$ (see Graham and Sloane [10]). For those matrices, there are many quantities equivalent to the condition number. One of them is as follows:

$$\chi(A) = \max_{i,j} |b_{ij}|$$

where $(b_{ij}) = A^{-1}$. Define

$$\chi(m) = \max_A \chi(A)$$

where A is over all $m \times m$ matrices with entries in $\{1,-1,0\}$. An important observation is as follows.

Lemma 16.4.1 $\gamma(m) \geq \chi(m)$.

Proof. Suppose $\chi(A) = \chi(m)$. Then A is a nonsingular matrix of order m. Without loss of generality, assume $\chi(A) = |\det A_{11}|/|\det A|$ where A_{11} is the submatrix of A, obtained by deleting the first row and the first column. Let L be an $m \times (m+1)$ matrix obtained from A by adding to its right a column $e_1 = (1,0,\cdots,0)^T$. Clearly, $rank(L) = m$. Without loss of generality, one may assume that $Lx = 0$ has a nonzero solution x with all coordinates non-negative. In fact, consider a nonzero solution x of $Lx = 0$ such that $x_{m+1} \geq 0$. If for some $1 \leq i \leq m, x_i < 0$, then, by changing the sign of entries in the ith column of A, the kernel of the new L would contain a nonzero vector with all coordinates non-negative.

By Lemma 16.3.3, there exists a minimum generator x' of K such that the sum of coordinates of x' is equal to

$$\begin{aligned} s(x') &= \frac{\sum_{i=1}^{m+1} |\det L_i|}{gcd(|\det L_1|, |\det L_2|, \cdots, |\det L_{m+1}|)} \\ &\geq \frac{|\det L_1|}{|\det L_{m+1}|} = \frac{|\det A_{11}|}{|\det A|} = \chi(A) = \chi(m) \end{aligned}$$

where L_i is obtained from L by deleting the ith column. $\square$

Lemma 16.4.1 indicates that to show a good lower bound for $\gamma(m)$, it suffices to construct an anti-Hadamard matrix A with large $\chi(A)$.

Lemma 16.4.2 *For $m = 2^k$, there exists an $m \times m$ matrix A with entries in $\{1,-1\}$ such that*

$$\chi(A) \geq 2^{(1/2)m \log m - m(1+o(1))}.$$

Proof. Let Ω be a set of k elements. Order all subsets of Ω, $\alpha_1, \alpha_2, \cdots, \alpha_m$ such that $|\alpha_i| \leq |\alpha_{i+1}| \leq |\alpha_i| + 1$ and $|\alpha_i \Delta \alpha_{i+1}| \leq 2$ where $\alpha_i \Delta \alpha_{i+1}$ represents the symmetric difference of α_i and α_{i+1}. To construct A, one first constructs a symmetric Hadamard matrix Q and a lower triangular matrix L as follows.

Let $Q = (q_{ij})$ where $q_{ij} = (-1)^{|\alpha_i \cap \alpha_j|}$. For $j < k$, there exists an element $a \in \alpha_k \setminus \alpha_j$. For every α_i with $a \notin \alpha_i$, denote $\alpha_{i'} = \alpha_i \cup \{a\}$.

$$
\begin{aligned}
q_{ij}q_{ik} &+ q_{i'j}q_{i'k} \\
&= (-1)^{|\alpha_i \cap \alpha_j| + |\alpha_i \cap \alpha_k|} + (-1)^{|\alpha_{i'} \cap \alpha_j| + |\alpha_{i'} \cap \alpha_k|} \\
&= (-1)^{|\alpha_i \cap \alpha_j| + |\alpha_i \cap \alpha_k|} + (-1)^{|\alpha_i \cap \alpha_j| + |\alpha_i \cap \alpha_k| + 1} \\
&= 0.
\end{aligned}
$$

Therefore, $\sum_{i=1}^{m} q_{ij}q_{ik} = 0$ for $j \neq k$. Moreover,

$$
\sum_{i=1}^{m} q_{ij}^2 = m.
$$

Hence,

$$
Q^2 = nI_m
$$

that is, Q is a symmetric Hadamard matrix.

To construct L, define

$$
F_i = \begin{cases} \{\alpha_s \mid \alpha_s \subseteq (\alpha_{i-1} \cup \alpha_i), |\alpha_s \cap (\alpha_{i-1}\Delta\alpha_i)| = 1\} & \text{if } |\alpha_{i-1}\Delta\alpha_i| = 2, \\ \{\alpha_s \mid \alpha_s \subseteq (\alpha_{i-1} \cup \alpha_i)\} & \text{if } |\alpha_{i-1}\Delta\alpha_i| = 1, \end{cases}
$$

that is,

$$
F_i = \begin{cases} \{\alpha_s \mid \alpha_s \subseteq \alpha_{i-1} \text{ or } \alpha_s \subseteq \alpha_i, \text{ but } \alpha_s \not\subseteq (\alpha_{i-1} \cap \alpha_i)\} & \text{if } |\alpha_{i-1}\Delta\alpha_i| = 2, \\ \{\alpha_s \mid \alpha_s \subseteq \alpha_i\} & \text{if } |\alpha_{i-1}\Delta\alpha_i| = 1. \end{cases}
$$

Here, denote $\alpha_0 = \emptyset$. It is easy to see from this representation that $s \leq i$ for $\alpha_s \in F_i$, $\alpha_{i-1}, \alpha_i \in F_i$ and $|F_i| = 2^{|\alpha_i|}$ for all i. Define $L = (l_{ij})$ by

$$
l_{ij} = \begin{cases} 0 & \text{if } \alpha_j \notin F_i, \\ (1/2)^{|\alpha_i|-1} - 1 & \text{if } j = i-1 \text{ and } \alpha_j \in F_i, \\ (1/2)^{|\alpha_i|-1} & \text{otherwise.} \end{cases}
$$

Clearly, L is a lower triangular matrix.

Set $A = LQ$. Then every entry a_{ij} of A is in $\{1, -1\}$. In fact,

$$
\begin{aligned}
a_{ij} = \sum_{s=1}^{m} l_{is}q_{sj} &= \sum_{\alpha_s \in F_i} (1/2)^{|\alpha_i|-1}(-1)^{|\alpha_s \cap \alpha_j|} + (-1)(-1)^{|\alpha_{i-1} \cap \alpha_i|} \\
&= (1/2)^{|\alpha_i|-1} \sum_{ij} + (-1)^{|\alpha_{i-1} \cap \alpha_i|+1}.
\end{aligned}
$$

(1) If $\alpha_j \cap (\alpha_{i-1} \cup \alpha_i) = \alpha_{i-1}\Delta\alpha_i$ and $|\alpha_{i-1}\Delta\alpha_i| = 2$, then $|\alpha_s \cap \alpha_j| = 1$ for every $\alpha_s \in F_i$ and hence $a_{ij} = -2 + 1 = -1$.

(2) If $\alpha_j \cap (\alpha_{i-1} \cup \alpha_i) = \emptyset$, then $|\alpha_s \cap \alpha_j| = 0$ for every $\alpha_s \in F_i$ and hence $a_{ij} = 2 - 1 = 1$.

(3) If neither (1) nor (2) occurs, then by a case argument it is not hard to prove $\Sigma_{ij} = 0$ and hence $a_{ij} = (-1)^{|\alpha_{i-1} \cap \alpha_j| + 1}$.

This lower triangular matrix L has a very important property. Let i_0 be the first index such that $|\alpha_{i_0}| = 3$. Let δ be the m-dimensional vector in which only one nonzero coordinate is equal to 1 and with index i_0. Suppose x is the solution of $Lx = \delta$. Then for $i \geq i_0$,

$$|x_i| \geq (2^{|\alpha_i|-1} - 2)|x_{i-1}|. \tag{16.9}$$

In fact, (16.9) can be proved by induction on i. First, note

$$\sum_{\alpha_j \in F_i} (1/2)^{|\alpha_i|-1} x_j - x_{i-1} = \delta_i.$$

Namely,

$$x_i = (2^{|\alpha_i|-1} - 1)x_{i-1} - \sum_{\alpha_j \in F_i \setminus \{\alpha_{i-1}, \alpha_i\}} x_j + 2^{|\alpha_i|-1}\delta.$$

Since for $i < i_0$ $\delta_i = 0$, one has $x_i = 0$ for $i < i_0$. Thus, $x_{i_0} = 2^{3-1}\delta_{i_0} = 4 > (2^{2-1} - 2)|x_{i_0-1}| = 0$. In general, for $i > i_0$,

$$x_i = (2^{|\alpha_i|-1} - 1)x_{i-1} - \sum_{\alpha_j \in F_i \setminus \{\alpha_{i-1}, \alpha_i\}} x_j.$$

By the induction hypothesis,

$$|x_{i-1}| \geq (2^{|\alpha_{i-1}|-1} - 2)|x_{i-2}| \geq 2|x_{i-2}|,$$

and

$$|x_{i-2}| \geq 2|x_{i_3}|, \cdots.$$

It follows that

$$(1/2)^t |x_{i-1}| \geq |x_{i-1-t}|.$$

Hence,

$$\left| \sum_{\alpha_j \in F_i \setminus \{\alpha_{i-1}, \alpha_i\}} x_j \right| \leq \sum_{\alpha_j \in F_i \setminus \{\alpha_{i-1}, \alpha_i\}} |x_j| \leq \sum_{t=1}^{\infty} (1/2)^t |x_{i-1}| = |x_{i-1}|.$$

Therefore,

$$|x_i| \geq |(2^{|\alpha_i|-1} - 1)x_{i-1}| - \left| \sum_{\alpha_j \in F_i \setminus \{\alpha_{i-1}, \alpha_i\}} x_j \right| \geq (2^{|\alpha_i|-1} - 2)|x_{i-1}|.$$

The following is an immediate consequence of (16.9).

$$x_m > \prod_{t=3}^{k} (2^{t-1} - 2)^{\binom{k}{t}} = \prod_{t=3}^{k} 2^{(t-1)\binom{k}{t}} \prod_{t=3}^{k} (1 - 2^{2-t})^{\binom{k}{t}}.$$

Note that

$$\sum_{t=3}^{k}(t-1)\binom{k}{t} = k2^{k-1} - 2^k + 1 - O(k^2) = (1/2)m\log m - (1+o(1))m.$$

Moreover, since $(1-\frac{1}{x})^x < 1/e < (1-\frac{1}{x})^{x-1} \le (1-\frac{1}{x})^{x/2}$ for $x \ge 2$, one has

$$\prod_{k=3}^{k}(1/e)^{2^{2-t}\binom{k}{t}} > \prod_{t=3}^{k}(1-2^{2-t})^{\binom{k}{t}} > \prod_{k=3}^{k}(1/e)^{2^{3-t}\binom{k}{t}}.$$

Hence,

$$\prod_{t=3}^{k}(1-2^{2-t})^{\binom{k}{t}} = 2^{O(1)(1+1/2)^k + O(k^2)} = 2^{o(m)}.$$

Therefore,

$$x_m \ge 2^{(1/2)m\log m - (1+o(1))m}.$$

Now, suppose y satisfies $Ay = \delta$. Then $|y_i| = |\delta A_{i_0 i}/\det A|$. Since $A = LQ$, $x = Qy$ and hence $y = (1/m)Qx$. Thus, $y_i = (1/m)\sum_{j=1}^{m} q_{ij}x_j$. Note that for $k \ge 4$, $|x_m| \ge (2^{|\alpha_m|-1} - 2)|x_{m-1}| \ge 4|x_{m-1}|$. Thus, $|x_m| > (1/2)^{t+1}|x_{m-t}|$. It follows that

$$|y_i| \ge (1/m)(|x_m| - \sum_{t=1}^{m-1}|x_t|) \ge (1/m)(|x_m|/2).$$

Hence,

$$|y_i| \ge 2^{(1/2)m\log m - (1+o(1))m}.$$

$\square$

It follows immediately from Lemma 16.4.2 that $\chi(m) \ge 2^{(1/2)m\log m + O(1)m}$ for $m = 2^k$. The following two lemmas are geared towards establishing a similar lower of $\chi(m)$ for general m.

Lemma 16.4.3 $\chi(m+m') \ge \chi(m)\chi(m')$.

Proof. Suppose

$$\chi(m) = \chi(A) = |\det A_{mm}|/|\det A|$$

and

$$\chi(m') = \chi(B) = |\det B_{11}|/|\det B|$$

where A_{ij} is obtained from A by deleting the ith row and the jth column. Consider matrx

$$R = \begin{pmatrix} A & 0 \\ C & B \end{pmatrix}$$

where

$$C = \begin{pmatrix} 0 & \cdots & 0 & 1 \\ 0 & \cdots & 0 & 0 \\ \cdot & \cdots & \cdot & \cdot \\ 0 & \cdots & 0 & 0 \end{pmatrix}.$$

Clearly,

$$\chi(m+m') \geq \chi(R) \geq \frac{|\det R_{m,(m+1)}|}{|\det R|} = \frac{|\det A_{mm}|}{|\det A|} \cdot \frac{|\det B_{11}|}{|\det B|} = \chi(m)\chi(m').$$

$\square$

Lemma 16.4.4 *Suppose* $q_1 > q_2 > \cdots > q_r \geq 0$ *are integers, and* $m_i = 2^{q_i}$, $m = \sum_{i=1}^{r} m_i$. *Then*

$$0 \leq m \log m - \sum_{i=1}^{r} m_i \log m_i \leq 2m.$$

Proof. We first show by induction on q_1 that

$$\sum_{i=2}^{r} (q_1 - q_i) 2^{q_i} \leq \sum_{i=1}^{r} 2^{q_i}. \tag{16.10}$$

It is trivial for $q_1 = 0, 1$. In general,

$$\sum_{i=2}^{r} (q_1 - q_i) 2^{q_i}$$

$$= \sum_{i=2}^{r} [(q_1 - 1) - q_i] 2^{q_i} + \sum_{i=2}^{r} 2^{q_i}$$

$$\leq \sum_{i=3}^{r} 2^{q_i} + \min(1, q_1 - 1 - q_2) 2^{q_2} + 2^{q_1 - 1} + \sum_{i=2}^{r} 2^{q_i}$$

(by the induction hypothesis)

$$\leq \sum_{i=1}^{r} 2^{q_i}.$$

Note that

$$\sum_{i=1}^{r} m_i \log m_i = \sum_{i=1}^{r} q_i 2^{q_i} = q_1 m - \sum_{i=2}^{r} (q_1 - q_i) 2^{q_i}.$$

By (16.10),

$$(q_1 - 1)m \leq \sum_{i=1}^{r} m_i \log m_i \leq q_1 m.$$

Moreover,

$$q_1 m \leq m \log m \leq (q_1 + 1)m.$$

Therefore,

$$0 \leq m \log m - \sum_{i=1}^{r} m_i \log m_i \leq 2m.$$

$\square$

Now, we are ready to show the lower bound of $\chi(m)$ for general m.

Lemma 16.4.5 *For any natural number m, $\chi(m) \geq 2^{(1/2)m \log m - O(1)m}$.*

Proof. Write m as a binary number $m = \sum_{i=1}^{r} 2^{q_i}$ where $q_1 > q_2 > \cdots > q_r \geq 0$. Denote $m_i = 2^{q_i}$. By Lemmas 16.4.2, 16.4.3, and 16.4.4,

$$\chi(m) \geq \prod_{i=1}^{r} \chi(m_i) \geq 2^{(1/2)\sum_{i=1}^{r} m_i \log m_i - O(1)m} \geq 2^{(1/2)m \log m - O(1)m}.$$

$\square$

Theorem 16.4.6 $n(m,2) = m^{(1/2+o(1))m}$.

Proof. It follows immediately from Lemmas 16.4.5, 16.4.1 and 16.3.8. $\square$

16.5 Coins with Arbitrary Weights

The all-equal problem has a general form as follows.

The General All-Equal Problem. Given a set of n coins of at most k different weights, determine whether all coins have the same weight or not.

Let $n(m,k)$ denote the maximum possible number of coins with at most k different weights for which the general all-equal problem can be solved in m weighings. Alon and Kozlov [2] proved the following.

Theorem 16.5.1 *There are two positive constants c_1 and c_2 such that for $k \geq 3$,*

$$c_1 \frac{m \log m}{\log k} < n(m,k) \leq c_2 \frac{m \log m}{\log k}.$$

When $k \geq m+1$, by Theorem 16.5.1,

$$n(m,k) \leq c_2 m.$$

In fact, Alon and Kozlov also proved that for $k \geq m+1$, $n(m,k) = m+1$.

Thus, for $k \geq 3$, $n(m,k)$ is much smaller than $n(m,2)$. But, with some condition on weights, the situation can be changed.

Kozlov and Vu [15] proposed the following condition.

Generic Weights. Let $w_1, \cdots, w_t$ be all different weights occurring among given coins. Those coins are said to have *generic weights* if there are no integers $\lambda_1, \cdots, \lambda_t$ such that not all λ_i's are equal to 0 and

$$\sum_{i=1}^{t} \lambda_i w_i = 0, \quad \sum_{i=1}^{t} \lambda_i = 0.$$

With this condition, all arguments in Secs. 5.3 and 5.4 can still go through. Therefore, $n(m, k)$ have the same magnitude of $n(m, 2)$. Note that two weights are always generic. Thus, this special case is a natural generalization of results on two weights.

Another condition was given by Alon and Vu [3]. They assume that a distinguished coin is known to be either the heaviest or the lightest one among the given n coins. In this case, $n(m, k)$ also have the same magnitude of $n(m, 2)$.

When three weights are not generic, they must satisfy a linear relation. Alon and Kozlov studied a simple one $w_1 + w_2 - 2w_3 = 0$, called *three weights in arithmetic progression*. Let $f(m)$ denote the maximum number n such that the general all-equal problem for n coins with possible three weights in an arithmetic progression can be solved using m weighings. They showed the following.

Theorem 16.5.2 *There are two positive constants c_1 and c_2 such that*

$$c_1 m \log m \le f(m) \le c_2 m \log m$$

for all m.

This theorem indicates that for some particular linear relations of weights, one may still do better than the general case. Is there a specific linear relation such that one cannot do better? This is an interesting open problem.

References

[1] M. Aigner, *Combinatorial Search* (Wiley-Teubner, New York-Stuttgart, 1988).

[2] N. Alon and D. Kozlov, Coins with arbitrary weights, *J. Algorithms* 25 (1997) 162-176.

[3] N. Alon and V.H. Vu, Anti-Hadamard matrices, coin weighting, theshold gates, and indecomposable hypergraphs, *J. Combin. Theory Ser. A* 79 (1997) 133-160.

[4] N. Alon, D. Kozlov, and V.H. Vu, The geometry of coin-weighting problems, *Proceedings of the 37th IEEE FOCS*, (IEEE, 1996) 524-532.

[5] I. Bošnjak, Some new results concerning three conterfeit coins problem, *Discrete Appl. Math.* 48 (1994) 81-85.

[6] A. De Bonis, A predetermined algorithm for detecting a counterfeit coin with a multi-arms balance, *Discrete Appl. Math.* 86 (1998) 181-200.

[7] A. De Bonis, L. Gargano, and U. Vaccaro, Optimal detection of a counterfeit coin with multi-arms balances, *Discrete Appl. Math.* 61 (1995) 121-131.

[8] D.Z. Du and F.K. Hwang, Competitive group testing, in L.A. McGeoch and D.D. Sleator (ed.) *On-Line Algorithm*, DIMACS Series in Discrete Mathematics and Theoretical Computer Science, Vol. 7 (AMS & ACM, 1992) 125-134. (Also in *Discrete Applied Mathematics* 45 (1993) 221-232.)

[9] L. Gargano, J. Körner, and U. Vaccaro, Search problems for two irregular coins with incomplete feedback: the underweight model, *Discrete Appl. Math.* 36 (1992) 191-197.

[10] R.L. Graham and N.J. Sloane, Anti-Hadamard matrices, *Linear Algebra and Its Applications* 62 (1984) 113-137.

[11] P.K. Guy and R.J. Nowakowsky, Coin-weighting problem, *Am. Math. Monthly* 102 (1992) 164-167.

[12] L. Halbeisen and N. Hungerbühler, The general counterfeit coin problem, *Discrete Math.* 147 (1995) 139-150.

[13] X.D. Hu, P.D. Chen, and F.K. Hwang, A new competitive algorithm for counterfeit coin problem, *Inform. Process. Lett.* 51 (1994) 213-218.

[14] X.D. Hu and F.K. Hwang, A competitive algorithm for the counterfeit coin problem, in D.-Z. Du and P.M. Pardalos (eds.) *Minimax and Applications* (Kluwer Acad. Publ, Dordrecht, 1995) 241-250.

[15] D.N. Kozlov and V.H. Vu, Coins and cones, *J. Combin. Theory Ser. A* 78 (1997) 1-14.

[16] A.P. Li, On the conjecture at two counterfeit coins, *Discrete Math.* 133 (1994) 301-306.

[17] A.P. Li, Three counterfeit coins problem, *J. Combin. Theory Ser. A* 66 (1994) 93-101.

[18] N. Linial and M. Tarsi, The counterfeit coin problem revisited, *SIAM J. Comput.* 11 (1982) 409-415.

[19] G.J. Manas and D.H. Meyer, On a problem of coin identification, *SIAM Review* 31 (1989) 114-117.

[20] B. Manvel, Counterfeit coin problems, *Math. Mag.* 50 (1977) 90-92.

[21] L. Pyber, How to find many counterfeit coins? *Graphs Combin.* 2 (1986) 173-177.

[22] A. Schrijver, *Theory of Linear and Integer Programming*, (Wiley, New York, 1986).

[23] R. Tošic, Two counterfeit coins, *Discrete Math.* 45 (1983) 295-298.

[24] P.-J. Wan and D.-Z. Du, A $(\log_2 3 + \frac{1}{2})$-competitive algorithm for the counterfeit coin problem, *Discrete Math.* 163 (1997) 173-200.

[25] P.-J. Wan, Q. Yang, and D. Kelley, A $\frac{3}{2}\log_2 3$-competitive algorithm for the counterfeit coin problem, *Theoret. Comput. Sci.* 181 (1997) 347-356.

Index

2-optimal, 233
μ-operation, 272

A-distinct, 40
A-sharp, 40
Aanderaa, 290
active user, 197
adjacent, 233
admissible algorithm, 14
Aigner, M., 219, 220, 233, 234, 236,
    242, 244, 250, 300
all-positive path, 40
Alon, N., 308, 314, 315
Althöfer, I., 236, 237
Andreae, T., 234, 245
Angluin, D., 98
anti-Hadamard matrices, 308
arithmetic progression, 315
Aslam, J.A., 101, 103, 104, 111, 278
Avriel, M., 261

balanced, 295
Balding, 170, 180, 183
Bar-Noy, A., 71
Barillot, E., 180
base pairs, 178
Bassalygo, 137
Beamer, J.H., 261
Ben-Or, M., 285
Bentley, J.L., 273, 274, 279
Berger, T., 205
Berlekamp, E.R., 90
BIBD, 144
bicolorable, 125
bin, 8
binary splitting, 24

binary tree, 13
bipartite graph, 233
Björner, A., 285
Blumenthal, S., 213
Boris, A.D., 190
Bose-Chaudhuri codes, 155
Bošnjak, I, 301
breadth-first search, 65
brute force, 110
Brylawski, T.H., 112
Bruno, W.J., 183, 185
Bush, K.A., 144
Busschbach, P., 164, 203

Cai, M.C., 152
candy factory model, 224
Cantor, D.G., 216, 217
Capetanakis, J.I., 198
Chang, G.J., 39, 40, 49, 233
Chang, X.M., 29, 51, 54, 209, 229
Chen, C.C., 45
Chen, R.W., 208
Cheng, S.-W., 71, 73, 82
Christen, C., 220, 224
classification problem, 189
clones, 177
cloning vector, 177
co-NP-complete, 118
Colbourn, C., 157
combinatorial group testing, 1, 4
competitive algorithm, 66, 302
competitive ratio, 66
complement, 118
complete, 118
completely separating system, 152
condition number, 308

319